99 Little Doilies

Leisure Arts, Inc.
Little Rock, Arkansas

EDITORIAL STAFF

Vice President and Editor-at-Large: Anne Van Wagner Childs
Vice President and Editor-in-Chief: Sandra Graham Case
Director of Designer Relations: Debra Nettles
Editorial Director: Susan Frantz Wiles
Publications Director: Susan White Sullivan
Creative Art Director: Gloria Bearden
Photography Director: Karen Smart Hall
Art Operations Director: Jeff Curtis

PRODUCTION

Managing Editor: Valesha M. Kirksey
Technical Editor: Linda Luder
Senior Instructional Editor: Susan Ackerman Carter
Instructional Editors: Sue Galucki, Sarah J. Green,
   Patricia Kowaleski, and Lois J. Long

EDITORIAL

Managing Editor: Suzie Puckett
Associate Editor: Taryn L. Stewart

ART

Graphics Art Director: Rhonda Hodge Shelby
Senior Graphics Illustrator: Lora Puls
Graphics Illustrator: Dana Vaughn
Color Technician: Mark Hawkins
Photography Stylists: Sondra Daniel, Tiffany Huffman, and
   Janna Laughlin
Staff Photographer: Russell Ganser
Publishing Systems Administrator: Becky Riddle
Publishing Systems Assistants: Myra S. Means and
   Chris Wertenberger

BUSINESS STAFF

Publisher: Rick Barton
Vice President, Finance: Tom Siebenmorgen
Director of Corporate Planning and Development:
   Laticia Mull Cornett
Vice President, Retail Marketing: Bob Humphrey
Retail Marketing Director: Margaret Sweetin
Vice President, Sales: Ray Shelgosh
Vice President, National Accounts: Pam Stebbins
Vice President, Operations: Jim Dittrich
Comptroller, Operations: Rob Thieme
Retail Customer Service Manager: Wanda Price
Print Production Manager: Fred F. Pruss

Softcover ISBN 1-57486-233-2

10   9

2

*M*any innovative "minis" await you in this exciting leaflet from Patricia Kristoffersen, today's master designer of exquisite threadwork. A book you'll treasure, it introduces scores of new designs as well as favorites from popular Leisure Arts publications. Expert crocheters will enjoy a challenge from time to time while creating Patricia's many lacy clusters, twists, picots, and other pretty pattern stitches, and the novice will find many opportunities to learn. Full-color photos illustrate the intricacies of every tiny masterpiece. With so many one-of-a-kind designs from which to choose, you can display doilies in every room and have gifts galore to spare!

1

Finished Size: 8" (straight edge to straight edge)

MATERIALS
Bedspread Weight Cotton Thread (size 10): 82 yards
Steel crochet hook, size 7 (1.65 mm) **or** size
needed for gauge

GAUGE SWATCH: 1$^1/_2$" diameter
Work same as Doily through Rnd 2.

STITCH GUIDE

TREBLE CROCHET (abbreviated tr)
YO twice, insert hook in st indicated, YO and pull
up a loop (4 loops on hook), (YO and draw through
2 loops on hook) 3 times.

PICOT
Ch 3, slip st in top of last st made **(Fig. 6a,
page 144)**.

BEGINNING DC CLUSTER (uses one sp)
Ch 2, ★ YO, insert hook in sp indicated, YO and
pull up a loop, YO and draw through 2 loops on
hook; repeat from ★ once **more**, YO and draw
through all 3 loops on hook.

DC CLUSTER (uses one ch-2 sp)
★ YO, insert hook in ch-2 sp indicated, YO and pull
up a loop, YO and draw through 2 loops on hook;
repeat from ★ 2 times **more**, YO and draw through
all 4 loops on hook.

TR CLUSTER (uses one ch-5 sp)
★ YO twice, insert hook in ch-5 sp indicated, YO
and pull up a loop, (YO and draw through 2 loops
on hook) twice; repeat from ★ once **more**, YO and
draw through all 3 loops on hook.

POPCORN
4 Dc in sp indicated, drop loop from hook, insert
hook in first dc of 4-dc group, hook dropped loop
and draw through.

TWISTED DECREASE (uses next 2 ch-3 sps)
YO twice, skip next ch-3 sp and next 9 sc, insert
hook in next ch-3 sp, YO and pull up a loop, (YO
and draw through 2 loops on hook) twice, YO twice,
working in **front** of first half of st, insert hook in
skipped ch-3 sp, YO and pull up a loop, (YO and
draw through 2 loops on hook) twice, YO and draw
through all 3 loops on hook **(counts as one tr)**.

DOILY
Ch 6; join with slip st to form a ring.

Rnd 1 (Right side)**:** Ch 3 **(counts as first dc, now
and throughout)**, dc in ring, (ch 2, 2 dc in ring) 7
times, ch 1, sc in first dc to form last ch-2 sp:
8 ch-2 sps.

Rnd 2: Ch 3, dc in last ch-2 sp made, 5 dc in next
ch-2 sp, ★ (2 dc, ch 2, 2 dc) in next ch-2 sp, 5 dc in
next ch-2 sp; repeat from ★ 2 times **more**, 2 dc in same
sp as first dc, ch 1, sc in first dc to form last ch-2 sp:
36 dc.

Rnd 3: Ch 3, dc in last ch-2 sp made, ch 3, skip next
4 dc, (sc, work Picot, sc) in next dc, ch 3, skip next 4 dc,
★ (2 dc, ch 2, 2 dc) in next ch-2 sp, ch 3, skip next
4 dc, (sc, work Picot, sc) in next dc, ch 3, skip next 4 dc;
repeat from ★ 2 times **more**, 2 dc in same sp as first dc,
ch 1, sc in first dc to form last ch-2 sp: 16 dc and
8 ch-3 sps.

Rnd 4: Ch 3, dc in last ch-2 sp made, ch 5, (sc in next
ch-3 sp, ch 5) twice, ★ (2 dc, ch 2, 2 dc) in next ch-2 sp,
ch 5, (sc in next ch-3 sp, ch 5) twice; repeat from ★
2 times **more**, 2 dc in same sp as first dc, ch 1, sc in
first dc to form last ch-2 sp: 16 dc and 12 ch-5 sps.

Rnd 5: Ch 3, dc in last ch-2 sp made, ch 3, sc in next
ch-5 sp, work tr Cluster in next ch-5 sp, (ch 2, work
tr Cluster in same sp) 4 times, sc in next ch-5 sp, ch 3,
★ (2 dc, ch 2, 2 dc) in next ch-2 sp, ch 3, sc in next
ch-5 sp, work tr Cluster in next ch-5 sp, (ch 2, work
tr Cluster in same sp) 4 times, sc in next ch-5 sp, ch 3;
repeat from ★ 2 times **more**, 2 dc in same sp as first dc,
ch 1, sc in first dc to form last ch-2 sp: 20 tr Clusters
and 28 sps.

Rnd 6: Ch 3, dc in last ch-2 sp made, ch 3, 2 sc in
each of next 2 sps, ch 2, (2 sc in next ch-2 sp, ch 2)
twice, 2 sc in each of next 2 sps, ch 3, ★ 2 dc in next
ch-2 sp, (ch 2, 2 dc in same sp) twice, ch 3, 2 sc in each
of next 2 sps, ch 2, (2 sc in next ch-2 sp, ch 2) twice,
2 sc in each of next 2 sps, ch 3; repeat from ★ 2 times
more, (2 dc, ch 2, 2 dc) in same sp as first dc, ch 1, sc
in first dc to form last ch-2 sp: 72 sts and 28 sps.

Rnd 7: Ch 3, dc in last ch-2 sp made, ch 3, ★ † 2 sc in
next ch-3 sp, sc in next sc, skip next 2 sc, sc in next sc,
2 sc in next ch-2 sp, (ch 2, 2 sc in next ch-2 sp) twice,
sc in next sc, skip next 2 sc, sc in next sc, 2 sc in next
ch-3 sp, ch 3 †, [(2 dc, ch 2, 2 dc) in next ch-2 sp, ch 3]
twice; repeat from ★ 2 times **more**, then repeat from
† to † once, (2 dc, ch 2, 2 dc) in next ch-2 sp, ch 3, 2 dc
in same sp as first dc, ch 1, sc in first dc to form last
ch-2 sp: 88 sts and 28 sps.

Rnd 8: Ch 3, dc in last ch-2 sp made, ★ † ch 3, (2 sc in next sp, sc in next 2 sc, skip next 2 sc, sc in next 2 sc, 2 sc in next sp, ch 3) twice, (2 dc, ch 2, 2 dc) in next ch-2 sp, ch 5, work Popcorn in next ch-3 sp, ch 5 †, (2 dc, ch 2, 2 dc) in next ch-2 sp; repeat from ★ 2 times **more**, then repeat from † to † once, 2 dc in same sp as first dc, ch 1, sc in first dc to form last ch-2 sp: 100 sts and 28 sps.

Rnd 9: Ch 3, dc in last ch-2 sp made, ★ † ch 3, 2 sc in next ch-3 sp, sc in next 2 sc, skip next 4 sc, sc in next 2 sc, 5 sc in next ch-3 sp, sc in next 2 sc, skip next 4 sc, sc in next 2 sc, 2 sc in next ch-3 sp, ch 3, (2 dc, ch 2, 2 dc) in next ch-2 sp, ch 5, work Popcorn in next ch-5 sp, ch 4, work Popcorn in next ch-5 sp, ch 5 †, (2 dc, ch 2, 2 dc) in next ch-2 sp; repeat from ★ 2 times **more**, then repeat from † to † once, 2 dc in same sp as first dc, ch 1, sc in first dc to form last ch-2 sp: 108 sts and 28 sps.

Rnd 10: Ch 3, dc in last ch-2 sp made, ★ † ch 3, 2 sc in next ch-3 sp, sc in next 2 sc, skip next 4 sc, sc in next 2 sc, 3 sc in next sc, sc in next 2 sc, skip next 4 sc, sc in next 2 sc, 2 sc in next ch-3 sp, ch 3, 2 dc in next ch-2 sp, (ch 2, 2 dc in same sp) twice, ch 5, (sc, work Picot, sc) in next ch-5 sp, ch 5, work Popcorn in next ch-4 sp, ch 5, (sc, work Picot, sc) in next ch-5 sp, ch 5 †, 2 dc in next ch-2 sp, (ch 2, 2 dc in same sp) twice; repeat from ★ 2 times **more**, then repeat from † to † once, (2 dc, ch 2, 2 dc) in same sp as first dc, ch 1, sc in first dc to form last ch-2 sp: 128 sts, 8 Picots, and 40 sps.

Rnd 11: Ch 3, dc in last ch-2 sp made, ch 3, ★ † 2 sc in next ch-3 sp, sc in next 2 sc, skip next 4 sc, sc in next sc, 3 sc in next sc, sc in next sc, skip next 4 sc, sc in next 2 sc, 2 sc in next ch-3 sp, [ch 3, (2 dc, ch 2, 2 dc) in next ch-2 sp] twice, ch 4, [(sc, work Picot, sc) in next ch-5 sp, ch 4] 4 times †, [(2 dc, ch 2, 2 dc) in next ch-2 sp, ch 3] twice; repeat from ★ 2 times **more**, then repeat from † to † once, (2 dc, ch 2, 2 dc) in next ch-2 sp, ch 3, 2 dc in same sp as first dc, ch 1, sc in first dc to form last ch-2 sp: 148 sts, 16 Picots, and 52 sps.

Rnd 12: Ch 3, dc in last ch-2 sp made, ch 3, ★ † 2 sc in next ch-3 sp, sc in next 2 sc, skip next 4 sc, sc in next sc, skip next 4 sc, sc in next 2 sc, 2 sc in next ch-3 sp, ch 3, (2 dc, ch 2, 2 dc) in next ch-2 sp, ch 3, sc in next ch-3 sp, ch 3, (2 dc, ch 2, 2 dc) in next ch-2 sp, ch 4, [(sc, work Picot, sc) in next ch-4 sp, ch 4] 5 times, (2 dc, ch 2, 2 dc) in next ch-2 sp, ch 3, sc in next ch-3 sp, ch 3 †, (2 dc, ch 2, 2 dc) in next ch-2 sp, ch 3; repeat from ★ 2 times **more**, then repeat from † to † once, 2 dc in same sp as first dc, ch 1, sc in first dc to form last ch-2 sp: 148 sts, 20 Picots, and 64 sps.

Rnd 13: Work Beginning dc Cluster in last ch-2 sp made, ★ † work Twisted decrease, work dc Cluster in next ch-2 sp, ch 5, 2 sc in next ch-3 sp, work Picot, 2 sc in next ch-3 sp, ch 5, work dc Cluster in next ch-2 sp, (sc, work Picot, sc) in next ch-4 sp, [ch 4, (sc, work Picot, sc) in next ch-4 sp] 5 times, work dc Cluster in next ch-2 sp, ch 5, 2 sc in next ch-3 sp, work Picot, 2 sc in next ch-3 sp †, ch 5, work dc Cluster in next ch-2 sp; repeat from ★ 2 times **more**, then repeat from † to † once, ch 1, tr in top of Beginning dc Cluster to form last ch-5 sp: 100 sts, 32 Picots, and 36 sps.

Rnd 14: Ch 1, (2 sc, hdc, dc, work Picot, hdc, 2 sc) in last ch-5 sp made, [ch 5, slip st in third ch from hook, ch 2, (2 sc, hdc, dc, work Picot, hdc, 2 sc) in next ch-5 sp] twice, ★ † ch 5, slip st in third ch from hook, ch 2, (sc in next ch-4 sp, ch 5, slip st in third ch from hook, ch 2) 5 times, (2 sc, hdc, dc, work Picot, hdc, 2 sc) in next ch-5 sp †, [ch 5, slip st in third ch from hook, ch 2, (2 sc, hdc, dc, work Picot, hdc, 2 sc) in next ch-5 sp] 3 times; repeat from ★ 2 times **more**, then repeat from † to † once, ch 5, slip st in third ch from hook, ch 2; join with slip st to first sc, finish off.

See Washing and Blocking, page 144.

Finished Size: 6" diameter

MATERIALS
Bedspread Weight Cotton Thread (size 10): 37 yards
Steel crochet hook, size 7 (1.65 mm) **or** size
  needed for gauge

GAUGE SWATCH: 2" diameter
Work same as Doily through Rnd 3.

STITCH GUIDE

TREBLE CROCHET (abbreviated tr)
YO twice, insert hook in sc indicated, YO and pull
up a loop (4 loops on hook), (YO and draw through
2 loops on hook) 3 times.

BEGINNING TR CLUSTER (uses first 4 sc)
Ch 4, YO twice, insert hook in Back Loop Only of
next sc, YO and pull up a loop, (YO and draw
through 2 loops on hook) twice, ★ YO twice, insert
hook in Front Loop Only of **next** sc, YO and pull
up a loop, (YO and draw through 2 loops on hook)
twice; repeat from ★ once **more**, YO and draw
through all 4 loops on hook.

TR CLUSTER (uses next 2 sc)
YO twice, insert hook in free loop of same sc as
third leg of previous tr Cluster *(Fig. 2a, page 144)*,
YO and pull up a loop, (YO and draw through
2 loops on hook) twice, YO twice, insert hook in
free loop of same sc as last leg of previous
tr Cluster, YO and pull up a loop, (YO and draw
through 2 loops on hook) twice, ★ YO twice, insert
hook in Front Loop Only of **next** sc, YO and pull
up a loop, (YO and draw through 2 loops on hook)
twice; repeat from ★ once **more**, YO and draw
through all 5 loops on hook.

ENDING TR CLUSTER
YO twice, insert hook in free loop of same sc as
third leg of previous tr Cluster, YO and pull up a
loop, (YO and draw through 2 loops on hook) twice,
YO twice, insert hook in free loop of same sc as last
leg of previous tr Cluster, YO and pull up a loop,
(YO and draw through 2 loops on hook) twice,
YO twice, insert hook in free loop of same sc as first
leg of Beginning tr Cluster, YO and pull up a loop,
(YO and draw through 2 loops on hook) twice,
YO twice, insert hook in free loop of same sc as
next leg of Beginning tr Cluster, YO and pull up a
loop, (YO and draw through 2 loops on hook) twice,
YO and draw through all 5 loops on hook.

DC CLUSTER (uses one ch-5 sp)
★ YO, insert hook in ch-5 sp indicated, YO and pull
up a loop, YO and draw through 2 loops on hook;
repeat from ★ 2 times **more**, YO and draw through
all 4 loops on hook.

BEGINNING POPCORN
Ch 3, 4 dc in sp indicated, drop loop from hook,
insert hook in first dc of 5-dc group, hook dropped
loop and draw through.

POPCORN
5 Dc in ch-3 sp indicated, drop loop from hook,
insert hook in first dc of 5-dc group, hook dropped
loop and draw through.

DOILY
Ch 7; join with slip st to form a ring.

Rnd 1 (Right side): Ch 1, 18 sc in ring; join with slip st
to Back Loop Only of first sc *(Fig. 1, page 143)*.

Rnd 2: Work Beginning tr Cluster, ch 5, (work
tr Cluster, ch 5) around, work Ending tr Cluster, ch 2, dc
in top of Beginning tr Cluster to form last ch-5 sp:
9 ch-5 sps.

Rnd 3: Ch 1, [sc, ch 2, slip st in top of last sc made
(Fig. 6a, page 144), sc] in last ch-5 sp made, ★ ch 6,
(sc, ch 2, slip st in top of last sc made, sc) in next
ch-5 sp; repeat from ★ around, ch 3, dc in first sc to
form last ch-6 sp.

Rnd 4: Ch 3 **(counts as first dc, now and
throughout)**, 3 dc in last ch-6 sp made, (4 dc, ch 2,
4 dc) in each ch-6 sp around, 4 dc in same sp as first dc,
ch 1, sc in first dc to form last ch-2 sp: 72 dc.

Rnd 5: Ch 1, sc in last ch-2 sp made, ch 9, ★ (sc, ch 3,
sc) in next ch-2 sp, ch 9; repeat from ★ around, sc in
same sp as first sc, dc in first sc to form last ch-3 sp:
18 sps.

Rnd 6: Work Beginning Popcorn in last ch-3 sp made,
ch 3, (4 sc, ch 3, 4 sc) in next ch-9 sp, ★ ch 3, work
Popcorn in next ch-3 sp, ch 3, (4 sc, ch 3, 4 sc) in next
ch-9 sp; repeat from ★ around, ch 1, hdc in top of
Beginning Popcorn to form last ch-3 sp: 27 ch-3 sps.

Rnd 7: Ch 1, 2 sc in last ch-3 sp made, (ch 5, 2 sc in
next ch-3 sp) around, ch 2, dc in first sc to form
last ch-5 sp.

Rnd 8: Ch 1, 2 sc in last ch-5 sp made, work
dc Cluster in next ch-5 sp, (ch 3, work dc Cluster in
same sp) twice, 2 sc in next ch-5 sp, ★ ch 5, 2 sc in
next ch-5 sp, work dc Cluster in next ch-5 sp, (ch 3,
work dc Cluster in same sp) twice, 2 sc in next ch-5 sp;
repeat from ★ around, ch 1, tr in first sc to form
last ch-5 sp.

Rnd 9: Ch 1, sc in last ch-5 sp made, ★ † (ch 2, sc in same sp) 3 times, sc in next 2 sc, (sc, ch 2, slip st in top of last sc made, 2 sc) in next ch-3 sp, ch 5, slip st in top of last sc made, (2 sc, ch 2, slip st in top of last sc made, sc) in next ch-3 sp, skip next dc Cluster, sc in next 2 sc †, sc in next ch-5 sp; repeat from ★ 7 times **more**, then repeat from † to † once; join with slip st to first sc, finish off.

See Washing and Blocking, page 144.

3

Finished Size: 4¹/₂" diameter

MATERIALS
Bedspread Weight Cotton Thread (size 10): 23 yards
Steel crochet hook, size 7 (1.65 mm) **or** size
   needed for gauge

GAUGE SWATCH: 2¹/₄" diameter
Work same as Doily through Rnd 3.

STITCH GUIDE

BEGINNING POPCORN
Ch 3, 4 dc in sp indicated, drop loop from hook, insert hook in first dc of 5-dc group, hook dropped loop and draw through.

POPCORN
5 Dc in ch-3 sp indicated, drop loop from hook, insert hook in first dc of 5-dc group, hook dropped loop and draw through.

CLUSTER (uses one dc)
★ YO, insert hook in dc indicated, YO and pull up a loop, YO and draw through 2 loops on hook; repeat from ★ once **more**, YO and draw through all 3 loops on hook.

DOILY

Ch 8; join with slip st to form a ring.

Rnd 1 (Right side)**:** Ch 3 **(counts as first dc, now and throughout)**, 23 dc in ring; join with slip st to first dc: 24 dc.

Rnd 2: Ch 6, dc in same st, skip next 2 dc, ★ (dc, ch 3, dc) in next dc, skip next 2 dc; repeat from ★ around; join with slip st to third ch of beginning ch-6: 8 ch-3 sps.

Rnd 3: (Slip st, work Beginning Popcorn) in first ch-3 sp, ch 5, sc in next 2 dc, ch 5, ★ work Popcorn in next ch-3 sp, ch 5, sc in next 2 dc, ch 5; repeat from ★ around; join with slip st to top of Beginning Popcorn: 16 ch-5 sps.

Rnd 4: (Slip st, ch 1, sc) in first ch-5 sp, ch 8, (sc in next 2 ch-5 sps, ch 8) around to last ch-5 sp, sc in last ch-5 sp; join with slip st to first sc: 16 sc and 8 ch-8 sps.

Rnd 5: Ch 1, sc in same st, 7 sc in next ch-8 sp, (sc in next 2 sc, 7 sc in next ch-8 sp) around to last sc, sc in last sc; join with slip st to first sc: 72 sc.

Rnd 6: Ch 2 **(counts as first hdc)**, sc in next 3 sc, 3 sc in next sc, sc in next 3 sc, ★ hdc in next 2 sc, sc in next 3 sc, 3 sc in next sc, sc in next 3 sc; repeat from ★ around to last sc, hdc in last sc; join with slip st to first hdc: 88 sts.

Rnd 7: Ch 3, working in Back Loops Only *(Fig. 1, page 143)*, dc in next 4 sc, 3 dc in next sc, ★ dc in next 10 sts, 3 dc in next sc; repeat from ★ around to last 5 sts, dc in last 5 sts; join with slip st to first dc: 104 dc.

Rnd 8: Working in both loops, slip st in next 3 dc, ch 1, sc in same st, ★ † ch 2, skip next 2 dc, work Cluster in next dc, (ch 3, work Cluster in same st) twice, ch 2, skip next 2 dc, sc in next dc, ch 8, skip next 6 sts †, sc in next dc; repeat from ★ 6 times **more**, then repeat from † to † once; join with slip st to first sc, finish off.

See Washing and Blocking, page 144.

Finished Size: 8" diameter

MATERIALS

Bedspread Weight Cotton Thread (size 10): 76 yards
Steel crochet hook, size 7 (1.65 mm) **or** size
    needed for gauge

GAUGE SWATCH: 2¹/₂" diameter
Work same as Doily through Rnd 3.

STITCH GUIDE

PICOT
Ch 2, slip st in top of last sc made *(Fig. 6a, page 144)*.

SPLIT TREBLE CROCHET
(abbreviated Split tr) (uses next 2 ch-3 sps)
★ YO twice, insert hook in **next** ch-3 sp, YO and pull up a loop, (YO and draw through 2 loops on hook) twice; repeat from ★ once **more**, YO and draw through all 3 loops on hook.

DECREASE
† YO twice, insert hook in next ch-3 sp, YO and pull up a loop, (YO and draw through 2 loops on hook) twice †, YO twice, skip next sc, insert hook in next sc, YO and pull up a loop, (YO and draw through 2 loops on hook) twice, YO 3 times, insert hook in next ch-2 sp, YO and pull up a loop, (YO and draw through 2 loops on hook) 3 times, YO twice, skip next sc, insert hook in next sc, YO and pull up a loop, (YO and draw through 2 loops on hook) twice, repeat from † to † once, YO and draw through all 6 loops on hook.

DOUBLE DECREASE
(uses 4 dc and 2 ch-2 sps)
(YO, insert hook in **next** dc, YO and pull up a loop, YO and draw through 2 loops on hook) twice, (YO, insert hook in **next** ch-2 sp, YO and pull up a loop, YO and draw through 2 loops on hook) twice, (YO, insert hook in **next** dc, YO and pull up a loop, YO and draw through 2 loops on hook) twice, YO and draw through all 7 loops on hook.

BEGINNING CLUSTER (uses next 2 dc)
Ch 2, ★ YO, insert hook in **next** dc, YO and pull up a loop, YO and draw through 2 loops on hook; repeat from ★ once **more**, YO and draw through all 3 loops on hook.

CLUSTER (uses next 2 dc and next ch-2 sp)
★ YO, insert hook in **next** dc, YO and pull up a loop, YO and draw through 2 loops on hook; repeat from ★ once **more**, YO, insert hook in next ch-2 sp, YO and pull up a loop, YO and draw through 2 loops on hook, YO and draw through all 4 loops on hook.

DOILY

Ch 6; join with slip st to form a ring.

Rnd 1 (Right side)**:** Ch 3 **(counts as first dc, now and throughout)**, 3 dc in ring, (ch 2, 4 dc in ring) 5 times, hdc in first dc to form last ch-2 sp: 6 ch-2 sps.

Rnd 2: Ch 3, (dc, ch 2, 2 dc) in last ch-2 sp made, ch 4, ★ (2 dc, ch 2, 2 dc) in next ch-2 sp, ch 4; repeat from ★ around; join with slip st to first dc: 12 sps.

Rnd 3: Slip st in next dc and in next ch-2 sp, ch 3, (dc, ch 2, 2 dc) in same sp, ch 3, (sc, work Picot, sc) in next ch-4 sp, ch 3, ★ (2 dc, ch 2, 2 dc) in next ch-2 sp, ch 3, (sc, work Picot, sc) in next ch-4 sp, ch 3; repeat from ★ around; join with slip st to first dc: 18 sps.

Rnd 4: Slip st in next dc and in next ch-2 sp, ch 3, (dc, ch 2, 2 dc) in same sp, ch 4, work Split tr, ch 4, ★ (2 dc, ch 2, 2 dc) in next ch-2 sp, ch 4, work Split tr, ch 4; repeat from ★ around; join with slip st to first dc: 6 Split tr and 18 sps.

Rnd 5: Slip st in next dc and in next ch-2 sp, ch 3, (2 dc, ch 2, 2 dc) in same sp, ch 3, 2 sc in next ch-4 sp, sc in next Split tr, work Picot, 2 sc in next ch-4 sp, ch 3, ★ (2 dc, ch 2, 2 dc) in next ch-2 sp, ch 3, 2 sc in next ch-4 sp, sc in next Split tr, work Picot, 2 sc in next ch-4 sp, ch 3; repeat from ★ around; join with slip st to first dc.

Rnd 6: Slip st in next dc and in next ch-2 sp, ch 3, [dc, (ch 2, 2 dc) twice] in same sp, ch 3, 2 sc in next ch-3 sp, ch 6, 2 sc in next ch-3 sp, ch 3, ★ 2 dc in next ch-2 sp, (ch 2, 2 dc in same sp) twice, ch 3, 2 sc in next ch-3 sp, ch 6, 2 sc in next ch-3 sp, ch 3; repeat from ★ around; join with slip st to first dc: 30 sps.

Rnd 7: Slip st in next dc and in next ch-2 sp, ch 3, (dc, ch 2, 2 dc) in same sp, ch 3, (2 dc, ch 2, 2 dc) in next ch-2 sp, ch 3, sc in next ch-3 sp, dc in next ch-6 sp, (ch 1, dc in same sp) 5 times, sc in next ch-3 sp, ch 3, ★ [(2 dc, ch 2, 2 dc) in next ch-2 sp, ch 3] twice, sc in next ch-3 sp, dc in next ch-6 sp, (ch 1, dc in same sp) 5 times, sc in next ch-3 sp, ch 3; repeat from ★ around; join with slip st to first dc: 60 sps.

Rnd 8: Slip st in next dc and in next ch-2 sp, ch 3, (dc, ch 2, 2 dc) in same sp, ★ ✝ ch 3, (sc, work Picot, sc) in next ch-3 sp, ch 3, (2 dc, ch 2, 2 dc) in next ch-2 sp, ch 3, 2 sc in next ch-3 sp, sc in next ch-1 sp, (ch 2, sc in next ch-1 sp) 4 times, 2 sc in next ch-3 sp, ch 3 ✝, (2 dc, ch 2, 2 dc) in next ch-2 sp; repeat from ★ 4 times **more**, then repeat from ✝ to ✝ once; join with slip st to first dc.

Rnd 9: Slip st in next dc and in next ch-2 sp, ch 3, (dc, ch 2, 2 dc) in same sp, ★ ✝ ch 3, [(sc, work Picot, sc) in next ch-3 sp, ch 3] twice, (2 dc, ch 2, 2 dc) in next ch-2 sp, ch 3, 2 sc in next ch-3 sp, sc in next ch-2 sp, (ch 2, sc in next ch-2 sp) 3 times, 2 sc in next ch-3 sp, ch 3 ✝, (2 dc, ch 2, 2 dc) in next ch-2 sp; repeat from ★ 4 times **more**, then repeat from ✝ to ✝ once; join with slip st to first dc.

Rnd 10: Slip st in next dc and in next ch-2 sp, ch 3, (dc, ch 2, 2 dc) in same sp, ★ ✝ ch 3, [(sc, work Picot, sc) in next ch-3 sp, ch 3] 3 times, (2 dc, ch 2, 2 dc) in next ch-2 sp, ch 3, 2 sc in next ch-3 sp, sc in next ch-2 sp, (ch 2, sc in next ch-2 sp) twice, 2 sc in next ch-3 sp, ch 3 ✝, (2 dc, ch 2, 2 dc) in next ch-2 sp; repeat from ★ 4 times **more**, then repeat from ✝ to ✝ once; join with slip st to first dc.

Rnd 11: Slip st in next dc and in next ch-2 sp, ch 3, (dc, ch 2, 2 dc) in same sp, ★ ✝ ch 3, [(sc, work Picot, sc) in next ch-3 sp, ch 3] 4 times, (2 dc, ch 2, 2 dc) in next ch-2 sp, ch 3, 2 sc in next ch-3 sp, sc in next ch-2 sp, ch 2, sc in next ch-2 sp, 2 sc in next ch-3 sp, ch 3 ✝, (2 dc, ch 2, 2 dc) in next ch-2 sp; repeat from ★ 4 times **more**, then repeat from ✝ to ✝ once; join with slip st to first dc.

Rnd 12: Slip st in next dc and in next ch-2 sp, ch 3, (dc, ch 2, 2 dc) in same sp, ch 3, [(sc, work Picot, sc) in next ch-3 sp, ch 3] 5 times, (2 dc, ch 2, 2 dc) in next ch-2 sp, decrease, ★ (2 dc, ch 2, 2 dc) in next ch-2 sp, ch 3, [(sc, work Picot, sc) in next ch-3 sp, ch 3] 5 times, (2 dc, ch 2, 2 dc) in next ch-2 sp, decrease; repeat from ★ around; join with slip st to first dc: 48 sps.

Rnd 13: Slip st in next dc and in next ch-2 sp, work Beginning Cluster, ch 6, (sc, work Picot, sc) in next ch-3 sp, [ch 5, slip st in third ch from hook, ch 2, (sc, work Picot, sc) in next ch-3 sp] 5 times, ch 6, ★ double decrease, ch 5, slip st in top of last st made *(Fig. 6b, page 144)*, ch 6, (sc, work Picot, sc) in next ch-3 sp, [ch 5, slip st in third ch from hook, ch 2, (sc, work Picot, sc) in next ch-3 sp] 5 times, ch 6; repeat from ★ around to last ch-2 sp, work Cluster; join with (slip st, ch 5, slip st) in top of Beginning Cluster; finish off.

See Washing and Blocking, page 144.

5 ▬▬▬

Finished Size: 6" x 10"

MATERIALS
Bedspread Weight Cotton Thread (size 10): 60 yards
Steel crochet hook, size 7 (1.65 mm) **or** size needed for gauge

GAUGE SWATCH: 2¼"w x 6"h
Work same as Doily through Rnd 3.

STITCH GUIDE

TREBLE CROCHET *(abbreviated tr)*
YO twice, insert hook in sc indicated, YO and pull up a loop (4 loops on hook), (YO and draw through 2 loops on hook) 3 times.

CLUSTER *(uses one ch-2 sp)*
★ YO, insert hook in ch-2 sp indicated, YO and pull up a loop, YO and draw through 2 loops on hook; repeat from ★ 2 times **more**, YO and draw through all 4 loops on hook.

SMALL PICOT
Ch 2, slip st in top of last sc made *(Fig. 6a, page 144)*.

LARGE PICOT
Ch 3, slip st in top of last tr made *(Fig. 6a, page 144)*.

DOILY
Ch 37.

Rnd 1 (Right side)**:** Dc in fourth ch from hook **(3 skipped chs count as first dc)**, ch 2, (2 dc in same ch, ch 2) 3 times, ✝ skip next 2 chs, sc in next 6 chs, ch 2, skip next 2 chs, ★ (2 dc, ch 2) twice in next ch, skip next 2 chs, sc in next 6 chs, ch 2, skip next 2 chs; repeat from ★ once **more** ✝, (2 dc, ch 2) 5 times in last ch; working in free loops of beginning ch *(Fig. 2b, page 144)*, repeat from ✝ to ✝ once, 2 dc in same ch as first dc, ch 1, sc in first dc to form last ch-2 sp: 36 dc and 36 sc.

Rnd 2: Ch 3 **(counts as first dc, now and throughout)**, dc in last ch-2 sp made, ✝ [ch 4, (2 dc, ch 2, 2 dc) in next ch-2 sp] 3 times, ch 2, skip next sc, sc in next 4 sc, ch 2, skip next ch-2 sp, ★ (2 dc, ch 2) 3 times in next ch-2 sp, skip next sc, sc in next 4 sc, ch 2, skip next ch-2 sp; repeat from ★ once **more** ✝, (2 dc, ch 2, 2 dc) in next ch-2 sp, repeat from ✝ to ✝ once, 2 dc in same sp as first dc, ch 1, sc in first dc to form last ch-2 sp; do **not** finish off: 56 dc and 24 sc.

Continued on page 10.

Rnd 3: Ch 3, dc in last ch-2 sp made, † [sc in next ch-4 sp, 2 dc in next ch-2 sp, (ch 2, 2 dc in same sp) twice] 3 times, ch 2, skip next sc, sc in next 2 sc, ch 2, skip next ch-2 sp, ★ (2 dc, ch 2, 2 dc) in next ch-2 sp, ch 4, (2 dc, ch 2, 2 dc) in next ch-2 sp, ch 2, skip next sc, sc in next 2 sc, ch 2, skip next ch-2 sp; repeat from ★ once **more** †, 2 dc in next ch-2 sp, (ch 2, 2 dc in same sp) twice, repeat from † to † once, (2 dc, ch 2, 2 dc) in same sp as first dc, ch 1, sc in first dc to form last ch-2 sp: 80 dc and 18 sc.

Rnd 4: Ch 3, dc in last ch-2 sp made, † skip next 2 dc, (dc, ch 2, dc) in next sc, [(2 dc, ch 2, 2 dc) in next 2 ch-2 sps, skip next 2 dc, (dc, ch 2, dc) in next sc] twice, [(2 dc, ch 2, 2 dc) in next sp, ch 4, work Cluster in next ch-2 sp, skip next 2 ch-2 sps, work Cluster in next ch-2 sp, ch 4] 3 times †, (2 dc, ch 2, 2 dc) in next ch-2 sp, repeat from † to † once, 2 dc in same sp as first dc, hdc in first dc to form last ch-2 sp: 12 Clusters and 76 dc.

Rnd 5: Ch 1, (sc, work Small Picot, sc) in last ch-2 sp made, ch 5, [(sc, work Small Picot, sc) in next ch-2 sp, ch 5] 8 times, † (sc, work Small Picot, sc) in next 2 ch-4 sps, ch 5, (sc, work Small Picot, sc) in next ch-2 sp, ch 5 †, repeat from † to † 2 times **more**, [(sc, work Small Picot, sc) in next ch-2 sp, ch 5] 8 times, repeat from † to † twice, (sc, work Small Picot, sc) in next 2 ch-4 sps, ch 2, dc in first sc to form last ch-5 sp: 28 ch-5 sps.

Rnd 6: Ch 1, (sc, work Small Picot, sc) in last ch-5 sp made, ★ ch 5, (sc, work Small Picot, sc) in next ch-5 sp; repeat from ★ around, ch 2, dc in first sc to form last ch-5 sp.

Rnd 7: Ch 1, (sc, work Small Picot, sc) in last ch-5 sp made, ★ ch 6, (sc, work Small Picot, sc) in next ch-5 sp; repeat from ★ around, ch 2, tr in first sc to form last ch-6 sp.

Rnd 8: Ch 1, sc in last ch-6 sp made, (ch 6, sc in next ch-6 sp) 4 times, (ch 7, sc in next ch-6 sp) 3 times, (ch 6, sc in next ch-6 sp) 11 times, (ch 7, sc in next ch-6 sp) 3 times, ch 6, (sc in next ch-6 sp, ch 6) around; join with slip st to first sc.

Rnd 9: Ch 1, sc in same st, (6 sc in next ch-6 sp, sc in next sc) 4 times, (7 sc in next ch-7 sp, sc in next sc) 3 times, (6 sc in next ch-6 sp, sc in next sc) 11 times, (7 sc in next ch-7 sp, sc in next sc) 3 times, 6 sc in next ch-6 sp, (sc in next sc, 6 sc in next ch-6 sp) around; join with slip st to first sc: 202 sc.

Rnd 10: Ch 1, sc in same st and in each sc around; join with slip st to first sc.

Rnd 11: Ch 1, sc in same st, [skip next 2 sc, (2 dc, tr) in next sc, work Large Picot, (tr, 2 dc) in next sc, skip next 2 sc, sc in next sc] 4 times, [skip next 2 sc, 3 dc in next sc, (tr, work Large Picot, tr) in next sc, 3 dc in next sc, skip next 2 sc, sc in next sc] 3 times, [skip next 2 sc, (2 dc, tr) in next sc, work Large Picot, (tr, 2 dc) in next sc, skip next 2 sc, sc in next sc] 11 times, [skip next 2 sc, 3 dc in next sc, (tr, work Large Picot, tr) in next sc, 3 dc in next sc, skip next 2 sc, sc in next sc] 3 times, skip next 2 sc, (2 dc, tr) in next sc, work Large Picot, (tr, 2 dc) in next sc, skip next 2 sc, [sc in next sc, skip next 2 sc, (2 dc, tr) in next sc, work Large Picot, (tr, 2 dc) in next sc, skip next 2 sc] around; join with slip st to first sc, finish off.

See Washing and Blocking, page 144.

6

Finished Size: 7" diameter

MATERIALS
Bedspread Weight Cotton Thread (size 10): 85 yards
Steel crochet hook, size 7 (1.65 mm) **or** size needed for gauge

GAUGE SWATCH: 2¹/₄" diameter
Work same as Doily through Rnd 3.

STITCH GUIDE

> **TREBLE CROCHET** *(abbreviated tr)*
> YO twice, insert hook in st indicated, YO and pull up a loop (4 loops on hook), (YO and draw through 2 loops on hook) 3 times.
>
> **TRIPLE TREBLE CROCHET**
> *(abbreviated tr tr)*
> YO 4 times, insert hook in sc indicated, YO and pull up a loop (6 loops on hook), (YO and draw through 2 loops on hook) 5 times.
>
> **BEGINNING DC CLUSTER** (uses next 3 dc)
> ★ YO, insert hook in **next** dc, YO and pull up a loop, YO and draw through 2 loops on hook; repeat from ★ 2 times **more**, YO and draw through all 4 loops on hook.
>
> **DC CLUSTER** (uses next 2 dc)
> YO, insert hook in same dc as last st made, YO and pull up a loop, YO and draw through 2 loops on hook, ★ YO, insert hook in **next** dc, YO and pull up a loop, YO and draw through 2 loops on hook; repeat from ★ once **more**, YO and draw through all 4 loops on hook.

TR CLUSTER (uses one st)
★ YO twice, insert hook in st indicated, YO and pull up a loop, (YO and draw through 2 loops on hook) twice; repeat from ★ once **more**, YO and draw through all 3 loops on hook.

BEGINNING 4-DC POPCORN
Ch 3, 3 dc in sp indicated, drop loop from hook, insert hook in top of beginning ch-3, hook dropped loop and draw through.

4-DC POPCORN
4 Dc in ch-2 sp indicated, drop loop from hook, insert hook in first dc of 4-dc group, hook dropped loop and draw through.

BEGINNING 5-DC POPCORN
Ch 3, 4 dc in sp indicated, drop loop from hook, insert hook in top of beginning ch-3, hook dropped loop and draw through.

5-DC POPCORN
5 Dc in ch-3 sp indicated, drop loop from hook, insert hook in first dc of 5-dc group, hook dropped loop and draw through.

TR DECREASE (uses next 2 sc)
★ YO twice, insert hook in **next** sc, YO and pull up a loop, (YO and draw through 2 loops on hook) twice; repeat from ★ once **more**, YO and draw through all 3 loops on hook.

SMALL PICOT
Ch 2, slip st in top of last sc made *(Fig. 6a, page 144)*.

LARGE PICOT
Ch 5, slip st in top of last sc made *(Fig. 6a, page 144)*.

DOILY

Rnd 1 (Right side)**:** Ch 4, tr in fourth ch from hook, (ch 3, work tr Cluster in same ch) 7 times, ch 2, sc in first tr to form last ch-3 sp: 8 ch-3 sps.

Rnd 2: Ch 1, 2 sc in last ch-3 sp made, (2 sc, ch 3, 2 sc) in each ch-3 sp around, 2 sc in same sp as first sc, dc in first sc to form last ch-3 sp: 32 sc and 8 ch-3 sps.

Rnd 3: Work Beginning 5-dc Popcorn in last ch-3 sp made, ch 4, skip next sc, tr decrease, ★ ch 4, skip next sc, work 5-dc Popcorn in next ch-3 sp, ch 4, skip next sc, tr decrease; repeat from ★ around to last sc, ch 1, skip last sc, dc in top of Beginning 5-dc Popcorn to form last ch-4 sp: 16 ch-4 sps.

Rnd 4: Ch 1, 4 sc in last ch-4 sp made, 5 sc in each ch-4 sp around, sc in same sp as first sc; join with slip st to Back Loop Only of first sc *(Fig. 1, page 143)*: 80 sc.

Rnd 5: Ch 1, sc in same st and in Back Loop Only of each sc around; join with slip st to **both** loops of first sc.

Rnds 6 and 7: Ch 1, working in both loops, sc in same st and in each sc around; join with slip st to first sc.

Rnd 8: Ch 1, sc in same st, ★ ch 2, skip next sc, sc in next sc; repeat from ★ around to last sc, skip last sc, hdc in first sc to form last ch-2 sp: 40 ch-2 sps.

Rnd 9: Work Beginning 4-dc Popcorn in last ch-2 sp made, (ch 3, work 4-dc Popcorn in next ch-2 sp) around, dc in top of Beginning 4-dc Popcorn to form last ch-3 sp: 40 4-dc Popcorns and 40 ch-3 sps.

Rnd 10: Tr tr in free loop of sc on Rnd 4 **below** last ch-3 sp made *(Fig. 2a, page 144)*, sc in last ch-3 sp made on Rnd 9, ★ sc in next ch-3 sp, skip next sc on Rnd 4, tr tr in free loop of next sc on Rnd 4, sc in same sp on Rnd 9; repeat from ★ around, sc in same sp as first sc; join with slip st to first tr tr: 120 sts.

Rnds 11-13: Ch 1, sc in same st and in each st around; join with slip st to first sc.

Rnd 14: Ch 1, sc in same st, ★ † ch 9, skip next 6 sc, sc in next sc, ch 3, skip next 3 sc, (2 dc, ch 2, 2 dc) in next sc †, ch 3, skip next 3 sc, sc in next sc; repeat from ★ 6 times **more**, then repeat from † to † once, skip last 3 sc, dc in first sc to form last ch-3 sp: 32 sps.

Rnd 15: Ch 1, sc in last ch-3 sp made, 11 dc in next ch-9 sp, sc in next ch-3 sp, ch 3, (2 dc, ch 2, 2 dc) in next ch-2 sp, ★ ch 3, sc in next ch-3 sp, 11 dc in next ch-9 sp, sc in next ch-3 sp, ch 3, (2 dc, ch 2, 2 dc) in next ch-2 sp; repeat from ★ around, dc in first sc to form last ch-3 sp: 120 dc and 24 sps.

Rnd 16: Ch 1, sc in last ch-3 sp made, skip next sc, work Beginning dc Cluster, (ch 3, work dc Cluster) 4 times, sc in next ch-3 sp and in next 2 dc, 3 sc in next ch-2 sp, ★ sc in next 2 dc and in next ch-3 sp, skip next sc, work Beginning dc Cluster, (ch 3, work dc Cluster) 4 times, sc in next ch-3 sp and in next 2 dc, 3 sc in next ch-2 sp; repeat from ★ around to last 2 dc, sc in last 2 dc; join with slip st to first sc: 32 ch-3 sps.

Rnd 17: Ch 1, sc in same st, ★ † (work Small Picot, 3 sc in next ch-3 sp) twice, work Large Picot, (3 sc in next ch-3 sp, work Small Picot) twice, skip next Cluster, sc in next 4 sc, (sc, work Small Picot, sc) in next sc †, sc in next 4 sc; repeat from ★ 6 times **more**, then repeat from † to † once, sc in last 3 sc; join with slip st to first sc, finish off.

See Washing and Blocking, page 144.

Finished Size: 4$^1/_2$" diameter

MATERIALS

Bedspread Weight Cotton Thread (size 10): 43 yards
Steel crochet hook, size 7 (1.65 mm) **or** size
  needed for gauge

GAUGE SWATCH: 1$^5/_8$" diameter
Work same as Doily through Rnd 4.

STITCH GUIDE

FRONT POST TREBLE CROCHET
  (abbreviated FPtr)
YO twice, insert hook from **front** to **back** around
post of dc indicated *(Fig. 7, page 144)*, YO and
pull up a loop (4 loops on hook), (YO and draw
through 2 loops on hook) 3 times.

FRONT POST DOUBLE TREBLE CROCHET
  (abbreviated FPdtr)
YO 3 times, insert hook from **front** to **back** around
post of FPtr indicated *(Fig. 7, page 144)*, YO and
pull up a loop (5 loops on hook), (YO and draw
through 2 loops on hook) 4 times.

PICOT
Ch 2, slip st in top of last sc made *(Fig. 6a,
page 144)*.

DOILY

Ch 10; join with slip st to form a ring.

Rnd 1 (Right side)**:** Ch 3 **(counts as first dc, now
and throughout)**, 23 dc in ring; join with slip st to first
dc: 24 dc.

Rnd 2: Ch 1, sc in same st, (ch 1, sc in next dc)
around, sc in first sc to form last ch-1 sp: 24 ch-1 sps.

Rnd 3: Ch 1, sc in last ch-1 sp made, ch 1, (sc in next
ch-1 sp, ch 1) around; join with slip st to first sc.

Rnd 4: Ch 1, sc in same st, work FPtr around first dc
on Rnd 1, (sc in next sc on Rnd 3, work FPtr around
next dc on Rnd 1) around; join with slip st to Back Loop
Only of first sc *(Fig. 1, page 143)*: 24 FPtr and 24 sc.

Rnd 5: Ch 1, sc in same st and in Back Loop Only of
each st around; join with slip st to **both** loops of first sc:
48 sc.

Rnd 6: Ch 1, working in both loops, sc in same st and
in each sc around; join with slip st to first sc.

Rnd 7: Ch 1, sc in same st, ★ ch 2, skip next sc, sc in
next sc; repeat from ★ around to last sc, ch 1, skip last
sc, sc in first sc to form last ch-2 sp: 24 ch-2 sps.

Rnd 8: Ch 1, sc in last ch-2 sp made, (ch 3, sc in next
ch-2 sp) around, ch 1, hdc in first sc to form last
ch-3 sp.

Rnd 9: Ch 1, sc in last ch-3 sp made, ch 4, (sc in next
ch-3 sp, ch 4) around; join with slip st to first sc.

Rnd 10: Ch 1, sc in same st, 3 sc in next ch-4 sp, sc in
next sc, work 5 FPdtr around FPtr on Rnd 4 (below next
ch-4 sp), skip next ch-4 sp on Rnd 9 (behind 5-FPdtr
group), ★ sc in next sc, 3 sc in next ch-4 sp, sc in next
sc, skip next FPtr on Rnd 4, work 5 FPdtr around next
FPtr, skip next ch-4 sp on Rnd 9 (behind 5-FPdtr group);
repeat from ★ around; join with slip st to first sc:
60 FPdtr and 60 sc.

Rnd 11: Slip st in next 2 sc, ch 1, (sc, work Picot, sc)
in same st, ch 5, (sc, work Picot, sc) in next skipped
ch-4 sp on Rnd 9, ★ ch 5, skip next 2 sc on Rnd 10,
(sc, work Picot, sc) in next sc, ch 5, (sc, work Picot, sc)
in next skipped ch-4 sp on Rnd 9; repeat from ★
around, ch 2, dc in first sc to form last ch-5 sp:
24 ch-5 sps.

Rnd 12: Ch 1, (sc, work Picot, sc) in last ch-5 sp
made, ★ ch 5, (sc, work Picot, sc) in next ch-5 sp;
repeat from ★ around, ch 2, dc in first sc to form
last ch-5 sp.

Rnd 13: Ch 1, (sc, work Picot, sc) in last ch-5 sp
made, ch 5, ★ (sc, work Picot, sc) in next ch-5 sp, ch 5;
repeat from ★ around; join with slip st to first sc,
finish off.

See Washing and Blocking, page 144.

Finished Size: 6¹/₂" diameter

MATERIALS
Bedspread Weight Cotton Thread (size 10): 46 yards
Steel crochet hook, size 7 (1.65 mm) **or** size
    needed for gauge

GAUGE SWATCH: 2¹/₄" diameter
Work same as Doily through Rnd 5.

STITCH GUIDE

CLUSTER (uses one sp)
★ YO, insert hook in sp indicated, YO and pull up a
loop, YO and draw through 2 loops on hook; repeat
from ★ once **more**, YO and draw through all
3 loops on hook.

DECREASE (uses next 2 dc)
★ YO, insert hook in **next** dc, YO and pull up a
loop, YO and draw through 2 loops on hook; repeat
from ★ once **more**, YO and draw through all
3 loops on hook **(counts as one dc)**.

SMALL PICOT
Ch 2, slip st in top of last sc made **(Fig. 6a,
page 144)**.

LARGE PICOT
Ch 3, slip st in top of last st made **(Fig. 6a,
page 144)**.

DOILY

Ch 7; join with slip st to form a ring.

Rnd 1 (Right side)**:** Ch 1, 12 sc in ring; join with slip st
to first sc.

Rnd 2: Ch 1, sc in same st, (ch 1, sc in next sc) around,
sc in first sc to form last ch-1 sp: 12 ch-1 sps.

Rnd 3: Ch 2, dc in last ch-1 sp made, (ch 3, work
Cluster in next ch-1 sp) around, ch 2, sc in first dc to
form last ch-3 sp.

Rnd 4: Ch 2, dc in last ch-3 sp made, work (Cluster,
ch 3, Cluster) in each ch-3 sp around, work Cluster in
same sp as first dc, ch 1, hdc in first dc to form last
ch-3 sp.

Rnd 5: Ch 1, 2 sc in last ch-3 sp made, sc in next
2 sts, (3 sc in next ch-3 sp, sc in next 2 Clusters) around,
sc in same sp as first sc; join with slip st to Back Loop
Only of first sc **(Fig. 1, page 143)**: 60 sc.

Rnd 6: Ch 1, sc in same st and in Back Loop Only of
each sc around; join with slip st to **both** loops of first sc.

Rnd 7: Ch 3 **(counts as first dc, now and
throughout)**, working in both loops, 2 dc in same st,
★ † ch 3, skip next 2 sc, sc in next sc, ch 5, skip next
3 sc, sc in next sc, ch 3, skip next 2 sc †, 3 dc in next
sc; repeat from ★ 4 times **more**, then repeat from † to †
once; join with slip st to first dc: 18 dc and 18 sps.

Rnd 8: Ch 3, dc in same st, 2 dc in each of next 2 dc,
ch 3, sc in next ch-3 sp, (ch 4, sc in next sp) twice, ch 3,
★ 2 dc in each of next 3 dc, ch 3, sc in next ch-3 sp,
(ch 4, sc in next sp) twice, ch 3; repeat from ★ around;
join with slip st to first dc: 36 dc and 24 sps.

Rnd 9: Ch 3, dc in same st and in next 4 dc, 2 dc in
next dc, ch 3, 2 sc in each of next 2 sps, ch 5, 2 sc in
each of next 2 sps, ch 3, ★ 2 dc in next dc, dc in next
4 dc, 2 dc in next dc, ch 3, 2 sc in each of next 2 sps,
ch 5, 2 sc in each of next 2 sps, ch 3; repeat from ★
around; join with slip st to first dc: 48 dc and 18 sps.

Rnd 10: Ch 2, dc in next 5 dc, decrease, ★ † ch 3,
2 sc in next ch-3 sp, sc in next sc, skip next 2 sc, sc in
next sc, (2 sc, ch 4, 2 sc) in next ch-5 sp, sc in next sc,
skip next 2 sc, sc in next sc, 2 sc in next ch-3 sp, ch 3 †,
decrease, dc in next 4 dc, decrease; repeat from ★
4 times **more**, then repeat from † to † once; join with
slip st to first dc: 72 sc and 36 dc.

Rnd 11: Ch 2, dc in next 3 dc, decrease, ★ † ch 3,
2 sc in next ch-3 sp, sc in next 2 sc, skip next 2 sc, sc in
next 2 sc, (2 sc, ch 4, 2 sc) in next ch-4 sp, sc in next
2 sc, skip next 2 sc, sc in next 2 sc, 2 sc in next ch-3 sp,
ch 3 †, decrease, dc in next 2 dc, decrease; repeat from
★ 4 times **more**, then repeat from † to † once; join with
slip st to first dc: 96 sc and 24 dc.

Rnd 12: Ch 2, dc in next dc, decrease, ★ † ch 3, 2 sc
in next ch-3 sp, sc in next 3 sc, skip next 2 sc, sc in next
3 sc, (2 sc, ch 4, 2 sc) in next ch-4 sp, sc in next 3 sc,
skip next 2 sc, sc in next 3 sc, 2 sc in next ch-3 sp,
ch 3 †, decrease twice; repeat from ★ 4 times **more**,
then repeat from † to † once; join with slip st to first dc:
120 sc and 12 dc.

Rnd 13: Ch 2, dc in next dc, work Large Picot,
★ † ch 3, 2 sc in next ch-3 sp, work Small Picot, (sc in
next 2 sc, work Small Picot) twice, skip next 2 sc, (sc in
next 2 sc, work Small Picot) twice, (2 sc, work Large
Picot, 2 sc) in next ch-4 sp, work Small Picot, (sc in next
2 sc, work Small Picot) twice, skip next 2 sc, (sc in next
2 sc, work Small Picot) twice, 2 sc in next ch-3 sp,
ch 3 †, decrease, work Large Picot; repeat from ★
4 times **more**, then repeat from † to † once; join with
slip st to first dc, finish off.

See Washing and Blocking, page 144.

Finished Size: 7$\frac{1}{4}$" diameter

MATERIALS
Bedspread Weight Cotton Thread (size 10): 68 yards
Steel crochet hook, size 7 (1.65 mm) **or** size
   needed for gauge

GAUGE SWATCH: 3$\frac{1}{4}$" diameter
Work same as Doily through Rnd 5.

STITCH GUIDE

DOUBLE TREBLE CROCHET
(abbreviated dtr)
YO 3 times, insert hook in ch-4 sp indicated, YO
and pull up a loop (5 loops on hook), (YO and draw
through 2 loops on hook) 4 times.

BEGINNING CLUSTER (uses next 2 sc)
Ch 2, ★ YO, insert hook in **next** sc, YO and pull up
a loop, YO and draw through 2 loops on hook;
repeat from ★ once **more**, YO and draw through all
3 loops on hook.

CLUSTER (uses next 2 sc)
YO, insert hook in same sc as last Cluster made, YO
and pull up a loop, YO and draw through 2 loops
on hook, ★ YO, insert hook in **next** sc, YO and pull
up a loop, YO and draw through 2 loops on hook;
repeat from ★ once **more**, YO and draw through all
4 loops on hook.

ENDING CLUSTER (uses last sc)
YO, insert hook in same sc as last Cluster made, YO
and pull up a loop, YO and draw through 2 loops
on hook, YO, insert hook in last sc, YO and pull up
a loop, YO and draw through 2 loops on hook, YO,
insert hook in same sc as beginning ch-2, YO and
pull up a loop, YO and draw through 2 loops on
hook, YO and draw through all 4 loops on hook.

FRONT POST TREBLE CROCHET
(abbreviated FPtr)
YO twice, insert hook from **front** to **back** around
post of st indicated **(Fig. 7, page 144)**, YO and
pull up a loop (4 loops on hook), (YO and draw
through 2 loops on hook) 3 times.

BEGINNING 4-DC POPCORN
Ch 3, 3 dc in st indicated, drop loop from hook,
insert hook in first dc of 4-dc group, hook dropped
loop and draw through.

4-DC POPCORN
4 Dc in sc indicated, drop loop from hook, insert
hook in first dc of 4-dc group, hook dropped loop
and draw through.

4-DTR POPCORN
4 Dtr in ch-4 sp indicated, drop loop from hook,
insert hook in first dtr of 4-dtr group, hook dropped
loop and draw through.

DECREASE
Pull up a loop in next 2 sc, YO and draw through all
3 loops on hook **(counts as one sc)**.

DOILY
Rnd 1 (Right side)**:** Ch 5, (dc, ch 1) 11 times in fifth ch
from hook; join with slip st to fourth ch of beginning
ch-5: 12 ch-1 sps.

Rnd 2: Ch 1, sc in same st and in next ch-1 sp, (sc in
next dc and in next ch-1 sp) around; join with slip st to
first sc: 24 sc.

Rnd 3: Work Beginning Cluster, ch 4, (work Cluster,
ch 4) around to last sc, work Ending Cluster, ch 1, dc in
top of Beginning Cluster to form last ch-4 sp:
12 ch-4 sps.

Rnd 4: Ch 3 **(counts as first dc, now and
throughout)**, (dc, ch 2, 2 dc) in last ch-4 sp made,
ch 1, work FPtr around center post of next Cluster,
ch 1, ★ (2 dc, ch 2, 2 dc) in next ch-4 sp, ch 1, work
FPtr around center post of next Cluster, ch 1; repeat
from ★ around; join with slip st to first dc: 12 FPtr and
12 ch-2 sps.

Rnd 5: Slip st in next dc and in next ch-2 sp, ch 1, sc
in same sp, ch 2, (dc, ch 2) twice in next FPtr, skip next
ch-1 sp, ★ sc in next ch-2 sp, ch 2, (dc, ch 2) twice in
next FPtr, skip next ch-1 sp; repeat from ★ around; join
with slip st to first sc: 36 ch-2 sps.

Rnd 6: Work Beginning 4-dc Popcorn in same st,
ch 4, skip next ch-2 sp, sc in next ch-2 sp, ch 4, ★ work
4-dc Popcorn in next sc, ch 4, skip next ch-2 sp, sc in
next ch-2 sp, ch 4; repeat from ★ around; join with
slip st to top of Beginning 4-dc Popcorn: 12 Popcorns
and 24 ch-4 sps.

Rnd 7: Slip st in first ch-4 sp, ch 1, 4 sc in same sp and in next ch-4 sp, ★ ch 3, 4 sc in each of next 2 ch-4 sps; repeat from ★ around, ch 2, sc in first sc to form last ch-3 sp: 96 sc and 12 ch-3 sps.

Rnd 8: Ch 1, sc in last ch-3 sp made and in next 8 sc, ★ (sc, ch 3, sc) in next ch-3 sp, sc in next 8 sc; repeat from ★ around, sc in same sp as first sc, ch 2, sc in first sc to form last ch-3 sp: 120 sc and 12 ch-3 sps.

Rnd 9: Ch 1, sc in last ch-3 sp made and in next 4 sc, decrease, sc in next 4 sc, ★ (sc, ch 3, sc) in next ch-3 sp, sc in next 4 sc, decrease, sc in next 4 sc; repeat from ★ around, sc in same sp as first sc, ch 2, sc in first sc to form last ch-3 sp: 132 sc and 12 ch-3 sps.

Rnd 10: Ch 1, sc in last ch-3 sp made, ch 3, skip next 2 sc, (sc in next sc, ch 3, skip next 2 sc) 3 times, ★ (sc, ch 2, sc) in next ch-3 sp, ch 3, skip next 2 sc, (sc in next sc, ch 3, skip next 2 sc) 3 times; repeat from ★ around, sc in same sp as first sc, hdc in first sc to form last ch-2 sp: 60 sps.

Rnd 11: Ch 1, 2 sc in last ch-2 sp made and in each of next 2 ch-3 sps, ch 4, 2 sc in each of next 2 ch-3 sps, ★ 3 sc in next ch-2 sp, 2 sc in each of next 2 ch-3 sps, ch 4, 2 sc in each of next 2 ch-3 sps; repeat from ★ around, sc in same sp as first sc; join with slip st to first sc: 132 sc and 12 ch-4 sps.

Rnd 12: Ch 1, sc in same st, skip next 5 sc, work 4-dtr Popcorn in next ch-4 sp, (ch 5, work 4-dtr Popcorn in same sp) 3 times, skip next 5 sc, ★ sc in next sc, skip next 5 sc, work 4-dtr Popcorn in next ch-4 sp, (ch 5, work 4-dtr Popcorn in same sp) 3 times, skip next 5 sc; repeat from ★ around; join with slip st to first sc: 36 ch-5 sps.

Rnd 13: Ch 1, sc in same st, 4 sc in next ch-5 sp, [hdc, 2 dc, ch 3, slip st in top of last dc made *(Fig. 6a, page 144)*, dc, hdc] in next ch-5 sp, 4 sc in next ch-5 sp, ★ sc in next sc, 4 sc in next ch-5 sp, (hdc, 2 dc, ch 3, slip st in top of last dc made, dc, hdc) in next ch-5 sp, 4 sc in next ch-5 sp; repeat from ★ around; join with slip st to first sc, finish off.

See Washing and Blocking, page 144.

10

Finished Size: 4¹/₂" diameter

MATERIALS
Bedspread Weight Cotton Thread (size 10): 22 yards
Steel crochet hook, size 7 (1.65 mm) **or** size
   needed for gauge

GAUGE SWATCH: 1³/₄" diameter
Work same as Doily through Rnd 4.

STITCH GUIDE

BEGINNING CLUSTER
Ch 2, ★ YO, insert hook in sp indicated, YO and pull up a loop, YO and draw through 2 loops on hook; repeat from ★ once **more**, YO and draw through all 3 loops on hook.

CLUSTER
★ YO, insert hook in sp indicated, YO and pull up a loop, YO and draw through 2 loops on hook; repeat from ★ 2 times **more**, YO and draw through all 4 loops on hook.

DECREASE (uses next 2 ch-2 sps)
YO twice, skip next ch-2 sp, insert hook in next ch-2 sp, YO and pull up a loop, (YO and draw through 2 loops on hook) twice, YO twice, working in **front** of first half of st, insert hook in skipped ch-2 sp, YO and pull up a loop, (YO and draw through 2 loops on hook) twice, YO and draw through all 3 loops on hook **(counts as one tr)**.

PICOT
Ch 3, slip st in top of last sc made *(Fig. 6a, page 144)*.

DOILY

Ch 6; join with slip st to form a ring.

Rnd 1 (Right side)**:** Work Beginning Cluster in ring, (ch 2, work Cluster in ring) 7 times, hdc in top of Beginning Cluster to form last ch-2 sp; do **not** finish off: 8 Clusters and 8 ch-2 sps.

Continued on page 16.

Rnd 2: Ch 1, 3 sc in last ch-2 sp made, ch 1, (3 sc in next ch-2 sp, ch 1) around; join with slip st to Back Loop Only of first sc *(Fig. 1, page 143)*: 24 sc and 8 ch-1 sps.

Rnd 3: Ch 1, sc in same st and in Back Loop Only of each sc and each ch around; join with slip st to **both** loops of first sc: 32 sc.

Rnd 4: Ch 1, working in both loops, sc in same st, ch 2, skip next sc, ★ sc in next sc, ch 2, skip next sc; repeat from ★ around; join with slip st to first sc: 16 ch-2 sps.

Rnd 5: [Slip st, ch 3 **(counts as first dc, now and throughout)**, dc, ch 2, 2 dc] in first ch-2 sp, ch 2, sc in next ch-2 sp, ch 2, ★ (2 dc, ch 2) twice in next ch-2 sp, sc in next ch-2 sp, ch 2; repeat from ★ around; join with slip st to first dc: 32 dc and 8 sc.

Rnd 6: Slip st in next dc and in next ch-2 sp, ch 3, (dc, ch 2, 2 dc) in same sp, ch 2, decrease, ch 2, ★ (2 dc, ch 2) twice in next ch-2 sp, decrease, ch 2; repeat from ★ around; join with slip st to first dc: 40 sts and 24 ch-2 sps.

Rnd 7: Slip st in next dc and in next ch-2 sp, ch 4, [dc, (ch 1, dc) 3 times] in same sp, skip next 2 dc and next ch-2 sp, dc in next tr, (ch 1, dc in same st) 4 times, skip next ch-2 sp and next 2 dc, ★ dc in next ch-2 sp, (ch 1, dc in same sp) 4 times, skip next 2 dc and next ch-2 sp, dc in next tr, (ch 1, dc in same st) 4 times, skip next ch-2 sp and next 2 sts; repeat from ★ around; join with slip st to third ch of beginning ch-4: 64 ch-1 sps.

Rnd 8: (Slip st, ch 1, sc) in first ch-1 sp, sc in next dc and in next ch-1 sp, (sc, work Picot, sc) in next dc, sc in next ch-1 sp and in next dc, sc in next ch-1 sp, skip next 2 dc, ★ sc in next ch-1 sp and in next dc, sc in next ch-1 sp, (sc, work Picot, sc) in next dc, sc in next ch-1 sp and in next dc, sc in next ch-1 sp, skip next 2 dc; repeat from ★ around; join with slip st to first sc, finish off.

See Washing and Blocking, page 144.

11

Finished Size: 7" square

MATERIALS
Bedspread Weight Cotton Thread (size 10): 58 yards
Steel crochet hook, size 7 (1.65 mm) **or** size needed for gauge

GAUGE SWATCH: 1¹/₄" square
Work same as Doily through Rnd 2.

STITCH GUIDE

TREBLE CROCHET *(abbreviated tr)*
YO twice, insert hook in ch-4 sp indicated, YO and pull up a loop (4 loops on hook), (YO and draw through 2 loops on hook) 3 times.

PICOT
Ch 3, slip st in top of last sc made *(Fig. 6a, page 144)*.

BEGINNING CLUSTER (uses next 3 dc)
★ YO, insert hook in **next** dc, YO and pull up a loop, YO and draw through 2 loops on hook; repeat from ★ 2 times **more**, YO and draw through all 4 loops on hook.

CLUSTER (uses next 2 dc)
YO, insert hook in same dc as last st made, YO and pull up a loop, YO and draw through 2 loops on hook, ★ YO, insert hook in **next** dc, YO and pull up a loop, YO and draw through 2 loops on hook; repeat from ★ once **more**, YO and draw through all 4 loops on hook.

DECREASE (uses next 2 dc)
★ YO, insert hook in **next** dc, YO and pull up a loop, YO and draw through 2 loops on hook; repeat from ★ once **more**, YO and draw through all 3 loops on hook.

LEFT DECREASE

(uses next 2 dc and next ch-2 sp)
★ YO, insert hook in **next** dc, YO and pull up a loop, YO and draw through 2 loops on hook; repeat from ★ once **more**, YO, insert hook in next ch-2 sp, YO and pull up a loop, YO and draw through 2 loops on hook, YO and draw through all 4 loops on hook.

RIGHT DECREASE

(uses next ch-2 sp and next 2 dc)
YO, insert hook in next ch-2 sp, YO and pull up a loop, YO and draw through 2 loops on hook,
★ YO, insert hook in **next** dc, YO and pull up a loop, YO and draw through 2 loops on hook; repeat from ★ once **more**, YO and draw through all 4 loops on hook.

DOILY

Rnd 1 (Right side)**:** Ch 4, 3 dc in fourth ch from hook **(3 skipped chs count as first dc)**, (ch 3, 4 dc in same ch) 3 times, ch 1, hdc in first dc to form last ch-3 sp: 16 dc and 4 ch-3 sps.

Rnd 2: Ch 3 **(counts as first dc, now and throughout)**, dc in last ch-3 sp made, ★ dc in each dc across to next corner ch-3 sp, (2 dc, ch 2, 2 dc) in corner ch-3 sp; repeat from ★ 2 times **more**, dc in each dc across, 2 dc in same sp as first dc, ch 1, sc in first dc to form last ch-2 sp: 32 dc.

Rnd 3: Ch 3, dc in last ch-2 sp made, ch 5, skip next 3 dc, sc in next dc, work Picot, sc in next dc, ch 5, ★ (2 dc, ch 2, 2 dc) in next corner ch-2 sp, ch 5, skip next 3 dc, sc in next dc, work Picot, sc in next dc, ch 5; repeat from ★ 2 times **more**, 2 dc in same sp as first dc, ch 1, sc in first dc to form last ch-2 sp: 12 sps.

Rnd 4: Ch 3, dc in last ch-2 sp made, ch 3, (sc, ch 3, sc) in next ch-5 sp, ch 4, (sc, ch 3) twice in next ch-5 sp, ★ (2 dc, ch 2, 2 dc) in next ch-2 sp, ch 3, (sc, ch 3, sc) in next ch-5 sp, ch 4, (sc, ch 3) twice in next ch-5 sp; repeat from ★ 2 times **more**, 2 dc in same sp as first dc, ch 1, sc in first dc to form last ch-2 sp: 24 sps.

Rnd 5: Ch 3, (dc, ch 2, 2 dc) in last ch-2 sp made, ch 3, (sc in next sp, ch 3) 5 times, ★ 2 dc in next corner ch-2 sp, (ch 2, 2 dc in same sp) twice, ch 3, (sc in next sp, ch 3) 5 times; repeat from ★ 2 times **more**, 2 dc in same sp as first dc, ch 1, sc in first dc to form last ch-2 sp: 32 sps.

Rnd 6: Ch 3, dc in last ch-2 sp made, ch 3, (2 dc, ch 2, 2 dc) in next ch-2 sp, ch 3, 2 sc in each of next 6 ch-3 sps, ch 3, ★ [(2 dc, ch 2, 2 dc) in next ch-2 sp, ch 3] twice, 2 sc in each of next 6 ch-3 sps, ch 3; repeat from ★ 2 times **more**, 2 dc in same sp as first dc, ch 1, sc in first dc to form last ch-2 sp: 20 sps.

Rnd 7: Ch 3, dc in last ch-2 sp made, ★ † ch 5, (sc, work Picot, sc) in next ch-3 sp, ch 5, (2 dc, ch 2, 2 dc) in next ch-2 sp, ch 3, 2 sc in next ch-3 sp, skip next 2 sc, sc in next 8 sc, skip next 2 sc, 2 sc in next ch-3 sp, ch 3 †, (2 dc, ch 2, 2 dc) in next ch-2 sp; repeat from ★ 2 times **more**, then repeat from † to † once, 2 dc in same sp as first dc, ch 1, sc in first dc to form last ch-2 sp: 24 sps.

Rnd 8: Ch 3, dc in last ch-2 sp made, ★ † ch 3, sc in next ch-5 sp, ch 8, sc in next ch-5 sp, ch 3, (2 dc, ch 2, 2 dc) in next ch-2 sp, ch 3, 2 sc in next ch-3 sp, skip next 2 sc, sc in next 8 sc, skip next 2 sc, 2 sc in next ch-3 sp, ch 3 †, (2 dc, ch 2, 2 dc) in next ch-2 sp; repeat from ★ 2 times **more**, then repeat from † to † once, 2 dc in same sp as first dc, ch 1, sc in first dc to form last ch-2 sp: 28 sps.

Rnd 9: Ch 3, dc in last ch-2 sp made, ★ † ch 3, sc in next ch-3 sp, 13 dc in next ch-8 sp, sc in next ch-3 sp, ch 3, (2 dc, ch 2, 2 dc) in next ch-2 sp, ch 3, 2 sc in next ch-3 sp, skip next 3 sc, sc in next 6 sc, skip next 3 sc, 2 sc in next ch-3 sp, ch 3 †, (2 dc, ch 2, 2 dc) in next ch-2 sp; repeat from ★ 2 times **more**, then repeat from † to † once, 2 dc in same sp as first dc, ch 1, sc in first dc to form last ch-2 sp: 84 dc and 24 sps.

Rnd 10: Ch 3, dc in last ch-2 sp made, ★ † ch 3, sc in next ch-3 sp, skip next sc, work Beginning Cluster, (ch 4, work Cluster) 5 times, sc in next ch-3 sp, ch 3, (2 dc, ch 2, 2 dc) in next ch-2 sp, ch 3, 2 sc in next ch-3 sp, skip next 3 sc, sc in next 4 sc, skip next 3 sc, 2 sc in next ch-3 sp, ch 3 †, (2 dc, ch 2, 2 dc) in next ch-2 sp; repeat from ★ 2 times **more**, then repeat from † to † once, 2 dc in same sp as first dc, ch 1, sc in first dc to form last ch-2 sp: 44 sps.

Rnd 11: Ch 3, dc in last ch-2 sp made, ★ † ch 3, 2 sc in next ch-3 sp, ch 7, 2 sc in next ch-4 sp, ch 4, dc in next ch-4 sp, ch 4, (tr, ch 4) twice in next ch-4 sp, dc in next ch-4 sp, ch 4, 2 sc in next ch-4 sp, ch 7, 2 sc in next ch-3 sp, ch 3, (2 dc, ch 2, 2 dc) in next ch-2 sp, ch 3, 2 sc in next ch-3 sp, skip next 3 sc, sc in next 2 sc, skip next 3 sc, 2 sc in next ch-3 sp, ch 3 †, (2 dc, ch 2, 2 dc) in next ch-2 sp; repeat from ★ 2 times **more**, then repeat from † to † once, 2 dc in same sp as first dc, ch 1, sc in first dc to form last ch-2 sp: 52 sps.

Rnd 12: Ch 2, decrease, ★ † ch 5, (2 sc in next sp, ch 4) 4 times, (sc, ch 4, sc) in next ch-4 sp, (ch 4, 2 sc in next sp) 4 times, ch 5, work left decrease, ch 5, slip st in fifth ch from hook, skip next 2 ch-3 sps and next 2 dc †, work right decrease; repeat from ★ 2 times **more**, then repeat from † to † once; join with slip st to first decrease, finish off.

See Washing and Blocking, page 144.

Finished Size: 4¼" x 9"

MATERIALS

Bedspread Weight Cotton Thread (size 10): 60 yards
Steel crochet hook, size 7 (1.65 mm) **or** size
needed for gauge

GAUGE SWATCH: 1¼"w x 5"h
Work same as Doily through Rnd 3.

STITCH GUIDE

FRONT POST TREBLE CROCHET
    (abbreviated FPtr)
YO twice, insert hook from **front** to **back** around
post of st indicated *(Fig. 7, page 144)*, YO and
pull up a loop (4 loops on hook), (YO and draw
through 2 loops on hook) 3 times.

SPLIT FRONT POST TREBLE CROCHET
    (abbreviated Split FPtr)
YO twice, insert hook from **front** to **back** around
post of same dc on Rnd 1 as last FPtr made, YO
and pull up a loop, (YO and draw through 2 loops
on hook) twice, YO twice, skip next 3 dc on Rnd 1,
insert hook from **front** to **back** around post of next
dc, YO and pull up a loop, (YO and draw through
2 loops on hook) twice, YO and draw through all
3 loops on hook.

BEGINNING CLUSTER (uses one sp)
Ch 2, ★ YO, insert hook in sp indicated, YO and
pull up a loop, YO and draw through 2 loops on
hook; repeat from ★ once **more**, YO and draw
through all 3 loops on hook.

CLUSTER (uses one sp)
★ YO, insert hook in sp indicated, YO and pull up a
loop, YO and draw through 2 loops on hook; repeat
from ★ 2 times **more**, YO and draw through all
4 loops on hook.

DOILY

Ch 34.

Rnd 1 (Right side)**:** 6 Dc in fourth ch from hook
(3 skipped chs count as first dc), dc in each ch
across to last ch, 7 dc in last ch; dc in free loop of next
29 chs *(Fig. 2b, page 144)*; join with slip st to first dc:
72 dc.

Rnd 2: Ch 3 **(counts as first dc)**, dc in same st, 2 dc
in each of next 6 dc, dc in next 29 dc, 2 dc in each of
next 7 dc, dc in each dc around; join with slip st to first
dc: 86 dc.

Rnd 3: Ch 1, sc in same st, work FPtr around first dc
on Rnd 1, † (sc in dc behind FPtr and in next dc, work
FPtr around next dc on Rnd 1) 6 times, sc in dc behind
FPtr, skip next 2 dc on Rnd 1, work FPtr around next
dc, skip dc behind FPtr, sc in next 3 dc, (work Split FPtr,
skip dc behind Split FPtr, sc in next 3 dc) 6 times, work
FPtr around same dc as last Split FPtr made, skip dc
behind FPtr †, sc in next dc, skip next 2 dc on Rnd 1,
work FPtr around next dc, repeat from † to † once; join
with slip st to first sc: 100 sts.

Rnd 4: Ch 1, sc in same st and in each st around; join
with slip st to first sc.

Rnd 5: Ch 1, sc in same st, ★ ch 3, skip next sc, sc in
next sc; repeat from ★ around to last sc, ch 1, skip last
sc, hdc in first sc to form last ch-3 sp: 50 ch-3 sps.

Rnd 6: Ch 1, sc in last ch-3 sp made, ch 3, (sc in next
ch-3 sp, ch 3) around; join with slip st to first sc.

Rnd 7: (Slip st, work Beginning Cluster) in first ch-3 sp,
(ch 3, work Cluster in next ch-3 sp) 10 times, (ch 2,
work Cluster in next ch-3 sp) 15 times, (ch 3, work
Cluster in next ch-3 sp) 10 times, ch 2, (work Cluster in
next ch-3 sp, ch 2) around; join with slip st to top of
Beginning Cluster: 50 Clusters.

Rnd 8: Slip st in first ch-3 sp, work (Beginning Cluster,
ch 2, Cluster) in same sp, work (Cluster, ch 2, Cluster) in
next 9 ch-3 sps, ch 2, (work Cluster in next ch-2 sp,
ch 2) 15 times, work (Cluster, ch 2, Cluster) in next
10 ch-3 sps, ch 2, (work Cluster in next ch-2 sp, ch 2)
around; join with slip st to top of Beginning Cluster:
70 Clusters and 52 ch-2 sps.

Rnd 9: (Slip st, ch 1, 2 sc) in first ch-2 sp, † ch 3, (2 sc
in next ch-2 sp, ch 3) 3 times, (hdc, ch 3, dc) in next
ch-2 sp, ch 1, (dc, ch 3, hdc) in next ch-2 sp, (ch 3, 2 sc
in next ch-2 sp) 4 times †, (ch 1, 2 sc in next ch-2 sp) 17
times, repeat from † to † once, ch 1, (2 sc in next
ch-2 sp, ch 1) around; join with slip st to first sc:
36 ch-1 sps and 20 ch-3 sps.

Rnd 10: Ch 1, sc in same st and in next sc, † ★ [2 sc,
ch 3, slip st in top of last sc made *(Fig. 6a, page 144)*,
sc] in next ch-3 sp, sc in next 2 sc; repeat from ★
2 times **more**, 3 sc in next ch-3 sp, (sc, ch 3, slip st in
top of last sc made, sc) in next ch-3 sp, sc in next dc,
(hdc, ch 5, slip st in top of last hdc made, hdc) in next
ch-1 sp, sc in next dc, (sc, ch 3, slip st in top of last sc
made, sc) in next ch-3 sp, 3 sc in next ch-3 sp, sc in
next 2 sc, [(2 sc, ch 3, slip st in top of last sc made, sc)
in next ch-3 sp, sc in next 2 sc] 3 times †, (ch 2, slip st
in top of last sc made, skip next ch-1 sp, sc in next
2 sc) 17 times, repeat from † to † once, ch 2, slip st in
top of last sc made, skip next ch-1 sp, (sc in next 2 sc,
ch 2, slip st in top of last sc made, skip next ch-1 sp)
around; join with slip st to first sc, finish off.

See Washing and Blocking, page 144.

13

Finished Size: $5^1/_2$" diameter

MATERIALS
Bedspread Weight Cotton Thread (size 10): 35 yards
Steel crochet hook, size 7 (1.65 mm) **or** size
    needed for gauge

GAUGE SWATCH: $2^1/_2$" diameter
Work same as Doily through Rnd 4.

STITCH GUIDE

TREBLE CROCHET (abbreviated tr)
YO twice, insert hook in sc indicated, YO and pull
up a loop (4 loops on hook), (YO and draw through
2 loops on hook) 3 times.

TRIPLE TREBLE CROCHET
    (abbreviated tr tr)
YO 4 times, insert hook in sc indicated, YO and pull
up a loop (6 loops on hook), (YO and draw through
2 loops on hook) 5 times.

BEGINNING CLUSTER
Ch 2, ★ YO, insert hook in sp indicated, YO and
pull up a loop, YO and draw through 2 loops on
hook; repeat from ★ once **more**, YO and draw
through all 3 loops on hook.

CLUSTER
★ YO, insert hook in sp indicated, YO and pull up a
loop, YO and draw through 2 loops on hook; repeat
from ★ 2 times **more**, YO and draw through all
4 loops on hook.

PICOT
Ch 3, slip st in top of last sc made (*Fig. 6a,
page 144*).

DOILY
Ch 6; join with slip st to form a ring.

Rnd 1 (Right side)**:** Work Beginning Cluster in ring,
(ch 3, work Cluster in ring) 7 times, ch 1, hdc in top of
Beginning Cluster to form last ch-3 sp: 8 ch-3 sps.

Rnd 2: Ch 1, sc in last ch-3 sp made, ch 5, (sc in next
ch-3 sp, ch 5) around; join with slip st to first sc.

Rnd 3: Ch 4 **(counts as first dc plus ch 1)**, (dc,
ch 1, dc) in same st, sc in next ch-5 sp, ★ dc in next sc,
(ch 1, dc in same st) 3 times, sc in next ch-5 sp; repeat
from ★ around, dc in same st as first dc, ch 1; join with
slip st to first dc: 32 dc and 24 ch-1 sps.

Rnd 4: (Slip st, ch 1, sc, ch 2, sc) in first ch-1 sp, sc in
next dc, sc in next ch-1 sp and in next dc, skip next sc,
sc in next dc, sc in next ch-1 sp and in next dc, ★ (sc,
ch 2, sc) in next ch-1 sp, sc in next dc, sc in next ch-1 sp
and in next dc, skip next sc, sc in next dc, sc in next
ch-1 sp and in next st; repeat from ★ around; join with
slip st to first sc: 8 ch-2 sps.

Rnd 5: (Slip st, ch 1, sc) in first ch-2 sp, ch 9, (sc in
next ch-2 sp, ch 9) around; join with slip st to first sc.

Rnd 6: Ch 1, sc in same st and in next 9 chs, (sc in
next sc and in next 9 chs) around; join with slip st to
Back Loop Only of first sc (*Fig. 1, page 143*): 80 sc.

Rnd 7: Ch 1, sc in same st and in Back Loop Only of
each sc around; join with slip st to **both** loops of first sc.

Rnd 8: Ch 1, working in both loops, sc in same st and
in next 4 sc, 3 sc in next sc, (sc in next 9 sc, 3 sc in next
sc) around to last 4 sc, sc in last 4 sc; join with slip st to
first sc: 96 sc.

Rnd 9: Ch 1, sc in same st and in next 5 sc, (sc, ch 1,
sc) in next sc, ★ sc in next 11 sc, (sc, ch 1, sc) in next sc;
repeat from ★ around to last 5 sc, sc in last 5 sc; join
with slip st to first sc: 104 sc and 8 ch-1 sps.

Rnd 10: Ch 1, sc in same st, working in free loops of
sc on Rnd 6 (*Fig. 2a, page 144*), skip first sc on
Rnd 6, (tr in next sc, skip sc behind tr, sc in next sc on
Rnd 9, skip next sc on Rnd 6) twice, ★ † tr in next sc,
skip sc behind tr, sc in next sc on Rnd 9, tr in same st on
Rnd 6, skip ch-1 sp behind tr, sc in next sc on Rnd 9, tr
in same st on Rnd 6, skip sc behind tr, sc in next sc on
Rnd 9, skip next sc on Rnd 6 †, (tr in next sc, skip sc
behind tr, sc in next sc on Rnd 9, skip next sc on
Rnd 6) 4 times; repeat from ★ 6 times **more**, then
repeat from † to † once, tr in next sc, skip sc behind tr,
sc in next sc on Rnd 9, skip next sc on Rnd 6, tr in next
sc on Rnd 6, skip sc behind tr; join with slip st to first sc:
56 tr and 56 sc.

Rnd 11: Slip st in next 3 sts, ch 1, sc in same st and in
next 3 sts, (sc, ch 4, sc) in next tr, sc in next 4 sts,
★ ch 7, skip next 5 sts, sc in next 4 sts, (sc, ch 4, sc) in
next tr, sc in next 4 sts; repeat from ★ 6 times **more**,
ch 1, skip remaining sts, tr tr in first sc to form last
ch-7 sp: 16 sps.

Rnd 12: Ch 1, (3 sc, work Picot, 3 sc) in last ch-7 sp
made, ★ † ch 6, slip st in third ch from hook, ch 3, (sc,
work Picot, sc) in next ch-4 sp, ch 6, slip st in third ch
from hook, ch 3 †, (3 sc, work Picot, 3 sc) in next
ch-7 sp; repeat from ★ 6 times **more**, then repeat from
† to † once; join with slip st to first sc, finish off.

See Washing and Blocking, page 144.

Finished Size: 5³/₄" diameter

MATERIALS
Bedspread Weight Cotton Thread (size 10): 62 yards
Steel crochet hook, size 7 (1.65 mm) **or** size
needed for gauge

GAUGE SWATCH: 2" diameter
Work same as Doily through Rnd 6.

STITCH GUIDE

TREBLE CROCHET *(abbreviated tr)*
YO twice, insert hook in sc indicated, YO and pull
up a loop (4 loops on hook), (YO and draw through
2 loops on hook) 3 times.

BEGINNING CLUSTER (uses first 4 sc)
Ch 3, YO twice, insert hook in Back Loop Only of
next sc *(Fig. 1, page 143)*, YO and pull up a loop,
(YO and draw through 2 loops on hook) twice,
★ YO twice, insert hook in Front Loop Only of **next**
sc, YO and pull up a loop, (YO and draw through
2 loops on hook) twice; repeat from ★ once **more**,
YO and draw through all 4 loops on hook.

CLUSTER (uses next 2 sc)
YO twice, insert hook in free loop of same st as
third leg of previous Cluster, YO and pull up a loop,
(YO and draw through 2 loops on hook) twice,
YO twice, insert hook in free loop of same st as last
leg of previous Cluster, YO and pull up a loop, (YO
and draw through 2 loops on hook) twice,
★ YO twice, insert hook in Front Loop Only of **next**
sc, YO and pull up a loop, (YO and draw through
2 loops on hook) twice; repeat from ★ once **more**,
YO and draw through all 5 loops on hook.

ENDING CLUSTER
YO twice, insert hook in free loop of same st as
third leg of previous Cluster, YO and pull up a loop,
(YO and draw through 2 loops on hook) twice,
YO twice, insert hook in free loop of same st as last
leg of previous Cluster, YO and pull up a loop, (YO
and draw through 2 loops on hook) twice, YO twice,
insert hook in free loop of same st as first leg of
Beginning Cluster, YO and pull up a loop, (YO and
draw through 2 loops on hook) twice, YO twice,
insert hook in free loop of same st as second leg of
Beginning Cluster, YO and pull up a loop, (YO and
draw through 2 loops on hook) twice, YO and draw
through all 5 loops on hook.

SPLIT TRIPLE TREBLE CROCHET
(abbreviated Split tr tr)
First Leg: YO 4 times, insert hook from **top** to
bottom in free loop of st indicated *(Fig. 2a,
page 144)*, YO and pull up a loop (6 loops on
hook), (YO and draw through 2 loops on hook) 4
times (2 loops remaining on hook).

Second Leg: YO 4 times, insert hook from
bottom to **top** in free loop of st indicated, YO and
pull up a loop (7 loops on hook), (YO and draw
through 2 loops on hook) 4 times, YO and draw
through all 3 loops on hook. Skip sc behind
Split tr tr.

PICOT
Ch 2, slip st in top of last sc made *(Fig. 6a,
page 144)*.

DOILY

Rnd 1 (Right side)**:** Ch 7, dc in seventh ch from hook
(6 skipped chs count as first dc plus ch 3), ch 3,
(dc in same ch, ch 3) 6 times; join with slip st to first dc:
8 dc and 8 ch-3 sps.

Rnd 2: Ch 1, sc in same st, (3 sc in next ch-3 sp, sc in
next dc) around to last ch-3 sp, place marker in Front
Loop Only of last sc made for st placement *(Fig. 1,
page 143)*, 3 sc in last ch-3 sp; join with slip st to Back
Loop Only of first sc: 32 sc.

Rnd 3: Ch 1, sc in same st and in Back Loop Only of
each sc around; join with slip st to **both** loops of first sc.

Rnd 4: Ch 1, sc in same st, ch 1, (sc in both loops of
next sc, ch 1) around; join with slip st to first sc.

Rnd 5: (Slip st, ch 1, sc) in first ch-1 sp, (ch 1, sc in
next ch-1 sp) around, sc in first sc to form last ch-1 sp.

Rnd 6: Ch 1, sc in last ch-1 sp made, ch 1, (sc in next
ch-1 sp, ch 1) around; join with slip st to first sc.

Rnd 7: Ch 1, work First Leg of Split tr tr in marked sc on Rnd 2, skip next 7 sc on Rnd 2, work Second Leg of Split tr tr in next sc, sc in next ch-1 sp on Rnd 6, (sc in next sc and in next ch-1 sp) 3 times, working in **front** of Second Leg of last Split tr tr made, skip next 3 sc on Rnd 2 from First Leg of same st, work First Leg of Split tr tr in next sc, skip next 7 sc on Rnd 2, work Second Leg of Split tr tr in next sc, sc in next ch-1 sp on Rnd 6, (sc in next sc and in next ch-1 sp) 3 times, ★ working in **front** of Second Leg of last Split tr tr made, work First Leg of Split tr tr in same st as Second Leg of next-to-the-last Split tr tr made, skip next 7 sc on Rnd 2, work Second Leg of Split tr tr in next sc, sc in next ch-1 sp on Rnd 6, (sc in next sc and in next ch-1 sp) 3 times; repeat from ★ 3 times **more**, working in **front** of Second Leg of last Split tr tr made, work First Leg of Split tr tr in same st as Second Leg of next-to-the-last Split tr tr made, skip next 7 sc on Rnd 2, work Second Leg of Split tr tr in same st as First Leg of first Split tr tr made, sc in next ch-1 sp on Rnd 6, (sc in next sc and in next ch-1 sp) 3 times, working in **front** of Second Leg of last Split tr tr made, work First Leg of Split tr tr in same st as Second Leg of next-to-the-last Split tr tr made, working **behind** First Leg of first Split tr tr made, work Second Leg of Split tr tr in same st as First Leg of second Split tr tr made, sc in next ch-1 sp on Rnd 6, (sc in next sc and in next ch-1 sp) 3 times; join with slip st to first Split tr tr: 8 Split tr tr and 56 sc.

Rnd 8: Ch 1, sc in same st and in each st around; join with slip st to first sc: 64 sc.

Rnd 9: Ch 1, sc in same st, ch 5, skip next 3 sc, ★ sc in next sc, ch 5, skip next 3 sc; repeat from ★ around; join with slip st to first sc: 16 ch-5 sps.

Rnd 10: Ch 4 **(counts as first tr)**, skip next 2 chs, 5 dc in next ch, skip next 2 chs, ★ tr in next sc, skip next 2 chs, 5 dc in next ch, skip next 2 chs; repeat from ★ around; join with slip st to first tr: 80 dc and 16 tr.

Rnd 11: Ch 1, sc in same st and in Back Loop Only of each st around; join with slip st to Back Loop Only of first sc: 96 sc.

Rnd 12: Work Beginning Cluster, ch 5, (work Cluster, ch 5) around, work Ending Cluster, ch 5; join with slip st to top of Beginning Cluster: 48 Clusters.

Rnd 13: (Slip st, ch 1, 3 sc) in first ch-5 sp, work Picot, (3 sc in next ch-5 sp, work Picot) around; join with slip st to first sc, finish off.

See Washing and Blocking, page 144.

See Washing and Blocking, page 144.

15 ▬▬▬▬▬▬▬

Finished Size: 7$\frac{1}{2}$" diameter

MATERIALS
Bedspread Weight Cotton Thread (size 10): 68 yards
Steel crochet hook, size 7 (1.65 mm) **or** size needed for gauge

GAUGE SWATCH: 2" diameter
Work same as Doily through Rnd 3.

STITCH GUIDE

> **BEGINNING POPCORN**
> Ch 3 **(counts as first dc, now and throughout)**, 3 dc in ring, drop loop from hook, insert hook in first dc of 4-dc group, hook dropped loop and draw through.
>
> **POPCORN**
> 4 Dc in sp indicated, drop loop from hook, insert hook in first dc of 4-dc group, hook dropped loop and draw through.
>
> **BEGINNING CLUSTER** (uses next 2 dc)
> Ch 2, ★ YO, insert hook in **next** dc, YO and pull up a loop, YO and draw through 2 loops on hook; repeat from ★ once **more**, YO and draw through all 3 loops on hook.
>
> **CLUSTER** (uses next 3 dc)
> ★ YO, insert hook in **next** dc, YO and pull up a loop, YO and draw through 2 loops on hook; repeat from ★ 2 times **more**, YO and draw through all 4 loops on hook.
>
> **PICOT**
> Ch 2, slip st in top of last sc made **(Fig. 6a, page 144)**.

DOILY
Ch 6; join with slip st to form a ring.

Rnd 1 (Right side)**:** Work Beginning Popcorn, ch 3, (work Popcorn in ring, ch 3) 5 times; join with slip st to top of Beginning Popcorn, do **not** finish off: 6 ch-3 sps.

Continued on page 22.

Rnd 2: (Slip st, ch 3, 5 dc) in first ch-3 sp, 6 dc in each ch-3 sp around; join with slip st to first dc: 36 dc.

Rnd 3: Ch 3 **(counts as first dc, now and throughout)**, (dc, ch 2, 2 dc) in same st, ch 3, skip next 2 dc, sc in next dc, ch 3, skip next 2 dc, ★ (2 dc, ch 2, 2 dc) in next dc, ch 3, skip next 2 dc, sc in next dc, ch 3, skip next 2 dc; repeat from ★ around; join with slip st to first dc: 18 sps.

Rnd 4: Slip st in next dc and in next ch-2 sp, ch 3, (dc, ch 2, 2 dc) in same sp, ch 3, sc in next ch-3 sp, ch 2, sc in next ch-3 sp, ch 3, ★ (2 dc, ch 2, 2 dc) in next ch-2 sp, ch 3, sc in next ch-3 sp, ch 2, sc in next ch-3 sp, ch 3; repeat from ★ around; join with slip st to first dc: 24 sps.

Rnd 5: Slip st in next dc and in next ch-2 sp, ch 3, (dc, ch 2, 2 dc) in same sp, ch 3, sc in next ch-3 sp, ch 1, work Popcorn in next ch-2 sp, ch 1, sc in next ch-3 sp, ch 3, ★ (2 dc, ch 2, 2 dc) in next ch-2 sp, ch 3, sc in next ch-3 sp, ch 1, work Popcorn in next ch-2 sp, ch 1, sc in next ch-3 sp, ch 3; repeat from ★ around; join with slip st to first dc: 6 Popcorns and 30 sps.

Rnd 6: Slip st in next dc and in next ch-2 sp, ch 3, [dc, (ch 2, 2 dc) twice] in same sp, ch 3, sc in next ch-3 sp, ch 1, (work Popcorn in next ch-1 sp, ch 1) twice, sc in next ch-3 sp, ch 3, ★ 2 dc in next ch-2 sp, (ch 2, 2 dc in same sp) twice, ch 3, sc in next ch-3 sp, ch 1, (work Popcorn in next ch-1 sp, ch 1) twice, sc in next ch-3 sp, ch 3; repeat from ★ around; join with slip st to first dc: 12 Popcorns and 42 sps.

Rnd 7: Slip st in next dc and in next ch-2 sp, ch 3, (dc, ch 2, 2 dc) in same sp, ch 3, (2 dc, ch 2, 2 dc) in next ch-2 sp, ch 3, ★ † sc in next ch-3 sp, ch 1, skip next ch-1 sp, work Popcorn in next ch-1 sp, ch 1, skip next ch-1 sp, sc in next ch-3 sp, ch 3 †, [(2 dc, ch 2, 2 dc) in next ch-2 sp, ch 3] twice; repeat from ★ 4 times **more**, then repeat from † to † once; join with slip st to first dc: 6 Popcorns.

Rnd 8: Slip st in next dc and in next ch-2 sp, ch 3, (dc, ch 2, 2 dc) in same sp, ★ † ch 4, sc in next ch-3 sp, ch 4, (2 dc, ch 2, 2 dc) in next ch-2 sp, ch 3, 2 sc in next ch-3 sp, sc in next 2 ch-1 sps, 2 sc in next ch-3 sp, ch 3 †, (2 dc, ch 2, 2 dc) in next ch-2 sp; repeat from ★ 4 times **more**, then repeat from † to † once; join with slip st to first dc: 36 sps.

Rnd 9: Slip st in next dc and in next ch-2 sp, ch 3, (dc, ch 2, 2 dc) in same sp, ★ † ch 7, 2 sc in each of next 2 ch-4 sps, ch 7, (2 dc, ch 2, 2 dc) in next ch-2 sp, 2 sc in next ch-3 sp, sc in next 2 sc, work Picot, skip next 2 sc, sc in next 2 sc, 2 sc in next ch-3 sp †, (2 dc, ch 2, 2 dc) in next ch-2 sp; repeat from ★ 4 times **more**, then repeat from † to † once; join with slip st to first dc: 24 sps.

Rnd 10: Slip st in next dc and in next ch-2 sp, ch 3, 2 dc in same sp, ch 3, 7 sc in next ch-7 sp, sc in next 4 sc, 7 sc in next ch-7 sp, ch 3, ★ 3 dc in each of next 2 ch-2 sps, ch 3, 7 sc in next ch-7 sp, sc in next 4 sc, 7 sc in next ch-7 sp, ch 3; repeat from ★ around to last ch-2 sp, 3 dc in last ch-2 sp; join with slip st to first dc: 36 dc and 108 sc.

Rnd 11: Work Beginning Cluster, ch 4, 2 sc in next ch-3 sp, ch 4, skip next 2 sc, (sc in next 2 sc, ch 4, skip next 2 sc) 4 times, 2 sc in next ch-3 sp, ch 4, ★ work Cluster twice, ch 4, 2 sc in next ch-3 sp, ch 4, skip next 2 sc, (sc in next 2 sc, ch 4, skip next 2 sc) 4 times, 2 sc in next ch-3 sp, ch 4; repeat from ★ around to last 3 dc, work Cluster; join with slip st to top of Beginning Cluster: 42 ch-4 sps.

Rnd 12: (Slip st, ch 1, 2 sc) in first ch-4 sp, ch 4, (2 sc in next ch-4 sp, ch 4) around; join with slip st to first sc.

Rnd 13: Slip st in next sc and in next ch-4 sp, ch 1, sc in same sp, (work Picot, sc in same sp) 3 times, ★ sc in next ch-4 sp, (work Picot, sc in same sp) 3 times; repeat from ★ around; join with slip st to first sc, finish off.

See Washing and Blocking, page 144.

Finished Size: 6¹/₄" diameter

MATERIALS

Bedspread Weight Cotton Thread (size 10): 51 yards
Steel crochet hook, size 7 (1.65 mm) **or** size
   needed for gauge

GAUGE SWATCH: 2¹/₂" diameter
Work same as Doily through Rnd 3.

STITCH GUIDE

TREBLE CROCHET (*abbreviated tr*)
YO twice, insert hook in sc indicated, YO and pull
up a loop (4 loops on hook), (YO and draw through
2 loops on hook) 3 times.

BEGINNING CLUSTER (uses next 2 sc)
★ YO, insert hook in **next** sc, YO and pull up a
loop, YO and draw through 2 loops on hook; repeat
from ★ once **more**, YO and draw through all
3 loops on hook.

CLUSTER (uses next 2 sc)
YO, insert hook in same sc as last st made, YO and
pull up a loop, YO and draw through 2 loops on
hook, ★ YO, insert hook in **next** sc, YO and pull up
a loop, YO and draw through 2 loops on hook;
repeat from ★ once **more**, YO and draw through all
4 loops on hook.

ENDING CLUSTER (uses last sc)
YO, insert hook in same sc as last st made, YO and
pull up a loop, YO and draw through 2 loops on
hook, YO, insert hook in last sc, YO and pull up a
loop, YO and draw through 2 loops on hook, YO,
insert hook in same sc as beginning ch-2, YO and
pull up a loop, YO and draw through 2 loops on
hook, YO and draw through all 4 loops on hook.

DOILY

Ch 8; join with slip st to form a ring.

Rnd 1 (Right side)**:** Ch 3 **(counts as first dc, now
and throughout)**, 23 dc in ring; join with slip st to first
dc: 24 dc.

Rnd 2: Ch 1, sc in same st and in next 3 dc, (ch 12, sc
in next 4 dc) around, ch 8, tr in first sc to form last loop:
24 sc and 6 loops.

Rnd 3: Ch 2 **(counts as first hdc)**, 3 hdc in last loop
made, skip next sc, sc in next 2 sc, skip next sc,
★ 15 hdc in next loop, skip next sc, sc in next 2 sc, skip
next sc; repeat from ★ around, 11 hdc in same loop as
first hdc; join with slip st to first hdc: 102 sts.

Rnd 4: Ch 1, sc in same st, ch 2, skip next 8 sts, sc in
next hdc, ch 5, skip next 2 hdc, sc in next hdc, ch 5,
skip next hdc, sc in next hdc, ★ ch 5, skip next 2 hdc, sc
in next hdc, ch 2, skip next 8 sts, sc in next hdc, ch 5,
skip next 2 hdc, sc in next hdc, ch 5, skip next hdc, sc in
next hdc; repeat from ★ around to last 2 hdc, ch 2, skip
last 2 hdc, dc in first sc to form last ch-5 sp: 24 sps.

Rnd 5: Ch 1, sc in last ch-5 sp made, ch 5, skip next
ch-2 sp, ★ (sc in next ch-5 sp, ch 5) 3 times, skip next
ch-2 sp; repeat from ★ 4 times **more**, sc in next
ch-5 sp, ch 5, sc in next ch-5 sp, ch 2, dc in first sc to
form last ch-5 sp: 18 ch-5 sps.

Rnd 6: Ch 1, sc in last ch-5 sp made, ch 7, (sc in next
ch-5 sp, ch 7) around; join with slip st to first sc.

Rnd 7: Ch 3, 4 dc in same st, sc in next ch-7 sp, (5 dc
in next sc, sc in next ch-7 sp) around; join with slip st to
first dc: 90 dc and 18 sc.

Rnd 8: Ch 1, sc in same st and in Back Loop Only of
each st around *(Fig. 1, page 143)*; join with slip st to
both loops of first sc: 108 sc.

Rnd 9: Ch 1, sc in same st and in both loops of each sc
around; join with slip st to first sc.

Rnd 10: Ch 2, work Beginning Cluster, ch 3, (work
Cluster, ch 3) around to last sc, work Ending Cluster,
ch 3; join with slip st to top of Beginning Cluster:
54 ch-3 sps.

Rnd 11: Ch 1, sc in same st, ch 4, slip st in third ch
from hook, ch 1, ★ sc in next Cluster, ch 4, slip st in
third ch from hook, ch 1; repeat from ★ around; join
with slip st to first sc, finish off.

See Washing and Blocking, page 144.

17

Finished Size: 6¹/₂" square

MATERIALS
Bedspread Weight Cotton Thread (size 10): 54 yards
Steel crochet hook, size 7 (1.65 mm) **or** size
   needed for gauge

GAUGE SWATCH: 2" square
Work same as Doily through Rnd 3.

STITCH GUIDE

CLUSTER (uses one sp)
★ YO, insert hook in sp indicated, YO and pull up a loop, YO and draw through 2 loops on hook; repeat from ★ once **more**, YO and draw through all 3 loops on hook.

PICOT
Ch 3, slip st in third ch from hook.

DOILY
Rnd 1 (Right side)**:** Ch 6, dc in sixth ch from hook **(5 skipped chs count as first dc plus ch 2)**, (ch 2, dc in same ch) 10 times, ch 1, sc in first dc to form last ch-2 sp: 12 ch-2 sps.

Rnd 2: Ch 2, dc in last ch-2 sp made, ch 2, sc in next ch-2 sp, ch 3, sc in next ch-2 sp, ch 2, ★ (work Cluster, ch 2) twice in next ch-2 sp, sc in next ch-2 sp, ch 3, sc in next ch-2 sp, ch 2; repeat from ★ 2 times **more**, work Cluster in same sp as first dc, ch 1, sc in first dc to form last ch-2 sp: 16 sps.

Rnd 3: Ch 2, dc in last ch-2 sp made, ch 2, sc in next ch-2 sp, work (Cluster, ch 2, Cluster) in next ch-3 sp, sc in next ch-2 sp, ch 2, ★ (work Cluster, ch 2) twice in next ch-2 sp, sc in next ch-2 sp, work (Cluster, ch 2, Cluster) in next ch-3 sp, sc in next ch-2 sp, ch 2; repeat from ★ 2 times **more**, work Cluster in same sp as first dc, ch 1, sc in first dc to form last ch-2 sp.

Rnd 4: Ch 2, dc in last ch-2 sp made, ch 2, sc in next ch-2 sp, (ch 4, sc in next ch-2 sp) twice, ch 2, ★ (work Cluster, ch 2) twice in next ch-2 sp, sc in next ch-2 sp, (ch 4, sc in next ch-2 sp) twice, ch 2; repeat from ★ 2 times **more**, work Cluster in same sp as first dc, ch 1, sc in first dc to form last ch-2 sp: 20 sps.

Rnd 5: Ch 2, dc in last ch-2 sp made, ch 2, ★ † sc in next ch-2 sp, [work Cluster in next ch-4 sp, (ch 2, work Cluster in same sp) twice] 2 times, sc in next ch-2 sp, ch 2 †, (work Cluster, ch 2) twice in next ch-2 sp; repeat from ★ 2 times **more**, then repeat from † to † once, work Cluster in same sp as first dc, ch 1, sc in first dc to form last ch-2 sp: 28 sps.

Rnd 6: Ch 2, dc in last ch-2 sp made, ch 2, ★ † sc in next ch-2 sp, (ch 4, sc in next ch-2 sp) twice, work Picot, sc in next ch-2 sp, (ch 4, sc in next ch-2 sp) twice, ch 2 †, (work Cluster, ch 2) twice in next ch-2 sp; repeat from ★ 2 times **more**, then repeat from † to † once, work Cluster in same sp as first dc, ch 1, sc in first dc to form last ch-2 sp.

Rnd 7: Ch 2, dc in last ch-2 sp made, ch 2, ★ † sc in next ch-2 sp, work Cluster in next ch-4 sp, (ch 2, work Cluster in same sp) twice, sc in next ch-4 sp, ch 6, sc in next ch-4 sp, work Cluster in next ch-4 sp, (ch 2, work Cluster in same sp) twice, sc in next ch-2 sp, ch 2 †, (work Cluster, ch 2) twice in next ch-2 sp; repeat from ★ 2 times **more**, then repeat from † to † once, work Cluster in same sp as first dc, ch 1, sc in first dc to form last ch-2 sp: 32 sps.

Rnd 8: Ch 2, dc in last ch-2 sp made, ch 2, ★ † sc in next ch-2 sp, (ch 4, sc in next ch-2 sp) twice, work Cluster in next ch-6 sp, (ch 2, work Cluster in same sp) 3 times, sc in next ch-2 sp, (ch 4, sc in next ch-2 sp) twice, ch 2 †, (work Cluster, ch 2) twice in next ch-2 sp; repeat from ★ 2 times **more**, then repeat from † to † once, work Cluster in same sp as first dc, ch 1, sc in first dc to form last ch-2 sp: 40 sps.

Rnd 9: Ch 2, (dc, ch 2, work Cluster) in last ch-2 sp made, ch 2, ★ † sc in next ch-2 sp, work (Cluster, ch 2, Cluster) in next ch-4 sp, work Cluster in next ch-4 sp, (ch 2, work Cluster in same sp) twice, sc in next ch-2 sp, (ch 4, sc in next ch-2 sp) twice, work Cluster in next ch-4 sp, (ch 2, work Cluster in same sp) twice, work (Cluster, ch 2, Cluster) in next ch-4 sp, sc in next ch-2 sp, ch 2 †, (work Cluster, ch 2) 3 times in next ch-2 sp; repeat from ★ 2 times **more**, then repeat from † to † once, work Cluster in same sp as first dc, ch 1, sc in first dc to form last ch-2 sp: 48 sps.

Rnd 10: Ch 2, dc in last ch-2 sp made, ★ † ch 4, (work Cluster, ch 2) twice in next ch-2 sp, sc in next 2 ch-2 sps, (ch 4, sc in next ch-2 sp) twice, 3 sc in each of next 2 ch-4 sps, (sc in next ch-2 sp, ch 4) twice, sc in next 2 ch-2 sps, ch 2 †, work (Cluster, ch 2, Cluster) in next ch-2 sp; repeat from ★ 2 times **more**, then repeat from † to † once, work Cluster in same sp as first dc, ch 1, sc in first dc to form last ch-2 sp: 36 sps.

Rnd 11: Ch 1, sc in last ch-2 sp made, ★ † work Cluster in next ch-4 sp, work (Picot, Cluster in same sp) twice, (sc, work Picot, sc) in next ch-2 sp, sc in next ch-2 sp, [work Cluster in next ch-4 sp, work (Picot, Cluster in same sp) twice] 2 times, skip next 3 sc, sc in next sc, work Picot, sc in next sc, [work Cluster in next ch-4 sp, work (Picot, Cluster in same sp) twice] 2 times, sc in next ch-2 sp †, (sc, work Picot, sc) in next ch-2 sp; repeat from ★ 2 times **more**, then repeat from † to † once, sc in same sp as first sc, work Picot; join with slip st to first sc, finish off.

See Washing and Blocking, page 144.

18 ▆▬▬▬▬▬▬▬▬▬▬

Finished Size: 6¹/₂" diameter

MATERIALS
Bedspread Weight Cotton Thread (size 10): 43 yards
Steel crochet hook, size 7 (1.65 mm) **or** size
   needed for gauge

GAUGE SWATCH: 2" diameter
Work same as Doily through Rnd 3.

STITCH GUIDE

TREBLE CROCHET (*abbreviated tr*)
YO twice, insert hook in sc indicated, YO and pull up a loop (4 loops on hook), (YO and draw through 2 loops on hook) 3 times.

DC CLUSTER (uses one ch-6 sp)
★ YO, insert hook in ch-6 sp indicated, YO and pull up a loop, YO and draw through 2 loops on hook; repeat from ★ 2 times **more**, YO and draw through all 4 loops on hook.

BEGINNING TR CLUSTER
  (uses one ch-1 sp)
Ch 3, ★ YO twice, insert hook in ch-1 sp indicated, YO and pull up a loop, (YO and draw through 2 loops on hook) twice; repeat from ★ once **more**, YO and draw through all 3 loops on hook.

TR CLUSTER (uses one ch-1 sp)
★ YO twice, insert hook in ch-1 sp indicated, YO and pull up a loop, (YO and draw through 2 loops on hook) twice; repeat from ★ 2 times **more**, YO and draw through all 4 loops on hook.

DOILY
Ch 7; join with slip st to form a ring.

Rnd 1 (Right side)**:** Ch 3 **(counts as first dc)**, 17 dc in ring; join with slip st to first dc: 18 dc.

Rnd 2: Ch 1, sc in same st, ch 1, (sc in next dc, ch 1) around; join with slip st to first sc.

Rnd 3: Slip st in first ch-1 sp, work Beginning tr Cluster in same sp, (ch 3, work tr Cluster in next ch-1 sp) around, dc in top of Beginning tr Cluster to form last ch-3 sp: 18 ch-3 sps.

Rnd 4: Ch 1, 2 sc in last ch-3 sp made, (ch 4, 2 sc in next ch-3 sp) around, ch 1, dc in first sc to form last ch-4 sp.

Rnd 5: Ch 1, 2 sc in last ch-4 sp made, (ch 5, 2 sc in next ch-4 sp) around, ch 2, dc in first sc to form last ch-5 sp.

Rnd 6: Ch 1, 2 sc in last ch-5 sp made, (ch 6, 2 sc in next ch-5 sp) around, ch 2, tr in first sc to form last ch-6 sp.

Rnd 7: Ch 1, sc in last ch-6 sp made, work dc Cluster in next ch-6 sp, (ch 3, work dc Cluster in same sp) 3 times, ★ 2 sc in next ch-6 sp, work dc Cluster in next ch-6 sp, (ch 3, work dc Cluster in same sp) 3 times; repeat from ★ around, sc in same sp as first sc; join with slip st to first sc: 27 ch-3 sps.

Rnd 8: Slip st in next dc Cluster and in next ch-3 sp, ch 1, 2 sc in same sp, (ch 4, 2 sc in next ch-3 sp) twice, ch 6, ★ 2 sc in next ch-3 sp, (ch 4, 2 sc in next ch-3 sp) twice, ch 6; repeat from ★ around; join with slip st to first sc: 18 ch-4 sps and 9 ch-6 sps.

Rnd 9: Slip st in next sc and in next ch-4 sp, ch 1, 2 sc in same sp, ch 4, 2 sc in next ch-4 sp, work dc Cluster in next ch-6 sp, (ch 3, work dc Cluster in same sp) 3 times, ★ 2 sc in next ch-4 sp, ch 4, 2 sc in next ch-4 sp, work dc Cluster in next ch-6 sp, (ch 3, work dc Cluster in same sp) 3 times; repeat from ★ around; join with slip st to first sc: 36 sps.

Rnd 10: Slip st in next sc and in next ch-4 sp, ch 1, 2 sc in same sp, (ch 5, 2 sc in next sp) around, ch 2, dc in first sc to form last ch-5 sp.

Rnd 11: Ch 1, 2 sc in last ch-5 sp made, ch 5, slip st in third ch from hook, ch 2, ★ 2 sc in next ch-5 sp, ch 5, slip st in third ch from hook, ch 2; repeat from ★ around; join with slip st to first sc, finish off.

See Washing and Blocking, page 144.

Finished Size: 6¹/₂" (point to straight edge)

MATERIALS

Bedspread Weight Cotton Thread (size 10): 57 yards
Steel crochet hook, size 7 (1.65 mm) **or** size
    needed for gauge

GAUGE SWATCH: 2" diameter
Work same as Doily through Rnd 3.

STITCH GUIDE

TREBLE CROCHET *(abbreviated tr)*
YO twice, insert hook in dc indicated, YO and pull
up a loop (4 loops on hook), (YO and draw through
2 loops on hook) 3 times.

BEGINNING CLUSTER (uses one sp)
Ch 2, ★ YO, insert hook in sp indicated, YO and
pull up a loop, YO and draw through 2 loops on
hook; repeat from ★ once **more**, YO and draw
through all 3 loops on hook.

CLUSTER (uses one sp)
★ YO, insert hook in sp indicated, YO and pull up a
loop, YO and draw through 2 loops on hook; repeat
from ★ 2 times **more**, YO and draw through all
4 loops on hook.

DOILY

Rnd 1 (Right side)**:** Ch 5, dc in fifth ch from hook
(4 skipped chs count as first dc plus ch 1), (ch 1,
dc in same ch) 10 times, sc in first dc to form last
ch-1 sp: 12 ch-1 sps.

Rnd 2: Work Beginning Cluster in last ch-1 sp made,
(ch 3, work Cluster in next ch-1 sp) around, dc in top of
Beginning Cluster to form last ch-3 sp.

Rnd 3: Work (Beginning Cluster, ch 2, Cluster) in last
ch-3 sp made, work (Cluster, ch 2, Cluster) in each
ch-3 sp around; join with slip st to top of Beginning
Cluster: 24 Clusters and 12 ch-3 sps.

Rnd 4: Ch 3 **(counts as first dc)**, 4 dc in next
ch-2 sp, ★ dc in next 2 Clusters, 4 dc in next ch-2 sp;
repeat from ★ around to last Cluster, dc in last Cluster;
join with slip st to first dc: 72 dc.

Rnd 5: Ch 1, sc in same st, tr in next dc pulling tr to
right side, (sc in next dc, tr in next dc pulling tr to right
side) around; join with slip st to Back Loop Only of first
sc *(Fig. 1, page 143)*.

Rnd 6: Ch 1, sc in same st and in Back Loop Only of
each st around; join with slip st to **both** loops of first sc.

Rnd 7: Ch 1, working in both loops, sc in same st,
★ ch 2, skip next sc, sc in next sc; repeat from ★ around
to last sc, ch 1, skip last sc, sc in first sc to form last
ch-2 sp: 36 ch-2 sps.

Rnd 8: Ch 1, sc in last ch-2 sp made, ch 3, (sc in next
ch-2 sp, ch 3) twice, work Cluster in next ch-2 sp,
★ ch 3, (sc in next ch-2 sp, ch 3) 3 times, work Cluster
in next ch-2 sp; repeat from ★ around, dc in first sc to
form last ch-3 sp: 9 Clusters and 36 ch-3 sps.

Rnd 9: (Work Beginning Cluster, ch 3, sc) in last
ch-3 sp made, ★ † 2 sc in next ch-3 sp, ch 2, 2 sc in
next ch-3 sp, (sc, ch 3, work Cluster) in next ch-3 sp †,
ch 3, (work Cluster, ch 3, sc) in next ch-3 sp; repeat
from ★ 7 times **more**, then repeat from † to † once,
ch 1, hdc in top of Beginning Cluster to form last
ch-3 sp: 54 sc, 18 Clusters, and 36 sps.

Rnd 10: Ch 1, sc in last ch-3 sp made, ch 5, ★ † (work
Cluster, ch 3, sc) in next ch-3 sp, 3 sc in next ch-2 sp,
(sc, ch 3, work Cluster) in next ch-3 sp †, ch 5, sc in
next ch-3 sp, ch 5; repeat from ★ 7 times **more**, then
repeat from † to † once, ch 2, dc in first sc to form
last ch-5 sp.

Rnd 11: Ch 1, 2 sc in last ch-5 sp made, ch 5, 2 sc in
next ch-5 sp, ch 4, work Cluster in each of next
2 ch-3 sps, ★ ch 4, 2 sc in next ch-5 sp, ch 5, 2 sc in
next ch-5 sp, ch 4, work Cluster in each of next
2 ch-3 sps; repeat from ★ around, ch 1, dc in first sc to
form last ch-4 sp: 27 sps.

Rnd 12: Ch 1, 3 sc in last ch-4 sp made, sc in next
2 sc, 5 sc in next ch-5 sp, sc in next 2 sc, ★ 4 sc in each
of next 2 ch-4 sps, sc in next 2 sc, 5 sc in next ch-5 sp,
sc in next 2 sc; repeat from ★ around to last ch-4 sp,
4 sc in last ch-4 sp, sc in same sp as first sc; join with
slip st to first sc: 153 sc.

Rnd 13: Ch 1, sc in same st and in next 6 sc, 3 sc in
next sc, (sc in next 16 sc, 3 sc in next sc) around to last
9 sc, sc in last 9 sc; join with slip st to first sc: 171 sc.

Rnd 14: Ch 1, sc in same st and in next 7 sc, 2 sc in
next sc, (sc in next 18 sc, 2 sc in next sc) around to last
10 sc, sc in last 10 sc; join with slip st to first sc,
finish off.

See Washing and Blocking, page 144.

Finished Size: $3^3/_4$" x $7^3/_4$"

MATERIALS

Bedspread Weight Cotton Thread (size 10): 39 yards
Steel crochet hook, size 7 (1.65 mm) **or** size
    needed for gauge

GAUGE SWATCH: $1^1/_8$"w x $4^7/_8$"h
Work same as Doily through Rnd 3.

STITCH GUIDE

> **BEGINNING CLUSTER** (uses one sp)
> Ch 2, ★ YO, insert hook in sp indicated, YO and
> pull up a loop, YO and draw through 2 loops on
> hook; repeat from ★ once **more**, YO and draw
> through all 3 loops on hook.
>
> **CLUSTER** (uses one sp)
> ★ YO, insert hook in sp indicated, YO and pull up a
> loop, YO and draw through 2 loops on hook; repeat
> from ★ 2 times **more**, YO and draw through all
> 4 loops on hook.
>
> **PICOT**
> Ch 2, slip st in top of last sc made *(Fig. 6a,
> page 144)*.

DOILY

Ch 36.

Rnd 1 (Right side)**:** 6 Dc in fourth ch from hook
(3 skipped chs count as first dc), dc in each ch
across to last ch, 7 dc in last ch; dc in free loop of next
31 chs *(Fig. 2b, page 144)*; join with slip st to first dc:
76 dc.

Rnd 2: Ch 1, sc in same st, (ch 1, sc in next dc) 6
times, (ch 1, skip next dc, sc in next dc) 16 times, (ch 1,
sc in next dc) 6 times, (ch 1, skip next dc, sc in next dc)
around to last dc, skip last dc, sc in first sc to form last
ch-1 sp: 44 ch-1 sps.

Rnd 3: Ch 1, sc in last ch-1 sp made, ch 1, sc in next
ch-1 sp, (ch 2, sc in next ch-1 sp) 5 times, (ch 1, sc in
next ch-1 sp) 17 times, (ch 2, sc in next ch-1 sp) 5
times, (ch 1, sc in next ch-1 sp) around, sc in first sc to
form last ch-1 sp.

Rnd 4: Work Beginning Cluster in last ch-1 sp made,
(ch 2, work Cluster in next sp) twice, (ch 3, sc in next sc,
ch 3, work Cluster in next ch-2 sp) 4 times, (ch 2, work
Cluster in next sp) 18 times, (ch 3, sc in next sc, ch 3,
work Cluster in next ch-2 sp) 4 times, (ch 2, work
Cluster in next ch-1 sp) around, ch 1, sc in top of
Beginning Cluster to form last ch-2 sp: 52 sps.

Rnd 5: Ch 1, sc in last ch-2 sp made, ch 5, (sc in next
sp, ch 5) 3 times, (sc in next 2 ch-3 sps, ch 5) 3 times,
(sc in next sp, ch 5) 20 times, (sc in next 2 ch-3 sps,
ch 5) 3 times, sc in next ch-3 sp, (ch 5, sc in next
ch-2 sp) around, ch 2, dc in first sc to form last ch-5 sp:
46 ch-5 sps.

Rnd 6: Ch 1, 2 sc in last ch-5 sp made and in each of
next 3 ch-5 sps, ch 5, (2 sc in next ch-5 sp, ch 5) 4
times, 2 sc in each of next 19 ch-5 sps, ch 5, (2 sc in
next ch-5 sp, ch 5) 4 times, 2 sc in each ch-5 sp around;
join with slip st to first sc: 92 sc and 10 ch-5 sps.

Rnd 7: Ch 1, sc in same st and in next 7 sc, 5 sc in
next ch-5 sp, (sc in next 2 sc, 5 sc in next ch-5 sp) 4
times, sc in each sc across to next ch-5 sp, 5 sc in
ch-5 sp, (sc in next 2 sc, 5 sc in next ch-5 sp) 4 times, sc
in each sc around; join with slip st to first sc: 142 sc.

Rnd 8: Ch 1, sc in same st, skip next 2 sc, 5 dc in next
sc, skip next 2 sc, † sc in next 3 sc, skip next sc, 5 dc in
next sc, skip next sc, (sc in next sc, skip next 2 sc, sc in
next sc, skip next sc, 5 dc in next sc, skip next sc) 4
times, sc in next 3 sc, skip next 2 sc, (5 dc in next sc,
skip next 2 sc, sc in next 2 sc, skip next 2 sc) twice, 3 dc
in each of next 2 sc, skip next 2 sc †, (sc in next 2 sc,
skip next 2 sc, 5 dc in next sc, skip next 2 sc) twice,
repeat from † to † once, sc in next 2 sc, skip next 2 sc,
5 dc in next sc, skip next 2 sc, sc in last sc; join with
slip st to first sc: 44 sc and 102 dc.

Rnd 9: Ch 1, sc in same st, ch 3, skip next 2 dc, (sc,
work Picot, sc) in next dc, ch 3, skip next 2 dc, † sc in
next 2 sc, work Picot, [sc in next sc, ch 3, skip next
2 dc, (sc, work Picot, sc) in next dc, ch 3, skip next 2 dc,
sc in next sc, work Picot] 5 times, sc in next 2 sc, ch 3,
skip next 2 dc, [(sc, work Picot, sc) in next dc, ch 3, skip
next 2 dc, sc in next sc, work Picot, sc in next sc, ch 3,
skip next 2 dc] twice, sc in next dc, work Picot, sc in
next dc, ch 3, skip next 2 dc †, [sc in next sc, work
Picot, sc in next sc, ch 3, skip next 2 dc, (sc, work Picot,
sc) in next dc, ch 3, skip next 2 dc] twice, repeat from
† to † once, sc in next sc, work Picot, sc in next sc,
ch 3, skip next 2 dc, (sc, work Picot, sc) in next dc, ch 3,
skip next 2 dc, sc in next sc, work Picot; join with slip st
to first sc, finish off.

See Washing and Blocking, page 144.

Finished Size: 5¹/₂" (straight edge to straight edge)

MATERIALS
Bedspread Weight Cotton Thread (size 10): 48 yards
Steel crochet hook, size 7 (1.65 mm) **or** size
    needed for gauge

GAUGE SWATCH: 2" diameter
Work same as Doily through Rnd 4.

STITCH GUIDE

TREBLE CROCHET (abbreviated tr)
YO twice, insert hook in sc indicated, YO and pull
up a loop (4 loops on hook), (YO and draw through
2 loops on hook) 3 times.

FRONT POST TREBLE CROCHET
    (abbreviated FPtr)
YO twice, insert hook from **front** to **back** around
post of st indicated **(Fig. 7, page 144)**, YO and
pull up a loop (4 loops on hook), (YO and draw
through 2 loops on hook) 3 times.

**SPLIT FRONT POST DOUBLE TREBLE
CROCHET (abbreviated Split FPdtr)**
YO 3 times, working in **front** of previous rnds and
around posts of FPtr of 3-FPtr group on Rnd 8,
insert hook from **front** to **back** around post of first
FPtr **(Fig. 7, page 144)**, YO and pull up a loop,
(YO and draw through 2 loops on hook) 3 times,
YO 3 times, skip next FPtr, insert hook from **front**
to **back** around post of next FPtr, YO and pull up a
loop, (YO and draw through 2 loops on hook) 3
times, YO and draw through all 3 loops on hook.

CROSS ST
Working in **front** of previous rnds and around posts
of tr on Rnd 8, skip first tr, work FPtr around next
tr, working in **front** of FPtr just made, work FPtr
around skipped tr.

PICOT
Ch 3, slip st in third ch from hook.

DOILY
Ch 7; join with slip st to form a ring.

Rnd 1 (Right side)**: Ch 3 (counts as first dc, now
and throughout)**, 23 dc in ring; join with slip st to first
dc: 24 dc.

Rnd 2: Ch 1, sc in same st and in each dc around; join
with slip st to first sc.

Rnd 3: Ch 1, sc in same st, ★ ch 3, skip next sc, sc in
next sc; repeat from ★ around to last sc, ch 1, skip last
sc, hdc in first sc to form last ch-3 sp: 12 ch-3 sps.

Rnd 4: Ch 1, sc in last ch-3 sp made, (ch 4, sc in next
ch-3 sp) around, ch 1, dc in first sc to form last ch-4 sp.

Rnd 5: Ch 3, 4 dc in last ch-4 sp made, ch 2, sc in
next ch-4 sp, ch 2, ★ 5 dc in next ch-4 sp, ch 2, sc in
next ch-4 sp, ch 2; repeat from ★ around; join with
slip st to first dc: 30 dc and 6 sc.

Rnd 6: Ch 3, dc in next dc, 3 dc in next dc, dc in next
2 dc, ch 3, sc in next sc, ch 3, ★ dc in next 2 dc, 3 dc in
next dc, dc in next 2 dc, ch 3, sc in next sc, ch 3; repeat
from ★ around; join with slip st to first dc: 42 dc and
6 sc.

Rnd 7: Ch 1, sc in same st, ★ † working in **front** of
previous rnd and in 5-dc group on Rnd 5, skip first dc of
5-dc group, work FPtr around next dc, skip dc behind
FPtr, sc in next 2 dc on Rnd 6, work FPtr around next
dc on Rnd 5, sc in same st on Rnd 6 as last sc made and
in next dc, work FPtr around next dc on Rnd 5, skip dc
behind FPtr, sc in next dc on Rnd 6, 3 sc in each of next
2 ch-3 sps †, sc in next dc; repeat from ★ 4 times
more, then repeat from † to † once; join with slip st to
first sc: 18 FPtr and 72 sc.

Rnd 8: Ch 1, sc in same st and in next 3 sts, ★ † 2 sc
in next FPtr, sc in next 4 sts, working in **front** of
previous rnd, tr in front 2 legs of next sc on Rnd 6
(Fig. 4, page 144), skip sc behind tr, sc in next 4 sc,
working in **front** of previous rnd, tr in front 2 legs of
same sc on Rnd 6, skip sc behind tr †, sc in next 4 sts;
repeat from ★ 4 times **more**, then repeat from † to †
once; join with slip st to first sc: 12 tr and 84 sc.

Rnd 9: Ch 1, sc in same st and in next 4 sc, ch 1, (sc
in next 16 sts, ch 1) 5 times, sc in each sc across; join
with slip st to first sc: 96 sc and 6 ch-1 sps.

Rnd 10: Ch 1, sc in same st and in each sc across to
next ch-1 sp, 2 sc in next ch-1 sp, (sc in each sc across
to next ch-1 sp, 2 sc in next ch-1 sp) 5 times, sc in each
sc across; join with slip st to first sc: 108 sc.

Rnd 11: Ch 1, sc in same st and in next 5 sc, work
Split FPdtr, sc in sc behind Split FPdtr and in next 7 sc,
work Cross St, ★ skip next 2 sc (behind Cross St), sc in
next 8 sc, work Split FPdtr, sc in sc behind Split FPdtr
and in next 7 sc, work Cross St; repeat from ★ around
to last 4 sc, skip next 2 sc (behind Cross St), sc in last
2 sc; join with slip st to first sc: 96 sc.

Rnd 12: Ch 1, sc in same st, ch 2, skip next sc, (sc in
next sc, ch 2, skip next sc) twice, 2 sc in next
Split FPdtr, ch 2, (skip next sc, sc in next sc, ch 2) 4
times, skip next 2 sts, ★ (sc in next sc, ch 2, skip next
sc) 4 times, 2 sc in next Split FPdtr, ch 2, (skip next sc,
sc in next sc, ch 2) 4 times, skip next 2 sts; repeat from
★ 4 times **more**, sc next sc, ch 1, skip last sc, sc in first
sc to form last ch-2 sp: 54 ch-2 sps.

Rnds 13 and 14: Ch 1, sc in last ch-2 sp made, (ch 3, sc in next sp) around, ch 1, hdc in first sc to form last ch-3 sp.

Rnd 15: Ch 1, sc in last ch-3 sp made, (sc, work Picot, sc) in next 4 ch-3 sps, [hdc, dc, ch 3, slip st in top of last dc made *(Fig. 6a, page 144)*, hdc] in next sc, ★ (sc, work Picot, sc) in next 9 ch-3 sps, (hdc, dc, ch 3, slip st in top of last dc made, hdc) in next sc; repeat from ★ around to last 4 ch-3 sps, (sc, work Picot, sc) in last 4 ch-3 sps, sc in same sp as first sc, work Picot; join with slip st to first sc, finish off.

See Washing and Blocking, page 144.

22

Finished Size: 9" diameter

MATERIALS
Bedspread Weight Cotton Thread (size 10): 69 yards
Steel crochet hook, size 7 (1.65 mm) **or** size needed for gauge

GAUGE SWATCH: 2$^{1}/_{8}$" diameter
Work same as Doily through Rnd 3.

STITCH GUIDE

PICOT
Ch 2, slip st in top of last st made *(Fig. 6a, page 144)*.

BEGINNING CLUSTER (uses next 3 dc)
★ YO, insert hook in **next** dc, YO and pull up a loop, YO and draw through 2 loops on hook; repeat from ★ 2 times **more**, YO and draw through all 4 loops on hook.

CLUSTER (uses next 2 dc)
YO, insert hook in same dc as last st made, YO and pull up a loop, YO and draw through 2 loops on hook, ★ YO, insert hook in **next** dc, YO and pull up a loop, YO and draw through 2 loops on hook; repeat from ★ once **more**, YO and draw through all 4 loops on hook.

DECREASE (uses next 2 dc)
★ YO, insert hook in **next** dc, YO and pull up a loop, YO and draw through 2 loops on hook; repeat from ★ once **more**, YO and draw through all 3 loops on hook.

CLUSTER DECREASE (uses next 5 sts)
★ † YO, insert hook in **next** dc, YO and pull up a loop, YO and draw through 2 loops on hook; repeat from ★ once **more** †, skip next sc, repeat from † to † once, YO and draw through all 5 loops on hook.

DOILY
Ch 8; join with slip st to form a ring.

Rnd 1 (Right side)**:** Ch 3 **(counts as first dc)**, dc in ring, work Picot, (3 dc in ring, work Picot) 5 times, dc in ring; join with slip st to first dc: 18 dc.

Rnd 2: Ch 4 **(counts as first dc plus ch 1, now and throughout)**, dc in same st, ch 4, skip next 2 dc, ★ (dc, ch 1, dc) in next dc, ch 4, skip next 2 dc; repeat from ★ around; join with slip st to first dc: 12 sps.

Rnd 3: (Slip st, ch 4, dc) in first ch-1 sp, ch 4, sc in next ch-4 sp, ch 4, ★ (dc, ch 1, dc) in next ch-1 sp, ch 4, sc in next ch-4 sp, ch 4; repeat from ★ around; join with slip st to first dc: 18 sps.

Rnd 4: (Slip st, ch 4, dc) in first ch-1 sp, ch 3, sc in next ch-4 sp, 3 dc in next sc, sc in next ch-4 sp, ch 3, ★ (dc, ch 1, dc) in next ch-1 sp, ch 3, sc in next ch-4 sp, 3 dc in next sc, sc in next ch-4 sp, ch 3; repeat from ★ around; join with slip st to first dc: 30 dc.

Rnd 5: (Slip st, ch 4, dc) in first ch-1 sp, ch 3, sc in next ch-3 sp, 3 dc in next sc, ch 1, skip next 3 dc, 3 dc in next sc, sc in next ch-3 sp, ch 3, ★ (dc, ch 1, dc) in next ch-1 sp, ch 3, sc in next ch-3 sp, 3 dc in next sc, ch 1, skip next 3 dc, 3 dc in next sc, sc in next ch-3 sp, ch 3; repeat from ★ around; join with slip st to first dc: 48 dc.

Rnd 6: (Slip st, ch 4, dc) in first ch-1 sp, ch 3, sc in next ch-3 sp, skip next sc, dc in next 3 dc, 3 dc in next ch-1 sp, dc in next 3 dc, sc in next ch-3 sp, ch 3, ★ (dc, ch 1, dc) in next ch-1 sp, ch 3, sc in next ch-3 sp, skip next sc, dc in next 3 dc, 3 dc in next ch-1 sp, dc in next 3 dc, sc in next ch-3 sp, ch 3; repeat from ★ around; join with slip st to first dc: 66 dc.

Rnd 7: (Slip st, ch 4, dc) in first ch-1 sp, ch 3, sc in next ch-3 sp, skip next sc, work Beginning Cluster, (ch 3, work Cluster) 3 times, sc in next ch-3 sp, ch 3, ★ (dc, ch 1, dc) in next ch-1 sp, ch 3, sc in next ch-3 sp, skip next sc, work Beginning Cluster, (ch 3, work Cluster) 3 times, sc in next ch-3 sp, ch 3; repeat from ★ around; join with slip st to first dc, do **not** finish off: 36 sps.

Continued on page 30.

Rnd 8: (Slip st, ch 4, dc, ch 1, dc) in first ch-1 sp, ★ † ch 3, sc in next ch-3 sp, 2 sc in next ch-3 sp, ch 5, (sc, work Picot, sc) in next ch-3 sp, ch 5, 2 sc in next ch-3 sp, sc in next ch-3 sp, ch 3 †, dc in next ch-1 sp, (ch 1, dc in same sp) twice; repeat from ★ 4 times **more**, then repeat from † to † once; join with slip st to first dc.

Rnd 9: (Slip st, ch 4, dc) in first ch-1 sp, ★ † ch 3, (dc, ch 1, dc) in next ch-1 sp, ch 3, sc in next ch-3 sp, work Picot, skip next sc, sc in next 2 sc, 3 sc in next ch-5 sp, ch 5, 3 sc in next ch-5 sp, sc in next 2 sc, work Picot, skip next sc, sc in next ch-3 sp, ch 3 †, (dc, ch 1, dc) in next ch-1 sp; repeat from ★ 4 times **more**, then repeat from † to † once; join with slip st to first dc.

Rnd 10: (Slip st, ch 4, dc) in first ch-1 sp, ★ † ch 4, sc in next ch-3 sp, work Picot, ch 4, (dc, ch 1, dc) in next ch-1 sp, ch 5, skip next 3 sc, sc in next 3 sc, work Picot, 5 sc in next ch-5 sp, work Picot, sc in next 3 sc, ch 5, skip next ch-3 sp †, (dc, ch 1, dc) in next ch-1 sp; repeat from ★ 4 times **more**, then repeat from † to † once; join with slip st to first dc.

Rnd 11: (Slip st, ch 4, dc) in first ch-1 sp, ★ † ch 4, (sc in next ch-4 sp, work Picot, ch 4) twice, (dc, ch 1, dc) in next ch-1 sp, 2 sc in next ch-5 sp, ch 7, skip next 5 sc, (sc, work Picot, sc) in next sc, ch 7, 2 sc in next ch-5 sp †, (dc, ch 1, dc) in next ch-1 sp; repeat from ★ 4 times **more**, then repeat from † to † once; join with slip st to first dc: 42 sps.

Rnd 12: (Slip st, ch 4, dc) in first ch-1 sp, ★ † ch 4, (sc in next ch-4 sp, work Picot, ch 4) 3 times, (dc, ch 1, dc) in next ch-1 sp, 3 sc in next ch-7 sp, ch 5, 3 sc in next ch-7 sp †, (dc, ch 1, dc) in next ch-1 sp; repeat from ★ 4 times **more**, then repeat from † to † once; join with slip st to first dc.

Rnd 13: (Slip st, ch 4, dc) in first ch-1 sp, ★ † ch 4, (sc in next ch-4 sp, work Picot, ch 4) 4 times, (dc, ch 1, dc) in next ch-1 sp, 5 sc in next ch-5 sp †, (dc, ch 1, dc) in next ch-1 sp; repeat from ★ 4 times **more**, then repeat from † to † once; join with slip st to first dc.

Rnd 14: (Slip st, ch 4, dc) in first ch-1 sp, ★ † ch 5, (sc in next ch-4 sp, work Picot, ch 5) 5 times, (dc, ch 1, dc) in next ch-1 sp, skip next 3 sts, sc in next sc †, (dc, ch 1, dc) in next ch-1 sp; repeat from ★ 4 times **more**, then repeat from † to † once; join with slip st to first dc: 48 sps.

Rnd 15: Ch 2, dc in next dc, ★ † ch 5, slip st in third ch from hook, ch 2, (sc in next ch-5 sp, work Picot, ch 5, slip st in third ch from hook, ch 2) 6 times †, work Cluster decrease, work Picot; repeat from ★ 4 times **more**, then repeat from † to † once, decrease; join with slip st to first dc, ch 2, slip st in joining st, finish off.

See Washing and Blocking, page 144.

23

Finished Size: 8" (point to point)

MATERIALS
Bedspread Weight Cotton Thread (size 10): 70 yards
Steel crochet hook, size 7 (1.65 mm) **or** size needed for gauge

GAUGE SWATCH: 1^1/$_2$" (point to point)
Work same as Doily through Rnd 2.

STITCH GUIDE

TREBLE CROCHET *(abbreviated tr)*
YO twice, insert hook in st indicated, YO and pull up a loop (4 loops on hook), (YO and draw through 2 loops on hook) 3 times.

PICOT
Ch 2, slip st in top of last sc made *(Fig. 6a, page 144)*.

2-DC CLUSTER (uses one sp)
★ YO, insert hook in sp indicated, YO and pull up a loop, YO and draw through 2 loops on hook; repeat from ★ once **more**, YO and draw through all 3 loops on hook.

3-DC CLUSTER (uses one ch-2 sp)
★ YO, insert hook in ch-2 sp indicated, YO and pull up a loop, YO and draw through 2 loops on hook; repeat from ★ 2 times **more**, YO and draw through all 4 loops on hook.

TR CLUSTER (uses one ch-5 sp)
★ YO twice, insert hook in ch-5 sp indicated, YO and pull up a loop, (YO and draw through 2 loops on hook) twice; repeat from ★ 2 times **more**, YO and draw through all 4 loops on hook.

DECREASE (uses next 4 sps)
★ YO twice, insert hook in **next** sp, YO and pull up a loop, (YO and draw through 2 loops on hook) twice; repeat from ★ 3 times **more**, YO and draw through all 5 loops on hook.

DOILY

Ch 7; join with slip st to form a ring.

Rnd 1 (Right side)**:** Ch 3 **(counts as first dc)**, dc in ring, (ch 2, 2 dc in ring) 7 times, ch 1, sc in first dc to form last ch-2 sp: 8 ch-2 sps.

Rnd 2: Ch 5 **(counts as first dc plus ch 2, now and throughout)**, 2 dc in last ch-2 sp made, ch 2, sc in next ch-2 sp, ch 2, ★ (2 dc, ch 2) twice in next ch-2 sp, sc in next ch-2 sp, ch 2; repeat from ★ 2 times **more**, dc in same sp as first dc; join with slip st to first dc: 12 ch-2 sps.

Rnd 3: (Slip st, ch 5, 2 dc) in first ch-2 sp, ch 3, 2 sc in next ch-2 sp, work Picot, 2 sc in next ch-2 sp, ch 3, ★ (2 dc, ch 2, 2 dc) in next ch-2 sp, ch 3, 2 sc in next ch-2 sp, work Picot, 2 sc in next ch-2 sp, ch 3; repeat from ★ 2 times **more**, dc in same sp as first dc; join with slip st to first dc.

Rnd 4: (Slip st, ch 5, 2 dc) in first ch-2 sp, ch 4, 2 sc in next ch-3 sp, ch 5, 2 sc in next ch-3 sp, ch 4, ★ (2 dc, ch 2, 2 dc) in next ch-2 sp, ch 4, 2 sc in next ch-3 sp, ch 5, 2 sc in next ch-3 sp, ch 4; repeat from ★ 2 times **more**, dc in same sp as first dc; join with slip st to first dc: 16 sps.

Rnd 5: (Slip st, ch 5, 2 dc, ch 2, 2 dc) in first ch-2 sp, ch 3, sc in next ch-4 sp, work 2-dc Cluster in next ch-5 sp, (ch 2, work 2-dc Cluster in same sp) 4 times, sc in next ch-4 sp, ch 3, ★ 2 dc in next ch-2 sp, (ch 2, 2 dc in same sp) twice, ch 3, sc in next ch-4 sp, work 2-dc Cluster in next ch-5 sp, (ch 2, work 2-dc Cluster in same sp) 4 times, sc in next ch-4 sp, ch 3; repeat from ★ 2 times **more**, dc in same sp as first dc; join with slip st to first dc: 32 sps.

Rnd 6: (Slip st, ch 5, 2 dc) in first ch-2 sp, ch 3, (2 dc, ch 2, 2 dc) in next ch-2 sp, ch 3, 2 sc in next ch-3 sp, sc in next ch-2 sp, (ch 3, sc in next ch-2 sp) 3 times, 2 sc in next ch-3 sp, ch 3, ★ [(2 dc, ch 2, 2 dc) in next ch-2 sp, ch 3] twice, 2 sc in next ch-3 sp, sc in next ch-2 sp, (ch 3, sc in next ch-2 sp) 3 times, 2 sc in next ch-3 sp, ch 3; repeat from ★ 2 times **more**, dc in same sp as first dc; join with slip st to first dc.

Rnd 7: (Slip st, ch 5, 2 dc) in first ch-2 sp, ★ † ch 3, sc in next ch-3 sp, ch 3, (2 dc, ch 2, 2 dc) in next ch-2 sp, ch 3, 2 sc in each of next 2 ch-3 sps, ch 3, sc in next ch-3 sp, ch 3, 2 sc in each of next 2 ch-3 sps, ch 3 †, (2 dc, ch 2, 2 dc) in next ch-2 sp; repeat from ★ 2 times **more**, then repeat from † to † once, dc in same sp as first dc; join with slip st to first dc: 40 sc and 32 dc.

Rnd 8: (Slip st, ch 5, 2 dc) in first ch-2 sp, ★ † ch 4, 3 sc in each of next 2 ch-3 sps, ch 4, (2 dc, ch 2, 2 dc) in next ch-2 sp, ch 4, 2 sc in next ch-3 sp, skip next 2 sc, sc in next 2 sc, 2 sc in next ch-3 sp, ch 4, 2 sc in next ch-3 sp, sc in next 2 sc, 2 sc in next ch-3 sp, ch 4 †, (2 dc, ch 2, 2 dc) in next ch-2 sp; repeat from ★ 2 times **more**, then repeat from † to † once, dc in same sp as first dc; join with slip st to first dc: 72 sc and 28 sps.

Rnd 9: (Slip st, ch 5, 2 dc) in first ch-2 sp, ★ † ch 4, 2 sc in next ch-4 sp, ch 5, 2 sc in next ch-4 sp, ch 4, (2 dc, ch 2, 2 dc) in next ch-2 sp, ch 4, 2 sc in next ch-4 sp, skip next 2 sc, sc in next 4 sc, (2 sc, ch 3, 2 sc) in next ch-4 sp, sc in next 4 sc, 2 sc in next ch-4 sp, ch 4 †, (2 dc, ch 2, 2 dc) in next ch-2 sp; repeat from ★ 2 times **more**, then repeat from † to † once, dc in same sp as first dc; join with slip st to first dc: 32 sps.

Rnd 10: (Slip st, ch 5, 2 dc) in first ch-2 sp, ★ † ch 4, 2 sc in next ch-4 sp, work tr Cluster in next ch-5 sp, (ch 4, work tr Cluster in same sp) 4 times, 2 sc in next ch-4 sp, ch 4, (2 dc, ch 2, 2 dc) in next ch-2 sp, ch 4, 2 sc in next ch-4 sp, ch 2, dc in next ch-3 sp, (ch 1, dc in same sp) 3 times, ch 2, 2 sc in next ch-4 sp, ch 4 †, (2 dc, ch 2, 2 dc) in next ch-2 sp; repeat from ★ 2 times **more**, then repeat from † to † once, dc in same sp as first dc; join with slip st to first dc: 60 sps.

Rnd 11: (Slip st, ch 5, 2 dc) in first ch-2 sp, ★ † ch 4, 2 sc in next ch-4 sp, ch 1, 2 sc in next ch-4 sp, (ch 4, 2 sc in next ch-4 sp) 3 times, ch 1, 2 sc in next ch-4 sp, ch 4, (2 dc, ch 2, 2 dc) in next ch-2 sp, ch 4, 2 sc in next ch-4 sp, sc in next 2 sps, ch 3, sc in next ch-1 sp, ch 3, sc in next 2 sps, 2 sc in next ch-4 sp, ch 4 †, (2 dc, ch 2, 2 dc) in next ch-2 sp; repeat from ★ 2 times **more**, then repeat from † to † once, dc in same sp as first dc; join with slip st to first dc: 52 sps.

Rnd 12: (Slip st, ch 5, 2 dc) in first ch-2 sp, ★ † ch 4, 2 sc in next ch-4 sp, sc in next 2 sc and in next ch-1 sp, sc in next 2 sc, 3 sc in next ch-4 sp, ch 4, 2 sc in next ch-4 sp, ch 4, 3 sc in next ch-4 sp, sc in next 2 sc and in next ch-1 sp, sc in next 2 sc, 2 sc in next ch-4 sp, ch 4, (2 dc, ch 2, 2 dc) in next ch-2 sp, ch 3, decrease, ch 3 †, (2 dc, ch 2, 2 dc) in next ch-2 sp; repeat from ★ 2 times **more**, then repeat from † to † once, dc in same sp as first dc; join with slip st to first dc: 88 sc and 32 sps.

Rnd 13: (Slip st, ch 5, 2 dc) in first ch-2 sp, ★ † ch 5, 3 sc in next ch-4 sp, sc in next 10 sc, 3 sc in next ch-4 sp, ch 4, 3 sc in next ch-4 sp, sc in next 10 sc, 3 sc in next ch-4 sp, ch 5, (2 dc, ch 2, 2 dc) in next ch-2 sp, tr in next decrease, skip next ch-3 sp †, (2 dc, ch 2, 2 dc) in next ch-2 sp; repeat from ★ 2 times **more**, then repeat from † to † once, dc in same sp as first dc; join with slip st to first dc: 128 sc and 20 sps.

Rnd 14: (Slip st, ch 2, work 2-dc Cluster) in first ch-2 sp, ★ † ch 3, 5 sc in next ch-5 sp, sc in next 16 sc, [3 sc, ch 3, slip st in top of last sc made *(Fig. 6a, page 144)*, 2 sc] in next ch-4 sp, sc in next 16 sc, 5 sc in next ch-5 sp, ch 3, work 3-dc Cluster in next ch-2 sp, ch 3, slip st in third ch from hook †, work 3-dc Cluster in next ch-2 sp; repeat from ★ 2 times **more**, then repeat from † to † once; join with slip st to top of first 2-dc Cluster, finish off.

See Washing and Blocking, page 144.

Finished Size: 4$\frac{1}{2}$" diameter

MATERIALS

Bedspread Weight Cotton Thread (size 10): 28 yards
Steel crochet hook, size 7 (1.65 mm) **or** size
   needed for gauge

GAUGE SWATCH: 1$\frac{3}{4}$" diameter
Work same as Doily through Rnd 4.

STITCH GUIDE

TREBLE CROCHET *(abbreviated tr)*
YO twice, insert hook in ch-6 sp indicated, YO and
pull up a loop (4 loops on hook), (YO and draw
through 2 loops on hook) 3 times.

DOUBLE TREBLE CROCHET
  (abbreviated dtr)
YO 3 times, insert hook in sc indicated, YO and pull
up a loop (5 loops on hook), (YO and draw through
2 loops on hook) 4 times.

FRONT POST TREBLE CROCHET
  (abbreviated FPtr)
YO twice, insert hook from **front** to **back** around
post of dc indicated *(Fig. 7, page 144)*, YO and
pull up a loop (4 loops on hook) (YO and draw
through 2 loops on hook) 3 times.

PICOT
Ch 2, slip st in top of last sc made *(Fig. 6a,*
page 144).

BEGINNING CLUSTER (uses one sp)
Ch 2, ★ YO, insert hook in sp indicated, YO and
pull up a loop, YO and draw through 2 loops on
hook; repeat from ★ once **more**, YO and draw
through all 3 loops on hook.

CLUSTER (uses one ch-6 sp)
★ YO, insert hook in ch-6 sp indicated, YO and pull
up a loop, YO and draw through 2 loops on hook;
repeat from ★ 2 times **more**, YO and draw through
all 4 loops on hook.

DOILY

Ch 7; join with slip st to form a ring.

Rnd 1 (Right side)**:** Ch 3 **(counts as first dc)**, 23 dc
in ring; join with slip st to first dc: 24 dc.

Rnd 2: Ch 1, sc in same st, (ch 1, sc in next dc)
around, sc in first dc to form last ch-1 sp.

Rnd 3: Ch 1, sc in last ch-1 sp made, (ch 2, sc in next
ch-1 sp) around, ch 1, sc in first sc to form last ch-2 sp.

Rnd 4: Ch 1, sc in last ch-2 sp made and in next
ch-2 sp, work FPtr around first dc on Rnd 1, sc in same
sp as last sc made on Rnd 3, ★ sc in next ch-2 sp, work
FPtr around next dc on Rnd 1, sc in same sp as last sc
made on Rnd 3; repeat from ★ around, sc in same sp as
first sc, work FPtr around last dc on Rnd 1; join with
slip st to first sc: 72 sts.

Rnd 5: Ch 1, sc in same st and in next sc, skip next
FPtr, (sc in next 2 sc, skip next FPtr) around; join with
slip st to first sc: 48 sc.

Rnd 6: Ch 1, sc in same st and in next 2 sc, work
Picot, (sc in next 3 sc, work Picot) around; join with
slip st to first sc: 16 Picots.

Rnd 7: (Slip st, ch 1, sc) in next sc, ★ ch 6, skip next
2 sc, sc in next sc; repeat from ★ around, ch 1, dtr in
first sc to form last ch-6 sp: 16 ch-6 sps.

Rnd 8: Work (Beginning Cluster, ch 3, tr, ch 3, Cluster)
in last ch-6 sp made, work (Cluster, ch 3, tr, ch 3,
Cluster) in each ch-6 sp around; join with slip st to top of
Beginning Cluster: 32 ch-3 sps.

Rnd 9: (Slip st, ch 1, 3 sc) in first ch-3 sp, (sc, ch 2, sc)
in next tr, ★ 3 sc in each of next 2 ch-3 sps, (sc, ch 2,
sc) in next tr; repeat from ★ around to last ch-3 sp, 3 sc
in last ch-3 sp; join with slip st to first sc, finish off.

See Washing and Blocking, page 144.

25 ▮▬▬▬▬▬

Finished Size: 5¹/₄" diameter

MATERIALS
Bedspread Weight Cotton Thread (size 10): 31 yards
Steel crochet hook, size 7 (1.65 mm) **or** size
   needed for gauge

GAUGE SWATCH: 2" diameter
Work same as Doily through Rnd 3.

STITCH GUIDE

BEGINNING CLUSTER
  (uses next 2 dc and next ch)
Ch 2, ★ YO, insert hook in **next** st, YO and pull up
a loop, YO and draw through 2 loops on hook;
repeat from ★ 2 times **more**, YO and draw through
all 4 loops on hook.

CLUSTER (uses next 2 dc and next 2 chs)
★ YO, insert hook in **next** st, YO and pull up a
loop, YO and draw through 2 loops on hook; repeat
from ★ 3 times **more**, YO and draw through all
5 loops on hook.

SMALL PICOT
Ch 2, slip st in top of last sc made *(Fig. 6a,
page 144)*.

LARGE PICOT
Ch 3, slip st in top of last sc made *(Fig. 6a,
page 144)*.

DOILY

Rnd 1 (Right side)**:** Ch 7, dc in seventh ch from hook
(6 skipped chs count as first dc plus ch 3), ch 3,
(dc in same ch, ch 3) 6 times; join with slip st to first dc:
8 ch-3 sps.

Rnd 2: (Slip st, ch 3, 2 dc, ch 3, slip st) in next ch-3 sp
and in each ch-3 sp around; join with slip st to first
slip st.

Rnd 3: Slip st in first 3 chs, work Beginning Cluster,
★ ch 8, skip next 2 slip sts and next 2 chs, work Cluster;
repeat from ★ around, ch 5, dc in top of Beginning
Cluster to form last ch-8 sp.

Rnd 4: Ch 1, (sc, ch 3, sc) in last ch-8 sp made, ★ sc in
next ch-8 sp, (ch 3, sc in same sp) 3 times; repeat from
★ around, (sc, ch 3, sc) in same sp as first sc, ch 1, hdc
in first sc to form last ch-3 sp: 24 ch-3 sps.

Rnd 5: Ch 1, 2 sc in last ch-3 sp made, ch 4, 2 sc in
next ch-3 sp, work Small Picot, 2 sc in next ch-3 sp,
★ (ch 4, 2 sc in next ch-3 sp) twice, work Small Picot,
2 sc in next ch-3 sp; repeat from ★ around, ch 1, dc in
first sc to form last ch-4 sp: 16 ch-4 sps.

Rnd 6: Ch 1, 2 sc in last ch-4 sp made, ch 5, (2 sc in
next ch-4 sp, ch 5) around; join with slip st to first sc:
32 sc.

Rnd 7: Ch 1, sc in same st and in next sc, 4 sc in next
ch-5 sp, (sc in next 2 sc, 4 sc in next ch-5 sp) around;
join with slip st to first sc: 96 sc.

Rnd 8: Ch 1, sc in same st and in each sc around; join
with slip st to first sc.

Rnd 9: Ch 1, sc in same st and in next sc, ch 5, skip
next 4 sc, ★ sc in next 2 sc, ch 5, skip next 4 sc; repeat
from ★ around; join with slip st to first sc: 32 sc and
16 ch-5 sps.

Rnd 10: Ch 1, sc in same st and in next sc, ch 6, (sc in
next 2 sc, ch 6) around; join with slip st to first sc.

Rnd 11: Ch 1, sc in same st and in next sc, ch 7, (sc in
next 2 sc, ch 7) around; join with slip st to first sc.

Rnd 12: Ch 1, sc in same st and in next sc, ch 8, (sc in
next 2 sc, ch 8) around; join with slip st to first sc.

Rnd 13: Ch 1, sc in same st and in next sc, 2 sc in
next ch-8 sp, work Large Picot, ch 6, ★ sc in next 2 sc,
2 sc in next ch-8 sp, work Large Picot, ch 6; repeat
from ★ around; join with slip st to first sc, finish off.

See Washing and Blocking, page 144.

Finished Size: 5" diameter

MATERIALS

Bedspread Weight Cotton Thread (size 10): 26 yards
Steel crochet hook, size 7 (1.65 mm) **or** size
   needed for gauge

GAUGE SWATCH: 2" diameter
Work same as Doily through Rnd 3.

STITCH GUIDE

TREBLE CROCHET *(abbreviated tr)*
YO twice, insert hook in sc indicated, YO and pull
up a loop (4 loops on hook), (YO and draw through
2 loops on hook) 3 times.

BEGINNING DC CLUSTER (uses one sp)
Ch 2, ★ YO, insert hook in sp indicated, YO and
pull up a loop, YO and draw through 2 loops on
hook; repeat from ★ once **more**, YO and draw
through all 3 loops on hook.

DC CLUSTER (uses one ch-2 sp)
★ YO, insert hook in ch-2 sp indicated, YO and pull
up a loop, YO and draw through 2 loops on hook;
repeat from ★ 2 times **more**, YO and draw through
all 4 loops on hook.

TR CLUSTER (uses one ch-2 sp)
★ YO twice, insert hook in ch-2 sp indicated, YO
and pull up a loop, (YO and draw through 2 loops
on hook) twice; repeat from ★ 2 times **more**, YO
and draw through all 4 loops on hook.

DECREASE
Pull up a loop in next 2 3-dc Clusters, YO and draw
through all 3 loops on hook.

PICOT
Ch 3, slip st in top of last st made *(Fig. 6a,
page 144)*.

DOILY

Rnd 1 (Right side)**:** Ch 4, 11 dc in fourth ch from hook
(3 skipped chs count as first dc); join with slip st to
first dc: 12 dc.

Rnd 2: Ch 1, sc in same st, ch 2, (sc in next dc, ch 2)
around; join with slip st to first sc: 12 ch-2 sps.

Rnd 3: Ch 1, sc in same st, ch 4, work tr Cluster in
next ch-2 sp, ★ ch 4, sc in next sc, ch 4, work tr Cluster
in next ch-2 sp; repeat from ★ around, tr in first sc to
form last ch-4 sp: 24 ch-4 sps.

Rnd 4: Ch 1, sc in last ch-4 sp made and in next
ch-4 sp, ch 5, (sc in next 2 ch-4 sps, ch 5) around; join
with slip st to first sc: 12 ch-5 sps.

Rnd 5: Slip st in next sc and in next ch-5 sp, ch 1, sc
in same sp, (ch 3, sc in same sp) twice, ★ sc in next
ch-5 sp, (ch 3, sc in same sp) twice; repeat from ★
around; join with slip st to first sc: 24 ch-3 sps.

Rnd 6: (Slip st, work Beginning dc Cluster) in first
ch-3 sp, ch 6, ★ work dc Cluster in each of next
2 ch-2 sps, ch 6; repeat from ★ around to last ch-2 sp,
work dc Cluster in last ch-2 sp; join with slip st to top of
Beginning dc Cluster: 24 dc Clusters and 12 ch-6 sps.

Rnd 7: (Slip st, ch 1, sc) in first ch-6 sp, (ch 3, sc in
same sp) 3 times, decrease, ★ sc in next ch-6 sp, (ch 3,
sc in same sp) 3 times, decrease; repeat from ★ around;
join with slip st to first sc: 36 ch-3 sps.

Rnd 8: (Slip st, ch 1, 3 sc) in first ch-3 sp, (3 dc, work
Picot, 2 dc) in next ch-3 sp, 3 sc in next ch-3 sp, work
Picot, ★ 3 sc in next ch-3 sp, (3 dc, work Picot, 2 dc) in
next ch-3 sp, 3 sc in next ch-3 sp, work Picot; repeat
from ★ around; join with slip st to first sc, finish off.

See Washing and Blocking, page 144.

Finished Size: 6$^1/_2$" diameter

MATERIALS

Bedspread Weight Cotton Thread (size 10): 65 yards
Steel crochet hook, size 7 (1.65 mm) **or** size
    needed for gauge

GAUGE SWATCH: 2" diameter
Work same as Doily through Rnd 4.

STITCH GUIDE

> **TREBLE CROCHET** *(abbreviated tr)*
> YO twice, insert hook in dc indicated, YO and pull
> up a loop (4 loops on hook), (YO and draw through
> 2 loops on hook) 3 times.
>
> **CLUSTER** (uses next 2 sc)
> ★ YO, insert hook in **next** sc, YO and pull up a
> loop, YO and draw through 2 loops on hook;
> repeat from ★ once **more**, YO and draw through
> all 3 loops on hook.
>
> **POPCORN**
> 4 Dc in ch-3 sp indicated, drop loop from hook,
> insert hook in first dc of 4-dc group, hook dropped
> loop and draw through.

DOILY

Ch 7; join with slip st to form a ring.

Rnd 1 (Right side)**:** Ch 3, 23 dc in ring; join with slip st
to top of beginning ch-3: 24 sts.

Rnd 2: Ch 1, 2 sc in same st, tr in next dc pulling tr to
right side, (2 sc in next dc, tr in next dc pulling tr to
right side) around; join with slip st to first sc: 36 sts.

Rnd 3: Ch 1, sc in same st and in each st around; join
with slip st to first sc.

Rnd 4: Ch 2, dc in next sc, ch 3, (work Cluster, ch 3)
around; join with slip st to first dc: 18 ch-3 sps.

Rnd 5: Slip st in first ch-3 sp, ch 1, (sc, ch 3, sc) in
same sp and in each ch-3 sp around; join with slip st to
first sc.

Rnd 6: Ch 1, sc in same st, ch 3, work Popcorn in
next ch-3 sp, ch 3, ★ sc in next 2 sc, ch 3, work
Popcorn in next ch-3 sp, ch 3; repeat from ★ around to
last sc, sc in last sc; join with slip st to first sc:
18 Popcorns.

Rnd 7: (Slip st, ch 1, 2 sc) in first ch-3 sp, ch 3, 2 sc in
next ch-3 sp, ch 1, ★ 2 sc in next ch-3 sp, ch 3, 2 sc in
next ch-3 sp, ch 1; repeat from ★ around; join with
slip st to first sc: 36 sps.

Rnd 8: Slip st in next sc and in next ch-3 sp, ch 1, sc
in same sp, dc in next ch-1 sp, (ch 1, dc in same sp)
twice, ★ sc in next ch-3 sp, dc in next ch-1 sp, (ch 1, dc
in same sp) twice; repeat from ★ around; join with
slip st to first sc: 72 sts and 36 ch-1 sps.

Rnd 9: Ch 1, sc in same st and in each st and each
ch-1 sp around; join with slip st to Back Loop Only of
first sc *(Fig. 1, page 143)*: 108 sc.

Rnd 10: Ch 1, sc in Back Loop Only of same st and
each sc around; join with slip st to **both** loops of
first sc.

Rnd 11: Ch 1, sc in same st, working in free loops of
sc on Rnd 9 *(Fig. 2a, page 144)*, skip first sc on
Rnd 9, dc in next sc, skip next sc on Rnd 10, ★ sc in
next sc, skip next sc on Rnd 9, dc in next sc, skip next
sc on Rnd 10; repeat from ★ around; join with slip st to
first sc.

Rnd 12: Ch 1, sc in same st and in next 2 sts, ch 16,
★ skip next 4 sts, sc in next 5 sts, ch 16; repeat from ★
around to last 6 sts, skip next 4 sts, sc in last 2 sts; join
with slip st to first sc: 12 loops.

Rnd 13: Ch 1, sc in same st, 26 dc in next loop, skip
next 2 sc, ★ sc in next sc, 26 dc in next loop, skip next
2 sc; repeat from ★ around; join with slip st to first sc:
312 dc.

Rnd 14: Slip st in next 7 dc, ch 1, sc in same st, (ch 5,
slip st in fourth ch from hook, ch 2, skip next 2 dc, sc in
next dc) twice, ch 3, slip st in third ch from hook, sc in
next dc, (ch 5, slip st in fourth ch from hook, ch 2, skip
next 2 dc, sc in next dc) twice, ch 2, skip next 13 sts,
★ sc in next dc, (ch 5, slip st in fourth ch from hook,
ch 2, skip next 2 dc, sc in next dc) twice, ch 3, slip st in
third ch from hook, sc in next dc, (ch 5, slip st in fourth
ch from hook, ch 2, skip next 2 dc, sc in next dc) twice,
ch 2, skip next 13 sts; repeat from ★ around; join with
slip st to first sc, finish off.

See Washing and Blocking, page 144.

Finished Size: 5³/₄" diameter

MATERIALS
Bedspread Weight Cotton Thread (size 10): 50 yards
Steel crochet hook, size 7 (1.65 mm) **or** size
   needed for gauge

GAUGE SWATCH: 2" diameter
Work same as Doily through Rnd 3.

STITCH GUIDE

TREBLE CROCHET *(abbreviated tr)*
YO twice, insert hook in st indicated, YO and pull
up a loop (4 loops on hook), (YO and draw through
2 loops on hook) 3 times.

PICOT
Ch 2, slip st in top of sc just made *(Fig. 6a,
page 144)*.

DECREASE (uses next 2 ch-2 sps)
YO twice, insert hook in next ch-2 sp, YO and pull
up a loop, (YO and draw through 2 loops on hook)
twice, YO twice, skip next Picot, insert hook in next
ch-2 sp, YO and pull up a loop, (YO and draw
through 2 loops on hook) twice, YO and draw
through all 3 loops on hook.

DOILY
Ch 7; join with slip st to form a ring.

Rnd 1 (Right side)**:** Ch 3 **(counts as first dc, now
and throughout)**, 2 dc in ring, ch 2, (3 dc in ring,
ch 2) 5 times; join with slip st to first dc: 18 dc and
6 ch-2 sps.

Rnd 2: Ch 1, sc in same st, ch 3, skip next dc, sc in
next dc, 2 sc in next ch-2 sp, ★ sc in next dc, ch 3, skip
next dc, sc in next dc, 2 sc in next ch-2 sp; repeat from
★ around; join with slip st to first sc: 24 sc and
6 ch-3 sps.

Rnd 3: (Slip st, ch 5, 2 dc) in first ch-3 sp, ch 2, skip
next sc, sc in next sc, work Picot, sc in next sc, ch 2,
★ (2 dc, ch 2) twice in next ch-3 sp, skip next sc, sc in
next sc, work Picot, sc in next sc, ch 2; repeat from ★
around, dc in same sp as beginning slip st; join with
slip st to third ch of beginning ch-5: 18 ch-2 sps.

Rnd 4: (Slip st, ch 1, sc) in first ch-2 sp, ch 5, decrease,
ch 5, ★ sc in next ch-2 sp, ch 5, decrease, ch 5; repeat
from ★ around; join with slip st to first sc: 12 ch-5 sps.

Rnd 5: Ch 1, sc in same st, (2 sc, ch 4, 2 sc) in next
2 ch-5 sps, ★ sc in next sc, (2 sc, ch 4, 2 sc) in next
2 ch-5 sps; repeat from ★ around; join with slip st to
first sc: 54 sc and 12 ch-4 sps.

Rnd 6: Ch 1, sc in same st, [dc in **next** ch-4 sp, (ch 1,
dc in **same** sp) 4 times] twice, skip next 2 sc, ★ sc in
next sc, [dc in **next** ch-4 sp, (ch 1, dc in **same** sp) 4
times] twice, skip next 2 sc; repeat from ★ around; join
with slip st to first sc: 48 ch-1 sps.

Rnd 7: Ch 4, dc in next ch-1 sp, (ch 2, dc in next
ch-1 sp) 7 times, skip next dc, ★ tr in next sc, dc in next
ch-1 sp, (ch 2, dc in next ch-1 sp) 7 times, skip next dc;
repeat from ★ around; join with slip st to top of
beginning ch-4: 42 ch-2 sps.

Rnd 8: Slip st in next dc and in next ch-2 sp, ch 1, 2 sc
in same sp, (sc in next dc, 2 sc in next ch-2 sp) 6 times,
pull up a loop in next dc, skip next tr, pull up a loop in
next dc, YO and draw through all 3 loops on hook,
★ 2 sc in next ch-2 sp, (sc in next dc, 2 sc in next
ch-2 sp) 6 times, pull up a loop in next st, skip next st,
pull up a loop in next st, YO and draw through all
3 loops on hook; repeat from ★ around; join with slip st
to Back Loop Only of first sc *(Fig. 1, page 143)*:
126 sts.

Rnd 9: Ch 1, sc in Back Loop Only of same st and
each st around; join with slip st to **both** loops of first sc.

Rnd 10: Ch 3, working in free loops of sts on Rnd 8
(Fig. 2a, page 144), skip first st on Rnd 8, tr in next st,
skip next sc on Rnd 9, ★ dc in next sc, skip next st on
Rnd 8, tr in next st, skip next sc on Rnd 9; repeat from
★ around; join with slip st to first dc.

Rnd 11: Ch 1, ★ sc from **front** to **back** around post
of next tr *(Fig. 7, page 144)*, sc from **back** to **front**
around post of next dc; repeat from ★ around; join with
slip st to first sc.

Rnd 12: Ch 1, sc in same st, ★ ch 3, skip next sc, sc in
next sc; repeat from ★ around to last sc, ch 1, skip last
sc, hdc in first sc to form last ch-3 sp: 63 ch-3 sps.

Rnd 13: Ch 1, sc in last ch-3 sp made, ch 4, slip st in
fourth ch from hook, ch 1, ★ sc in next ch-3 sp, ch 4,
slip st in fourth ch from hook, ch 1; repeat from ★
around; join with slip st to first sc, finish off.

See Washing and Blocking, page 144.

Finished Size: 5³/₄" diameter

MATERIALS
Bedspread Weight Cotton Thread (size 10): 45 yards
Steel crochet hook, size 7 (1.65 mm) **or** size
 needed for gauge

GAUGE SWATCH: 1¹/₂" diameter
Work same as Doily through Rnd 2.

STITCH GUIDE

TREBLE CROCHET *(abbreviated tr)*
YO twice, insert hook in sp indicated, YO and pull
up a loop (4 loops on hook), (YO and draw through
2 loops on hook) 3 times.

BEGINNING CLUSTER (uses one sp)
Ch 2, ★ YO, insert hook in sp indicated, YO and
pull up a loop, YO and draw through 2 loops on
hook; repeat from ★ once **more**, YO and draw
through all 3 loops on hook.

CLUSTER (uses one sp)
★ YO, insert hook in sp indicated, YO and pull up a
loop, YO and draw through 2 loops on hook; repeat
from ★ 2 times **more**, YO and draw through all
4 loops on hook.

BEGINNING POPCORN
Ch 3, 3 dc in sp indicated, drop loop from hook,
insert hook in top of beginning ch-3, hook dropped
loop and draw through.

POPCORN
4 Dc in ch-4 sp indicated, drop loop from hook,
insert hook in first dc of 4-dc group, hook dropped
loop and draw through.

DOILY
Ch 6; join with slip st to form a ring.

Rnd 1 (Right side)**:** Work Beginning Cluster in ring,
ch 3, (work Cluster in ring, ch 3) 5 times; join with slip st
to top of Beginning Cluster: 6 Clusters and 6 ch-3 sps.

Rnd 2: Ch 1, sc in same st, (sc, ch 5, sc) in next
ch-3 sp, ★ sc in next Cluster, (sc, ch 5, sc) in next
ch-3 sp; repeat from ★ around; join with slip st to first
sc: 18 sc and 6 ch-5 sps.

Rnd 3: Ch 1, sc in same st, 7 hdc in next ch-5 sp, skip
next sc, ★ sc in next sc, 7 hdc in next ch-5 sp, skip next
sc; repeat from ★ around; join with slip st to first sc:
48 sts.

Rnd 4: (Slip st, ch 1, sc) in next hdc, (ch 3, skip next
hdc, sc in next hdc) 3 times, skip next sc, ★ sc in next
hdc, (ch 3, skip next hdc, sc in next hdc) 3 times, skip
next st; repeat from ★ around; join with slip st to first sc:
18 ch-3 sps.

Rnd 5: (Slip st, ch 1, 2 sc) in first ch-3 sp, ch 4, 2 sc in
next ch-3 sp, ch 4, ★ 2 sc in each of next 2 ch-3 sps,
ch 4, 2 sc in next ch-3 sp, ch 4; repeat from ★ around
to last ch-3 sp, 2 sc in last ch-3 sp; join with slip st to
first sc: 12 ch-4 sps.

Rnd 6: Slip st in next sc and in next ch-4 sp, work
(Beginning Popcorn, ch 8, Popcorn) in same sp, work
(Popcorn, ch 8, Popcorn) in each ch-4 sp around; join
with slip st to top of Beginning Popcorn: 24 Popcorns.

Rnd 7: Slip st in first ch-8 sp, ch 1, (sc, ch 3) 4 times in
same sp and in each ch-8 sp around; join with slip st to
first sc: 48 ch-3 sps.

Rnd 8: (Slip st, ch 1, sc) in first ch-3 sp, (ch 4, sc in
next ch-3 sp) twice, ★ (ch 1, sc in next ch-3 sp) twice,
(ch 4, sc in next ch-3 sp) twice; repeat from ★ around to
last ch-3 sp, ch 1, sc in last ch-3 sp, ch 1; join with
slip st to first sc.

Rnd 9: Slip st in first 2 chs, ch 1, sc in same sp, ch 4,
sc in next ch-4 sp, skip next ch-1 sp, tr in next ch-1 sp,
ch 4, working in **front** of last tr made, tr in skipped
ch-1 sp, ★ sc in next ch-4 sp, ch 4, sc in next ch-4 sp,
skip next ch-1 sp, tr in next ch-1 sp, ch 4, working in
front of last tr made, tr in skipped ch-1 sp; repeat from
★ around; join with slip st to first sc: 24 ch-4 sps.

Rnd 10: Slip st in first 2 chs, ch 1, sc in same sp, tr in
next ch-4 sp, (ch 1, tr in same sp) 6 times, ★ sc in next
ch-4 sp, tr in next ch-4 sp, (ch 1, tr in same sp) 6 times;
repeat from ★ around; join with slip st to first sc:
72 ch-1 sps.

Rnd 11: Ch 1, sc in same st and in next ch-1 sp, (ch 4,
sc in next ch-1 sp) 5 times, skip next tr, ★ sc in next sc
and in next ch-1 sp, (ch 4, sc in next ch-1 sp) 5 times,
skip next tr; repeat from ★ around; join with slip st to
first sc, finish off.

See Washing and Blocking, page 144.

Finished Size: 4³/₄" (point to point)

MATERIALS

Bedspread Weight Cotton Thread (size 10): 40 yards
Steel crochet hook, size 7 (1.65 mm) **or** size
    needed for gauge

GAUGE SWATCH: 1³/₄" diameter
Work same as Doily through Rnd 3.

STITCH GUIDE

BEGINNING CLUSTER (uses one sp)
Ch 2, ★ YO, insert hook in sp indicated, YO and
pull up a loop, YO and draw through 2 loops on
hook; repeat from ★ once **more**, YO and draw
through all 3 loops on hook.

CLUSTER (uses one sp)
★ YO, insert hook in sp indicated, YO and pull up a
loop, YO and draw through 2 loops on hook; repeat
from ★ 2 times **more**, YO and draw through all
4 loops on hook.

DOILY

Ch 7; join with slip st to form a ring.

Rnd 1 (Right side)**:** Work Beginning Cluster in ring,
(ch 3, work Cluster in ring) 7 times, ch 2, sc in top of
Beginning Cluster to form last ch-3 sp: 8 Clusters and
8 ch-3 sps.

Rnd 2: Ch 1, sc in last ch-3 sp made, (sc, ch 3, 2 sc,
ch 3, sc) in next ch-3 sp and in each ch-3 sp around, (sc,
ch 3, 2 sc) in same sp as first sc, ch 1, hdc in first sc to
form last ch-3 sp: 16 ch-3 sps.

Rnd 3: Ch 1, 2 sc in last ch-3 sp made and in next
ch-3 sp, (ch 4, 2 sc in each of next 2 ch-3 sps) around,
ch 3, sc in first sc to form last ch-4 sp: 8 ch-4 sps.

Rnd 4: Work Beginning Cluster in last ch-4 sp made,
skip next 3 sc, dc in next sc, working in **front** of last dc
made, dc in first skipped sc, ★ work Cluster in next
ch-4 sp, (ch 4, work Cluster in same sp) twice, skip next
3 sc, dc in next sc, working in **front** of last dc made, dc
in first skipped sc; repeat from ★ around, work (Cluster,
ch 4, Cluster) in same sp as Beginning Cluster, ch 3, sc
in top of Beginning Cluster to form last ch-4 sp: 16 dc
and 16 ch-4 sps.

Rnd 5: Ch 1, sc in last ch-4 sp made, skip next Cluster,
sc in next 2 dc and in next ch-4 sp, (ch 3, sc in same sp)
twice, ★ sc in next ch-4 sp, (ch 3, sc in same sp) twice,
skip next Cluster, sc in next 2 dc and in next ch-4 sp,
(ch 3, sc in same sp) twice; repeat from ★ around, (sc,
ch 3, sc) in same sp as first sc, dc in first sc to form last
ch-3 sp: 32 ch-3 sps.

Rnd 6: Ch 1, 2 sc in last ch-3 sp made, (ch 1, 2 sc in
next ch-3 sp) twice, ch 2, 2 sc in next ch-3 sp, ★ (ch 1,
2 sc in next ch-3 sp) 3 times, ch 2, 2 sc in next ch-3 sp;
repeat from ★ around, ch 1; join with slip st to first sc:
64 sc and 32 sps.

Rnd 7: Ch 1, sc in same st and in next sc, (sc in next
ch-1 sp and in next 2 sc) twice, 3 sc in next ch-2 sp, sc
in next 2 sc, ★ (sc in next ch-1 sp and in next 2 sc) 3
times, 3 sc in next ch-2 sp, sc in next 2 sc; repeat from
★ around to last ch-1 sp, sc in last ch-1 sp; join with
slip st to first sc: 112 sc.

Rnd 8: Ch 1, sc in same st, ch 3, skip next 3 sc, sc in
next 2 sc, hdc in next 2 sc, dc in next sc, 3 dc in next sc,
dc in next sc, hdc in next 2 sc, ★ sc in next 2 sc, ch 3,
skip next 3 sc, sc in next 2 sc, hdc in next 2 sc, dc in
next sc, 3 dc in next sc, dc in next sc, hdc in next 2 sc;
repeat from ★ around to last sc, sc in last sc; join with
slip st to first sc: 104 sts and 8 ch-3 sps.

Rnd 9: (Slip st, ch 1, sc, ch 3, sc) in first ch-3 sp, ch 4,
skip next 4 sts, sc in next dc, ch 3, skip next dc, (sc,
ch 3) twice in next dc, skip next dc, sc in next dc, ch 4,
★ (sc, ch 3, sc) in next ch-3 sp, ch 4, skip next 4 sts, sc
in next dc, ch 3, skip next dc, (sc, ch 3) twice in next dc,
skip next dc, sc in next dc, ch 4; repeat from ★ around;
join with slip st to first sc: 48 sps.

Rnd 10: Slip st in first ch-3 sp, ch 1, (sc, ch 3) twice in
same sp, 2 sc in next ch-4 sp, sc in next ch-3 sp, ch 3,
(sc, ch 3) twice in next ch-3 sp, sc in next ch-3 sp, 2 sc
in next ch-4 sp, ch 3, ★ (sc, ch 3) twice in next ch-3 sp,
2 sc in next ch-4 sp, sc in next ch-3 sp, ch 3, (sc, ch 3)
twice in next ch-3 sp, sc in next ch-3 sp, 2 sc in next
ch-4 sp, ch 3; repeat from ★ around; join with slip st to
first sc, finish off.

See Washing and Blocking, page 144.

Finished Size: $4^1/_2$" diameter

MATERIALS

Bedspread Weight Cotton Thread (size 10): 30 yards
Steel crochet hook, size 7 (1.65 mm) **or** size
   needed for gauge

GAUGE SWATCH: 1" diameter
Work same as Doily through Rnd 2.

STITCH GUIDE

TREBLE CROCHET *(abbreviated tr)*
YO twice, insert hook in st or sp indicated, YO and
pull up a loop (4 loops on hook), (YO and draw
through 2 loops on hook) 3 times.

BEGINNING CLUSTER (uses one sp)
Ch 2, ★ YO, insert hook in sp indicated, YO and
pull up a loop, YO and draw through 2 loops on
hook; repeat from ★ once **more**, YO and draw
through all 3 loops on hook.

CLUSTER (uses one sp)
★ YO, insert hook in sp indicated, YO and pull up a
loop, YO and draw through 2 loops on hook; repeat
from ★ 2 times **more**, YO and draw through all
4 loops on hook.

PICOT
Ch 2, slip st in top of last sc made *(Fig. 6a,
page 144)*.

DOILY

Ch 7; join with slip st to form a ring.

Rnd 1 (Right side)**:** Work Beginning Cluster in ring,
ch 3, (work Cluster in ring, ch 3) 7 times; join with slip st
to top of Beginning Cluster: 8 Clusters and 8 ch-3 sps.

Rnd 2: Ch 1, sc in same st, 3 sc in next ch-3 sp, (sc in
next Cluster, 3 sc in next ch-3 sp) around; join with
slip st to Back Loop Only of first sc *(Fig. 1, page 143)*:
32 sc.

Rnd 3: Ch 1, working in Back Loops Only, sc in same
st and in next 2 sc, ch 3, (sc in same st and in next 4 sc,
ch 3) around to last sc, sc in same st and in last sc; join
with slip st to **both** loops of first sc: 40 sc and
8 ch-3 sps.

Rnd 4: Ch 3, dc in next ch-3 sp, (ch 2, dc in same
sp) 3 times, skip next 2 sc, ★ dc in next sc and in next
ch-3 sp, (ch 2, dc in same sp) 3 times, skip next 2 sc;
repeat from ★ around; join with slip st to top of
beginning ch-3: 24 ch-2 sps.

Rnd 5: (Slip st, ch 1, sc) in next dc, 2 sc in next
ch-2 sp, sc in next dc, 3 sc in next ch-2 sp, sc in next
dc, 2 sc in next ch-2 sp, sc in next dc, skip next dc, ★ sc
in next dc, 2 sc in next ch-2 sp, sc in next dc, 3 sc in
next ch-2 sp, sc in next dc, 2 sc in next ch-2 sp, sc in
next dc, skip next st; repeat from ★ around; join with
slip st to first sc: 88 sc.

Rnd 6: Slip st in next 3 sc, ch 1, sc in same st, (ch 3,
skip next sc, sc in next sc) twice, ★ ch 6, skip next 6 sc,
sc in next sc, (ch 3, skip next sc, sc in next sc) twice;
repeat from ★ around to last 6 sts, ch 2, skip last 6 sts,
tr in first sc to form last ch-6 sp: 24 sc and 8 ch-6 sps.

Rnd 7: Ch 5 **(counts as first tr plus ch 1)**, tr in last
ch-6 sp made, (ch 1, tr in same sp) 5 times, skip next sc,
sc in next sc, ★ tr in next ch-6 sp, (ch 1, tr in same sp) 8
times, skip next sc, sc in next sc; repeat from ★ around,
(tr, ch 1, tr) in same sp as first tr, sc in first tr to form last
ch-1 sp: 72 tr and 64 ch-1 sps.

Rnd 8: Ch 1, sc in last ch-1 sp made and in next tr,
work Picot, (sc in next ch-1 sp and in next tr, work
Picot) 5 times, sc in next 2 ch-1 sps and in next tr, work
Picot, ★ (sc in next ch-1 sp and in next tr, work Picot) 6
times, sc in next 2 ch-1 sps and in next tr, work Picot;
repeat from ★ around; join with slip st to first sc: 120 sc.

Rnd 9: Ch 1, sc in same st, ch 5, (skip next Picot, sc in
next sc, ch 5) 5 times, skip next 2 Picots, ★ sc in next
sc, ch 5, (skip next Picot, sc in next sc, ch 5) 5 times,
skip next 2 Picots; repeat from ★ around; join with
slip st to first sc, finish off.

See Washing and Blocking, page 144.

Finished Size: 7¼" (point to point)

MATERIALS

Bedspread Weight Cotton Thread (size 10): 55 yards
Steel crochet hook, size 7 (1.65 mm) **or** size
needed for gauge

GAUGE SWATCH: 1⅞" diameter
Work same as Doily through Rnd 3.

STITCH GUIDE

> **CLUSTER** (uses one ch-2 sp)
> ★ YO, insert hook in ch-2 sp indicated, YO and pull up a loop, YO and draw through 2 loops on hook; repeat from ★ 2 times **more**, YO and draw through all 4 loops on hook.
>
> **PICOT**
> Ch 2, slip st in top of last sc made *(Fig. 6a, page 144)*.

DOILY

Ch 7; join with slip st to form a ring.

Rnd 1 (Right side)**:** Ch 3 **(counts as first dc, now and throughout)**, 23 dc in ring; join with slip st to first dc: 24 dc.

Rnd 2: Ch 1, sc in same st, ch 2, skip next dc, ★ sc in next dc, ch 2, skip next dc; repeat from ★ around; join with slip st to first sc: 12 ch-2 sps.

Rnd 3: Ch 1, sc in same st, ch 3, work Cluster in next ch-2 sp, ★ ch 3, sc in next sc, ch 3, work Cluster in next ch-2 sp; repeat from ★ around, dc in first sc to form last ch-3 sp: 24 ch-3 sps.

Rnd 4: Ch 1, sc in last ch-3 sp made, ch 3, sc in next ch-3 sp, ★ ch 2, sc in next ch-3 sp, ch 3, sc in next ch-3 sp; repeat from ★ around, ch 1, sc in first sc to form last ch-2 sp.

Rnd 5: Ch 1, sc in last ch-2 sp made, ch 4, (sc, work Picot, sc) in next ch-3 sp, ★ ch 4, sc in next ch-2 sp, ch 4, (sc, work Picot, sc) in next ch-3 sp; repeat from ★ around, ch 2, hdc in first sc to form last ch-4 sp.

Rnd 6: Ch 1, sc in last ch-4 sp made, (ch 4, sc in next ch-4 sp) around, ch 1, dc in first sc to form last ch-4 sp.

Rnd 7: Ch 5 **(counts as first dc plus ch 2, now and throughout)**, 2 dc in last ch-4 sp made, ch 2, sc in next ch-4 sp, ch 2, ★ (2 dc, ch 2) twice in next ch-4 sp, sc in next ch-4 sp, ch 2; repeat from ★ around, dc in same sp as first dc; join with slip st to first dc: 36 ch-2 sps.

Rnd 8: (Slip st, ch 5, 2 dc) in first ch-2 sp, ch 3, sc in next ch-2 sp and in next sc, sc in next ch-2 sp, ch 3, ★ (2 dc, ch 2, 2 dc) in next ch-2 sp, ch 3, sc in next ch-2 sp and in next sc, sc in next ch-2 sp, ch 3; repeat from ★ around, dc in same sp as first dc; join with slip st to first dc.

Rnd 9: (Slip st, ch 5, 2 dc) in first ch-2 sp, ch 3, sc in next ch-3 sp and in next 3 sc, sc in next ch-3 sp, ch 3, ★ (2 dc, ch 2, 2 dc) in next ch-2 sp, ch 3, sc in next ch-3 sp and in next 3 sc, sc in next ch-3 sp, ch 3; repeat from ★ around, dc in same sp as first dc; join with slip st to first dc.

Rnd 10: (Slip st, ch 5, 2 dc) in first ch-2 sp, ch 1, dc in next ch-3 sp, ch 7, dc in next ch-3 sp, ch 1, ★ (2 dc, ch 2, 2 dc) in next ch-2 sp, ch 1, dc in next ch-3 sp, ch 7, dc in next ch-3 sp, ch 1; repeat from ★ around, dc in same sp as first dc; join with slip st to first dc: 48 sps.

Rnd 11: (Slip st, ch 5, 2 dc) in first ch-2 sp, ch 3, sc in next ch-1 sp, 9 hdc in next ch-7 sp, sc in next ch-1 sp, ch 3, ★ (2 dc, ch 2, 2 dc) in next ch-2 sp, ch 3, sc in next ch-1 sp, 9 hdc in next ch-7 sp, sc in next ch-1 sp, ch 3; repeat from ★ around, dc in same sp as first dc; join with slip st to first dc: 36 sps.

Rnd 12: (Slip st, ch 3, 2 dc, ch 4, slip st in third ch from hook, ch 2, 3 dc) in first ch-2 sp, dc in next ch-3 sp, skip next 3 sts, sc in next hdc, (ch 4, slip st in third ch from hook, ch 2, skip next hdc, sc in next hdc) twice, dc in next ch-3 sp, ★ (3 dc, ch 4, slip st in third ch from hook, ch 2, 3 dc) in next ch-2 sp, dc in next ch-3 sp, skip next 3 sts, sc in next hdc, (ch 4, slip st in third ch from hook, ch 2, skip next hdc, sc in next hdc) twice, dc in next ch-3 sp; repeat from ★ around; join with slip st to first dc, finish off.

See Washing and Blocking, page 144.

33 ▮

Finished Size: 8¹/₂" (corner to corner)

MATERIALS
Bedspread Weight Cotton Thread (size 10): 85 yards
Steel crochet hook, size 7 (1.65 mm) **or** size
    needed for gauge

GAUGE SWATCH: 2" (corner to corner)
Work same as Doily through Rnd 3.

STITCH GUIDE

> **TREBLE CROCHET** *(abbreviated tr)*
> YO twice, insert hook in ch-5 sp indicated, YO and
> pull up a loop (4 loops on hook), (YO and draw
> through 2 loops on hook) 3 times.
>
> **CLUSTER** *(uses one st or sp)*
> ★ YO, insert hook in st or sp indicated, YO and pull
> up a loop, YO and draw through 2 loops on hook;
> repeat from ★ once **more**, YO and draw through all
> 3 loops on hook.
>
> **DECREASE** *(uses next 6 sc)*
> † YO twice, insert hook in **next** sc, YO and pull up
> a loop, (YO and draw through 2 loops on hook)
> twice †, repeat from † to † once **more**, skip next
> 2 sc, repeat from † to † twice, YO and draw through
> all 5 loops on hook.
>
> **PICOT**
> Ch 2, slip st in top of last sc made *(Fig. 6a,
> page 144)*.

DOILY
Ch 6; join with slip st to form a ring.

Rnd 1 (Right side)**:** Ch 3 **(counts as first dc, now
and throughout)**, 4 dc in ring, (ch 2, 5 dc in ring) 3
times, ch 1, sc in first dc to form last ch-2 sp: 20 dc and
4 ch-2 sps.

Rnd 2: Ch 3, dc in last ch-2 sp made, ch 2, skip next
dc, sc in next 3 dc, ch 2, ★ (2 dc, ch 2) twice in next
ch-2 sp, skip next dc, sc in next 3 dc, ch 2; repeat from
★ 2 times **more**, 2 dc in same sp as first dc, ch 1, sc in
first dc to form last ch-2 sp: 12 ch-2 sps.

Rnd 3: Ch 3, dc in last ch-2 sp made and in next 2 dc,
ch 2, skip next sc, sc in next sc, ch 2, skip next sc, dc in
next 2 dc, ★ (2 dc, ch 2, 2 dc) in next ch-2 sp, dc in
next 2 dc, ch 2, skip next sc, sc in next sc, ch 2, skip
next sc, dc in next 2 dc; repeat from ★ 2 times **more**,
2 dc in same sp as first dc, ch 1, sc in first dc to form
last ch-2 sp: 32 dc.

Rnd 4: Ch 3, dc in last ch-2 sp made, ch 2, skip next
dc, sc in next 3 dc, ch 5, skip next sc, sc in next 3 dc,
ch 2, ★ (2 dc, ch 2) twice in next ch-2 sp, skip next dc,
sc in next 3 dc, ch 5, skip next sc, sc in next 3 dc, ch 2;
repeat from ★ 2 times **more**, 2 dc in same sp as first dc,
ch 1, sc in first dc to form last ch-2 sp: 16 sps.

Rnd 5: Ch 3, dc in last ch-2 sp made, ch 2, sc in next
ch-2 sp, tr in next ch-5 sp, (ch 1, tr in same sp) 7 times,
sc in next ch-2 sp, ch 2, ★ (2 dc, ch 2) twice in next
ch-2 sp, sc in next ch-2 sp, tr in next ch-5 sp, (ch 1, tr in
same sp) 7 times, sc in next ch-2 sp, ch 2; repeat from
★ 2 times **more**, 2 dc in same sp as first dc, ch 1, sc in
first dc to form last ch-2 sp: 40 sps.

Rnd 6: Ch 3, (dc, ch 2, 2 dc) in last ch-2 sp made,
ch 2, ★ † sc in next ch-2 sp, work Cluster in next
ch-1 sp, (ch 2, work Cluster in next ch-1 sp) 6 times, sc
in next ch-2 sp, ch 2 †, (2 dc, ch 2) 3 times in next
ch-2 sp; repeat from ★ 2 times **more**, then repeat from
† to † once, 2 dc in same sp as first dc, ch 1, sc in first
dc to form last ch-2 sp: 28 Clusters.

Rnd 7: Ch 3, dc in last ch-2 sp made, ★ † ch 4, (2 dc,
ch 2) twice in next ch-2 sp, sc in next 2 ch-2 sps, ch 3,
(sc in next ch-2 sp, ch 3) 4 times, sc in next 2 ch-2 sps,
ch 2 †, (2 dc, ch 2, 2 dc) in next ch-2 sp; repeat from ★
2 times **more**, then repeat from † to † once, 2 dc in
same sp as first dc, ch 1, sc in first dc to form
last ch-2 sp.

Rnd 8: Ch 3, dc in last ch-2 sp made, ★ † ch 3, 3 sc in
next ch-4 sp, ch 3, (2 dc, ch 2) twice in next ch-2 sp, sc
in next 2 sps, ch 3, (sc in next ch-3 sp, ch 3) 3 times, sc
in next 2 sps, ch 2 †, (2 dc, ch 2, 2 dc) in next ch-2 sp;
repeat from ★ 2 times **more**, then repeat from † to †
once, 2 dc in same sp as first dc, ch 1, sc in first dc to
form last ch-2 sp.

Rnd 9: Ch 3, dc in last ch-2 sp made, ★ † ch 4, sc in
next ch-3 sp, skip next sc, work (Cluster, ch 5, Cluster)
in next sc, sc in next ch-3 sp, ch 4, (2 dc, ch 2, 2 dc) in
next ch-2 sp, ch 3, sc in next 2 sps, ch 3, (sc in next
ch-3 sp, ch 3) twice, sc in next 2 sps, ch 3 †, (2 dc,
ch 2, 2 dc) in next ch-2 sp; repeat from ★ 2 times
more, then repeat from † to † once, 2 dc in same sp as
first dc, ch 1, sc in first dc to form last ch-2 sp.

Rnd 10: Ch 3, dc in last ch-2 sp made, ★ † ch 4, 2 sc
in next ch-4 sp, work Cluster in next ch-5 sp, (ch 2,
work Cluster in same sp) 4 times, 2 sc in next ch-4 sp,
ch 4, (2 dc, ch 2, 2 dc) in next ch-2 sp, ch 3, sc in next
2 ch-3 sps, ch 4, sc in next ch-3 sp, ch 4, sc in next
2 ch-3 sps, ch 3 †, (2 dc, ch 2, 2 dc) in next ch-2 sp;
repeat from ★ 2 times **more**, then repeat from † to †
once, 2 dc in same sp as first dc, ch 1, sc in first dc to
form last ch-2 sp; do **not** finish off: 48 sps.

Continued on page 42.

Rnd 11: Ch 3, dc in last ch-2 sp made, ★ † ch 4, 3 sc in next ch-4 sp, sc in next 2 sc, (sc, ch 2, sc) in next 4 ch-2 sps, skip next Cluster, sc in next 2 sc, 3 sc in next ch-4 sp, ch 4, (2 dc, ch 2, 2 dc) in next ch-2 sp, ch 7, sc in next ch-3 sp, 2 sc in next ch-4 sp, ch 7, 2 sc in next ch-4 sp, sc in next ch-3 sp, ch 7 †, (2 dc, ch 2, 2 dc) in next ch-2 sp; repeat from ★ 2 times **more**, then repeat from † to † once, 2 dc in same sp as first dc, ch 1, sc in first dc to form last ch-2 sp: 44 sps.

Rnd 12: Ch 3, dc in last ch-2 sp made, ★ † ch 4, 3 sc in next ch-4 sp, sc in next 3 sc, (dc, ch 4, dc) in next 4 ch-2 sps, skip next 3 sc, sc in next 3 sc, 3 sc in next ch-4 sp, ch 4, (2 dc, ch 2, 2 dc) in next ch-2 sp, 2 sc in next ch-7 sp, 4 sc in next ch-7 sp, 2 sc in next ch-7 sp †, (2 dc, ch 2, 2 dc) in next ch-2 sp; repeat from ★ 2 times **more**, then repeat from † to † once, 2 dc in same sp as first dc, ch 1, sc in first dc to form last ch-2 sp: 32 sps.

Rnd 13: Ch 3, dc in last ch-2 sp made, ★ † ch 4, 3 sc in next ch-4 sp, sc in next 4 sc, work [Cluster, (ch 2, Cluster) twice] in each of next 4 ch-4 sps, skip next 3 sts, sc in next 4 sc, 3 sc in next ch-4 sp, ch 4, (2 dc, ch 2, 2 dc) in next ch-2 sp, skip next 3 sts, decrease †, (2 dc, ch 2, 2 dc) in next ch-2 sp; repeat from ★ 2 times **more**, then repeat from † to † once, 2 dc in same sp as first dc, ch 2; join with slip st to first dc: 48 sps.

Rnd 14: Slip st in next dc and in next ch-4 sp, ch 1, 5 sc in same sp, ★ † sc in next 7 sc, (2 sc, work Picot, sc) in next 8 ch-2 sps, skip next Cluster, sc in next 7 sc, 5 sc in next ch-4 sp, ch 3, 2 dc in next ch-2 sp, ch 3, slip st in top of last dc made, 2 dc in next ch-2 sp, ch 3 †, 5 sc in next ch-4 sp; repeat from ★ 2 times **more**, then repeat from † to † once; join with slip st to first sc, finish off.

See Washing and Blocking, page 144.

34 ▬▬▬▬▬▬

Finished Size: 7" diameter

MATERIALS

Bedspread Weight Cotton Thread (size 10): 85 yards
Steel crochet hook, size 7 (1.65 mm) **or** size needed for gauge

GAUGE SWATCH: 1½" diameter
Work same as Doily through Rnd 7.

STITCH GUIDE

CLUSTER (uses one ch-1 sp)
★ YO, insert hook in ch-1 sp indicated, YO and pull up a loop, YO and draw through 2 loops on hook; repeat from ★ 2 times **more**, YO and draw through all 4 loops on hook.

BEGINNING CROSS ST (uses next 2 ch-2 sps)
Skip next ch-2 sp, dc in next ch-2 sp, ch 3, working in **front** of dc just made, dc in skipped ch-2 sp.

CROSS ST (uses next ch-2 sp)
Dc in next ch-2 sp, ch 3, working in **front** of dc just made, dc in same ch-2 sp as first dc of previous Cross St.

DOILY

Rnd 1 (Right side)**:** Ch 2, 6 sc in second ch from hook; join with slip st to first sc.

Note: Loop a short piece of thread around any stitch to mark Rnd 1 as **right** side.

Rnd 2: Ch 1, 2 sc in same st and in each sc around; join with slip st to first sc: 12 sc.

Rnd 3: Ch 1, sc in same st, 2 sc in next sc, (sc in next sc, 2 sc in next sc) around; join with slip st to first sc: 18 sc.

Rnd 4: Ch 1, sc in same st and in next sc, 2 sc in next sc, (sc in next 2 sc, 2 sc in next sc) around; join with slip st to first sc: 24 sc.

Rnd 5: Ch 1, sc in same st, 2 sc in next sc, (sc in next sc, 2 sc in next sc) around; join with slip st to first sc: 36 sc.

Rnd 6: Ch 1, sc in same st and in each sc around; join with slip st to first sc.

Rnd 7: Ch 1, sc in same st and in next sc, 2 sc in next sc, (sc in next 2 sc, 2 sc in next sc) around; join with slip st to first sc: 48 sc.

Rnds 8 and 9: Repeat Rnds 6 and 7: 64 sc.

Rnds 10 and 11: Ch 1, sc in same st and in each sc around; join with slip st to first sc.

Rnd 12: Ch 1, sc in same st and in next 6 sc, 2 sc in next sc, (sc in next 7 sc, 2 sc in next sc) around; join with slip st to first sc: 72 sc.

Rnd 13: Ch 1, sc in same st and in each sc around; join with slip st to first sc.

Rnd 14: Ch 1, sc in same st and in next 2 sc, 2 sc in next sc, (sc in next 3 sc, 2 sc in next sc) around; join with slip st to first sc: 90 sc.

Rnd 15: Ch 1, sc in same st and in next 3 sc, 2 sc in next sc, (sc in next 4 sc, 2 sc in next sc) around; join with slip st to first sc: 108 sc.

Rnd 16: Ch 1, sc in same st and in next 7 sc, 2 sc in next sc, (sc in next 8 sc, 2 sc in next sc) around; join with slip st to first sc: 120 sc.

Rnd 17: Ch 1, sc in same st and in each sc around; join with slip st to Front Loop Only of first sc *(Fig. 1, page 143)*.

Rnd 18: Ch 1, **turn**; sc in same st, ch 4, slip st in fourth ch from hook, ch 1, skip next 3 sc, ★ sc in Back Loop Only of next sc, ch 4, slip st in fourth ch from hook, ch 1, skip next 3 sc; repeat from ★ around; join with slip st to **both** loops of first sc, finish off.

Rnd 19: With **right** side facing, working in Back Loops Only of skipped sc and in free loops of sc on Rnd 17 *(Fig. 2a, page 144)*, join thread with sc in first sc *(see Joining With Sc, page 143)*; sc in each sc around; join with slip st to **both** loops of first sc: 120 sc.

Rnd 20: Ch 1, sc in same st, ch 2, skip next sc, ★ sc in next sc, ch 2, skip next sc; repeat from ★ around; join with slip st to first sc: 60 ch-2 sps.

Rnd 21: [Slip st, ch 5 **(counts as first dc plus ch 2, now and throughout)**, 2 dc] in first ch-2 sp, skip next 2 ch-2 sps, (dc, ch 6, dc) in next ch-2 sp, skip next 2 ch-2 sps, ★ (2 dc, ch 2, 2 dc) in next ch-2 sp, skip next 2 ch-2 sps, (dc, ch 6, dc) in next ch-2 sp, skip next 2 ch-2 sps; repeat from ★ around, dc in same sp as first dc; join with slip st to first dc: 60 dc and 20 sps.

Rnd 22: (Slip st, ch 5, 2 dc) in first ch-2 sp, dc in next ch-6 sp, (ch 1, dc in same sp) 6 times, ★ (2 dc, ch 2, 2 dc) in next ch-2 sp, dc in next ch-6 sp, (ch 1, dc in same sp) 6 times; repeat from ★ around, dc in same sp as first dc; join with slip st to first dc: 110 dc and 70 sps.

Rnd 23: (Slip st, ch 5, 2 dc) in first ch-2 sp, work Cluster in next ch-1 sp, (ch 2, work Cluster in next ch-1 sp) 5 times, ★ (2 dc, ch 2, 2 dc) in next ch-2 sp, work Cluster in next ch-1 sp, (ch 2, work Cluster in next ch-1 sp) 5 times; repeat from ★ around, dc in same sp as first dc; join with slip st to first dc: 60 ch-2 sps.

Rnd 24: (Slip st, ch 3, 6 dc) in first ch-2 sp, work Beginning Cross St, work 3 Cross Sts, ★ 7 dc in next ch-2 sp, work Beginning Cross St, work 3 Cross Sts; repeat from ★ around; join with slip st to top of beginning ch-3: 40 Cross Sts.

Rnd 25: Ch 1, sc in same st, ch 5, slip st in fourth ch from hook, ch 2, skip next 5 dc, sc in next dc, 2 sc in next ch-3 sp, (ch 3, slip st in third ch from hook, ch 1, 2 sc in next ch-3 sp) 3 times, skip next dc, ★ sc in next dc, ch 5, slip st in fourth ch from hook, ch 2, skip next 5 dc, sc in next dc, 2 sc in next ch-3 sp, (ch 3, slip st in third ch from hook, ch 1, 2 sc in next ch-3 sp) 3 times, skip next dc; repeat from ★ around; join with slip st to first sc, finish off.

See Washing and Blocking, page 144.

Finished Size: 6$^1/_2$" diameter

MATERIALS
Bedspread Weight Cotton Thread (size 10): 75 yards
Steel crochet hook, size 7 (1.65 mm) **or** size
needed for gauge

GAUGE SWATCH: 1$^1/_2$" diameter
Work same as Doily through Rnd 7.

STITCH GUIDE

BEGINNING POPCORN
Ch 3, 2 dc in sp indicated, drop loop from hook,
insert hook in top of beginning ch-3, hook dropped
loop and draw through.

POPCORN
3 Dc in ch-2 sp indicated, drop loop from hook,
insert hook in first dc of 3-dc group, hook dropped
loop and draw through.

BEGINNING SHELL
Ch 3 **(counts as first dc)**, (dc, ch 2, 2 dc) in
same sp.

SHELL
(2 Dc, ch 2, 2 dc) in sp indicated.

FRONT POST DOUBLE TREBLE CROCHET
(abbreviated FPdtr)
YO 3 times, insert hook from **front** to **back** around
post of dc indicated **(Fig. 7, page 144)**, YO and
pull up a loop (5 loops on hook), (YO and draw
through 2 loops on hook) 4 times.

DOILY

Rnd 1 (Right side)**:** Ch 2, 6 sc in second ch from hook;
join with slip st to first sc.

Note: Loop a short piece of thread around any stitch to
mark Rnd 1 as **right** side.

Rnd 2: Ch 1, 2 sc in same st and in each sc around;
join with slip st to first sc: 12 sc.

Rnd 3: Ch 1, sc in same st, 2 sc in next sc, (sc in next
sc, 2 sc in next sc) around; join with slip st to first sc:
18 sc.

Rnd 4: Ch 1, sc in same st and in next sc, 2 sc in next
sc, (sc in next 2 sc, 2 sc in next sc) around; join with
slip st to first sc: 24 sc.

Rnd 5: Ch 1, sc in same st, 2 sc in next sc, (sc in next
sc, 2 sc in next sc) around; join with slip st to first sc:
36 sc.

Rnd 6: Ch 1, sc in same st and in each sc around; join
with slip st to first sc.

Rnd 7: Ch 1, sc in same st and in next sc, 2 sc in next
sc, (sc in next 2 sc, 2 sc in next sc) around; join with
slip st to first sc: 48 sc.

Rnds 8 and 9: Repeat Rnds 6 and 7: 64 sc.

Rnds 10 and 11: Ch 1, sc in same st and in each sc
around; join with slip st to first sc.

Rnd 12: Ch 1, sc in same st and in next 6 sc, 2 sc in
next sc, (sc in next 7 sc, 2 sc in next sc) around; join
with slip st to first sc: 72 sc.

Rnd 13: Ch 1, sc in same st and in each sc around;
join with slip st to first sc.

Rnd 14: Ch 1, sc in same st and in next 2 sc, 2 sc in
next sc, (sc in next 3 sc, 2 sc in next sc) around; join
with slip st to first sc: 90 sc.

Rnd 15: Ch 1, sc in same st and in next 3 sc, 2 sc in
next sc, (sc in next 4 sc, 2 sc in next sc) around; join
with slip st to first sc: 108 sc.

Rnd 16: Ch 1, sc in same st and in next 7 sc, 2 sc in
next sc, (sc in next 8 sc, 2 sc in next sc) around; join
with slip st to first sc: 120 sc.

Rnd 17: Ch 1, sc in same st and in each sc around;
join with slip st to Front Loop Only of first sc **(Fig. 1,
page 143)**.

Rnd 18: Ch 1, **turn**; working in Back Loops Only, sc
in same st and in next 3 sc, skip next sc, dc in next sc,
(ch 1, dc in same st) twice, ★ skip next sc, sc in next
5 sc, skip next sc, dc in next sc, (ch 1, dc in same st)
twice; repeat from ★ around to last 2 sc, skip next sc, sc
in last sc; join with slip st to **both** loops of first sc:
120 sts and 30 ch-1 sps.

Rnd 19: Ch 1, sc in same st, (skip next st, sc in next st)
twice, sc in next ch-1 sp, [sc, ch 2, slip st in top of sc
just made **(Fig. 6a, page 144)**, sc] in next dc, sc in next
ch-1 sp and in next dc, ★ (skip next st, sc in next st) 3
times, sc in next ch-1 sp, (sc, ch 2, slip st in top of sc
just made, sc) in next dc, sc in next ch-1 sp and in next
dc; repeat from ★ around to last sc, skip last sc; join with
slip st to first sc, finish off.

Rnd 20: With **right** side facing, working in Back Loops Only of skipped sc and in free loops of sc on Rnd 17 *(Fig. 2a, page 144)*, join thread with sc in first sc *(see Joining With Sc, page 143)*; sc in each sc around; join with slip st to **both** loops of first sc: 120 sc.

Rnd 21: Ch 1, sc in same st, ch 2, skip next sc, ★ sc in next sc, ch 2, skip next sc; repeat from ★ around; join with slip st to first sc: 60 ch-2 sps.

Rnd 22: (Slip st, work Beginning Popcorn) in first ch-2 sp, ch 3, (work Popcorn in next ch-2 sp, ch 3) around; join with slip st to top of Beginning Popcorn.

Rnd 23: (Slip st, work Beginning Shell) in first ch-3 sp, ch 2, sc in next ch-3 sp, 2 sc in each of next 2 ch-3 sps, sc in next ch-3 sp, ch 2, ★ work Shell in next ch-3 sp, ch 2, sc in next ch-3 sp, 2 sc in each of next 2 ch-3 sps, sc in next ch-3 sp, ch 2; repeat from ★ around; join with slip st to first dc: 72 sc and 12 Shells.

Rnd 24: Ch 3, dc in next dc, work Shell in next ch-2 sp, dc in next 2 dc, ch 2, sc in next ch-2 sp, skip next 2 sc, sc in next sc, ch 3, slip st in third ch from hook, sc in next sc and in next ch-2 sp, ch 2, ★ dc in next 2 dc, work Shell in next ch-2 sp, dc in next 2 dc, ch 2, sc in next ch-2 sp, skip next 2 sc, sc in next sc, ch 3, slip st in third ch from hook, sc in next sc and in next ch-2 sp, ch 2; repeat from ★ around; join with slip st to top of beginning ch-3.

Rnd 25: Ch 1, sc in same st, work FPdtr around first dc of first Shell on Rnd 23, ★ † skip next dc on Rnd 24, sc in next dc, work FPdtr around next dc of Shell on Rnd 23, skip next dc on Rnd 24, (sc, ch 3, slip st in third ch from hook, sc) in next ch-2 sp, (work FPdtr around next dc of Shell on Rnd 23, skip next dc on Rnd 24, sc in next dc) twice, sc in next ch-2 sp, ch 4, slip st in third ch from hook, ch 2 †, sc in next ch-2 sp and in next dc, work FPdtr around first dc of next Shell on Rnd 23; repeat from ★ 10 times **more**, then repeat from † to † once, sc in last ch-2 sp; join with slip st to first sc, finish off.

See and Washing and Blocking, page 144.

36

Finished Size: 6" (point to point)

MATERIALS
Bedspread Weight Cotton Thread (size 10): 55 yards
Steel crochet hook, size 7 (1.65 mm) **or** size needed for gauge

GAUGE SWATCH: 1⁷/₈" diameter
Work same as Doily through Rnd 3.

STITCH GUIDE

BEGINNING CLUSTER (uses one sp)
Ch 2, ★ YO, insert hook in sp indicated, YO and pull up a loop, YO and draw through 2 loops on hook; repeat from ★ once **more**, YO and draw through all 3 loops on hook.

CLUSTER (uses one sp)
★ YO, insert hook in sp indicated, YO and pull up a loop, YO and draw through 2 loops on hook; repeat from ★ 2 times **more**, YO and draw through all 4 loops on hook.

PICOT
Ch 2, slip st in top of last sc made *(Fig. 6a, page 144)*.

POPCORN
3 Dc in ch-1 sp indicated, drop loop from hook, insert hook in first dc of 3-dc group, hook dropped loop and draw through.

FRONT POST DOUBLE CROCHET
   (abbreviated FPdc)
YO, insert hook from **front** to **back** around post of dc indicated *(Fig. 7, page 144)*, YO and pull up a loop (3 loops on hook), (YO and draw through 2 loops on hook) twice.

DOILY
Ch 6; join with slip st to form a ring.

Rnd 1 (Right side)**:** Work Beginning Cluster in ring, ch 3, (work Cluster in ring, ch 3) 5 times; join with slip st to top of Beginning Cluster: 6 Clusters and 6 ch-3 sps.

Rnd 2: (Slip st, ch 1, 4 sc) in first ch-3 sp, (ch 2, 4 sc in next ch-3 sp) around, ch 1, sc in first sc to form last ch-2 sp; do **not** finish off: 24 sc and 6 ch-2 sps.

Continued on page 46.

Rnd 3: Ch 5 **(counts as first dc plus ch 2, now and throughout)**, 2 dc in last ch-2 sp made, ch 2, skip next sc, sc in next sc, work Picot, sc in next sc, ch 2, ★ (2 dc, ch 2) twice in next ch-2 sp, skip next sc, sc in next sc, work Picot, sc in next sc, ch 2; repeat from ★ around, dc in same sp as first dc; join with slip st to first dc: 18 ch-2 sps.

Rnd 4: (Slip st, ch 5, 2 dc) in first ch-2 sp, ch 2, sc in next ch-2 sp, ch 5, sc in next ch-2 sp, ch 2, ★ (2 dc, ch 2) twice in next ch-2 sp, sc in next ch-2 sp, ch 5, sc in next ch-2 sp, ch 2; repeat from ★ around, dc in same sp as first dc; join with slip st to first dc: 24 sps.

Rnd 5: (Slip st, ch 5, 2 dc) in first ch-2 sp, ch 2, sc in next ch-2 sp, 6 sc in next ch-5 sp, sc in next ch-2 sp, ch 2, ★ (2 dc, ch 2) twice in next ch-2 sp, sc in next ch-2 sp, 6 sc in next ch-5 sp, sc in next ch-2 sp, ch 2; repeat from ★ around, dc in same sp as first dc; join with slip st to first dc: 72 sts and 18 ch-2 sps.

Rnd 6: (Slip st, ch 5, 2 dc) in first ch-2 sp, ch 3, sc in next ch-2 sp, skip next sc, dc in next sc, (ch 1, dc in next sc) 5 times, sc in next ch-2 sp, ch 3, ★ (2 dc, ch 2, 2 dc) in next ch-2 sp, ch 3, sc in next ch-2 sp, skip next sc, dc in next sc, (ch 1, dc in next sc) 5 times, sc in next ch-2 sp, ch 3; repeat from ★ around, dc in same sp as first dc; join with slip st to first dc: 48 sps.

Rnd 7: [Slip st, ch 3 **(counts as first dc, now and throughout)**, dc, ch 2, 2 dc] in first ch-2 sp, ch 3, sc in next ch-3 sp, work Popcorn in next ch-1 sp, (ch 3, work Popcorn in next ch-1 sp) 4 times, sc in next ch-3 sp, ch 3, ★ (2 dc, ch 2, 2 dc) in next ch-2 sp, ch 3, sc in next ch-3 sp, work Popcorn in next ch-1 sp, (ch 3, work Popcorn in next ch-1 sp) 4 times, sc in next ch-3 sp, ch 3; repeat from ★ around; join with slip st to first dc: 24 dc and 42 sps.

Rnd 8: Ch 3, dc in next dc, 5 dc in next ch-2 sp, dc in next 2 dc, ch 2, sc in next ch-3 sp, (sc, ch 3, sc) in next 4 ch-3 sps, sc in next ch-3 sp, ★ ch 2, dc in next 2 dc, 5 dc in next ch-2 sp, dc in next 2 dc, ch 2, sc in next ch-3 sp, (sc, ch 3, sc) in next 4 ch-3 sps, sc in next ch-3 sp; repeat from ★ around, ch 1, sc in first dc to form last ch-2 sp: 54 dc and 36 sps.

Rnd 9: Ch 1, sc in last ch-2 sp made and in next 4 dc, 3 sc in next dc, sc in next 4 dc and in next ch-2 sp, 2 sc in next ch-3 sp, (ch 3, 2 sc in next ch-3 sp) 3 times, ★ sc in next ch-2 sp and in next 4 dc, 3 sc in next dc, sc in next 4 dc and in next ch-2 sp, 2 sc in next ch-3 sp, (ch 3, 2 sc in next ch-3 sp) 3 times; repeat from ★ around; join with slip st to first sc: 126 sc and 18 ch-3 sps.

Rnd 10: Ch 1, sc in same st and in next 5 sc, (sc, ch 1, sc) in next sc, sc in next 8 sc, 2 sc in next ch-3 sp, (ch 3, 2 sc in next ch-3 sp) twice, ★ sc in next 8 sc, (sc, ch 1, sc) in next sc, sc in next 8 sc, 2 sc in next ch-3 sp, (ch 3, 2 sc in next ch-3 sp) twice; repeat from ★ around to last 2 sc, sc in last 2 sc; join with slip st to first sc: 144 sc and 12 ch-3 sps.

Rnd 11: Ch 1, sc in same st, work FPdc around first dc on Rnd 8, ★ † sc in next sc on Rnd 10, skip next dc on Rnd 8, work FPdc around next dc, sc in next 2 sc on Rnd 10, skip next dc on Rnd 8, work FPdc around next dc, 3 sc in next ch-1 sp on Rnd 10, work FPdc around same dc on Rnd 8 as last FPdc, sc in next 2 sc on Rnd 10, skip next dc on Rnd 8, work FPdc around next dc, sc in next sc on Rnd 10, skip next dc on Rnd 8, work FPdc around next dc, sc in next sc on Rnd 10, skip next sc, sc in next 3 sc, 3 sc in next ch-3 sp, ch 3, 3 sc in next ch-3 sp, sc in next 3 sc, skip next sc †, sc in next sc, work FPdc around next dc on Rnd 8; repeat from ★ 4 times **more**, then repeat from † to † once; join with slip st to first sc: 174 sts and 6 ch-3 sps.

Rnd 12: Ch 1, sc in same st and in next FPdc, ★ † work Picot, sc in next 2 sts, work Picot, sc in next 3 sts, work Picot, (sc in next 2 sts, work Picot) twice, sc in next 3 sts, work Picot, sc in next 2 sts, work Picot, sc in next sc, skip next sc, sc in next 5 sc, (2 sc, work Picot, 2 sc) in next ch-3 sp, sc in next 5 sc, skip next sc †, sc in next sc and in next FPdc; repeat from ★ 4 times **more**, then repeat from † to † once; join with slip st to first sc, finish off.

See Washing and Blocking, page 144.

Finished Size: $5^1/2$" (point to point)

MATERIALS
Bedspread Weight Cotton Thread (size 10): 40 yards
Steel crochet hook, size 7 (1.65 mm) **or** size
   needed for gauge

GAUGE SWATCH: 1" diameter
Work same as Doily through Rnd 2.

STITCH GUIDE

TREBLE CROCHET *(abbreviated tr)*
YO twice, insert hook in ch-2 sp indicated, YO and
pull up a loop (4 loops on hook), (YO and draw
through 2 loops on hook) 3 times.

BEGINNING POPCORN
Ch 3, 3 dc in sp indicated, drop loop from hook,
insert hook in first dc of 4-dc group, hook dropped
loop and draw through.

POPCORN
4 Dc in ch-2 sp indicated, drop loop from hook,
insert hook in first dc of 4-dc group, hook dropped
loop and draw through.

DC CLUSTER (uses one ch-1 sp)
★ YO, insert hook in ch-1 sp indicated, YO and pull
up a loop, YO and draw through 2 loops on hook;
repeat from ★ once **more**, YO and draw through all
3 loops on hook.

TR CLUSTER (uses one ch-4 sp)
★ YO twice, insert hook in ch-4 sp indicated, YO
and pull up a loop, (YO and draw through 2 loops
on hook) twice; repeat from ★ once **more**, YO and
draw through all 3 loops on hook.

DOILY
Ch 7; join with slip st to form a ring.

Rnd 1 (Right side)**:** Ch 3 **(counts as first dc, now
and throughout)**, 19 dc in ring; join with slip st to first
dc: 20 dc.

Rnd 2: Ch 1, sc in same st, ch 2, skip next dc, ★ sc in
next dc, ch 2, skip next dc; repeat from ★ around; join
with slip st to first sc: 10 ch-2 sps.

Rnd 3: (Slip st, work Beginning Popcorn) in first
ch-2 sp, (ch 4, work Popcorn in next ch-2 sp) around,
ch 2, hdc in top of Beginning Popcorn to form last
ch-4 sp.

Rnd 4: Ch 1, 3 sc in last ch-4 sp made, (3 sc, ch 4,
3 sc) in each ch-4 sp around, 3 sc in same sp as first sc,
ch 1, dc in first sc to form last ch-4 sp.

Rnd 5: Ch 4 **(counts as first dc plus ch 1)**, (dc,
ch 1, dc) in last ch-4 sp made, skip next 2 sc, dc in next
2 sc, ★ dc in next ch-4 sp, (ch 1, dc in same sp) 3 times,
skip next 2 sc, dc in next 2 sc; repeat from ★ around, dc
in same sp as first dc, ch 1; join with slip st to first dc:
60 dc and 30 ch-1 sps.

Rnd 6: Ch 1, sc in same st, ch 2, work (dc Cluster,
ch 4, dc Cluster) in next ch-1 sp, ch 2, sc in next dc,
2 sc in next ch-1 sp, sc in next dc, skip next 2 dc, sc in
next dc, 2 sc in next ch-1 sp, ★ sc in next dc, ch 2,
work (dc Cluster, ch 4, dc Cluster) in next ch-1 sp, ch 2,
sc in next dc, 2 sc in next ch-1 sp, sc in next dc, skip
next 2 dc, sc in next dc, 2 sc in next ch-1 sp; repeat
from ★ around; join with slip st to first sc: 10 ch-4 sps.

Rnd 7: Slip st in first ch-2 sp, ch 4 **(counts as first
tr)**, work tr Cluster in next ch-4 sp, (ch 2, work
tr Cluster in same sp) 4 times, ★ tr in next 2 ch-2 sps,
work tr Cluster in next ch-4 sp, (ch 2, work tr Cluster in
same sp) 4 times; repeat from ★ around to last ch-2 sp,
tr in last ch-2 sp; join with slip st to first tr: 70 sts and
40 ch-2 sps.

Rnd 8: Ch 1, sc in same st and in next tr Cluster, 2 sc
in next ch-2 sp, sc in next tr Cluster, 2 sc in next
ch-2 sp, 3 sc in next tr Cluster, 2 sc in next ch-2 sp, sc
in next tr Cluster, 2 sc in next ch-2 sp, ★ sc in next
4 sts, 2 sc in next ch-2 sp, sc in next tr Cluster, 2 sc in
next ch-2 sp, 3 sc in next tr Cluster, 2 sc in next
ch-2 sp, sc in next tr Cluster, 2 sc in next ch-2 sp;
repeat from ★ around to last 2 sts, sc in last 2 sts; join
with slip st to first sc: 170 sc.

Rnd 9: (Slip st, ch 1, sc) in next sc, ★ † (ch 3, slip st in
third ch from hook, ch 1, skip next 2 sc, sc in next sc)
twice, [sc, ch 4, slip st in top of sc just made *(Fig. 6a,
page 144)*, sc] in next sc, sc in next sc, (ch 3, slip st in
third ch from hook, ch 1, skip next 2 sc, sc in next sc)
twice, skip next 2 sts †, sc in next sc; repeat from ★
8 times **more**, then repeat from † to † once; join with
slip st to first sc, finish off.

See Washing and Blocking, page 144.

Finished Size: 9¹⁄₂" (corner to corner)

MATERIALS

Bedspread Weight Cotton Thread (size 10): 115 yards
Steel crochet hook, size 7 (1.65 mm) **or** size
   needed for gauge

GAUGE SWATCH: 2¹⁄₄" (corner to corner)
Work same as Doily through Rnd 5.

STITCH GUIDE

TREBLE CROCHET *(abbreviated tr)*
YO twice, insert hook in sp indicated, YO and pull
up a loop (4 loops on hook), (YO and draw through
2 loops on hook) 3 times.

DOUBLE TREBLE CROCHET
   (abbreviated dtr)
YO 3 times, insert hook in sp indicated, YO and pull
up a loop (5 loops on hook), (YO and draw through
2 loops on hook) 4 times.

POPCORN
3 Dc in sc indicated, drop loop from hook, insert
hook in first dc of 3-dc group, hook dropped loop
and draw through.

CLUSTER *(uses one ch-1 sp)*
★ YO, insert hook in ch-1 sp indicated, YO and pull
up a loop, YO and draw through 2 loops on hook;
repeat from ★ once **more**, YO and draw through all
3 loops on hook.

SPLIT CLUSTER *(uses next 2 sc)*
★ YO, insert hook in **next** sc, YO and pull up a
loop, YO and draw through 2 loops on hook; repeat
from ★ once **more**, YO and draw through all
3 loops on hook.

PICOT
Ch 2, slip st in top of last sc made *(Fig. 6a,
page 144)*.

FRONT POST SINGLE CROCHET
   (abbreviated FPsc)
Insert hook from **front** to **back** around post of st
indicated *(Fig. 7, page 144)*, YO and pull up a
loop, YO and draw through both loops on hook.

FRONT POST TRIPLE TREBLE CROCHET
   (abbreviated FPtr tr)
YO 4 times, insert hook from **front** to **back** around
post of sc indicated *(Fig. 7, page 144)*, YO and
pull up a loop (6 loops on hook), (YO and draw
through 2 loops on hook) 5 times.

DECREASE *(uses next 3 sps)*
† YO twice, insert hook in **next** ch-3 sp, YO and
pull up a loop, (YO and draw through 2 loops on
hook) twice †, pull up a loop in next ch-7 sp
(3 loops on hook), repeat from † to † once, YO and
draw through all 4 loops on hook.

DOILY

Ch 7; join with slip st to form a ring.

Rnd 1 (Right side)**:** Ch 1, 16 sc in ring; join with slip st
to Back Loop Only of first sc *(Fig. 1, page 143)*.

Rnd 2: Ch 1, sc in Back Loop Only of same st and
each sc around; join with slip st to **both** loops of first sc.

Rnd 3: Ch 1, sc in same st and in next 3 sc, (ch 3, sc
in next 4 sc) around, ch 1, hdc in first sc to form last
ch-3 sp: 16 sc and 4 ch-3 sps.

Rnd 4: Ch 5 **(counts as first dc plus ch 2, now
and throughout)**, 2 dc in last ch-3 sp made, sc in next
2 sc, ch 3, sc in next 2 sc, ★ (2 dc, ch 2, 2 dc) in next
ch-3 sp, sc in next 2 sc, ch 3, sc in next 2 sc; repeat
from ★ 2 times **more**, dc in same sp as first dc; join
with slip st to first dc: 32 sts and 8 sps.

Rnd 5: (Slip st, ch 5, 2 dc) in first ch-2 sp, ch 1, sc in
next 4 sts, (sc, ch 3, sc) in next ch-3 sp, sc in next 4 sts,
ch 1, ★ (2 dc, ch 2, 2 dc) in next ch-2 sp, ch 1, sc in
next 4 sts, (sc, ch 3, sc) in next ch-3 sp, sc in next 4 sts,
ch 1; repeat from ★ 2 times **more**, dc in same sp as first
dc; join with slip st to first dc: 16 sps.

Rnd 6: (Slip st, ch 5, 2 dc) in first ch-2 sp, ch 3, sc in
next ch-1 sp, ch 4, 2 sc in next ch-3 sp, ch 4, sc in next
ch-1 sp, ch 3, ★ (2 dc, ch 2, 2 dc) in next ch-2 sp, ch 3,
sc in next ch-1 sp, ch 4, 2 sc in next ch-3 sp, ch 4, sc in
next ch-1 sp, ch 3; repeat from ★ 2 times **more**, dc in
same sp as first dc; join with slip st to first dc: 20 sps.

Rnd 7: (Slip st, ch 5, 2 dc) in first ch-2 sp, ch 3, sc in
next ch-3 sp, ch 2, sc in next ch-4 sp, work Popcorn in
next sc, ch 6, work Popcorn in next sc, sc in next
ch-4 sp, ch 2, sc in next ch-3 sp, ch 3, ★ (2 dc, ch 2,
2 dc) in next ch-2 sp, ch 3, sc in next ch-3 sp, ch 2, sc
in next ch-4 sp, work Popcorn in next sc, ch 6, work
Popcorn in next sc, sc in next ch-4 sp, ch 2, sc in next
ch-3 sp, ch 3; repeat from ★ 2 times **more**, dc in same
sp as first dc; join with slip st to first dc: 24 sps.

Rnd 8: (Slip st, ch 5, 2 dc, ch 2, 2 dc) in first ch-2 sp, ch 3, 2 sc in next ch-3 sp, sc in next ch-2 sp, dc in next ch-6 sp, (ch 1, dc in same sp) 6 times, sc in next ch-2 sp, 2 sc in next ch-3 sp, ch 3, ★ 2 dc in next ch-2 sp, (ch 2, 2 dc in same sp) twice, ch 3, 2 sc in next ch-3 sp, sc in next ch-2 sp, dc in next ch-6 sp, (ch 1, dc in same sp) 6 times, sc in next ch-2 sp, 2 sc in next ch-3 sp, ch 3; repeat from ★ 2 times **more**, dc in same sp as first dc; join with slip st to first dc: 40 sps.

Rnd 9: (Slip st, ch 5, 2 dc) in first ch-2 sp, (ch 2, 2 dc) twice in next ch-2 sp, ch 3, 2 sc in next ch-3 sp, work Cluster in next ch-1 sp, (ch 3, work Cluster in next ch-1 sp) 5 times, 2 sc in next ch-3 sp, ch 3, ★ (2 dc, ch 2) twice in next ch-2 sp, (2 dc, ch 2, 2 dc) in next ch-2 sp, ch 3, 2 sc in next ch-3 sp, work Cluster in next ch-1 sp, (ch 3, work Cluster in next ch-1 sp) 5 times, 2 sc in next ch-3 sp, ch 3; repeat from ★ 2 times **more**, dc in same sp as first dc; join with slip st to first dc.

Rnd 10: (Slip st, ch 5, 2 dc) in first ch-2 sp, ★ † ch 3, sc in next ch-2 sp, ch 3, (2 dc, ch 2, 2 dc) in next ch-2 sp, ch 3, 2 sc in each of next 2 ch-3 sps, (work Picot, 2 sc in same sp and in next ch-3 sp) 5 times, ch 3 †, (2 dc, ch 2, 2 dc) in next ch-2 sp; repeat from ★ 2 times **more**, then repeat from † to † once, dc in same sp as first dc; join with slip st to first dc: 24 sps.

Rnd 11: (Slip st, ch 5, 2 dc) in first ch-2 sp, ★ † ch 3, 2 sc in each of next 2 ch-3 sps, ch 3, (2 dc, ch 2, 2 dc) in next ch-2 sp, ch 3, sc in next ch-3 sp, skip next 2 sc, dc in next sc, ch 4, skip next Picot and next sc, (work Split Cluster, ch 4, skip next Picot and next sc) 4 times, dc in next sc, sc in next ch-3 sp, ch 3 †, (2 dc, ch 2, 2 dc) in next ch-2 sp; repeat from ★ 2 times **more**, then repeat from † to † once, dc in same sp as first dc; join with slip st to first dc: 24 sc and 44 sps.

Rnd 12: (Slip st, ch 5, 2 dc) in first ch-2 sp, ★ † ch 3, 2 sc in next ch-3 sp, sc in next 4 sc, 2 sc in next ch-3 sp, ch 3, (2 dc, ch 2, 2 dc) in next ch-2 sp, ch 3, sc in next ch-3 sp, 2 sc in next ch-4 sp, (ch 5, 2 sc in next ch-4 sp) 4 times, sc in next ch-3 sp, ch 3 †, (2 dc, ch 2, 2 dc) in next ch-2 sp; repeat from ★ 2 times **more**, then repeat from † to † once, dc in same sp as first dc; join with slip st to first dc: 80 sc and 40 sps.

Rnd 13: (Slip st, ch 5, 2 dc) in first ch-2 sp, ★ † ch 3, 2 sc in next ch-3 sp, sc in next 8 sc, 2 sc in next ch-3 sp, ch 3, (2 dc, ch 2, 2 dc) in next ch-2 sp, ch 3, sc in next 2 sps, [(dc, ch 1) twice in next sc, (dc, ch 1, dc) in next sc, sc in next ch-5 sp] 3 times, sc in next ch-3 sp, ch 3 †, (2 dc, ch 2, 2 dc) in next ch-2 sp; repeat from ★ 2 times **more**, then repeat from † to † once, dc in same sp as first dc; join with slip st to first dc: 72 sc and 60 sps.

Rnd 14: (Slip st, ch 5, 2 dc) in first ch-2 sp, ★ † ch 3, 2 sc in next ch-3 sp, sc in next 12 sc, 2 sc in next ch-3 sp, ch 3, (2 dc, ch 2, 2 dc) in next ch-2 sp, ch 3, sc in next 2 sps, ch 3, (sc in next ch-1 sp, ch 3, sc in next 2 ch-1 sps, ch 3) 3 times †, (2 dc, ch 2, 2 dc) in next ch-2 sp; repeat from ★ 2 times **more**, then repeat from † to † once, dc in same sp as first dc; join with slip st to first dc: 108 sc and 48 sps.

Rnd 15: (Slip st, ch 5, 2 dc) in first ch-2 sp, ★ † ch 4, 2 sc in next ch-3 sp, sc in next 2 sc, dc in ch-3 sp **before** 2 sc 2 rnds **below**, skip next sc on Rnd 14, sc in next sc, tr in ch-3 sp **before** 2 sc 3 rnds **below**, skip next sc on Rnd 14, sc in next sc, dtr in ch-3 sp **before** 2 sc 4 rnds **below**, skip next sc on Rnd 14, sc in next sc, work FPtr tr around sc 5 rnds **below**, sc in next sc on Rnd 14, dtr in ch-3 sp **after** 2 sc 4 rnds **below**, skip next sc on Rnd 14, sc in next sc, tr in ch-3 sp **after** 2 sc 3 rnds **below**, skip next sc on Rnd 14, sc in next sc, dc in ch-3 sp **after** 2 sc 2 rnds **below**, skip next sc on Rnd 14, sc in next 2 sc, 2 sc in next ch-3 sp, ch 4, (2 dc, ch 2, 2 dc) in next ch-2 sp, ch 3, sc in next 2 ch-3 sps, ch 3, (sc in next ch-3 sp and in next 2 sc, sc in next ch-3 sp, ch 3) twice, sc in next 2 ch-3 sps, ch 3 †, (2 dc, ch 2, 2 dc) in next ch-2 sp; repeat from ★ 2 times **more**, then repeat from † to † once, dc in same sp as first dc; join with slip st to first dc: 164 sts and 36 sps.

Rnd 16: (Slip st, ch 5, 2 dc) in first ch-2 sp, ★ † ch 4, 3 sc in next ch-4 sp, sc in next 2 sc, dc in ch-3 sp **before** 2 sc 2 rnds **below**, skip next sc on Rnd 15, sc in next sc, (work FPsc around next st, sc in next sc) 7 times, dc in ch-3 sp **after** 2 sc 2 rnds **below**, skip next sc on Rnd 15, sc in next 2 sc, 3 sc in next ch-4 sp, ch 4, (2 dc, ch 2, 2 dc) in next ch-2 sp, ch 3, sc in next ch-3 sp, (2 sc, work Picot, sc) in next ch-3 sp, [skip next sc, sc in next 2 sc, (2 sc, work Picot, sc) in next ch-3 sp] twice, sc in next ch-3 sp, ch 3 †, (2 dc, ch 2, 2 dc) in next ch-2 sp; repeat from ★ 2 times **more**, then repeat from † to † once, dc in same sp as first dc; join with slip st to first dc: 24 sps.

Rnd 17: (Slip st, ch 5, 2 dc) in first ch-2 sp, ★ † ch 4, 3 sc in next ch-4 sp, sc in next 3 sc, dc in ch-3 sp **before** 2 sc 2 rnds **below**, skip next sc on Rnd 16, sc in next sc, work FPsc around next dc, sc in next 15 sts, work FPsc around next dc, sc in next sc, dc in ch-3 sp **after** 2 sc 2 rnds **below**, skip next sc on Rnd 16, sc in next 3 sc, 3 sc in next ch-4 sp, ch 4, (2 dc, ch 2, 2 dc) in next ch-2 sp, ch 3, sc in next ch-3 sp, ch 3, skip next Picot and next 2 sc, sc in next sc, ch 6, skip next Picot and next sc, sc in next sc, ch 3, sc in next ch-3 sp, ch 3 †, (2 dc, ch 2, 2 dc) in next ch-2 sp; repeat from ★ 2 times **more**, then repeat from † to † once, dc in same sp as first dc; join with slip st to first dc, do **not** finish off: 180 sts and 36 sps.

Continued on page 50.

Rnd 18: (Slip st, ch 5, 2 dc) in first ch-2 sp, ★ † ch 4, 3 sc in next ch-4 sp, sc in next 3 sc, dc in ch-4 sp **before** 3 sc 2 rnds **below**, skip next sc on Rnd 17, sc in next 2 sc, work FPsc around next dc, sc in next 19 sts, work FPsc around next dc, sc in next 2 sc, dc in ch-4 sp **after** 3 sc 2 rnds **below**, skip next sc on Rnd 17, sc in next 3 sc, 3 sc in next ch-4 sp, ch 4, (2 dc, ch 2, 2 dc) in next ch-2 sp, ch 3, sc in next ch-3 sp, skip next ch-3 sp, (3 sc, ch 7, 3 sc) in next ch-6 sp, skip next ch-3 sp, sc in next ch-3 sp, ch 3 †, (2 dc, ch 2, 2 dc) in next ch-2 sp; repeat from ★ 2 times **more**, then repeat from † to † once, dc in same sp as first dc; join with slip st to first dc: 220 sts and 28 sps.

Rnd 19: (Slip st, ch 5, 2 dc) in first ch-2 sp, ★ † ch 4, 3 sc in next ch-4 sp, sc in next 3 sc, dc in ch-4 sp **before** 3 sc 2 rnds **below**, skip next sc on Rnd 18, sc in next 2 sc, work FPsc around next dc, sc in next 25 sts, work FPsc around next dc, sc in next 2 sc, dc in ch-4 sp **after** 3 sc 2 rnds **below**, skip next sc on Rnd 18, sc in next 3 sc, 3 sc in next ch-4 sp, ch 4, (2 dc, ch 2, 2 dc) in next ch-2 sp, decrease †, (2 dc, ch 2, 2 dc) in next ch-2 sp; repeat from ★ 2 times **more**, then repeat from † to † once, dc in same sp as first dc; join with slip st to first dc: 216 sts and 16 sps.

Rnd 20: [Slip st, ch 3 (**counts as first dc**), dc] in first ch-2 sp, ★ † ch 4, 4 sc in next ch-4 sp, dc in ch-4 sp **before** 3 sc one rnd **below**, skip next sc on Rnd 19, sc in next 2 sc, dc in ch-4 sp **before** 3 sc 2 rnds **below**, skip next sc on Rnd 19, sc in next 2 sc, work FPsc around next dc, sc in next 31 sts, work FPsc around next dc, sc in next 2 sc, dc in ch-4 sp **after** 3 sc 2 rnds **below**, skip next sc on Rnd 19, sc in next 2 sc, dc in ch-4 sp **after** 3 sc one rnd **below**, 4 sc in next ch-4 sp, ch 4 †, 2 dc in each of next 2 ch-2 sps; repeat from ★ 2 times **more**, then repeat from † to † once, 2 dc in last ch-2 sp; join with slip st to first dc: 228 sts and 8 ch-4 sps.

Rnd 21: Slip st in next dc, ch 1, ★ 4 sc in next ch-4 sp, dc in ch-4 sp **before** 4 sc one rnd **below**, skip next sc on Rnd 20, sc in next 51 sts, dc in ch-4 sp **after** 4 sc one rnd **below**, 4 sc in next ch-4 sp, skip next 2 dc, (sc, work Picot, sc) in ch-4 sp **before** next st; repeat from ★ around; join with slip st to first sc, finish off.

See Washing and Blocking, page 144.

39 ▰

Finished Size: 7^{1}/$_{4}$" diameter

MATERIALS
   Bedspread Weight Cotton Thread (size 10): 95 yards
   Steel crochet hook, size 7 (1.65 mm) **or** size
      needed for gauge

GAUGE SWATCH: 1^{1}/$_{2}$" diameter
Work same as Doily through Rnd 7.

STITCH GUIDE

> **TREBLE CROCHET** (*abbreviated tr*)
> YO twice, insert hook in sc indicated, YO and pull up a loop (4 loops on hook), (YO and draw through 2 loops on hook) 3 times.
>
> **BEGINNING POPCORN**
> Ch 3, 3 dc in sp indicated, drop loop from hook, insert hook in top of beginning ch-3, hook drooped loop and draw through.
>
> **POPCORN**
> 4 Dc in ch-3 sp indicated, drop loop from hook, insert hook in first dc of 4-dc group, hook dropped loop and draw through.
>
> **PICOT**
> Ch 5, slip st in fourth ch from hook.

DOILY

Rnd 1 (Right side)**:** Ch 2, 6 sc in second ch from hook; join with slip st to first sc.

Note: Loop a short piece of thread around any stitch to mark Rnd 1 as **right** side.

Rnd 2: Ch 1, 2 sc in same st and in each sc around; join with slip st to first sc: 12 sc.

Rnd 3: Ch 1, sc in same st, 2 sc in next sc, (sc in next sc, 2 sc in next sc) around; join with slip st to first sc: 18 sc.

Rnd 4: Ch 1, sc in same st and in next sc, 2 sc in next sc, (sc in next 2 sc, 2 sc in next sc) around; join with slip st to first sc: 24 sc.

Rnd 5: Ch 1, sc in same st, 2 sc in next sc, (sc in next sc, 2 sc in next sc) around; join with slip st to first sc: 36 sc.

Rnd 6: Ch 1, sc in same st and in each sc around; join with slip st to first sc.

Rnd 7: Ch 1, sc in same st and in next sc, 2 sc in next sc, (sc in next 2 sc, 2 sc in next sc) around; join with slip st to first sc: 48 sc.

Rnds 8 and 9: Repeat Rnds 6 and 7: 64 sc.

Rnds 10 and 11: Ch 1, sc in same st and in each sc around; join with slip st to first sc.

Rnd 12: Ch 1, sc in same st and in next 6 sc, 2 sc in next sc, (sc in next 7 sc, 2 sc in next sc) around; join with slip st to first sc: 72 sc.

Rnd 13: Ch 1, sc in same st and in each sc around; join with slip st to first sc.

Rnd 14: Ch 1, sc in same st and in next 2 sc, 2 sc in next sc, (sc in next 3 sc, 2 sc in next sc) around; join with slip st to first sc: 90 sc.

Rnd 15: Ch 1, sc in same st and in next 3 sc, 2 sc in next sc, (sc in next 4 sc, 2 sc in next sc) around; join with slip st to first sc: 108 sc.

Rnd 16: Ch 1, sc in same st and in next 7 sc, 2 sc in next sc, (sc in next 8 sc, 2 sc in next sc) around; join with slip st to first sc: 120 sc.

Rnd 17: Ch 1, sc in same st and in next 5 sc, place marker in Front Loop Only of last sc made for st placement *(Fig. 1, page 143)*, sc in each sc around; join with slip st to Back Loop Only of first sc.

Rnd 18: Ch 1, sc in Back Loop Only of same st and each sc around; join with slip st to **both** loops of first sc.

Rnd 19: Ch 1, sc in same st and in each sc around; join with slip st to first sc.

Rnd 20: Ch 1, sc in same st, ch 2, skip next sc, sc in next sc, (dc, ch 5, dc) in marked sc on Rnd 17, do **not** remove marker, skip next 5 sc on Rnd 19, ★ sc in next sc, ch 2, skip next sc, sc in next sc, skip next 7 sc on Rnd 17, (dc, ch 5, dc) in free loop of next sc *(Fig. 2a, page 144)*, skip next 5 sc on Rnd 19; repeat from ★ around; join with slip st to first sc: 30 sps.

Rnd 21: (Slip st, ch 1, 2 sc) in first ch-2 sp, dc in next ch-5 sp, (ch 1, dc in same sp) 5 times, ★ 2 sc in next ch-2 sp, dc in next ch-5 sp, (ch 1, dc in same sp) 5 times; repeat from ★ around; join with slip st to first sc: 75 ch-1 sps.

Rnd 22: Slip st in next 2 sts and in next ch-1 sp, ch 1, sc in same sp, ch 3, (sc in next ch-1 sp, ch 3) 3 times, ★ sc in next 2 ch-1 sps, ch 3, (sc in next ch-1 sp, ch 3) 3 times; repeat from ★ around to last ch-1 sp, sc in last ch-1 sp; join with slip st to first sc: 60 ch-3 sps.

Rnd 23: (Slip st, work Beginning Popcorn) in first ch-3 sp, ch 3, (work Popcorn in next ch-3 sp, ch 3) twice, ★ work Popcorn in next 2 ch-3 sps, ch 3, (work Popcorn in next ch-3 sp, ch 3) twice; repeat from ★ around to last ch-3 sp, work Popcorn in last ch-3 sp; join with slip st to top of Beginning Popcorn: 45 ch-3 sps.

Rnd 24: (Slip st, ch 1, sc) in first ch-3 sp, (ch 3, sc in same sp) twice, ★ sc in next ch-3 sp, (ch 3, sc in same sp) twice; repeat from ★ around; join with slip st to first sc: 90 ch-3 sps.

Rnd 25: (Slip st, ch 1, sc) in first ch-3 sp, ch 2, hdc in next ch-3 sp, ch 2, dc in next ch-3 sp, work Picot, ch 2, dc in next ch-3 sp, ch 2, hdc in next ch-3 sp, ch 2, ★ sc in next 2 ch-3 sps, ch 2, hdc in next ch-3 sp, ch 2, dc in next ch-3 sp, work Picot, ch 2, dc in next ch-3 sp, ch 2, hdc in next ch-3 sp, ch 2; repeat from ★ around to last ch-3 sp, sc in last ch-3 sp; join with slip st to first sc, finish off.

Rnd 26: With **right** side facing and working in free loops of sc on Rnd 17, join thread with slip st in marked sc (**between** base of 2 dc worked on Rnd 20); slip st in next sc, sc in next sc, slip st in next sc, ch 3, slip st in third ch from hook, skip next sc, slip st in next sc, sc in next sc, slip st in next sc, ★ slip st in next sc (**between** base of 2 dc worked on Rnd 20) and in next sc, sc in next sc, slip st in next sc, ch 3, slip st in third ch from hook, skip next sc, slip st in next sc, sc in next sc, slip st in next sc; repeat from ★ around; join with slip st to first slip st.

Rnd 27: Ch 1, ★ tr in center sc of skipped 5-sc group on Rnd 19, sc in next sc on Rnd 26, work Picot, ch 2, sc in next sc; repeat from ★ around; join with slip st to first tr, finish off.

See Washing and Blocking, page 144.

Finished Size: 6¼" diameter

MATERIALS

Bedspread Weight Cotton Thread (size 10): 55 yards
Steel crochet hook, size 7 (1.65 mm) **or** size
     needed for gauge

GAUGE SWATCH: 2" diameter
Work same as Doily through Rnd 7.

STITCH GUIDE

FRONT POST CLUSTER
  (abbreviated FP Cluster) (uses one dc)
★ YO, insert hook from **front** to **back** around post
of dc indicated *(Fig. 7, page 144)*, YO and pull up
a loop, YO and draw through 2 loops on hook;
repeat from ★ 2 times **more**, YO and draw through
all 4 loops on hook.

2-DC CLUSTER (uses one sp)
★ YO, insert hook in sp indicated, YO and pull up a
loop, YO and draw through 2 loops on hook; repeat
from ★ once **more**, YO and draw through all
3 loops on hook.

BEGINNING 4-DC CLUSTER
  (uses one ch-3 sp)
Ch 2, ★ YO, insert hook in sp indicated, YO and
pull up a loop, YO and draw through 2 loops on
hook; repeat from ★ 2 times **more**, YO and draw
through all 4 loops on hook.

4-DC CLUSTER (uses one ch-3 sp)
★ YO, insert hook in ch-3 sp indicated, YO and pull
up a loop, YO and draw through 2 loops on hook;
repeat from ★ 3 times **more**, YO and draw through
all 5 loops on hook.

DECREASE
  (uses next 6 sc and next 2 ch-2 sps)
† YO twice, insert hook in **next** ch-2 sp, YO and
pull up a loop, (YO and draw through 2 loops on
hook) twice †, ★ YO twice, skip **next** 2 sc, insert
hook in **next** sc, YO and pull up a loop, (YO and
draw through 2 loops on hook) twice; repeat from ★
once **more**, then repeat from † to † once, YO and
draw through all 5 loops on hook.

PICOT
Ch 2, slip st in top of last st made *(Fig. 6a,
page 144)*.

DOILY

Ch 6; join with slip st to form a ring.

Rnd 1 (Right side)**:** Ch 3 **(counts as first dc)**, 23 dc
in ring; join with slip st to first dc: 24 dc.

Rnd 2: Ch 1, sc in same st, ch 2, skip next dc, ★ sc in
next dc, ch 2, skip next dc; repeat from ★ around; join
with slip st to first sc: 12 sc and 12 ch-2 sps.

Rnd 3: Ch 1, sc in same st and in next ch-2 sp, work
FP Cluster around first skipped dc on Rnd 1, ★ sc in
next sc on Rnd 2 and in next ch-2 sp, work FP Cluster
around next skipped dc on Rnd 1; repeat from ★
around; join with slip st to first sc: 36 sts.

Rnd 4: Ch 1, sc in same st and in each st around; join
with slip st to first sc.

Rnd 5: Ch 1, sc in same st and in next sc, 2 sc in next
sc, (sc in next 2 sc, 2 sc in next sc) around; join with
slip st to first sc: 48 sc.

Rnd 6: Ch 1, sc in same st and in each sc around; join
with slip st to first sc.

Rnd 7: Ch 1, sc in same st, ch 3, skip next sc, ★ sc in
next sc, ch 3, skip next sc; repeat from ★ around; join
with slip st to first sc: 24 ch-3 sps.

Rnd 8: (Slip st, work Beginning 4-dc Cluster) in first
ch-3 sp, ch 4, (work 4-dc Cluster in next ch-3 sp, ch 4)
around; join with slip st to top of Beginning 4-dc Cluster.

Rnd 9: (Slip st, ch 1, sc) in first ch-4 sp, (ch 3, sc in
same sp) twice, ★ sc in next ch-4 sp, (ch 3, sc in same
sp) twice; repeat from ★ around; join with slip st to first
sc: 48 ch-3 sps.

Rnd 10: (Slip st, ch 1, sc) in first ch-3 sp, ch 3, (sc in
next ch-3 sp, ch 3) around; join with slip st to first sc.

Rnd 11: (Slip st, ch 2, dc, ch 2, work 2-dc Cluster) in
first ch-3 sp, ch 2, sc in next ch-3 sp, 2 sc in next
ch-3 sp, sc in next ch-3 sp, ch 2, ★ (work 2-dc Cluster,
ch 2) twice in next ch-3 sp, sc in next ch-3 sp, 2 sc in
next ch-3 sp, sc in next ch-3 sp, ch 2; repeat from ★
around; join with slip st to first dc: 48 sc and
36 ch-2 sps.

Rnd 12: (Slip st, ch 2, dc, ch 2, work 2-dc Cluster) in
first ch-2 sp, ch 2, sc in next ch-2 sp, sc in next 4 sc and
in next ch-2 sp, ch 2, ★ (work 2-dc Cluster, ch 2) twice
in next ch-2 sp, sc in next ch-2 sp, sc in next 4 sc and in
next ch-2 sp, ch 2; repeat from ★ around; join with
slip st to first dc: 72 sc.

Rnd 13: (Slip st, ch 2, dc, ch 2, work 2-dc Cluster) in
first ch-2 sp, ch 2, sc in next ch-2 sp, sc in next 6 sc and
in next ch-2 sp, ch 2, ★ (work 2-dc Cluster, ch 2) twice
in next ch-2 sp, sc in next ch-2 sp, sc in next 6 sc and in
next ch-2 sp, ch 2; repeat from ★ around; join with
slip st to first dc: 96 sc.

Rnd 14: (Slip st, ch 2, dc, ch 2, work 2-dc Cluster) in first ch-2 sp, ch 5, decrease, ch 5, ★ work (2-dc Cluster, ch 2, 2-dc Cluster) in next ch-2 sp, ch 5, decrease, ch 5; repeat from ★ around; join with slip st to first dc: 36 sps.

Rnd 15: Ch 1, sc in same st, (sc, dc, work Picot, sc) in next ch-2 sp, sc in next 2-dc Cluster, (3 sc, work Picot, 2 sc) in next 2 ch-5 sps, ★ sc in next 2-dc Cluster, (sc, dc, work Picot, sc) in next ch-2 sp, sc in next 2-dc Cluster, (3 sc, work Picot, 2 sc) in next 2 ch-5 sps; repeat from ★ around; join with slip st to first sc, finish off.

See Washing and Blocking, page 144.

41 ▬▬▬

Finished Size: 5$\frac{1}{4}$" diameter

MATERIALS
Bedspread Weight Cotton Thread (size 10): 50 yards
Steel crochet hook, size 7 (1.65 mm) **or** size
   needed for gauge

GAUGE SWATCH: 1$\frac{1}{4}$" diameter
Work same as Doily through Rnd 4.

STITCH GUIDE

BEGINNING 3-DC CLUSTER (uses one sp)
Ch 2, ★ YO, insert hook in sp indicated, YO and pull up a loop, YO and draw through 2 loops on hook; repeat from ★ once **more**, YO and draw through all 3 loops on hook.

3-DC CLUSTER (uses one sp)
★ YO, insert hook in sp indicated, YO and pull up a loop, YO and draw through 2 loops on hook; repeat from ★ 2 times **more**, YO and draw through all 4 loops on hook.

4-DC CLUSTER (uses one ch-2 sp)
★ YO, insert hook in ch-2 sp indicated, YO and pull up a loop, YO and draw through 2 loops on hook; repeat from ★ 3 times **more**, YO and draw through all 5 loops on hook.

FRONT POST TRIPLE TREBLE CROCHET
   (abbreviated FPtr tr)
YO 4 times, insert hook from **front** to **back** around post of sc indicated *(Fig. 7, page 144)*, YO and pull up a loop (6 loops on hook), (YO and draw through 2 loops on hook) 5 times.

DOILY
Ch 7; join with slip st to form a ring.

Rnd 1 (Right side)**:** Ch 1, 12 sc in ring; join with slip st to Back Loop Only of first sc *(Fig. 1, page 143)*.

Rnd 2: Ch 1, 2 sc in Back Loop Only of same st and each sc around; join with slip st to **both** loops of first sc: 24 sc.

Rnd 3: Ch 1, sc in same st, ch 2, skip next sc, sc in next sc, place marker around sc just made for st placement, ch 2, skip next sc, ★ sc in next sc, ch 2, skip next sc; repeat from ★ around; join with slip st to first sc: 12 ch-2 sps.

Rnd 4: (Slip st, ch 2, work 3-dc Cluster) in first ch-2 sp, ch 4, (work 4-dc Cluster in next ch-2 sp, ch 4) around; join with slip st to top of first 3-dc Cluster.

Rnd 5: (Slip st, ch 1, sc) in first ch-4 sp, (ch 3, sc in same sp) twice, ★ sc in next ch-4 sp, (ch 3, sc in same sp) twice; repeat from ★ around; join with slip st to first sc: 24 ch-3 sps.

Rnd 6: (Slip st, ch 1, 2 sc) in first ch-3 sp, (ch 3, 2 sc in next ch-3 sp) around, ch 1, hdc in first sc to form last ch-3 sp.

Rnd 7: Ch 1, 2 sc in last ch-3 sp made, sc in next ch-3 sp, work FPtr tr around marked sc on Rnd 3, sc in same sp on Rnd 6, ★ (2 sc, ch 2, 2 sc) in next ch-3 sp, sc in next ch-3 sp, work FPtr tr around next sc on Rnd 3, sc in same sp on Rnd 6; repeat from ★ around, 2 sc in same sp as first sc, ch 1, sc in first sc to form last ch-2 sp: 72 sc and 12 ch-2 sps.

Rnd 8: Ch 1, 2 sc in last ch-2 sp made, sc in next 3 sc, skip next FPtr tr, sc in next 3 sc, ★ 3 sc in next ch-2 sp, sc in next 3 sc, skip next FPtr tr, sc in next 3 sc; repeat from ★ around, sc in same sp as first sc; join with slip st to first sc: 108 sc.

Rnd 9: Ch 1, sc in same st, ★ ch 4, skip next 2 sc, sc in next sc; repeat from ★ around to last 2 sc, ch 1, skip last 2 sc, dc in first sc to form last ch-4 sp: 36 ch-4 sps.

Rnd 10: Ch 1, sc in last ch-4 sp made, ch 5, (2 sc in each of next 3 ch-4 sps, ch 5) around to last 2 ch-4 sps, 2 sc in each of last 2 ch-4 sps, sc in same sp as first sc; join with slip st to first sc: 72 sc and 12 ch-5 sps.

Rnd 11: Ch 1, sc in same st and in next ch-5 sp, (ch 3, sc in same sp) 3 times, ★ sc in next 6 sc and in next ch-5 sp, (ch 3, sc in same sp) 3 times; repeat from ★ around to last 5 sc, sc in last 5 sc; join with slip st to first sc, do **not** finish off: 120 sc and 36 ch-3 sps.

Continued on page 54.

Rnd 12: Slip st in next sc and in next ch-3 sp, work Beginning 3-dc Cluster in same sp, ch 4, sc in next sc, ch 4, work 3-dc Cluster in next ch-3 sp, ch 4, sc in next sc, ch 4, ★ work 3-dc Cluster in next 2 ch-3 sps, ch 4, sc in next sc, ch 4, work 3-dc Cluster in next ch-3 sp, ch 4, sc in next sc, ch 4; repeat from ★ around to last ch-3 sp, work 3-dc Cluster in last ch-3 sp; join with slip st to top of Beginning 3-dc Cluster: 48 ch-4 sps.

Rnd 13: (Slip st, ch 1, 2 sc) in first ch-4 sp, ch 3, 2 sc in each of next 2 ch-4 sps, ch 3, 2 sc in next ch-4 sp, skip next 3-dc Cluster, dc in sp **before** next 3-dc Cluster, ★ 2 sc in next ch-4 sp, ch 3, 2 sc in each of next 2 ch-4 sps, ch 3, 2 sc in next ch-4 sp, skip next 3-dc Cluster, dc in sp **before** next 3-dc Cluster; repeat from ★ around; join with slip st to first sc: 108 sts and 24 ch-3 sps.

Rnd 14: Ch 1, sc in same st, 5 sc in next ch-3 sp, sc in next 4 sc, 5 sc in next ch-3 sp, ★ skip next sc, sc in next 3 sts, 5 sc in next ch-3 sp, sc in next 4 sc, 5 sc in next ch-3 sp; repeat from ★ around to last 3 sts, skip next sc, sc in last 2 sts; join with slip st to first sc, finish off.

See Washing and Blocking, page 144.

42 ▬▬▬▬

Finished Size: 5" x 8"

MATERIALS
Bedspread Weight Cotton Thread (size 10): 80 yards
Steel crochet hook, size 7 (1.65 mm) **or** size
　　needed for gauge

GAUGE SWATCH: $1^1/_2$"w x $4^1/_4$"h
Work same as Doily through Rnd 3.

STITCH GUIDE

TREBLE CROCHET *(abbreviated tr)*
YO twice, insert hook in sc indicated, YO and pull up a loop (4 loops on hook), (YO and draw through 2 loops on hook) 3 times.

FRONT POST TREBLE CROCHET
　　(abbreviated FPtr)
YO twice, insert hook from **front** to **back** around post of st indicated *(Fig. 7, page 144)*, YO and pull up a loop (4 loops on hook), (YO and draw through 2 loops on hook) 3 times.

BEGINNING DECREASE (uses next 2 chs)
Ch 2, ★ YO, insert hook in **next** ch, YO and pull up a loop, YO and draw through 2 loops on hook; repeat from ★ once **more**, YO and draw through all 3 loops on hook.

DECREASE (uses next 3 chs)
★ YO, insert hook in **next** ch, YO and pull up a loop, YO and draw through 2 loops on hook; repeat from ★ 2 times **more**, YO and draw through all 4 loops on hook.

CLUSTER (uses one sp)
★ YO, insert hook in sp indicated, YO and pull up a loop, YO and draw through 2 loops on hook; repeat from ★ 2 times **more**, YO and draw through all 4 loops on hook.

BEGINNING CROSS ST
Skip next 2 sc, work FPtr around next dc, working in **front** of last FPtr made, work FPtr around first dc.

CROSS ST
Skip next 2 sc, work FPtr around next st, working in **front** of last FPtr made, work FPtr around same st as first FPtr of last Cross St made.

ENDING CROSS ST
Skip next 2 sts, work FPtr around same dc as second FPtr of Beginning Cross St working **above** FPtr, working in **front** of last FPtr made, work FPtr around same st as last Cross St made.

DOILY

Foundation Row: Ch 5, slip st in fifth ch from hook to form a ring, ch 23, slip st in fifth ch from hook to form a ring: 2 rings and 18 chs.

Rnd 1 (Right side)**:** Slip st in next ch, work beginning decrease, ch 3, (decrease, ch 3) 5 times, (work Cluster, ch 3) 4 times in next ring; working in free loops of beginning ch *(Fig. 2b, page 144)*, (decrease, ch 3) 6 times, (work Cluster, ch 3) 4 times in next ring; join with slip st to top of beginning decrease: 20 ch-3 sps.

Rnd 2: (Slip st, ch 1, 2 sc) in first ch-3 sp, (ch 5, 2 sc in next ch-3 sp) around, ch 2, dc in first sc to form last ch-5 sp.

Rnd 3: Ch 1, 2 sc in last ch-5 sp made, (ch 1, 2 sc in next ch-5 sp) 5 times, ch 3, 2 sc in next ch-5 sp, ch 4, (3 sc in next ch-5 sp, ch 4) twice, 2 sc in next ch-5 sp, ch 3, 2 sc in next ch-5 sp, (ch 1, 2 sc in next ch-5 sp) 5 times, ch 3, 2 sc in next ch-5 sp, ch 4, (3 sc in next ch-5 sp, ch 4) twice, 2 sc in last ch-5 sp, ch 3; join with slip st to first sc: 44 sc.

Rnd 4: Ch 1, sc in same st and in next sc, sc in next ch-1 sp, place marker around sc just made for st placement, sc in next 2 sc, (sc in next ch-1 sp and in next 2 sc) 4 times, 3 sc in next ch-3 sp, sc in next 2 sc, 4 sc in next ch-4 sp, sc in next 3 sc, 5 sc in next ch-4 sp, sc in next 3 sc, 4 sc in next ch-4 sp, sc in next 2 sc, 3 sc in next ch-3 sp, sc in next 2 sc, (sc in next ch-1 sp and in next 2 sc) 5 times, 3 sc in next ch-3 sp, sc in next 2 sc, 4 sc in next ch-4 sp, sc in next 3 sc, 5 sc in next ch-4 sp, sc in next 3 sc, 4 sc in next ch-4 sp, sc in next 2 sc, 3 sc in last ch-3 sp; join with slip st to Back Loop Only of first sc *(Fig. 1, page 143)*: 92 sc.

Rnd 5: Ch 1, working in Back Loops Only, sc in same st and in next 30 sc, 3 sc in next sc, sc in next 45 sc, 3 sc in next sc, sc in last 14 sc; join with slip st to **both** loops of first sc: 96 sc.

Rnd 6: Ch 1, sc in same st and in next 23 sc, ch 2, sc in next 8 sc, (sc, ch 1, sc) in next sc, sc in next 8 sc, ch 2, sc in next 31 sc, ch 2, sc in next 8 sc, (sc, ch 1, sc) in next sc, sc in next 8 sc, ch 2, sc in last 7 sc; join with slip st to first sc: 98 sc and 6 sps.

Rnd 7: Ch 1, working in sc and ch-2 sps on Rnd 6 and in free loops of sc on Rnd 4 *(Fig. 2a, page 144)*, sc in same st and in next sc, dc in marked sc on Rnd 4, (skip next sc on Rnd 6, sc in next 2 sc, skip next 2 sc on Rnd 4, dc in next sc) 7 times, † skip next sc on Rnd 6, 3 sc in next ch-2 sp, dc in next sc on Rnd 4, skip next sc on Rnd 6, sc in next 2 sc, (skip next 2 sc on Rnd 4, dc in next sc, skip next sc on Rnd 6, sc in next 2 sc) twice, tr in next sc on Rnd 4, skip next ch-1 sp on Rnd 6, sc in next 2 sc, dc in next sc on Rnd 4, skip next sc on Rnd 6, (sc in next 2 sc, skip next 2 sc on Rnd 4, dc in next sc, skip next sc on Rnd 6) twice, 3 sc in next ch-2 sp, dc in next sc on Rnd 4 †, (skip next sc on Rnd 6, sc in next 2 sc, skip next 2 sc on Rnd 4, dc in next sc) 10 times, repeat from † to † once, skip next sc on Rnd 6, (sc in next 2 sc, skip next 2 sc on Rnd 4, dc in next sc, skip next sc on Rnd 6) twice; join with slip st to first sc: 112 sts.

Rnd 8: Slip st in next 2 sts, ch 3 **(counts as first dc)**, work Beginning Cross St, dc in same dc as first FPtr of last Cross St made, (work Cross St, dc in same dc as first FPtr of last Cross St made) 6 times, † dc in next sc, work Cross St, dc in second skipped sc and in same dc as first FPtr of last Cross St made, (work Cross St, dc in same dc as first FPtr of last Cross St made) twice, work Cross St, 3 dc in same tr as first FPtr of last Cross St made, (work Cross St, dc in same dc as first FPtr of last Cross St made) 3 times, dc in next sc, work Cross St, dc in second skipped sc and in same dc as first FPtr of last Cross St made †, (work Cross St, dc in same dc as first FPtr of last Cross St made) 10 times, repeat from † to † once, (work Cross St, dc in same dc as first FPtr of last Cross St made) twice, work Ending Cross St; join with slip st to first dc: 120 sts.

Rnd 9: Ch 1, sc in same st and in next 23 sts, ch 2, sc in next 12 sts, (sc, ch 2, sc) in next dc, sc in next 12 sts, ch 2, sc in next 35 sts, ch 2, sc in next 12 sts, (sc, ch 2, sc) in next dc, sc in next 12 sts, ch 2, sc in last 11 sts; join with slip st to first sc: 122 sts and 6 ch-2 sps.

Rnd 10: Ch 1, sc in same st and in next 23 sc, 3 sc in next ch-2 sp, (sc in next 13 sc, 3 sc in next ch-2 sp) twice, sc in next 35 sc, 3 sc in next ch-2 sp, (sc in next 13 sc, 3 sc in next ch-2 sp) twice, sc in last 11 sc; join with slip st to first sc: 140 sc.

Rnd 11: Ch 1, sc in same st, ch 3, (skip next 2 sc, sc in next sc, ch 3) 8 times, skip next sc, sc in next sc, ch 3, (skip next 2 sc, sc in next sc, ch 3) 10 times, skip next sc, sc in next sc, ch 3, (skip next 2 sc, sc in next sc, ch 3) 12 times, skip next sc, sc in next sc, ch 3, (skip next 2 sc, sc in next sc, ch 3) 10 times, skip next sc, sc in next sc, (ch 3, skip next 2 sc, sc in next sc) 3 times, ch 1, skip last 2 sc, hdc in first sc to form last ch-3 sp: 48 ch-3 sps.

Rnd 12: Ch 1, sc in last ch-3 sp made, (ch 3, sc in next ch-3 sp) around, ch 1, hdc in first sc to form last ch-3 sp.

Rnd 13: Ch 1, sc in last ch-3 sp made, (ch 4, sc in next ch-3 sp) around, ch 2, hdc in first sc to form last ch-4 sp.

Rnd 14: Ch 1, sc in last ch-4 sp made, dc in next ch-4 sp, (ch 1, dc in same sp) 4 times, ★ sc in next ch-4 sp, dc in next ch-4 sp, (ch 1, dc in same sp) 4 times; repeat from ★ around; join with slip st to first sc: 96 ch-1 sps.

Rnd 15: Slip st in next dc and in next ch-1 sp, ch 1, sc in same sp, ch 3, sc in next ch-1 sp, ch 4, sc in next ch-1 sp, ch 3, sc in next ch-1 sp, ch 1, ★ sc in next ch-1 sp, ch 3, sc in next ch-1 sp, ch 4, sc in next ch-1 sp, ch 3, sc in next ch-1 sp, ch 1; repeat from ★ around; join with slip st to first sc, finish off.

See Washing and Blocking, page 144.

Finished Size: 8" (point to point)

MATERIALS

Bedspread Weight Cotton Thread (size 10): 100 yards
Steel crochet hook, size 7 (1.65 mm) **or** size
needed for gauge

GAUGE SWATCH: 1³/₄" diameter
Work same as Doily through Rnd 5.

STITCH GUIDE

BEGINNING POPCORN
Ch 3, 3 dc in sp indicated, drop loop from hook,
insert hook in top of beginning ch-3, hook dropped
loop and draw through.

POPCORN
4 Dc in sp indicated, drop loop from hook, insert
hook in first dc of 4-dc group, hook dropped loop
and draw through.

2-DC DECREASE (uses next 2 ch-2 sps)
★ YO, insert hook in **next** ch-2 sp, YO and pull up
a loop, YO and draw through 2 loops on hook;
repeat from ★ once **more**, YO and draw through all
3 loops on hook.

BEGINNING 3-DC DECREASE
(uses next 2 dc)
Ch 2, ★ YO, insert hook in **next** dc, YO and pull
up a loop, YO and draw through 2 loops on hook;
repeat from ★ once **more**, YO and draw through all
3 loops on hook.

3-DC DECREASE (uses next 3 dc)
★ YO, insert hook in **next** dc, YO and pull up a
loop, YO and draw through 2 loops on hook; repeat
from ★ 2 times **more**, YO and draw through all
4 loops on hook.

4-DC DECREASE (uses next 4 sc)
★ YO, insert hook in **next** sc, YO and pull up a
loop, YO and draw through 2 loops on hook; repeat
from ★ 3 times **more**, YO and draw through all
5 loops on hook.

PICOT
Ch 2, slip st in top of last sc made **(Fig. 6a,
page 144)**.

2-DC CLUSTER (uses one sp)
★ YO, insert hook in sp indicated, YO and pull up a
loop, YO and draw through 2 loops on hook; repeat
from ★ once **more**, YO and draw through all
3 loops on hook.

3-DC CLUSTER (uses one ch-2 sp)
★ YO, insert hook in ch-2 sp indicated, YO and pull
up a loop, YO and draw through 2 loops on hook;
repeat from ★ 2 times **more**, YO and draw through
all 4 loops on hook.

DOILY

Ch 7; join with slip st to form a ring.

Rnd 1 (Right side): Ch 1, 18 sc in ring; join with slip st
to Back Loop Only of first sc **(Fig. 1, page 143)**.

Rnd 2: Ch 1, working in Back Loops Only, sc in same
st and in next sc, 2 sc in next sc, (sc in next 2 sc, 2 sc in
next sc) around; join with slip st to **both** loops of first sc:
24 sc.

Rnd 3: Ch 1, sc in same st and in each sc around; join
with slip st to first sc.

Rnd 4: Ch 1, sc in same st, ch 2, skip next sc, ★ sc in
next sc, ch 2, skip next sc; repeat from ★ around; join
with slip st to first sc: 12 ch-2 sps.

Rnd 5: (Slip st, work Beginning Popcorn) in first
ch-2 sp, ch 4, (work Popcorn in next ch-2 sp, ch 4)
around; join with slip st to top of Beginning Popcorn.

Rnd 6: [Slip st, ch 3 **(counts as first dc)**, 5 dc] in first
ch-4 sp, ch 3, sc in next ch-4 sp, ch 3, ★ 6 dc in next
ch-4 sp, ch 3, sc in next ch-4 sp, ch 3; repeat from ★
around; join with slip st to first dc: 36 dc.

Rnd 7: Work beginning 3-dc decrease, ch 5, work
3-dc decrease, ch 3, (sc in next ch-3 sp, ch 3) twice,
★ work 3-dc decrease, ch 5, work 3-dc decrease, ch 3,
(sc in next ch-3 sp, ch 3) twice; repeat from ★ around;
join with slip st to top of beginning 3-dc decrease:
24 sps.

Rnd 8: (Slip st, ch 1, sc) in first ch-5 sp, (ch 3, sc in
same sp) twice, 2 sc in next ch-3 sp, ch 3, sc in next
ch-3 sp, ch 3, 2 sc in next ch-3 sp, ★ sc in next ch-5 sp,
(ch 3, sc in same sp) twice, 2 sc in next ch-3 sp, ch 3, sc
in next ch-3 sp, ch 3, 2 sc in next ch-3 sp; repeat from
★ around; join with slip st to first sc.

Rnd 9: [Slip st, ch 5 **(counts as first dc plus ch 2, now and throughout)**, 2 dc] in first ch-3 sp, (ch 2, 2 dc) twice in next ch-3 sp, ch 3, 2 sc in next ch-3 sp, work Picot, 2 sc in next ch-3 sp, ch 3, ★ (2 dc, ch 2) twice in next ch-3 sp, (2 dc, ch 2, 2 dc) in next ch-3 sp, ch 3, 2 sc in next ch-3 sp, work Picot, 2 sc in next ch-3 sp, ch 3; repeat from ★ around, dc in same sp as first dc; join with slip st to first dc: 30 sps.

Rnd 10: (Slip st, ch 5, 2 dc) in first ch-2 sp, ch 2, sc in next ch-2 sp, ch 2, (2 dc, ch 2) twice in next ch-2 sp, sc in next ch-3 sp, ch 5, sc in next ch-3 sp, ch 2, ★ (2 dc, ch 2) twice in next ch-2 sp, sc in next ch-2 sp, ch 2, (2 dc, ch 2) twice in next ch-2 sp, sc in next ch-3 sp, ch 5, sc in next ch-3 sp, ch 2; repeat from ★ around, dc in same sp as first dc; join with slip st to first dc: 42 sps.

Rnd 11: (Slip st, ch 5, 2 dc) in first ch-2 sp, ch 2, 2 sc in each of next 2 ch-2 sps, ch 2, (2 dc, ch 2) twice in next ch-2 sp, sc in next ch-2 sp, work 2-dc Cluster in next ch-5 sp, (ch 1, work 2-dc Cluster in same sp) 3 times, sc in next ch-2 sp, ch 2, ★ (2 dc, ch 2) twice in next ch-2 sp, 2 sc in each of next 2 ch-2 sps, ch 2, (2 dc, ch 2) twice in next ch-2 sp, sc in next ch-2 sp, work 2-dc Cluster in next ch-5 sp, (ch 1, work 2-dc Cluster in same sp) 3 times, sc in next ch-2 sp, ch 2; repeat from ★ around, dc in same sp as first dc; join with slip st to first dc: 54 sps.

Rnd 12: (Slip st, ch 5, 2 dc) in first ch-2 sp, ch 2, 2 sc in next ch-2 sp, sc in next 4 sc, 2 sc in next ch-2 sp, ch 2, (2 dc, ch 2) twice in next ch-2 sp, sc in next ch-2 sp, work 2-dc Cluster in next ch-1 sp, (ch 2, work 2-dc Cluster in next ch-1 sp) twice, sc in next ch-2 sp, ch 2, ★ (2 dc, ch 2) twice in next ch-2 sp, 2 sc in next ch-2 sp, sc in next 4 sc, 2 sc in next ch-2 sp, ch 2, (2 dc, ch 2) twice in next ch-2 sp, sc in next ch-2 sp, work 2-dc Cluster in next ch-1 sp, (ch 2, work 2-dc Cluster in next ch-1 sp) twice, sc in next ch-2 sp, ch 2; repeat from ★ around, dc in same sp as first dc; join with slip st to first dc: 48 ch-2 sps.

Rnd 13: (Slip st, ch 5, 2 dc) in first ch-2 sp, ch 2, 2 sc in next ch-2 sp, sc in next 8 sc, 2 sc in next ch-2 sp, ch 2, (2 dc, ch 2) twice in next ch-2 sp, sc in next ch-2 sp, work 2-dc Cluster in next ch-2 sp, ch 2, work 2-dc Cluster in next ch-2 sp, sc in next ch-2 sp, ch 2, ★ (2 dc, ch 2) twice in next ch-2 sp, 2 sc in next ch-2 sp, sc in next 8 sc, 2 sc in next ch-2 sp, ch 2, (2 dc, ch 2) twice in next ch-2 sp, sc in next ch-2 sp, work 2-dc Cluster in next ch-2 sp, ch 2, work 2-dc Cluster in next ch-2 sp, sc in next ch-2 sp, ch 2; repeat from ★ around, dc in same sp as first dc; join with slip st to first dc: 42 ch-2 sps.

Rnd 14: (Slip st, ch 5, 2 dc) in first ch-2 sp, ch 2, 2 sc in next ch-2 sp, sc in next 12 sc, 2 sc in next ch-2 sp, ch 2, (2 dc, ch 2) twice in next ch-2 sp, sc in next ch-2 sp, work 2-dc Cluster in next ch-2 sp, sc in next ch-2 sp, ch 2, ★ (2 dc, ch 2) twice in next ch-2 sp, 2 sc in next ch-2 sp, sc in next 12 sc, 2 sc in next ch-2 sp, ch 2, (2 dc, ch 2) twice in next ch-2 sp, sc in next ch-2 sp, work 2-dc Cluster in next ch-2 sp, sc in next ch-2 sp, ch 2; repeat from ★ around, dc in same sp as first dc; join with slip st to first dc: 36 ch-2 sps.

Rnd 15: (Slip st, ch 5, 2 dc) in first ch-2 sp, ch 2, 2 sc in next ch-2 sp, sc in next 16 sc, 2 sc in next ch-2 sp, (ch 2, 2 dc) twice in next ch-2 sp, work 2-dc decrease, ★ (2 dc, ch 2) twice in next ch-2 sp, 2 sc in next ch-2 sp, sc in next 16 sc, 2 sc in next ch-2 sp, (ch 2, 2 dc) twice in next ch-2 sp, work 2-dc decrease; repeat from ★ around, dc in same sp as first dc; join with slip st to first dc: 24 ch-2 sps.

Rnd 16: (Slip st, ch 2, work 2-dc Cluster) in first ch-2 sp, ch 5, 2 sc in next ch-2 sp, ch 2, work 4-dc decrease, (ch 5, work 4-dc decrease) 4 times, ch 2, 2 sc in next ch-2 sp, ch 5, ★ work 3-dc Cluster in next 2 ch-2 sps, ch 5, 2 sc in next ch-2 sp, ch 2, work 4-dc decrease, (ch 5, work 4-dc decrease) 4 times, ch 2, 2 sc in next ch-2 sp, ch 5; repeat from ★ around to last ch-2 sp, work 3-dc Cluster in last ch-2 sp; join with slip st to top of first 2-dc Cluster: 48 sps.

Rnd 17: [Slip st, ch 2 **(counts as first hdc)**, 4 hdc] in first ch-5 sp, hdc in next 2 sc, 2 sc in next ch-2 sp, 4 sc in each of next 4 ch-5 sps, 2 sc in next ch-2 sp, hdc in next 2 sc, 5 hdc in next ch-5 sp, skip next 3-dc Cluster, 4 dc in sp **before** next 3-dc Cluster, ★ 5 hdc in next ch-5 sp, hdc in next 2 sc, 2 sc in next ch-2 sp, 4 sc in each of next 4 ch-5 sps, 2 sc in next ch-2 sp, hdc in next 2 sc, 5 hdc in next ch-5 sp, skip next 3-dc Cluster, 4 dc in sp **before** next 3-dc Cluster; repeat from ★ around; join with slip st to first hdc: 228 sts.

Rnd 18: Ch 1, sc in same st and in next 34 sts, 2 sc in each of next 2 dc, (sc in next 36 sts, 2 sc in each of next 2 dc) around to last dc, sc in last dc; join with slip st to first sc, finish off.

See Washing and Blocking, page 144.

Finished Size: 5" diameter

MATERIALS

Bedspread Weight Cotton Thread (size 10): 50 yards
Steel crochet hook, size 7 (1.65 mm) **or** size
   needed for gauge

GAUGE SWATCH: $1^1/2$" diameter
Work same as Doily through Rnd 3.

STITCH GUIDE

BACK POST SINGLE CROCHET
(abbreviated BPsc)
Insert hook from **back** to **front** around post of dc
indicated *(Fig. 7, page 144)*, YO and pull up a
loop, YO and draw through both loops on hook.

FRONT POST SINGLE CROCHET
(abbreviated FPsc)
Insert hook from **front** to **back** around post of
FPdc indicated *(Fig. 7, page 144)*, YO and pull up
a loop, YO and draw through both loops on hook.
Skip st behind FPsc.

FRONT POST DOUBLE CROCHET
(abbreviated FPdc)
YO, insert hook from **front** to **back** around post of
dc indicated *(Fig. 7, page 144)*, YO and pull up a
loop (3 loops on hook), (YO and draw through
2 loops on hook) twice. Skip st behind FPdc.

FRONT POST DOUBLE TREBLE CROCHET
(abbreviated FPdtr)
YO 3 times, insert hook from **front** to **back** around
post of FPsc indicated *(Fig. 7, page 144)*, YO and
pull up a loop (5 loops on hook), (YO and draw
through 2 loops on hook) 4 times.

BEGINNING POPCORN
Ch 3, 3 dc in sp indicated, drop loop from hook,
insert hook in first dc of 4-dc group, hook dropped
loop and draw through.

POPCORN
4 Dc in ch-2 sp indicated, drop loop from hook,
insert hook in first dc of 4-dc group, hook dropped
loop and draw through.

DOILY

Ch 7; join with slip st to form a ring.

Rnd 1 (Right side)**:** Ch 3 **(counts as first dc, now
and throughout)**, 23 dc in ring; join with slip st to first
dc: 24 dc.

Rnd 2: Ch 1, 2 sc in same st, work FPdc around next
dc, (2 sc in next dc, work FPdc around next dc) around;
join with slip st to first sc: 12 FPdc.

Rnd 3: Slip st in next sc, ch 1, work FPsc around next
FPdc, (ch 5, work FPsc around next FPdc) around, ch 2,
dc in first FPsc to form last ch-5 sp: 12 ch-5 sps.

Rnd 4: Ch 3, 4 dc in last ch-5 sp made, work FPdtr
around last FPsc made on Rnd 3, skip next FPsc and
next ch-5 sp, work FPdtr around next FPsc, working
behind FPdtr, 5 dc in skipped ch-5 sp, working in **front**
of last FPdtr made, work FPdtr around skipped FPsc,
skip next ch-5 sp, ★ work FPdtr around next FPsc,
working **behind** FPdtr, 5 dc in skipped ch-5 sp, working
in **front** of last FPdtr made, work FPdtr around same
FPsc as second-to-the-last FPdtr, skip next ch-5 sp;
repeat from ★ 8 times **more**, work FPdtr around same
FPsc as first FPdtr working **above** first FPdtr, working
behind FPdtr, 5 dc in skipped ch-5 sp, working in **front**
of last FPdtr made, work FPdtr around same FPsc as
second-to-the-last FPdtr, working **behind** first FPdtr,
work FPdtr around same FPsc as third FPdtr working
above third FPdtr; join with slip st to first dc: 60 dc and
24 FPdtr.

Rnd 5: Ch 1, sc in same st and in next 4 dc, skip next
2 FPdtr, (sc in next 5 dc, skip next 2 FPdtr) around; join
with slip st to first sc: 60 sc.

Rnd 6: Ch 1, sc in same st and in next sc, 3 sc in next
sc, (sc in next 4 sc, 3 sc in next sc) around to last 2 sc,
sc in last 2 sc; join with slip st to first sc: 84 sc.

Rnd 7: Ch 1, sc in same st and in next 2 sc, 3 sc in
next sc, (sc in next 6 sc, 3 sc in next sc) around to last
3 sc, sc in last 3 sc; join with slip st to first sc: 108 sc.

Rnd 8: Slip st in next 4 sc, ch 1, sc in same st, ch 7,
skip next 8 sc, ★ sc in next sc, ch 7, skip next 8 sts;
repeat from ★ around; join with slip st to first sc:
12 ch-7 sps.

Rnd 9: (Slip st, ch 3, 10 dc) in first ch-7 sp, 11 dc in
each ch-7 sp around; join with slip st to first dc: 132 dc.

Rnd 10: Ch 1, work BPsc around same st, ch 2, skip
next dc, (work BPsc around next dc, ch 2, skip next
dc) 4 times, ★ work BPsc around each of next 2 dc,
ch 2, skip next dc, (work BPsc around next dc, ch 2,
skip next dc) 4 times; repeat from ★ 10 times **more**,
work BPsc around last dc; join with slip st to first BPsc:
60 ch-2 sps.

Rnd 11: (Slip st, work Beginning Popcorn) in first ch-2 sp, ch 3, (work Popcorn in next ch-2 sp, ch 3) 3 times, ★ work Popcorn in next 2 ch-2 sps, ch 3, (work Popcorn in next ch-2 sp, ch 3) 3 times; repeat from ★ around to last ch-2 sp, work Popcorn in last ch-2 sp; join with slip st to top of Beginning Popcorn: 48 ch-3 sps.

Rnd 12: Slip st in first ch-3 sp, ch 1, (sc, ch 3, sc) in same sp and in each ch-3 sp around; join with slip st to first sc, finish off.

See Washing and Blocking, page 144.

45 ▮▬▬▬

Finished Size: 6" diameter

MATERIALS
Bedspread Weight Cotton Thread (size 10): 50 yards
Steel crochet hook, size 7 (1.65 mm) **or** size
    needed for gauge

GAUGE SWATCH: 1" diameter
Work same as Doily through Rnd 1.

STITCH GUIDE

> **TREBLE CROCHET** (abbreviated tr)
> YO twice, insert hook in dc indicated, YO and pull up a loop (4 loops on hook), (YO and draw through 2 loops on hook) 3 times.

DOILY
Ch 7; join with slip st to form a ring.

Rnd 1 (Right side): Ch 3 **(counts as first dc, now and throughout)**, 2 dc in ring, ch 2, (3 dc in ring, ch 2) 5 times; join with slip st to first dc: 18 dc and 6 ch-2 sps.

Rnd 2: Ch 1, sc in same st, (sc, ch 4, sc) in next dc, sc in next dc, (sc, ch 1, sc) in next ch-2 sp, ★ sc in next dc, (sc, ch 4, sc) in next dc, sc in next dc, (sc, ch 1, sc) in next ch-2 sp; repeat from ★ around; join with slip st to first sc: 36 sc and 12 sps.

Rnd 3: Slip st in next sc and in next ch-4 sp, ch 3, 8 dc in same sp, skip next 3 sc, sc in next ch-1 sp, ★ 9 dc in next ch-4 sp, skip next 3 sc, sc in next ch-1 sp; repeat from ★ around; join with slip st to first dc: 54 dc.

Rnd 4: Ch 1, sc in same st, tr in next dc pulling tr to right side **now and throughout**, sc in next dc, tr in next dc, (sc, tr, sc) in next dc, (tr in next dc, sc in next dc) twice, skip next sc, ★ (sc in next dc, tr in next dc) twice, (sc, tr, sc) in next dc, (tr in next dc, sc in next dc) twice, skip next sc; repeat from ★ around; join with slip st to first sc: 66 sts.

Rnd 5: Slip st in next tr, ch 1, sc in same st and in next 3 sts, 3 sc in next tr, sc in next 4 sts, ★ ch 3, skip next 2 sc, sc in next 4 sts, 3 sc in next tr, sc in next 4 sts; repeat from ★ around to last 2 sts, ch 1, skip last 2 sts, hdc in first sc to form last ch-3 sp: 66 sc and 6 ch-3 sps.

Rnd 6: Ch 1, sc in last ch-3 sp made, ch 6, skip next 5 sc, sc in next sc, ch 6, ★ sc in next ch-3 sp, ch 6, skip next 5 sc, sc in next sc, ch 6; repeat from ★ around; join with slip st to first sc: 12 ch-6 sps.

Rnd 7: Ch 1, sc in same st, (ch 4, sc) twice in next ch-6 sp, ★ ch 4, sc in next sc, (ch 4, sc) twice in next ch-6 sp; repeat from ★ around, ch 2, hdc in first sc to form last ch-4 sp: 36 ch-4 sps.

Rnds 8 and 9: Ch 1, sc in last ch-4 sp made, (ch 4, sc in next ch-4 sp) around, ch 2, hdc in first sc to form last ch-4 sp.

Rnd 10: Ch 1, sc in last ch-4 sp made, 5 dc in next ch-4 sp, (sc in next ch-4 sp, 5 dc in next ch-4 sp) around; join with slip st to first sc: 108 sts.

Rnd 11: Ch 1, sc in same st, tr in next dc, (sc in next st, tr in next dc) around; join with slip st to first sc.

Rnd 12: Ch 1, sc in same st, skip next 2 sts, dc in next tr, (ch 1, dc in same st) 4 times, skip next 2 sts, ★ sc in next sc, skip next 2 sts, dc in next tr, (ch 1, dc in same st) 4 times, skip next 2 sts; repeat from ★ around; join with slip st to first sc: 72 ch-1 sps.

Rnd 13: Slip st in next dc, ch 1, sc in same st and in next ch-1 sp, (ch 3, sc in next ch-1 sp) 3 times, sc in next dc, skip next sc, ★ sc in next dc and in next ch-1 sp, (ch 3, sc in next ch-1 sp) 3 times, sc in next dc, skip next st; repeat from ★ around; join with slip st to first sc, finish off.

See Washing and Blocking, page 144.

Finished Size: 5¹/₂" (point to point)

MATERIALS

Bedspread Weight Cotton Thread (size 10): 50 yards
Steel crochet hook, size 7 (1.65 mm) **or** size
  needed for gauge

GAUGE SWATCH: 1³/₄" diameter
Work same as Doily through Rnd 3.

STITCH GUIDE

TREBLE CROCHET *(abbreviated tr)*
YO twice, insert hook in sc indicated, YO and pull
up a loop (4 loops on hook), (YO and draw through
2 loops on hook) 3 times.

BEGINNING CLUSTER (uses one sp)
Ch 2, ★ YO, insert hook in sp indicated, YO and
pull up a loop, YO and draw through 2 loops on
hook; repeat from ★ once **more**, YO and draw
through all 3 loops on hook.

CLUSTER (uses one sp)
★ YO, insert hook in sp indicated, YO and pull up a
loop, YO and draw through 2 loops on hook; repeat
from ★ 2 times **more**, YO and draw through all
4 loops on hook.

POPCORN
4 Dc in ch-3 sp indicated, drop loop from hook,
insert hook in first dc of 4-dc group, hook dropped
loop and draw through.

DECREASE (uses next 5 dc)
YO, insert hook in next dc, YO and pull up a loop,
YO and draw through 2 loops on hook, ★ YO, skip
next dc, insert hook in **next** dc, YO and pull up a
loop, YO and draw through 2 loops on hook; repeat
from ★ once **more**, YO and draw through all
4 loops on hook.

PICOT
Ch 2, slip st in top of sc just made *(Fig. 6a,
page 144)*.

DOILY

Ch 8; join with slip st to form a ring.

Rnd 1 (Right side)**:** Work Beginning Cluster in ring,
ch 3, (work Cluster in ring, ch 3) 7 times; join with slip st
to top of Beginning Cluster: 8 ch-3 sps.

Rnd 2: Slip st in first ch-3 sp, ch 1, (sc, ch 3, sc) in
same sp and in each ch-3 sp around; join with slip st to
first sc.

Rnd 3: Ch 1, sc in same st, ch 3, work Popcorn in
next ch-3 sp, ch 3, ★ sc in next 2 sc, ch 3, work
Popcorn in next ch-3 sp, ch 3; repeat from ★ around to
last sc, sc in last sc; join with slip st to first sc:
16 ch-3 sps.

Rnd 4: (Slip st, ch 1, 3 sc) in first ch-3 sp, ch 3, (3 sc in
each of next 2 ch-3 sps, ch 3) around to last ch-3 sp,
3 sc in last ch-3 sp; join with slip st to first sc: 48 sc and
8 ch-3 sps.

Rnd 5: (Slip st, ch 1, sc) in next sc, ch 3, 5 dc in next
ch-3 sp, ch 3, skip next sc, sc in next sc, skip next 2 sc,
★ sc in next sc, ch 3, 5 dc in next ch-3 sp, ch 3, skip
next sc, sc in next sc, skip next 2 sts; repeat from ★
around; join with slip st to first sc: 40 dc and
16 ch-3 sps.

Rnd 6: (Slip st, ch 1, 2 sc) in first ch-3 sp, ch 4,
decrease, ch 4, 2 sc in next ch-3 sp, ★ ch 3, 2 sc in next
ch-3 sp, ch 4, decrease, ch 4, 2 sc in next ch-3 sp;
repeat from ★ around, ch 1, hdc in first sc to form last
ch-3 sp: 24 sps.

Rnd 7: Ch 1, sc in last ch-3 sp made, ch 3, (2 sc in
next ch-4 sp, ch 3) twice, ★ sc in next ch-3 sp, ch 3,
(2 sc in next ch-4 sp, ch 3) twice; repeat from ★ around;
join with slip st to first sc.

Rnd 8: (Slip st, ch 1, 3 sc) in first ch-3 sp, sc in next
2 sc and in next ch-3 sp, ch 5, sc in same sp and in next
2 sc, ★ 3 sc in each of next 2 ch-3 sps, sc in next 2 sc
and in next ch-3 sp, ch 5, sc in same sp and in next
2 sc; repeat from ★ around to last ch-3 sp, 3 sc in last
ch-3 sp; join with slip st to first sc: 96 sc and 8 ch-5 sps.

Rnd 9: Ch 1, sc in same st and in next 5 sc, (sc, ch 3,
sc, ch 4, sc, ch 3, sc) in next ch-5 sp, sc in next 6 sc,
★ ch 4, sc in next 6 sc, (sc, ch 3, sc, ch 4, sc, ch 3, sc)
in next ch-5 sp, sc in next 6 sc; repeat from ★ around,
ch 2, hdc in first sc to form last ch-4 sp: 32 sps.

Rnd 10: Ch 1, sc in last ch-4 sp made, ★ † skip next
5 sc, tr in next sc, ch 4, working in **front** of last tr
made, tr in first skipped sc, sc in next sc, 2 sc in each of
next 2 sps, ch 2, 2 sc in same sp and in next ch-3 sp, sc
in next sc, skip next 5 sc, tr in next sc, ch 4, working in
front of last tr made, tr in first skipped sc †, sc in next
ch-4 sp; repeat from ★ 6 times **more**, then repeat from
† to † once; join with slip st to first sc: 24 sps.

Rnd 11: Slip st in next tr and in next ch-4 sp, ch 1, (2 sc, ch 2, 2 sc) in same sp, ch 6, 2 sc in next ch-2 sp, ch 6, ★ (2 sc, ch 2, 2 sc) in next 2 ch-4 sps, ch 6, 2 sc in next ch-2 sp, ch 6; repeat from ★ around to last ch-4 sp, (2 sc, ch 2, 2 sc) in last ch-4 sp; join with slip st to first sc: 32 sps.

Rnd 12: Slip st in next sc and in next ch-2 sp, ch 1, (sc, work Picot, sc) in same sp, ch 2, 5 sc in next ch-6 sp, sc in next sc, work Picot, sc in next sc, 5 sc in next ch-6 sp, ch 2, (sc, work Picot, sc) in next ch-2 sp, ch 1, ★ (sc, work Picot, sc) in next ch-2 sp, ch 2, 5 sc in next ch-6 sp, sc in next sc, work Picot, sc in next sc, 5 sc in next ch-6 sp, ch 2, (sc, work Picot, sc) in next ch-2 sp, ch 1; repeat from ★ around; join with slip st to first sc, finish off.

See Washing and Blocking, page 144.

47 ▰▰▰

Finished Size: 6" diameter

MATERIALS
Bedspread Weight Cotton Thread (size 10): 60 yards
Steel crochet hook, size 7 (1.65 mm) **or** size
   needed for gauge

GAUGE SWATCH: 2" diameter
Work same as Doily through Rnd 3.

STITCH GUIDE

2-DC CLUSTER (uses one ch-1 sp)
★ YO, insert hook in ch-1 sp indicated, YO and pull up a loop, YO and draw through 2 loops on hook; repeat from ★ once **more**, YO and draw through all 3 loops on hook.

3-DC CLUSTER (uses one ch-2 sp)
★ YO, insert hook in ch-2 sp indicated, YO and pull up a loop, YO and draw through 2 loops on hook; repeat from ★ 2 times **more**, YO and draw through all 4 loops on hook.

BEGINNING POPCORN
Ch 3 **(counts as first dc)**, 5 dc in ch-3 sp indicated, drop loop from hook, insert hook in first dc of 6-dc group, hook dropped loop and draw through.

POPCORN
6 Dc in ch-3 sp indicated, drop loop from hook, insert hook in first dc of 6-dc group, hook dropped loop and draw through.

PICOT
Ch 3, slip st in third ch from hook, ch 1.

DOILY
Ch 7; join with slip st to form a ring.

Rnd 1 (Right side)**:** Ch 1, 18 sc in ring; join with slip st to first sc.

Rnd 2: Ch 4, (dc in next sc, ch 1) around; join with slip st to third ch of beginning ch-4: 18 ch-1 sps.

Rnd 3: (Slip st, ch 2, dc) in first ch-1 sp, ch 2, (work 2-dc Cluster in next ch-1 sp, ch 2) around; join with slip st to first dc.

Rnd 4: (Slip st, ch 1, sc) in first ch-2 sp, ch 3, (sc in next ch-2 sp, ch 3) around; join with slip st to first sc.

Rnd 5: Slip st in first ch-3 sp, work Beginning Popcorn, (ch 6, work Popcorn) around, ch 3, dc in top of Beginning Popcorn to form last ch-6 sp.

Rnd 6: Ch 1, sc in last ch-6 sp made, ch 3, (sc, ch 3) twice in each ch-6 sp around, sc in same sp as first sc, ch 1, hdc in first sc to form last ch-3 sp: 36 ch-3 sps.

Rnd 7: Ch 1, sc in last ch-3 sp made, ch 3, (sc in next ch-3 sp, ch 3) around; join with slip st to first sc.

Rnd 8: Slip st in first ch-3 sp, ch 1, 3 sc in same sp and in each ch-3 sp around; join with slip st to first sc: 108 sc.

Rnd 9: Ch 1, sc in same st and in next 3 sc, 2 sc in next sc, (sc in next 5 sc, 2 sc in next sc) around to last sc, sc in last sc; join with slip st to first sc: 126 sc.

Rnd 10: Ch 1, sc in same st and in each sc around; join with slip st to first sc.

Rnd 11: Ch 1, sc in same st, ch 2, skip next sc, ★ sc in next sc, ch 2, skip next sc; repeat from ★ around; join with slip st to first sc: 63 ch-2 sps.

Rnd 12: (Slip st, ch 1, sc) in first ch-2 sp, ch 3, sc in next ch-2 sp, ch 3, work 3-dc Cluster in next ch-2 sp, ch 3, ★ (sc in next ch-2 sp, ch 3) twice, work 3-dc Cluster in next ch-2 sp, ch 3; repeat from ★ around; join with slip st to first sc.

Rnd 13: [Slip st, ch 1, sc, ch 2, slip st in top of last sc made *(Fig. 6a, page 144)*, sc] in first ch-3 sp, 2 sc in next ch-3 sp, work Picot, 2 sc in next ch-3 sp, ★ (sc, ch 2, slip st in top of last sc made, sc) in next ch-3 sp, 2 sc in next ch-3 sp, work Picot, 2 sc in next ch-3 sp; repeat from ★ around; join with slip st to first sc, finish off.

See Washing and Blocking, page 144.

48 ▰▰▰

Finished Size: 5^1/$_2$" diameter

MATERIALS
Bedspread Weight Cotton Thread (size 10): 40 yards
Steel crochet hook, size 7 (1.65 mm) **or** size
   needed for gauge

GAUGE SWATCH: 2" diameter
Work same as Doily through Rnd 4.

STITCH GUIDE

2-DC CLUSTER (uses one sp)
★ YO, insert hook in sp indicated, YO and pull up a loop, YO and draw through 2 loops on hook; repeat from ★ once **more**, YO and draw through all 3 loops on hook.

3-DC CLUSTER (uses one sp)
★ YO, insert hook in sp indicated, YO and pull up a loop, YO and draw through 2 loops on hook; repeat from ★ 2 times **more**, YO and draw through all 4 loops on hook.

4-DC CLUSTER (uses one ch-2 sp)
★ YO, insert hook in ch-2 sp indicated, YO and pull up a loop, YO and draw through 2 loops on hook; repeat from ★ 3 times **more**, YO and draw through all 5 loops on hook.

SPLIT TREBLE CROCHET
  (abbreviated Split tr) (uses 2 ch-3 sps)
YO twice, working in **front** of same sp *(Fig. 5, page 144)*, insert hook in ch-3 sp **before** sc one rnd **below**, YO and pull up a loop, (YO and draw through 2 loops on hook) twice, YO twice, insert hook in next ch-3 sp **after** same sc, YO and pull up a loop, (YO and draw through 2 loops on hook) twice, YO and draw through all 3 loops on hook.

DOILY

Rnd 1 (Right side)**:** Ch 4, 11 dc in fourth ch from hook **(3 skipped chs count as first dc)**; join with slip st to first dc: 12 dc.

Rnd 2: Ch 1, 2 sc in same st and in each dc around; join with slip st to first sc: 24 sc.

Rnd 3: Ch 1, sc in same st, ch 2, skip next sc, ★ sc in next sc, ch 2, skip next sc; repeat from ★ around; join with slip st to first sc: 12 ch-2 sps.

Rnd 4: (Slip st, ch 2, work 3-dc Cluster) in first ch-2 sp, (ch 4, work 4-dc Cluster in next ch-2 sp) around, ch 2, hdc in top of first 3-dc Cluster to form last ch-4 sp.

Rnd 5: Ch 1, (sc, ch 3, sc) in last ch-4 sp made, ★ sc in next ch-4 sp, (ch 3, sc in same sp) twice; repeat from ★ around, sc in same sp as first sc, ch 1, hdc in first sc to form last ch-3 sp: 24 ch-3 sps.

Rnd 6: Ch 1, 2 sc in last ch-3 sp made, ch 1, (2 sc in next ch-3 sp, ch 1) around; join with slip st to first sc: 48 sc and 24 ch-1 sps.

Rnd 7: Ch 1, sc in same st and in each sc and each ch-1 sp around; join with slip st to first sc: 72 sc.

Rnd 8: Ch 1, sc in same st, ch 2, skip next sc, ★ sc in next sc, ch 2, skip next sc; repeat from ★ around; join with slip st to first sc: 36 ch-2 sps.

Rnd 9: (Slip st, ch 2, work 2-dc Cluster) in first ch-2 sp, ch 2, (work 3-dc Cluster in next ch-2 sp, ch 2) around; join with slip st to top of first 2-dc Cluster.

Rnd 10: (Slip st, ch 2, work 2-dc Cluster) in first ch-2 sp, ch 3, sc in next ch-2 sp, ch 3, ★ work 3-dc Cluster in next ch-2 sp, ch 3, sc in next ch-2 sp, ch 3; repeat from ★ around; join with slip st to top of first 2-dc Cluster.

Rnd 11: (Slip st, ch 1, sc) in first ch-3 sp, ch 6, (sc in next 2 ch-3 sps, ch 6) around to last ch-3 sp, sc in last ch-3 sp; join with slip st to first sc: 18 ch-6 sps.

Rnd 12: (Slip st, ch 1, 3 sc) in first ch-6 sp, work Split tr, ★ 3 sc in same sp on Rnd 11 and in next ch-6 sp, work Split tr; repeat from ★ around, 3 sc in same sp on Rnd 11; join with slip st to first sc: 126 sts.

Rnd 13: Ch 1, sc in same st, ch 3, slip st in third ch from hook, ch 1, skip next 2 sc, (sc, ch 4, slip st in fourth ch from hook, sc) in next Split tr, ch 3, slip st in third ch from hook, ch 1, ★ skip next 2 sc, sc in next 2 sc, ch 3, slip st in third ch from hook, ch 1, skip next 2 sc, (sc, ch 4, slip st in fourth ch from hook, sc) in next Split tr, ch 3, slip st in third ch from hook, ch 1; repeat from ★ around to last 3 sc, skip next 2 sc, sc in last sc; join with slip st to first sc, finish off.

See Washing and Blocking, page 144.

Finished Size: 5" diameter

MATERIALS

Bedspread Weight Cotton Thread (size 10): 40 yards
Steel crochet hook, size 7 (1.65 mm) **or** size
    needed for gauge

GAUGE SWATCH: 1¼" diameter
Work same as Doily through Rnd 3.

STITCH GUIDE

TREBLE CROCHET *(abbreviated tr)*
YO twice, insert hook in ch-5 sp indicated, YO and
pull up a loop (4 loops on hook), (YO and draw
through 2 loops on hook) 3 times.

CLUSTER (uses one sp)
★ YO, insert hook in sp indicated, YO and pull up a
loop, YO and draw through 2 loops on hook; repeat
from ★ once **more**, YO and draw through all
3 loops on hook.

PICOT
Ch 2, slip st in top of sc just made **(Fig. 6a,
page 144)**.

DOILY

Ch 6; join with slip st to form a ring.

Rnd 1 (Right side)**:** Ch 2, dc in ring, ch 2, (work
Cluster in ring, ch 2) 9 times; join with slip st to first dc:
10 ch-2 sps.

Rnd 2: Ch 1, sc in same st, 2 sc in next ch-2 sp, (sc in
next Cluster, 2 sc in next ch-2 sp) around; join with
slip st to Back Loop Only of first sc **(Fig. 1, page 143)**:
30 sc.

Rnd 3: Ch 1, working in Back Loops Only, sc in same
st and in next sc, 2 sc in next sc, (sc in next 2 sc, 2 sc in
next sc) around; join with slip st to **both** loops of first sc:
40 sc.

Rnd 4: Ch 5 **(counts as first dc plus ch 2, now
and throughout)**, 2 dc in same st, ch 1, skip next 3 sc,
★ (2 dc, ch 2, 2 dc) in next sc, ch 1, skip next 3 sc;
repeat from ★ around, dc in same st as first dc; join with
slip st to first dc: 20 sps.

Rnd 5: (Slip st, ch 5, 2 dc) in first ch-2 sp, ch 2, sc in
next ch-1 sp, ch 2, ★ (2 dc, ch 2) twice in next ch-2 sp,
sc in next ch-1 sp, ch 2; repeat from ★ around, dc in
same sp as first dc; join with slip st to first dc:
30 ch-2 sps.

Rnd 6: Ch 1, sc in same st, (sc, ch 3, sc) in next
ch-2 sp, sc in next 2 dc and in next ch-2 sp, ch 1, ★ sc
in next ch-2 sp and in next 2 dc, (sc, ch 3, sc) in next
ch-2 sp, sc in next 2 dc and in next ch-2 sp, ch 1;
repeat from ★ around to last ch-2 sp, sc in last ch-2 sp
and in last dc; join with slip st to first sc: 80 sc and
20 sps.

Rnd 7: Slip st in next sc and in next ch-3 sp, ch 1, 3 sc
in same sp, ch 5, place marker around ch-5 just made
for st placement, (sc, work Picot, sc) in next ch-1 sp,
ch 5, ★ 3 sc in next ch-3 sp, ch 5, (sc, work Picot, sc) in
next ch-1 sp, ch 5; repeat from ★ around; join with
slip st to first sc: 50 sc and 20 ch-5 sps.

Rnd 8: Ch 1, sc in same st and in next 2 sc, 2 sc in
next ch-5 sp, ch 4, 2 sc in next ch-5 sp, ★ sc in next
3 sc, 2 sc in next ch-5 sp, ch 4, 2 sc in next ch-5 sp;
repeat from ★ around; join with slip st to first sc: 70 sc
and 10 ch-4 sps.

Rnd 9: Ch 1, sc in same st and in next 4 sc, 5 sc in
next ch-4 sp, (sc in next 7 sc, 5 sc in next ch-4 sp)
around to last 2 sc, sc in last 2 sc; join with slip st to first
sc: 120 sc.

Rnd 10: Ch 1, sc in same st and in next 6 sc, 2 sc in
next sc, (sc in next 11 sc, 2 sc in next sc) around to last
4 sc, sc in last 4 sc; join with slip st to first sc: 130 sc.

Rnd 11: Ch 1, sc in same st, working in **front** of
previous rnds **(Fig. 5, page 144)**, tr in marked ch-5 sp
on Rnd 7, working in **front** of tr just made, tr in
previous ch-5 sp, skip next sc on Rnd 10, sc in next
6 sc, ch 1, ★ sc in next 6 sc, working in **front** of
previous rnds, skip next ch-5 sp on Rnd 7, tr in next
ch-5 sp, working in **front** of tr just made, tr in skipped
ch-5 sp, skip next sc on Rnd 10, sc in next 6 sc, ch 1;
repeat from ★ around to last 5 sc, sc in last 5 sc; join
with slip st to first sc: 120 sc and 20 tr.

Rnd 12: Ch 1, sc in same st, skip next 2 tr, sc in next
sc, hdc in next 2 sc, dc in next 3 sc, 3 dc in next
ch-1 sp, dc in next 3 sc, hdc in next 2 sc, ★ sc in next
sc, skip next 2 tr, sc in next sc, hdc in next 2 sc, dc in
next 3 sc, 3 dc in next ch-1 sp, dc in next 3 sc, hdc in
next 2 sc; repeat from ★ around; join with slip st to first
sc, finish off.

See Washing and Blocking, page 144.

50 ▰▰▰▰▰▰▰

Finished Size: $8^1/_2$" x $4^1/_4$"

MATERIALS

Bedspread Weight Cotton Thread (size 10): 80 yards
Steel crochet hook, size 7 (1.65 mm) **or** size
needed for gauge

GAUGE SWATCH: $5^3/_4$" x $1^1/_4$"
Work same as Doily through Rnd 2.

STITCH GUIDE

TREBLE CROCHET *(abbreviated tr)*
YO twice, insert hook in st indicated, YO and pull
up a loop (4 loops on hook), (YO and draw through
2 loops on hook) 3 times.

BEGINNING CLUSTER
Ch 2, ★ YO, insert hook in ring indicated, YO and
pull up a loop, YO and draw through 2 loops on
hook; repeat from ★ once **more**, YO and draw
through all 3 loops on hook.

CLUSTER
★ YO, insert hook in ring indicated, YO and pull up
a loop, YO and draw through 2 loops on hook;
repeat from ★ 2 times **more**, YO and draw through
all 4 loops on hook.

BACK POST DOUBLE CROCHET
(abbreviated BPdc)
YO, insert hook from **back** to **front** around post of
dc indicated *(Fig. 7, page 144)*, YO and pull up a
loop (3 loops on hook), (YO and draw through
2 loops on hook) twice.

DOILY

Foundation Row: Ch 4, tr in fourth ch from hook to
form a ring, ★ ch 3, dc in third ch from hook to form a
ring, ch 4, tr in fourth ch from hook to form a ring;
repeat from ★ 3 times **more**: 9 rings.

Rnd 1 (Right side)**:** Work Beginning Cluster in last ring
made, **[**(ch 3, work Cluster in same ring) 3 times, sc in
next ring, work Cluster in next ring**]** 4 times, (ch 3, work
Cluster in same ring) 7 times, sc in next ring, **[**work
Cluster in next ring, (ch 3, work Cluster in same ring) 3
times, sc in next ring**]** 3 times, work Cluster in same ring
as Beginning Cluster, (ch 3, work Cluster in same ring) 3
times, ch 2, sc in top of Beginning Cluster to form last
ch-3 sp: 32 ch-3 sps.

Rnd 2: Ch 1, sc in last ch-3 sp made, † (sc, ch 3, sc) in
next 3 ch-3 sps, ★ skip next Cluster, slip st in next sc,
(sc, ch 3, sc) in next 3 ch-3 sps; repeat from ★ 3 times
more †, (sc, ch 6, sc) in next ch-3 sp; repeat from † to †
once, sc in same sp as first sc, ch 3, dc in first sc to form
last ch-6 sp.

Rnd 3: Ch 1, sc in last ch-6 sp made, ch 4, (sc in next
ch-3 sp, ch 4) 15 times, (sc, ch 4) twice in next ch-6 sp,
(sc in next ch-3 sp, ch 4) 15 times, sc in same sp as first
sc, ch 2, hdc in first sc to form last ch-4 sp: 34 ch-4 sps.

Rnd 4: Ch 1, sc in last ch-4 sp made, † 6 dc in next
ch-4 sp, 3 dc in each of next 14 ch-4 sps, 6 dc in next
ch-4 sp †, (sc, ch 5, sc) in next ch-4 sp, repeat from
† to † once, sc in same sp as first sc, ch 2, dc in first sc
to form last ch-5 sp: 108 dc and 2 ch-5 sps.

Rnd 5: Ch 1, 2 sc in last ch-5 sp made, † (work BPdc
around next dc, ch 1) 5 times, work BPdc around each
of next 44 dc, (ch 1, work BPdc around next dc) 5
times †, 3 sc in next ch-5 sp, repeat from † to † once, sc
in same sp as first sc; join with slip st to first sc: 114 sts
and 20 ch-1 sps.

Rnd 6: Ch 1, sc in same st, † ch 3, (sc in next ch-1 sp,
ch 3) 5 times, skip next BPdc, sc in next BPdc, ch 3,
(skip next BPdc, sc in next 2 BPdc, ch 3) 13 times, skip
next BPdc, sc in next BPdc, ch 3, (sc in next ch-1 sp,
ch 3) 5 times, skip next 2 sts †, sc in next sc, repeat
from † to † once; join with slip st to first sc: 52 ch-3 sps.

Rnd 7: Slip st in first ch-3 sp, ch 1, (sc, ch 3, sc) in
same sp and in each ch-3 sp around; join with slip st to
first sc.

Rnds 8 and 9: Slip st in first sp, ch 1, (sc, ch 4, sc) in
same sp and in each sp around; join with slip st to
first sc.

Finish off.

See Washing and Blocking, page 144.

91

47

81

74

85

12

3

13

32

53

42

5

26

8

76

52

77

54

95

68

64

80

71

63

58

40

96

51

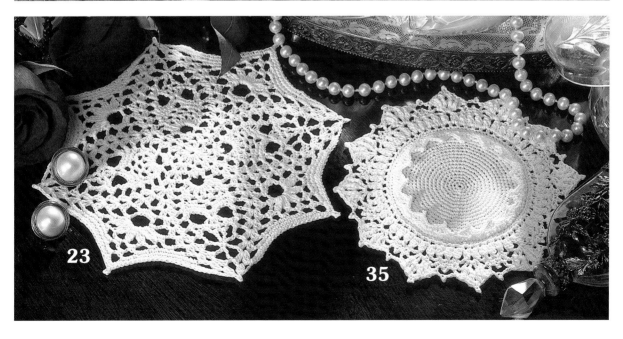

23

35

71

72

87

79

89

84

19

43

34

44

38

65

57

67

60

61

59

98

73

56

88

83

15

16

46

97

33

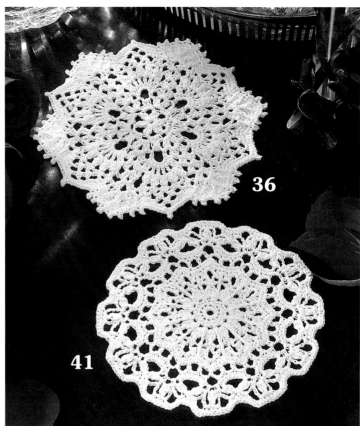

94

49

21

11

22

2

66

45

31

28

27

29

80

51

Finished Size: $4^7/8"$ x $8^1/4"$

MATERIALS

Bedspread Weight Cotton Thread (size 10): 75 yards
Steel crochet hook, size 7 (1.65 mm) **or** size
   needed for gauge

GAUGE SWATCH: 1" x $4^1/4"$
Work same as Doily through Rnd 1.

STITCH GUIDE

TREBLE CROCHET (abbreviated tr)
YO twice, insert hook in st indicated, YO and pull
up a loop (4 loops on hook), (YO and draw through
2 loops on hook) 3 times.

CLUSTER (uses one sp)
★ YO, insert hook in sp indicated, YO and pull up a
loop, YO and draw through 2 loops on hook; repeat
from ★ 2 times **more**, YO and draw through all
4 loops on hook.

FRONT POST TREBLE CROCHET
   (abbreviated FPtr)
YO twice, insert hook from **front** to **back** around
post of dc indicated **(Fig. 7, page 144)**, YO and
pull up a loop (4 loops on hook), (YO and draw
through 2 loops on hook) 3 times.

PICOT
Ch 2, slip st in top of last sc made **(Fig. 6a,
page 144)**.

DOILY

Foundation Row: Ch 8, slip st in eighth ch from
hook to form a ring, (ch 9, tr in fourth ch from hook to
form a ring) twice, ch 13, slip st in eighth ch from hook
to form a ring: 4 rings.

Rnd 1 (Right side)**:** Slip st in next 3 chs, ch 1, sc in
same ch, † work Cluster in next ring, [(ch 4, work
Cluster in same ring) 3 times, skip next 2 chs, sc in next
ch, work Cluster in next ring] twice, (ch 4, work Cluster
in same ring) 7 times †; working in free loops of
beginning ch **(Fig. 2b, page 144)**, skip next 2 chs, sc
in next ch, repeat from † to † once; join with slip st to
first sc: 26 ch-4 sps.

Rnd 2: Slip st in next Cluster and in next ch-4 sp,
ch 1, 2 sc in same sp, [(ch 3, 2 sc in next ch-4 sp)
twice, ch 1, 2 sc in next ch-4 sp] twice, (ch 3, 2 sc in
next ch-4 sp) 6 times, ch 1, 2 sc in next ch-4 sp, [(ch 3,
2 sc in next ch-4 sp) twice, ch 1, 2 sc in next ch-4 sp]
twice, (ch 3, 2 sc in next ch-4 sp) 6 times, ch 1; join
with slip st to first sc: 20 ch-3 sps and 6 ch-1 sps.

Rnd 3: Slip st in next sc and in next ch-3 sp, ch 3
(counts as first dc), 3 dc in same sp, 4 dc in next
ch-3 sp, ch 1, skip next ch-1 sp, 4 dc in each of next
2 ch-3 sps, ch 1, skip next ch-1 sp, 4 dc in next
ch-3 sp, (ch 2, 4 dc in next ch-3 sp) 5 times, (ch 1, skip
next ch-1 sp, 4 dc in each of next 2 ch-3 sps) twice,
ch 1, skip next ch-1 sp, 4 dc in next ch-3 sp, (ch 2, 4 dc
in next ch-3 sp) 5 times, ch 1, skip last ch-1 sp; join
with slip st to first dc: 80 dc.

Rnd 4: Ch 1, sc in same st and in next 7 dc, sc in next
ch-1 sp and in next 8 dc, sc in next ch-1 sp and in next
4 dc, (2 sc in next ch-2 sp, sc in next 4 dc) 5 times, (sc
in next ch-1 sp and in next 8 dc) twice, sc in next
ch-1 sp and in next 4 dc, (2 sc in next ch-2 sp, sc in
next 4 dc) 5 times, sc in last ch-1 sp; join with slip st to
first sc: 106 sc.

Rnd 5: Ch 1, sc in same st and in next 22 sc, ch 1, (sc
in next sc, 2 sc in next sc, sc in next 2 sc, 2 sc in next
sc, sc in next sc, ch 1) 4 times, sc in next 29 sc, ch 1,
(sc in next sc, 2 sc in next sc, sc in next 2 sc, 2 sc in
next sc, sc in next sc, ch 1) 4 times, sc in last 6 sc; join
with slip st to first sc: 122 sc and 10 ch-1 sps.

Rnd 6: Ch 1, sc in same st, work FPtr around fourth
dc of first 4-dc group on Rnd 3, working in **front** of
FPtr just made, work FPtr around first dc of same
group, skip next 2 sc on Rnd 5, † [sc in next 2 sc, work
FPtr around fourth dc of next 4-dc group on Rnd 3,
working in **front** of FPtr just made, work FPtr around
first dc of same group, skip next 2 sc on Rnd 5, sc in
next 3 sc, work FPtr around fourth dc of next
4-dc group on Rnd 3, working in **front** of FPtr just
made, work FPtr around first dc of same group, skip
next 2 sc on Rnd 5] twice, sc in next 2 sc and in next
ch-1 sp, [sc in next 3 sc, work FPtr around fourth dc of
next 4-dc group on Rnd 3, working in **front** of FPtr just
made, work FPtr around first dc of same group, skip
next 2 sc on Rnd 5, sc in next 3 sc and in next
ch-1 sp] 4 times, sc in next 2 sc, work FPtr around
fourth dc of next 4-dc group on Rnd 3, working in
front of FPtr just made, work FPtr around first dc of
same group, skip next 2 sc on Rnd 5 †, sc in next 3 sc,
work FPtr around fourth dc of next 4-dc group on
Rnd 3, working in **front** of FPtr just made, work FPtr
around first dc of same group, skip next 2 sc on Rnd 5,
repeat from † to † once, sc in last 2 sc; join with slip st
to first sc, do **not** finish off: 92 sc and 40 FPtr.

Continued on page 82.

Rnd 7: Ch 1, sc in same st and in each st around; join with slip st to first sc: 132 sc.

Rnd 8: Ch 1, sc in same st, ch 4, skip next 2 sc, ★ sc in next sc, ch 4, skip next 2 sc; repeat from ★ around; join with slip st to first sc: 44 ch-4 sps.

Rnd 9: Slip st in first 2 chs, ch 1, sc in same sp, (ch 5, sc in next ch-4 sp) around, ch 2, dc in first sc to form last ch-5 sp.

Rnd 10: Ch 1, sc in last ch-5 sp made, (ch 5, sc in next ch-5 sp) around, ch 2, dc in first sc to form last ch-5 sp.

Rnd 11: Ch 1, sc in last ch-5 sp made, [dc in next ch-5 sp, (ch 1, dc in same sp) 3 times, sc in next ch-5 sp] 4 times, † dc in next ch-5 sp, (ch 1, dc in same sp) 4 times, sc in next ch-5 sp, [dc in next ch-5 sp, (ch 1, dc in same sp) 5 times, sc in next ch-5 sp] 4 times, dc in next ch-5 sp, (ch 1, dc in same sp) 4 times, sc in next ch-5 sp †, [dc in next ch-5 sp, (ch 1, dc in same sp) 3 times, sc in next ch-5 sp] 5 times, repeat from † to † once, dc in last ch-5 sp, (ch 1, dc in same sp) 3 times; join with slip st to first sc.

Rnd 12: Slip st in first dc, ch 1, sc in same st and in next ch-1 sp, work Picot, (sc in next dc and in next ch-1 sp, work Picot) twice, [sc in next dc, skip next sc, (sc in next dc and in next ch-1 sp, work Picot) 3 times] 3 times, † sc in next dc, skip next sc, (sc in next dc and in next ch-1 sp, work Picot) 4 times, sc in next dc, skip next sc, [(sc in next dc and in next ch-1 sp, work Picot) 5 times, sc in next dc, skip next sc] 4 times, (sc in next dc and in next ch-1 sp, work Picot) 4 times †, [sc in next dc, skip next sc, (sc in next dc and in next ch-1 sp, work Picot) 3 times] 5 times, repeat from † to † once, sc in next dc, skip next sc, (sc in next dc and in next ch-1 sp, work Picot) 3 times, sc in next dc, skip last sc; join with slip st to first sc, finish off.

See Washing and Blocking, page 144.

52 ▆

Finished Size: $8^1/_2$" x $6^1/_2$"

MATERIALS
Bedspread Weight Cotton Thread (size 10): 80 yards
Steel crochet hook, size 7 (1.65 mm) **or** size needed for gauge

GAUGE SWATCH: $3^1/_2$" x $2^1/_4$"
Work same as Doily through Rnd 5.

STITCH GUIDE

TREBLE CROCHET (*abbreviated tr*)
YO twice, insert hook in free loop of sc indicated **(Fig. 2a, page 144)**, YO and pull up a loop (4 loops on hook), (YO and draw through 2 loops on hook) 3 times.

2-DC CLUSTER (uses one sp)
★ YO, insert hook in sp indicated, YO and pull up a loop, YO and draw through 2 loops on hook; repeat from ★ once **more**, YO and draw through all 3 loops on hook.

3-DC CLUSTER (uses one ch-1 sp)
★ YO, insert hook in ch-1 sp indicated, YO and pull up a loop, YO and draw through 2 loops on hook; repeat from ★ 2 times **more**, YO and draw through all 4 loops on hook.

PICOT
Ch 3, slip st in third ch from hook, ch 1.

DOILY
Ch 7; join with slip st to form a ring.

Rnd 1 (Right side)**:** Ch 3 **(counts as first dc)**, 10 dc in ring, ch 3, 11 dc in ring, ch 3; join with slip st to first dc: 22 dc and 2 ch-3 sps.

Rnd 2: Ch 1, sc in same st, ch 2, (skip next dc, sc in next dc, ch 2) 5 times, (sc, ch 2) twice in next ch-3 sp, sc in next dc, ch 2, (skip next dc, sc in next dc, ch 2) 5 times, (sc, ch 2, sc) in last ch-3 sp, hdc in first sc to form last ch-2 sp: 16 ch-2 sps.

Rnd 3: Ch 1, sc in last ch-2 sp made, ch 3, (sc in next ch-2 sp, ch 3) 6 times, (dc, ch 3) twice in next ch-2 sp, (sc in next ch-3 sp, ch 3) 7 times, (dc, ch 3, dc) in last ch-2 sp, dc in first sc to form last ch-3 sp: 18 ch-3 sps.

Rnd 4: Ch 1, 3 sc in last ch-3 sp made and in each of next 7 ch-3 sps, ch 3, sc in next ch-3 sp, ch 3, 3 sc in each of next 8 ch-3 sps, ch 3, sc in next ch-3 sp, dc in first sc to form last ch-3 sp: 50 sc and 4 ch-3 sps.

Rnd 5: Ch 1, 3 sc in last ch-3 sp made, sc in Back Loop Only of next 24 sc *(Fig. 1, page 143)*, 3 sc in next ch-3 sp, ch 3, 3 sc in next ch-3 sp, sc in Back Loop Only of next 24 sc, 3 sc in next ch-3 sp, ch 1, hdc in **both** loops of first sc to form last ch-3 sp: 60 sc and 2 ch-3 sps.

Rnd 6: Ch 1, 3 sc in last ch-3 sp made, working in both loops, sc in each sc across to next ch-3 sp, 5 sc in next ch-3 sp, sc in each sc across, 2 sc in same sp as first sc; join with slip st to first sc: 70 sc.

Rnd 7: Ch 1, sc in same st, (ch 3, skip next 2 sc, sc in next sc) twice, † tr in free loop of center sc of 3-sc group 2 rnds **below** *(Fig. 2a, page 144)*, skip next sc on Rnd 6 from last sc made, ★ sc in next 2 sc, tr in free loop of center sc of next 3-sc group 2 rnds **below**, skip next sc on Rnd 6 from last sc made; repeat from ★ 6 times **more**, sc in next sc, ch 3, skip next 2 sc, sc in next sc, ch 3, skip next 2 sc †, (sc, ch 3) twice in next sc, skip next 2 sc, sc in next sc, ch 3, skip next 2 sc, sc in next sc, repeat from † to † once, sc in same st as first sc, ch 3; join with slip st to first sc: 56 sts and 10 ch-3 sps.

Rnd 8: [Slip st, ch 4 **(counts as first dc plus ch 1, now and throughout)**, dc] in first ch-3 sp, (ch 1, dc in same sp) 3 times, † 2 sc in next ch-3 sp, skip next sc, sc in next tr, (ch 4, skip next 2 sc, sc in next tr) 7 times, 2 sc in next ch-3 sp, dc in next ch-3 sp, (ch 1, dc in same sp) 4 times, sc in next ch-3 sp †, dc in next ch-3 sp, (ch 1, dc in same sp) 4 times, repeat from † to † once; join with slip st to first dc: 46 sts and 30 sps.

Rnd 9: (Slip st, ch 1, sc) in first ch-1 sp, (ch 3, sc in next ch-1 sp) 3 times, † skip next dc, sc in next 2 sc, (sc, ch 4, sc) in next 7 ch-4 sps, skip next sc, sc in next 2 sc †, sc in next ch-1 sp, (ch 3, sc in next ch-1 sp) 7 times, repeat from † to † once, (sc in next ch-1 sp, ch 3) 4 times; join with slip st to first sc: 52 sc and 28 sps.

Rnds 10 and 11: Slip st in first ch-3 sp, ch 1, (sc, ch 3, sc) in same sp and in next 2 ch-3 sps, † skip next sc, sc in next 2 sc, (sc, ch 4, sc) in next 7 ch-4 sps, skip next sc, sc in next 2 sc †, (sc, ch 3, sc) in next 7 ch-3 sps, repeat from † to † once, (sc, ch 3, sc) in last 4 ch-3 sps; join with slip st to first sc.

Rnd 12: (Slip st, ch 4, dc) in first ch-3 sp, (ch 1, dc in same sp) 3 times, sc in next ch-3 sp, dc in next ch-3 sp, (ch 1, dc in same sp) 4 times, † 2 sc in next ch-4 sp, [dc in next ch-4 sp, (ch 1, dc in same sp) 5 times, 2 sc in next ch-4 sp] 3 times †, dc in next ch-3 sp, (ch 1, dc in same sp) 4 times, [sc in next ch-3 sp, dc in next ch-3 sp, (ch 1, dc in same sp) 4 times] 3 times, repeat from † to † once, [dc in next ch-3 sp, (ch 1, dc in same sp) 4 times, sc in next ch-3 sp] twice; join with slip st to first dc: 62 ch-1 sps.

Rnd 13: (Slip st, ch 2, work 2-dc Cluster) in first ch-1 sp, [ch 3, (work 3-dc Cluster in next ch-1 sp, ch 3) twice, work 3-dc Cluster in next 2 ch-1 sps] twice, † [ch 3, (work 3-dc Cluster in next ch-1 sp, ch 3) 3 times, work 3-dc Cluster in next 2 ch-1 sps] 3 times †, [ch 3, (work 3-dc Cluster in next ch-1 sp, ch 3) twice, work 3-dc Cluster in next 2 ch-1 sps] 4 times, repeat from † to † once, ch 3, (work 3-dc Cluster in next ch-1 sp, ch 3) twice, work 3-dc Cluster in next 2 ch-1 sps, (ch 3, work 3-dc Cluster in next ch-1 sp) 3 times; join with slip st to top of first 2-dc Cluster: 48 ch-3 sps.

Rnd 14: (Slip st, ch 1, sc) in first ch-3 sp, (ch 4, sc in next ch-3 sp) 23 times, ch 6, sc in next ch-3 sp, (ch 4, sc in next ch-3 sp) around, ch 6; join with slip st to first sc.

Rnd 15: Slip st in first ch-4 sp, ch 1, (2 sc, work Picot, 2 sc) in same sp and in each ch-4 sp across to next ch-6 sp, work (sc, Picot, 2-dc Cluster) in next ch-6 sp, ch 4, slip st in third ch from hook, ch 2, work (2-dc Cluster, Picot, sc) in same ch-6 sp, (2 sc, work Picot, 2 sc) in each ch-4 sp across to last ch-6 sp, work (sc, Picot, 2-dc Cluster) in last ch-6 sp, ch 4, slip st in third ch from hook, ch 2, work (2-dc Cluster, Picot, sc) in same ch-6 sp; join with slip st to first sc, finish off.

See Washing and Blocking, page 144.

Finished Size: 6¹/₄" (edge to edge)

MATERIALS

Bedspread Weight Cotton Thread (size 10): 55 yards
Steel crochet hook, size 7 (1.65 mm) **or** size
needed for gauge

GAUGE SWATCH: 1⁷/₈" (point to point)
Work same as Doily through Rnd 3.

STITCH GUIDE

BEGINNING POPCORN
Ch 3, 3 dc in sp indicated, drop loop from hook,
insert hook in first dc of 4-dc group, hook dropped
loop and draw through.

POPCORN
4 Dc in ch-3 sp indicated, drop loop from hook,
insert hook in first dc of 4-dc group, hook dropped
loop and draw through.

**BEGINNING SPLIT DOUBLE TREBLE
CROCHET**
(abbreviated Beginning Split dtr)
First Leg: YO 3 times, insert hook from **front** to
back in second marked dc on Rnd 1, YO and pull
up a loop, (YO and draw through 2 loops on
hook) 3 times (2 loops remaining on hook).

Second Leg: YO 3 times, working in **front** of
First Leg, insert hook from **back** to **front** in first
marked dc, YO and pull up a loop, (YO and draw
through 2 loops on hook) 3 times, YO and draw
through all 3 loops on hook.

SPLIT DOUBLE TREBLE CROCHET
(abbreviated Split dtr)
First Leg: YO 3 times, skip next 3 dc from
First Leg of last Split dtr made on Rnd 1, insert
hook from **front** to **back** in next dc (dc below next
Popcorn), YO and pull up a loop, (YO and draw
through 2 loops on hook) 3 times (2 loops
remaining on hook).

Second Leg: YO 3 times, working in **front** of
First Leg, insert hook from **back** to **front** in **same**
dc as First Leg of last Split dtr made, YO and pull up
a loop, (YO and draw through 2 loops on hook) 3
times, YO and draw through all 3 loops on hook.

SMALL PICOT
Ch 3, slip st in third ch from hook.

LARGE PICOT
Ch 5, slip st in fourth ch from hook.

DOILY

Ch 7; join with slip st to form a ring.

Rnd 1 (Right side)**:** Ch 3 **(counts as first dc, now
and throughout)**, dc in ring, place first marker around
dc just made for st placement, 4 dc in ring, place second
marker around last dc made for st placement, 18 dc in
ring; join with slip st to first dc: 24 dc.

Rnd 2: Ch 1, sc in same st, ch 3, skip next dc, ★ sc in
next dc, ch 3, skip next dc; repeat from ★ around; join
with slip st to first sc: 12 ch-3 sps.

Rnd 3: (Slip st, work Beginning Popcorn) in first
ch-3 sp, ch 5, sc in next ch-3 sp, ch 5, ★ work Popcorn
in next ch-3 sp, ch 5, sc in next ch-3 sp, ch 5; repeat
from ★ around; join with slip st to top of Beginning
Popcorn.

Rnd 4: (Slip st, ch 1, 5 sc) in first ch-5 sp, work
Beginning Split dtr, 5 sc in next ch-5 sp, ch 3, 5 sc in
next ch-5 sp, ★ work Split dtr, 5 sc in next ch-5 sp,
ch 3, 5 sc in next ch-5 sp; repeat from ★ 3 times **more**,
YO 3 times, skip next 3 dc from First Leg of last
Split dtr made on Rnd 1, insert hook from **front** to
back in **same** st as Second Leg of Beginning Split dtr,
YO and pull up a loop, (YO and draw through 2 loops
on hook) 3 times (2 loops remaining on hook), work
Second Leg of Split dtr, 5 sc in last ch-5 sp, ch 1, hdc in
first sc to form last ch-3 sp: 6 ch-3 sps.

Rnd 5: Ch 1, sc in last ch-3 sp made, ch 15, (sc in next
ch-3 sp, ch 15) around; join with slip st to first sc:
6 loops.

Rnd 6: Slip st in first loop, ch 1, 19 sc in same loop
and in each loop around; join with slip st to first sc:
114 sc.

Rnd 7: (Slip st, ch 1, sc) in next sc, (ch 3, skip next sc,
sc in next sc) 8 times, skip next 2 sc, ★ sc in next sc,
(ch 3, skip next sc, sc in next sc) 8 times, skip next 2 sts;
repeat from ★ around; join with slip st to first sc:
48 ch-3 sps.

Rnd 8: (Slip st, ch 1, sc) in first ch-3 sp, ch 4, (sc in
next ch-3 sp, ch 4) 6 times, ★ sc in next 2 ch-3 sps,
ch 4, (sc in next ch-3 sp, ch 4) 6 times; repeat from ★
around to last ch-3 sp, sc in last ch-3 sp; join with slip st
to first sc: 42 ch-4 sps.

Rnd 9: (Slip st, ch 3, dc) in first ch-4 sp, 3 dc in each of
next 2 ch-4 sps, 5 dc in next ch-4 sp, 3 dc in each of
next 2 ch-4 sps, ★ 2 dc in each of next 2 ch-4 sps, 3 dc
in each of next 2 ch-4 sps, 5 dc in next ch-4 sp, 3 dc in
each of next 2 ch-4 sps; repeat from ★ around to last
ch-4 sp, 2 dc in last ch-4 sp; join with slip st to first dc:
126 dc.

Rnd 10: (Slip st, ch 1, sc) in next dc, ch 4, skip next
2 dc, ★ sc in next dc, ch 4, skip next 2 sts; repeat from
★ around; join with slip st to first sc: 42 ch-4 sps.

Rnd 11: Slip st in first 2 chs, ch 1, sc in same sp, dc in next ch-4 sp, (ch 1, dc in same sp) 4 times, sc in next ch-4 sp, ch 5, ★ sc in next ch-4 sp, [dc in next ch-4 sp, (ch 1, dc in same sp) 4 times, sc in next ch-4 sp] 3 times, ch 5; repeat from ★ 4 times **more**, [sc in next ch-4 sp, dc in next ch-4 sp, (ch 1, dc in same sp) 4 times] twice; join with slip st to first sc: 78 sps.

Rnd 12: Slip st in next dc and in next ch-1 sp, ch 1, sc in same sp, work Small Picot, ch 1, sc in next ch-1 sp, work Large Picot, ch 2, sc in next ch-1 sp, work Small Picot, ch 1, sc in next ch-1 sp, [3 sc, ch 2, slip st in top of last sc made *(Fig. 6a, page 144)*, 3 sc] in next ch-5 sp, ★ (sc in next ch-1 sp, work Small Picot, ch 1, sc in next ch-1 sp, work Large Picot, ch 2, sc in next ch-1 sp, work Small Picot, ch 1, sc in next ch-1 sp) 3 times, (3 sc, ch 2, slip st in top of last sc made, 3 sc) in next ch-5 sp; repeat from ★ 4 times **more**, (sc in next ch-1 sp, work Small Picot, ch 1, sc in next ch-1 sp, work Large Picot, ch 2, sc in next ch-1 sp, work Small Picot, ch 1, sc in next ch-1 sp) twice; join with slip st to first sc, finish off.

See Washing and Blocking, page 144.

54 ▰

Finished Size: $6^1/_2$" diameter

MATERIALS
Bedspread Weight Cotton Thread (size 10): 45 yards
Steel crochet hook, size 7 (1.65 mm) **or** size
    needed for gauge

GAUGE SWATCH: $2^1/_2$" diameter
Work same as Doily through Rnd 4.

STITCH GUIDE

BEGINNING CLUSTER (uses one ch-3 sp)
Ch 2, ★ YO, insert hook in ch-3 sp indicated, YO and pull up a loop, YO and draw through 2 loops on hook; repeat from ★ 2 times **more**, YO and draw through all 4 loops on hook.

CLUSTER (uses one ch-3 sp)
★ YO, insert hook in ch-3 sp indicated, YO and pull up a loop, YO and draw through 2 loops on hook; repeat from ★ 3 times **more**, YO and draw through all 5 loops on hook.

PICOT
Ch 3, slip st in third ch from hook, ch 1.

DOILY
Ch 7; join with slip st to form a ring.

Rnd 1 (Right side)**:** Ch 3 **(counts as first dc, now and throughout)**, 19 dc in ring; join with slip st to first dc: 20 dc.

Rnd 2: Ch 1, sc in same st, 2 sc in next dc, (sc in next dc, 2 sc in next dc) around; join with slip st to first sc: 30 sc.

Rnd 3: Ch 1, sc in same st, ★ ch 3, skip next sc, sc in next sc; repeat from ★ around to last sc, skip last sc, dc in first sc to form last ch-3 sp: 15 ch-3 sps.

Rnd 4: Work Beginning Cluster in last ch-3 sp made, (ch 4, work Cluster in next ch-3 sp) around, ch 1, dc in top of Beginning Cluster to form last ch-4 sp.

Rnd 5: Ch 1, (sc, ch 2, sc) in last ch-4 sp made, ★ sc in next ch-4 sp, (ch 2, sc in same sp) twice; repeat from ★ around, sc in same sp as first sc, ch 1, sc in first sc to form last ch-2 sp: 30 ch-2 sps.

Rnd 6: Ch 1, sc in last ch-2 sp made, (ch 3, sc in next ch-2 sp) around, dc in first sc to form last ch-3 sp.

Rnd 7: Ch 3, 2 dc in last ch-3 sp made, 3 dc in each ch-3 sp around; join with slip st to first dc: 90 dc.

Rnd 8: Ch 1, sc in same st, ch 3, ★ skip next dc, sc in next 2 dc, ch 3; repeat from ★ around to last 2 dc, skip next dc, sc in last dc; join with slip st to first sc: 30 ch-3 sps.

Rnd 9: (Slip st, ch 7, dc) in first ch-3 sp, (dc, ch 4, dc) in each ch-3 sp around; join with slip st to third ch of beginning ch-7.

Rnd 10: Slip st in first ch-4 sp, ch 5, (dc, ch 2, dc) in same sp and in next ch-4 sp, ★ dc in next ch-4 sp, (ch 2, dc in same sp) twice, (dc, ch 2, dc) in next ch-4 sp; repeat from ★ around; join with slip st to third ch of beginning ch-5: 45 ch-2 sps.

Rnd 11: (Slip st, ch 1, 2 sc) in first ch-2 sp, work Picot, 2 sc in next ch-2 sp, (3 dc, work Picot, 3 dc) in next ch-2 sp, ★ 2 sc in next ch-2 sp, work Picot, 2 sc in next ch-2 sp, (3 dc, work Picot, 3 dc) in next ch-2 sp; repeat from ★ around; join with slip st to first sc, finish off.

See Washing and Blocking, page 144.

Finished Size: 7¹/₈" square

MATERIALS

Bedspread Weight Cotton Thread (size 10): 79 yards
Steel crochet hook, size 7 (1.65 mm) **or** size
    needed for gauge

GAUGE SWATCH: 1¹/₂" square
Work same Doily through Rnd 2.

STITCH GUIDE

BACK POST SINGLE CROCHET
(abbreviated BPsc)
Insert hook from **back** to **front** around post of dc
indicated *(Fig. 7, page 144)*, YO and pull up a
loop, YO and draw through both loops on hook.

BACK POST DOUBLE CROCHET
(abbreviated BPdc)
YO, insert hook from **back** to **front** around post of
st indicated *(Fig. 7, page 144)*, YO and pull up a
loop (3 loops on hook), (YO and draw through
2 loops on hook) twice.

FRONT POST TREBLE CROCHET
(abbreviated FPtr)
YO twice, insert hook from **front** to **back** around
post of dc indicated *(Fig. 7, page 144)*, YO and
pull up a loop (4 loops on hook), (YO and draw
through 2 loops on hook) 3 times.

SPLIT FRONT POST TREBLE CROCHET
(abbreviated Split FPtr)
YO twice, insert hook from **front** to **back** around
post of first dc of 4-dc group just worked into
(Fig. 7, page 144), YO and pull up a loop, (YO
and draw through 2 loops on hook) twice, YO twice,
insert hook from **front** to **back** around post of last
dc of same 4-dc group, YO and pull up a loop, (YO
and draw through 2 loops on hook) twice, YO and
draw through all 3 loops on hook.

DECREASE *(uses next 3 sps)*
★ YO, insert hook in **next** sp, YO and pull up a
loop, YO and draw through 2 loops on hook; repeat
from ★ 2 times **more**, YO and draw through all
4 loops on hook.

PICOT
Ch 2, slip st in top of last dc made *(Fig. 6a,
page 144)*.

SCALLOP
Ch 2, ★ YO, insert hook in top of last dc made, YO
and pull up a loop, YO and draw through 2 loops
on hook; repeat from ★ once **more**, YO and draw
through all 3 loops on hook, ch 2, slip st in top of
last st made *(Fig. 6b, page 144)*, ch 2, † YO,
insert hook in same st, YO and pull up a loop, YO
and draw through 2 loops on hook †; repeat from
† to † once **more**, YO and draw through all 3 loops
on hook.

DOILY

Ch 8; join with slip st to form a ring.

Rnd 1 (Right side)**:** Ch 3 **(counts as first dc, now
and throughout)**, 3 dc in ring, (ch 2, 4 dc in ring) 3
times, ch 1, sc in first dc to form last ch-2 sp:
four 4-dc groups and 4 ch-2 sps.

Rnd 2: Ch 3, dc in last ch-2 sp made and in next 2 dc,
work Split FPtr, working **behind** Split FPtr just made, dc
in next 2 dc, ★ (2 dc, ch 2, 2 dc) in next ch-2 sp, dc in
next 2 dc, work Split FPtr, working **behind** Split FPtr
just made, dc in next 2 dc; repeat from ★ 2 times **more**,
2 dc in same sp as first dc, ch 1, sc in first dc to form
last ch-2 sp: 36 sts.

Rnd 3: Ch 3, dc in last ch-2 sp made, ch 3, skip next
2 dc, sc in next dc, ch 5, skip next 3 sts, sc in next dc,
ch 3, ★ (2 dc, ch 2, 2 dc) in next ch-2 sp, ch 3, skip
next 2 dc, sc in next dc, ch 5, skip next 3 sts, sc in next
dc, ch 3; repeat from ★ 2 times **more**, 2 dc in same sp
as first dc, ch 1, sc in first dc to form last ch-2 sp:
16 sps.

Rnd 4: Ch 3, dc in last ch-2 sp made, ch 3, sc in next
ch-3 sp, dc in next ch-5 sp, (ch 1, dc in same sp) 5
times, sc in next ch-3 sp, ch 3, ★ (2 dc, ch 2, 2 dc) in
next ch-2 sp, ch 3, sc in next ch-3 sp, dc in next
ch-5 sp, (ch 1, dc in same sp) 5 times, sc in next
ch-3 sp, ch 3; repeat from ★ 2 times **more**, 2 dc in
same sp as first dc, ch 1, sc in first dc to form last
ch-2 sp: 48 sts and 32 sps.

Rnd 5: Ch 3, dc in last ch-2 sp made, ch 3, sc in next
ch-3 sp, skip next sc, work BPsc around next dc, (ch 3,
work BPsc around next dc) 5 times, sc in next ch-3 sp,
ch 3, ★ 2 dc in next ch-2 sp, (ch 2, 2 dc in same sp)
twice, ch 3, sc in next ch-3 sp, skip next sc, work BPsc
around next dc, (ch 3, work BPsc around next dc) 5
times, sc in next ch-3 sp, ch 3; repeat from ★ 2 times
more, (2 dc, ch 2, 2 dc) in same sp as first dc, ch 1, sc
in first dc to form last ch-2 sp: 36 sps.

Rnd 6: Ch 3, dc in last ch-2 sp made, ★ † ch 3, sc in next 2 ch-3 sps, ch 3, (sc in next ch-3 sp, ch 3) 3 times, sc in next 2 ch-3 sps, ch 3, (2 dc, ch 2, 2 dc) in next ch-2 sp, skip next dc, work FPtr around next dc, ch 3, working in **front** of last FPtr made, work FPtr around skipped dc †, (2 dc, ch 2, 2 dc) in next ch-2 sp; repeat from ★ 2 times **more**, then repeat from † to † once, 2 dc in same sp as first dc, ch 1, sc in first dc to form last ch-2 sp: 8 FPtr and 36 sps.

Rnd 7: Ch 3, dc in last ch-2 sp made, ★ † ch 3, sc in next 2 ch-3 sps, ch 3, (sc in next ch-3 sp, ch 3) twice, sc in next 2 ch-3 sps, ch 3, (2 dc, ch 2, 2 dc) in next ch-2 sp, work BPdc around next FPtr, ch 4, sc in next ch-3 sp, ch 4, work BPdc around next FPtr †, (2 dc, ch 2, 2 dc) in next ch-2 sp; repeat from ★ 2 times **more**, then repeat from † to † once, 2 dc in same sp as first dc, ch 1, sc in first dc to form last ch-2 sp: 8 BPdc and 36 sps.

Rnd 8: Ch 3, dc in last ch-2 sp made, ★ † ch 3, sc in next 2 ch-3 sps, dc in next ch-3 sp, (ch 1, dc in same sp) 3 times, sc in next 2 ch-3 sps, ch 3, (2 dc, ch 2, 2 dc) in next ch-2 sp, work BPdc around next BPdc, ch 4, 2 sc in each of next 2 ch-4 sps, ch 4, work BPdc around next BPdc †, (2 dc, ch 2, 2 dc) in next ch-2 sp; repeat from ★ 2 times **more**, then repeat from † to † once, 2 dc in same sp as first dc, ch 1, sc in first dc to form last ch-2 sp: 88 sts and 36 sps.

Rnd 9: Ch 3, dc in last ch-2 sp made, ★ † ch 3, sc in next ch-3 sp, skip next 2 sc, work BPsc around next dc, (ch 3, work BPsc around next dc) 3 times, sc in next ch-3 sp, ch 3, (2 dc, ch 2, 2 dc) in next ch-2 sp, work BPdc around next BPdc, ch 4, 2 sc in next ch-4 sp, sc in next 4 sc, 2 sc in next ch-4 sp, ch 4, work BPdc around next BPdc †, (2 dc, ch 2, 2 dc) in next ch-2 sp; repeat from ★ 2 times **more**, then repeat from † to † once, 2 dc in same sp as first dc, ch 1, sc in first dc to form last ch-2 sp: 96 sts and 36 sps.

Rnd 10: Ch 3, dc in last ch-2 sp made, ★ † ch 3, sc in next 2 ch-3 sps, ch 3, sc in next ch-3 sp, ch 3, sc in next 2 ch-3 sps, ch 3, (2 dc, ch 2, 2 dc) in next ch-2 sp, work BPdc around next BPdc, ch 4, 2 sc in next ch-4 sp, sc in next 8 sc, 2 sc in next ch-4 sp, ch 4, work BPdc around next BPdc †, (2 dc, ch 2, 2 dc) in next ch-2 sp; repeat from ★ 2 times **more**, then repeat from † to † once, 2 dc in same sp as first dc, ch 1, sc in first dc to form last ch-2 sp: 108 sts and 32 sps.

Rnd 11: Ch 3, dc in last ch-2 sp made, ★ † ch 3, sc in next 2 ch-3 sps, (2 dc, ch 1, 2 dc) in next sc, sc in next 2 ch-3 sps, ch 3, (2 dc, ch 2, 2 dc) in next ch-2 sp, work BPdc around next BPdc, ch 4, 2 sc in next ch-4 sp, ch 2, skip next sc, (sc in next sc, ch 2, skip next sc) twice, sc in next 2 sc, ch 2, (skip next sc, sc in next sc, ch 2) twice, 2 sc in next ch-4 sp, ch 4, work BPdc around next BPdc †, (2 dc, ch 2, 2 dc) in next ch-2 sp; repeat from ★ 2 times **more**, then repeat from † to † once, 2 dc in same sp as first dc, ch 1, sc in first dc to form last ch-2 sp: 112 sts and 52 sps.

Rnd 12: Ch 3, dc in last ch-2 sp made, ★ † ch 3, decrease, ch 3, (2 dc, ch 2, 2 dc) in next ch-2 sp, work BPdc around next BPdc, ch 4, 2 sc in next ch-4 sp, ch 2, (sc in next ch-2 sp, ch 2) 6 times, 2 sc in next ch-4 sp, ch 4, work BPdc around next BPdc †, (2 dc, ch 2, 2 dc) in next ch-2 sp; repeat from ★ 2 times **more**, then repeat from † to † once, 2 dc in same sp as first dc, ch 1, sc in first dc to form last ch-2 sp: 84 sts and 52 sps.

Rnd 13: Ch 3, dc in last ch-2 sp made, ★ † ch 7, skip next 2 ch-3 sps, (2 dc, ch 2, 2 dc) in next ch-2 sp, work BPdc around next BPdc, ch 4, 2 sc in next ch-4 sp, ch 2, (sc in next ch-2 sp, ch 2) 7 times, 2 sc in next ch-4 sp, ch 4, work BPdc around next BPdc †, (2 dc, ch 2, 2 dc) in next ch-2 sp; repeat from ★ 2 times **more**, then repeat from † to † once, 2 dc in same sp as first dc, hdc in first dc to form last ch-2 sp.

Rnd 14: Ch 1, sc in last ch-2 sp made, ★ † dc in next ch-7 sp, (work Picot, dc in same sp) 3 times, work Scallop, dc in same sp as last dc made, (work Picot, dc in same sp) 3 times, sc in next ch-2 sp, skip next 2 dc, work BPdc around next BPdc, ch 4, 2 sc in next ch-4 sp, dc in next ch-2 sp, (work Picot, dc in same sp) 3 times, sc in next ch-2 sp, dc in next ch-2 sp, (work Picot, dc in same sp) 3 times, sc in next 2 ch-2 sps, dc in next ch-2 sp, (work Picot, dc in same sp) 3 times, sc in next ch-2 sp, dc in next ch-2 sp, (work Picot, dc in same sp) 3 times, 2 sc in next ch-4 sp, ch 4, work BPdc around next BPdc †, sc in next ch-2 sp; repeat from ★ 2 times **more**, then repeat from † to † once; join with slip st to first sc, finish off.

See Washing and Blocking, page 144.

Finished Size: 6" (point to point)

MATERIALS

Bedspread Weight Cotton Thread (size 10): 59 yards
Steel crochet hook, size 7 (1.65 mm) **or** size
   needed for gauge

GAUGE SWATCH: 1" diameter
Work same as Doily through Rnd 1.

STITCH GUIDE

BEGINNING POPCORN
Ch 3, 3 dc in sp indicated, drop loop from hook,
insert hook in first dc of 4-dc group, hook dropped
loop and draw through.

POPCORN
4 Dc in sp indicated, drop loop from hook, insert
hook in first dc of 4-dc group, hook dropped loop
and draw through.

CLUSTER (uses one sc)
★ YO twice, insert hook in **front** 2 legs of sc
indicated *(Fig. 4, page 144)*, YO and pull up a
loop, (YO and draw through 2 loops on hook) twice;
repeat from ★ once **more**, YO and draw through all
3 loops on hook.

DECREASE
Pull up a loop in next 2 ch-1 sps, YO and draw
through all 3 loops on hook.

FRONT POST SINGLE CROCHET
   (abbreviated FPsc)
Insert hook from **front** to **back** around post of FPtr
indicated *(Fig. 7, page 144)*, YO and pull up a
loop, YO and draw through both loops on hook.

FRONT POST DOUBLE CROCHET
   (abbreviated FPdc)
YO, insert hook from **front** to **back** around post of
Cluster indicated *(Fig. 7, page 144)*, YO and pull
up a loop (3 loops on hook), (YO and draw through
2 loops on hook) twice.

FRONT POST TREBLE CROCHET
   (abbreviated FPtr)
YO twice, insert hook from **front** to **back** around
post of FPdc indicated *(Fig. 7, page 144)*, YO and
pull up a loop (4 loops on hook), (YO and draw
through 2 loops on hook) 3 times.

PICOT
Ch 3, slip st in top of last FPsc made *(Fig. 6a,
page 144)*.

DOILY

Ch 6; join with slip st to form a ring.

Rnd 1 (Right side)**:** Ch 3 **(counts as first dc, now
and throughout)**, 23 dc in ring; join with slip st to first
dc: 24 dc.

Rnd 2: Ch 1, sc in same st, ch 2, skip next dc, ★ sc in
next dc, ch 2, skip next dc; repeat from ★ around; join
with slip st to first sc: 12 ch-2 sps.

Rnd 3: (Slip st, work Beginning Popcorn) in first
ch-2 sp, ch 4, sc in next ch-2 sp, ch 4, ★ work Popcorn
in next ch-2 sp, ch 4, sc in next ch-2 sp, ch 4; repeat
from ★ around; join with slip st to top of Beginning
Popcorn: 6 Popcorns and 12 ch-4 sps.

Rnd 4: Ch 1, (sc, ch 5, sc) in each ch-4 sp around; join
with slip st to first sc.

Rnd 5: Slip st in next 2 chs, ch 1, sc in same ch-5 sp,
ch 6, sc in next ch-5 sp, place marker around sc just
made for st placement, ch 6, (sc in next ch-5 sp, ch 6)
around; join with slip st to first sc.

Rnd 6: Ch 1, sc in first ch-6 sp, (ch 4, sc in same sp) 3
times, ★ sc in next ch-6 sp, (ch 4, sc in same sp) 3
times; repeat from ★ around; join with slip st to first sc:
36 ch-4 sps.

Rnd 7: (Slip st, ch 1, sc) in first ch-4 sp, ch 4, sc in
next ch-4 sp, ch 4, ★ sc in next 2 ch-4 sps, ch 4, sc in
next ch-4 sp, ch 4; repeat from ★ around to last
ch-4 sp, sc in last ch-4 sp; join with slip st to first sc:
36 sc and 24 ch-4 sps.

Rnd 8: (Slip st, ch 1, sc) in first ch-4 sp, (dc, ch 4, dc)
in next sc, sc in next ch-4 sp, ch 1, work Cluster in
marked sc on Rnd 5, ch 1, ★ sc in next ch-4 sp on
Rnd 7, (dc, ch 4, dc) in next sc, sc in next ch-4 sp, ch 1,
work Cluster in next sc on Rnd 5, ch 1; repeat from ★
around; join with slip st to first sc: 12 Clusters and
36 sps.

Rnd 9: Ch 1, sc in same st and in next dc, 5 sc in next ch-4 sp, sc in next 2 sts, decrease, ★ sc in next 2 sts, 5 sc in next ch-4 sp, sc in next 2 sts, decrease; repeat from ★ around; join with slip st to first sc: 120 sts.

Rnd 10: Ch 1, sc in same st and in next 3 sc, 3 sc in next sc, sc in next 4 sc, work FPdc around next Cluster on Rnd 8, skip next decrease on Rnd 9, ★ sc in next 4 sc, 3 sc in next sc, sc in next 4 sc, work FPdc around next Cluster on Rnd 8, skip next decrease on Rnd 9; repeat from ★ around; join with slip st to first sc: 12 FPdc and 132 sc.

Rnd 11: Ch 1, sc in same st, (ch 2, skip next sc, sc in next sc) 5 times, skip next FPdc, ★ sc in next sc, (ch 2, skip next sc, sc in next sc) 5 times, skip next FPdc; repeat from ★ around; join with slip st to first sc: 60 ch-2 sps.

Rnd 12: (Slip st, ch 1, sc) in first ch-2 sp, ch 3, (sc in next ch-2 sp, ch 3) 3 times, ★ sc in next 2 ch-2 sps, ch 3, (sc in next ch-2 sp, ch 3) 3 times; repeat from ★ around to last ch-2 sp, sc in last ch-2 sp; join with slip st to first sc: 48 ch-3 sps.

Rnd 13: (Slip st, ch 1, sc) in first ch-3 sp, (ch 4, sc in next ch-3 sp) 3 times, work FPtr around next FPdc on Rnd 10, ★ sc in next ch-3 sp on Rnd 12, (ch 4, sc in next ch-3 sp) 3 times, work FPtr around next FPdc on Rnd 10; repeat from ★ around; join with slip st to first sc: 36 ch-4 sps.

Rnd 14: Ch 1, 4 sc in first ch-4 sp, (sc, ch 4, slip st in third ch from hook, ch 2, sc) in next ch-4 sp, 4 sc in next ch-4 sp, work FPsc around next FPtr, work Picot, ★ 4 sc in next ch-4 sp, (sc, ch 4, slip st in third ch from hook, ch 2, sc) in next ch-4 sp, 4 sc in next ch-4 sp, work FPsc around next FPtr, work Picot; repeat from ★ around; join with slip st to first sc, finish off.

See Washing and Blocking, page 144.

57 ▇

Finished Size: 7" (point to point)

MATERIALS
Bedspread Weight Cotton Thread (size 10): 59 yards
Steel crochet hook, size 7 (1.65 mm) **or** size
    needed for gauge

GAUGE SWATCH: 1^1/$_2$" diameter
Work same as Doily through Rnd 4.

STITCH GUIDE

FRONT POST TREBLE CROCHET
    (abbreviated FPtr)
YO twice, insert hook from **front** to **back** around post of dc indicated *(Fig. 7, page 144)*, YO and pull up a loop (4 loops on hook), (YO and draw through 2 loops on hook) 3 times.

SPLIT DOUBLE TREBLE CROCHET
    (abbreviated Split dtr)
First Leg: YO 3 times, working in **front** of previous rnds *(Fig. 5, page 144)*, insert hook in dc indicated, YO and pull up a loop, (YO and draw through 2 loops on hook) 3 times (2 loops remaining on hook).

Second Leg: YO 3 times, insert hook in next dc on Rnd 7, YO and pull up a loop, (YO and draw through 2 loops on hook) 3 times, YO and draw through all 3 loops on hook.

PICOT
Ch 3, slip st in third ch from hook.

POPCORN
4 Dc in ch-3 sp indicated, drop loop from hook, insert hook in first dc of 4-dc group, hook dropped loop and draw through.

DOILY
Ch 8; join with slip st to form a ring.

Rnd 1 (Right side)**:** Ch 3 **(counts as first dc, now and throughout)**, 5 dc in ring, place marker around last dc made for st placement, 18 dc in ring; join with slip st to first dc: 24 dc.

Rnd 2: Ch 1, sc in same st, ch 2, skip next dc, ★ sc in next dc, ch 2, skip next dc; repeat from ★ around; join with slip st to first sc, do **not** finish off: 12 sc and 12 ch-2 sps.

Continued on page 90.

Rnd 3: Ch 1, sc in same st, work FPtr around marked dc on Rnd 1, ★ sc in next ch-2 sp on Rnd 2 and in next sc, skip next dc on Rnd 1 from last FPtr made, work FPtr around next dc; repeat from ★ around to last ch-2 sp on Rnd 2, sc in last ch-2 sp; join with slip st to first sc: 12 FPtr and 24 sc.

Rnd 4: Ch 1, sc in same st, 2 sc in next FPtr, (sc in next 2 sc, 2 sc in next FPtr) around to last sc, sc in last sc; join with slip st to first sc: 48 sc.

Rnd 5: Ch 1, sc in same st, ch 2, ★ skip next sc, sc in next 3 sc, ch 2; repeat from ★ around to last 3 sc, skip next sc, sc in last 2 sc; join with slip st to first sc: 12 ch-2 sps.

Rnd 6: (Slip st, ch 3, dc, ch 2, 2 dc) in first ch-2 sp, (2 dc, ch 2, 2 dc) in each ch-2 sp around; join with slip st to first dc.

Rnd 7: Slip st in next dc and in next ch-2 sp, ch 3, (dc, ch 2, 2 dc) in same sp, place marker around last dc made for st placement, ch 3, ★ (2 dc, ch 2, 2 dc) in next ch-2 sp, ch 3; repeat from ★ around; join with slip st to first dc: 24 sps.

Rnd 8: Slip st in next dc and in next ch-2 sp, ch 3, (dc, ch 2, 2 dc) in same sp, ch 2, sc in next ch-3 sp, ch 2, ★ (2 dc, ch 2) twice in next ch-2 sp, sc in next ch-3 sp, ch 2; repeat from ★ around; join with slip st to first dc: 36 ch-2 sps.

Rnd 9: Slip st in next dc and in next ch-2 sp, ch 3, (dc, ch 2, 2 dc) in same sp, ch 2, 2 sc in each of next 2 ch-2 sps, ch 2, ★ (2 dc, ch 2) twice in next ch-2 sp, 2 sc in each of next 2 ch-2 sps, ch 2; repeat from ★ around; join with slip st to first dc: 48 sc and 36 ch-2 sps.

Rnd 10: Slip st in next dc and in next ch-2 sp, ch 3, (dc, ch 2, 2 dc) in same sp, ch 3, 2 sc in next ch-2 sp, sc in next sc, skip next 2 sc, sc in next sc, 2 sc in next ch-2 sp, ch 3, ★ (2 dc, ch 2, 2 dc) in next ch-2 sp, ch 3, 2 sc in next ch-2 sp, sc in next sc, skip next 2 sc, sc in next sc, 2 sc in next ch-2 sp, ch 3; repeat from ★ around; join with slip st to first dc: 72 sc and 36 sps.

Rnd 11: Slip st in next dc and in next ch-2 sp, ch 3, (dc, ch 2, 2 dc) in same sp, ch 3, 2 sc in next ch-3 sp, ch 2, work First Leg of Split dtr in marked dc on Rnd 7, work Second Leg of Split dtr, ch 2, 2 sc in next ch-3 sp on Rnd 10, ch 3, ★ (2 dc, ch 2, 2 dc) in next ch-2 sp, ch 3, 2 sc in next ch-3 sp, ch 2, skip next 2 dc on Rnd 7 from last Split dtr made, work First Leg of Split dtr in next dc, work Second Leg of Split dtr, ch 2, 2 sc in next ch-3 sp on Rnd 10, ch 3; repeat from ★ around; join with slip st to first dc: 60 sps.

Rnd 12: Ch 1, sc in same st, ch 3, sc in next dc, 3 sc in next ch-2 sp, sc in next dc, ch 3, sc in next dc, 3 sc in next ch-3 sp, skip next ch-2 sp, dc in next ch-2 sp, ch 3, working in **front** of last dc made, dc in skipped ch-2 sp, 3 sc in next ch-3 sp, ★ (sc in next dc, ch 3, sc in next dc, 3 sc in next sp) twice, skip next ch-2 sp, dc in next ch-2 sp, ch 3, working in **front** of last dc made, dc in skipped ch-2 sp, 3 sc in next ch-3 sp; repeat from ★ around; join with slip st to first sc: 180 sts and 36 ch-3 sps.

Rnd 13: (Slip st, ch 1, sc) in first ch-3 sp, ★ † ch 2, skip next 2 sc, (dc, work Picot, ch 1, dc) in next sc, ch 2, sc in next ch-3 sp, ch 3, skip next 2 sc, sc in next sc, ch 1, work Popcorn in next ch-3 sp, ch 1, skip next 2 sts, sc in next sc, ch 3 †, sc in next ch-3 sp; repeat from ★ 10 times **more**, then repeat from † to † once; join with slip st to first sc, finish off.

See Washing and Blocking, page 144.

58

Finished Size: 6¼" diameter

MATERIALS
Bedspread Weight Cotton Thread (size 10): 77 yards
Steel crochet hook, size 7 (1.65 mm) **or** size needed for gauge

GAUGE SWATCH: 1½" diameter
Work same as Doily through Rnd 4.

STITCH GUIDE

TREBLE CROCHET (abbreviated tr)
YO twice, insert hook in st indicated, YO and pull up a loop (4 loops on hook), (YO and draw through 2 loops on hook) 3 times.

SPLIT FRONT POST TREBLE CROCHET (abbreviated Split FPtr)
First Leg: YO twice, insert hook from **front** to **back** around post of st indicated (*Fig. 7, page 144*), YO and pull up a loop, (YO and draw through 2 loops on hook) twice (2 loops remaining on hook).

Second Leg: YO twice, insert hook from **front** to **back** around post of st indicated, YO and pull up a loop, (YO and draw through 2 loops on hook) twice, YO and draw through all 3 loops on hook.

CLUSTER
★ YO twice, insert hook from **front** to **back** around post of tr indicated *(Fig. 7, page 144)*, YO and pull up a loop, (YO and draw through 2 loops on hook) twice; repeat from ★ 2 times **more**, YO and draw through all 4 loops on hook.

PICOT
Ch 3, slip st in third ch from hook.

DOILY

Rnd 1 (Right side): Ch 4, dc in fourth ch from hook, place marker around dc just made for st placement, 14 dc in same ch; join with slip st to top of beginning ch-4: 16 sts.

Rnd 2: (Slip st, ch 1, sc) in next dc, ch 3, skip next dc, ★ sc in next dc, ch 3, skip next st; repeat from ★ around; join with slip st to first sc: 8 sc and 8 ch-3 sps.

Rnd 3: Ch 1, sc in same st and in next ch-3 sp, work First Leg of Split FPtr around marked dc on Rnd 1, skip next dc, ★ work Second Leg of Split FPtr around next dc, sc in same sp as last sc made on Rnd 2, sc in next sc and in next ch-3 sp, work First Leg of Split FPtr around same dc as Second Leg of last Split FPtr, skip next st on Rnd 1; repeat from ★ 6 times **more**, working **above** First Leg of first Split FPtr, work Second Leg of Split FPtr, sc in same sp as last sc made on Rnd 2; join with slip st to first sc: 8 Split FPtr and 24 sc.

Rnd 4: Ch 1, sc in same st and in next sc, 2 sc in next Split FPtr, place marker around last sc made for st placement, (sc in next 3 sc, 2 sc in next Split FPtr) around to last sc, sc in last sc; join with slip st to Back Loop Only of first sc *(Fig. 1, page 143)*: 40 sc.

Rnd 5: Ch 3 **(counts as first dc, now and throughout)**, dc in Back Loop Only of next sc and each sc around; join with slip st to **both** loops of first dc.

Rnd 6: Ch 1, sc in same st, tr in free loop of marked sc on Rnd 4 *(Fig. 2a, page 144)*, place marker around tr just made for st placement, ★ working **behind** tr just made, sc in **both** loops of next 2 dc on Rnd 5, skip next sc on Rnd 4, tr in free loop of next sc; repeat from ★ around to last dc on Rnd 5, working **behind** last tr made, sc in **both** loops of last dc; join with slip st to first sc: 60 sts.

Rnd 7: Ch 1, sc in same st and in each st around; join with slip st to first sc.

Rnd 8: Ch 1, sc in same st, ch 4, skip next 2 sc, ★ sc in next sc, ch 4, skip next 2 sc; repeat from ★ around; join with slip st to first sc: 20 sc and 20 ch-4 sps.

Rnd 9: Ch 1, sc in same st, 3 sc in next ch-4 sp, work Cluster around marked tr on Rnd 6, ★ sc in next sc on Rnd 8, 3 sc in next ch-4 sp, work Cluster around next tr on Rnd 6; repeat from ★ around; join with slip st to first sc: 20 Clusters and 80 sc.

Rnd 10: Slip st in next 2 sc, ch 1, sc in same st, ch 5, skip next 4 sts, ★ sc in next sc, ch 5, skip next 4 sts; repeat from ★ around; join with slip st to first sc: 20 sc and 20 ch-5 sps.

Rnd 11: (Slip st, ch 3, 4 dc) in first ch-5 sp, 5 dc in each ch-5 sp around; join with slip st to first dc: 20 5-dc groups.

Rnd 12: Ch 3, dc in next 2 dc, work First Leg of Split FPtr around first dc of 5-dc group just worked into, work Second Leg of Split FPtr around last dc of same 5-dc group, ★ working **behind** Split FPtr, dc in same st as last dc made and in next 5 dc, work First Leg of Split FPtr around first dc of 5-dc group just worked into, work Second Leg of Split FPtr around last dc of same 5-dc group; repeat from ★ around to last 2 dc, working **behind** Split FPtr, dc in same st as last dc made and in last 2 dc; join with slip st to first dc: 20 Split FPtr and 120 dc.

Rnd 13: Ch 1, sc in same st and in next 2 dc, (skip next Split FPtr, sc in next 6 dc) around to last 4 sts, skip next Split FPtr, sc in last 3 dc; join with slip st to first sc: 120 sc.

Rnd 14: Ch 3, dc in next 5 sc, work First Leg of Split FPtr around Second Leg of Split FPtr 2 rnds **below**, work Second Leg of Split FPtr around First Leg of next Split FPtr, ★ working **behind** Split FPtr just made, dc in next 6 sc on Rnd 13, work First Leg of Split FPtr around Second Leg of Split FPtr 2 rnds **below**, work Second Leg of Split FPtr around First Leg of next Split FPtr; repeat from ★ around; join with slip st to first dc: 20 Split FPtr and 120 dc.

Rnd 15: Ch 1, sc in same st, tr in next dc pulling tr to right side, (sc in next st, tr in next st pulling tr to right side) around; join with slip st to first sc: 140 sts.

Rnd 16: Ch 1, 2 sc in same st, sc in next tr and in each st around; join with slip st to first sc: 141 sc.

Rnd 17: Ch 1, sc in same st, work Picot, ch 1, skip next 2 sc, ★ sc in next sc, work Picot, ch 1, skip next 2 sc; repeat from ★ around; join with slip st to first sc, finish off.

See Washing and Blocking, page 144.

Finished Size: 6" diameter

MATERIALS

Bedspread Weight Cotton Thread (size 10): 70 yards
Steel crochet hook, size 7 (1.65 mm) **or** size
  needed for gauge

GAUGE SWATCH: 1³/₄" diameter
Work same as Doily through Rnd 4.

STITCH GUIDE

TREBLE CROCHET *(abbreviated tr)*
YO twice, insert hook in dc indicated, YO and pull
up a loop (4 loops on hook), (YO and draw through
2 loops on hook) 3 times.

BACK POST SINGLE CROCHET
  (abbreviated BPsc)
Insert hook from **back** to **front** around post of dc
indicated *(Fig. 7, page 144)*, YO and pull up a
loop, YO and draw through both loops on hook.

SPLIT FRONT POST TREBLE CROCHET
  (abbreviated Split FPtr)
First Leg: YO twice, insert hook from **front** to
back around post of dc indicated *(Fig. 7,
page 144)*, YO and pull up a loop, (YO and draw
through 2 loops on hook) twice (2 loops remaining
on hook).

Second Leg: YO twice, insert hook from **front** to
back around post of next dc, YO and pull up a
loop, (YO and draw through 2 loops on hook) twice,
YO and draw through all 3 loops on hook.

SPLIT DOUBLE TREBLE CROCHET
  (abbreviated Split dtr)
First Leg: YO 3 times, working in **front** of
previous rnds *(Fig. 5, page 144)*, insert hook from
back to **front** in sc indicated, YO and pull up a
loop, (YO and draw through 2 loops on hook) 3
times (2 loops remaining on hook).

Second Leg: YO 3 times, insert hook from **front**
to **back** in sc indicated, YO and pull up a loop, (YO
and draw through 2 loops on hook) 3 times, YO and
draw through all 3 loops on hook.

PICOT
Ch 3, slip st in third ch from hook.

DOILY

Ch 10; join with slip st to form a ring.

Rnd 1 (Right side)**:** Ch 3 **(counts as first dc, now
and throughout)**, 2 dc in ring, place marker around
last dc made for st placement, 21 dc in ring; join with
slip st to first dc: 24 dc.

Rnd 2: Ch 1, sc in same st, ch 3, skip next dc, ★ sc in
next dc, ch 3, skip next dc; repeat from ★ around; join
with slip st to first sc: 12 sc and 12 ch-3 sps.

Rnd 3: Ch 1, sc in same st and in next ch-3 sp, work
First Leg of Split FPtr around marked dc on Rnd 1, work
Second Leg of Split FPtr, working **behind** Split FPtr, sc
in same sp as last sc made on Rnd 2, ★ sc in next sc and
in next ch-3 sp, work First Leg of Split FPtr around next
dc on Rnd 1, work Second Leg of Split FPtr, working
behind Split FPtr, sc in same sp on Rnd 2 as last sc
made; repeat from ★ around; join with slip st to first sc:
36 sc and 12 Split FPtr.

Rnd 4: Ch 1, sc in same st and in each st around; join
with slip st to Back Loop Only of first sc *(Fig. 1,
page 143)*: 48 sc.

Rnd 5: Ch 3, working in Back Loops Only, dc in next
sc, 2 dc in next sc, (dc in next 3 sc, 2 dc in next sc)
around to last sc, dc in last sc; join with slip st to **both**
loops of first dc: 60 dc.

Rnd 6: Ch 1, sc in same st, working in both loops, tr in
next dc pulling tr to right side, (sc in next dc, tr in next
dc pulling tr to right side) around; join with slip st to
first sc.

Rnd 7: Ch 1, sc in same st and in each st around; join
with slip st to first sc.

Rnd 8: Ch 1, sc in same st and in next sc, 2 sc in next
sc, (sc in next 2 sc, 2 sc in next sc) around, place marker
in last sc made for st placement; join with slip st to first
sc: 80 sc.

Rnd 9: Ch 1, sc in same st, ch 3, skip next sc, ★ sc in
next sc, ch 3, skip next sc; repeat from ★ around; join
with slip st to first sc: 40 ch-3 sps.

Rnd 10: (Slip st, ch 3, 2 dc) in first ch-3 sp, 3 dc in
each ch-3 sp around; join with slip st to first dc: 120 dc.

Rnd 11: Ch 1, sc in same st, work First Leg of Split dtr in marked sc on Rnd 8, skip next 3 sc, work Second Leg of Split dtr in next sc, skip next dc on Rnd 10 from last sc made, sc in next 2 dc, working in **front** of Second Leg of last Split dtr made, skip next sc on Rnd 8 from First Leg of same st, work First Leg of Split dtr in next sc, ★ skip next 3 sc, work Second Leg of Split dtr in next sc, skip next dc on Rnd 10 from last sc made, sc in next 2 dc, working in **front** of Second Leg of last Split dtr made, work First Leg of Split dtr in same st on Rnd 8 as Second Leg of next-to-the-last Split dtr made; repeat from ★ around to last 5 dc, work Second Leg of Split dtr in same st as First Leg of first Split dtr made, skip next dc on Rnd 10 from last sc made, sc in next 2 dc, working in **front** of Second Leg of last Split dtr made, work First Leg of Split dtr in same st as Second Leg of next-to-the-last Split dtr made, working **behind** First Leg of first Split dtr made, work Second Leg of Split dtr in same st as First Leg of second Split dtr made, skip next dc on Rnd 10 from last sc made, sc in last dc; join with slip st to first sc: 40 Split dtr and 80 sc.

Rnds 12 and 13: Ch 1, sc in same st and in each st around; join with slip st to first sc: 120 sc.

Rnd 14: Ch 1, sc in same st, skip next 2 sc, dc in next sc, (ch 1, dc in same st) 4 times, skip next 2 sc, sc in next sc, ★ ch 6, skip next 3 sc, sc in next sc, skip next 2 sc, dc in next sc, (ch 1, dc in same st) 4 times, skip next 2 sc, sc in next sc; repeat from ★ around to last 3 sc, ch 4, skip last 3 sc, hdc in first sc to form last ch-6 sp: 60 dc and 12 ch-6 sps.

Rnd 15: Ch 1, 2 sc in last ch-6 sp made, skip next sc, work BPsc around next dc, (work Picot, ch 1, work BPsc around next dc) 4 times, ★ (2 sc, ch 4, slip st in third ch from hook, ch 2, 2 sc) in next ch-6 sp, skip next sc, work BPsc around next dc, (work Picot, ch 1, work BPsc around next dc) 4 times; repeat from ★ around, 2 sc in same sp as first sc, ch 4, slip st in third ch from hook, ch 2; join with slip st to first sc, finish off.

See Washing and Blocking, page 144.

60 ▰

Finished Size: 6¹/₂" diameter

MATERIALS
Bedspread Weight Cotton Thread (size 10): 62 yards
Steel crochet hook, size 7 (1.65 mm) **or** size needed for gauge

GAUGE SWATCH: 2¹/₄" diameter
Work same as Doily through Rnd 5.

STITCH GUIDE

BACK POST DOUBLE CROCHET
(abbreviated BPdc)
YO, insert hook from **back** to **front** around post of dc indicated *(Fig. 7, page 144)*, YO and pull up a loop (3 loops on hook), (YO and draw through 2 loops on hook) twice.

FRONT POST CLUSTER
(abbreviated FP Cluster)
★ YO, insert hook from **front** to **back** around post of st indicated *(Fig. 7, page 144)*, YO and pull up a loop, YO and draw through 2 loops on hook; repeat from ★ 2 times **more**, YO and draw through all 4 loops on hook.

SPLIT TREBLE CROCHET
(abbreviated Split tr)
First Leg: YO twice, insert hook from **top** to **bottom** in free loop of sc indicated *(Fig. 2a, page 144)*, YO and pull up a loop, (YO and draw through 2 loops on hook) twice (2 loops remaining on hook).

Second Leg: YO twice, insert hook from **bottom** to **top** in free loop of sc indicated, YO and pull up a loop, (YO and draw through 2 loops on hook) twice, YO and draw through all 3 loops on hook.

BEGINNING POPCORN
Ch 3, 3 dc in ch-3 sp indicated, drop loop from hook, insert hook in first dc of 4-dc group, hook dropped loop and draw through.

POPCORN
4 Dc in ch-3 sp indicated, drop loop from hook, insert hook in first dc of 4-dc group, hook dropped loop and draw through.

PICOT
Ch 2, slip st in top of last dc made *(Fig. 6a, page 144)*.

Continued on page 94.

DOILY

Rnd 1 (Right side)**:** Ch 5, (dc, ch 1) 11 times in fifth ch from hook; join with slip st to fourth ch of beginning ch-5: 12 sts and 12 ch-1 sps.

Rnd 2: (Slip st, ch 1, sc) in first ch-1 sp, (ch 3, sc in next ch-1 sp) around, dc in first sc to form last ch-3 sp: 12 ch-3 sps.

Rnd 3: Ch 1, sc in last ch-3 sp made, work FP Cluster around dc one rnd **below**, sc in same sp on Rnd 2 as last sc made, ★ ch 3, sc in next ch-3 sp, work FP Cluster around next dc one rnd **below**, sc in same sp on Rnd 2 as last sc made; repeat from ★ around, dc in first sc to form last ch-3 sp.

Rnd 4: Ch 3 **(counts as first dc, now and throughout)**, 3 dc in last ch-3 sp made, ch 1, (4 dc in next ch-3 sp, ch 1) around; join with slip st to first dc: 48 dc and 12 ch-1 sps.

Rnd 5: Ch 1, sc in same st and in each dc and each ch-1 sp around, place marker around last sc made for st placement; join with slip st to Back Loop Only of first sc **(Fig. 1, page 143)**: 60 sc.

Rnd 6: Ch 1, working in Back Loops Only, sc in same st and in next 3 sc, 2 sc in next sc, (sc in next 4 sc, 2 sc in next sc) around; join with slip st to **both** loops of first sc: 72 sc.

Rnd 7: Ch 1, sc in both loops of same st and each sc around; join with slip st to first sc.

Rnd 8: Ch 1, sc in same st, ch 3, skip next 2 sc, ★ sc in next sc, ch 3, skip next 2 sc; repeat from ★ around; join with slip st to first sc: 24 sc and 24 ch-3 sps.

Rnd 9: (Slip st, ch 1, sc) in first ch-3 sp, work First Leg of Split tr in marked sc on Rnd 5, ★ skip next 4 sc, work Second Leg of Split tr in next sc, sc in same sp on Rnd 8 as last sc made, ch 3, (sc, ch 3) twice in next ch-3 sp, sc in next ch-3 sp, work First Leg of Split tr in same st as Second Leg of last Split tr made; repeat from ★ around to last ch-3 sp, work Second Leg of Split tr in same st as First Leg of first Split tr, sc in same sp on Rnd 8 as last sc made, (ch 3, sc) twice in last ch-3 sp, dc in first sc to form last ch-3 sp: 36 ch-3 sps.

Rnd 10: Ch 1, sc in last ch-3 sp made, (ch 4, sc in next ch-3 sp) around, ch 1, dc in first sc to form last ch-4 sp.

Rnd 11: Ch 1, sc last ch-4 sp made, 5 dc in next ch-4 sp, sc in next ch-4 sp, ★ ch 4, sc in next ch-4 sp, 5 dc in next ch-4 sp, sc in next ch-4 sp; repeat from ★ around; ch 3, sc in first sc to form last ch-4 sp: 60 dc and 12 ch-4 sps.

Rnd 12: Ch 1, sc in last ch-4 sp made, skip next sc, work BPdc around next dc, (ch 1, work BPdc around next dc) 4 times, ★ (sc, ch 3, sc) in next ch-4 sp, skip next sc, work BPdc around next dc, (ch 1, work BPdc around next dc) 4 times; repeat from ★ around, sc in same sp as first sc, ch 1, hdc in first sc to form last ch-3 sp: 60 sps.

Rnd 13: Work Beginning Popcorn in last ch-3 sp made, ch 2, sc in next ch-1 sp, (ch 3, sc in next ch-1 sp) 3 times, ★ ch 2, work Popcorn in next ch-3 sp, ch 2, sc in next ch-1 sp, (ch 3, sc in next ch-1 sp) 3 times; repeat from ★ around, ch 1, sc in top of Beginning Popcorn to form last ch-2 sp.

Rnd 14: Ch 1, sc in last ch-2 sp made and in next ch-2 sp, ★ ch 3, (sc in next ch-3 sp, ch 3) 3 times, sc in next 2 ch-2 sps; repeat from ★ around to last 3 ch-3 sps, (ch 3, sc in next ch-3 sp) 3 times, dc in first sc to form last ch-3 sp: 48 ch-3 sps.

Rnd 15: Ch 1, sc in last ch-3 sp made, (ch 3, sc in next ch-3 sp) around, ch 1, hdc in first sc to form last ch-3 sp.

Rnd 16: Ch 1, sc in last ch-3 sp made, dc in next ch-3 sp, (work Picot, dc in same sp) 4 times, ★ sc in next ch-3 sp, dc in next ch-3 sp, (work Picot, dc in same sp) 4 times; repeat from ★ around; join with slip st to first sc, finish off.

See Washing and Blocking, page 144.

61 ▰▰▰▰▰▰▰▰▰

Finished Size: 6" diameter

MATERIALS
Bedspread Weight Cotton Thread (size 10): 65 yards
Steel crochet hook, size 7 (1.65 mm) **or** size needed for gauge

GAUGE SWATCH: 2" diameter
Work same as Doily through Rnd 5.

STITCH GUIDE

> **TREBLE CROCHET** *(abbreviated tr)*
> YO twice, insert hook in st indicated, YO and pull up a loop (4 loops on hook), (YO and draw through 2 loops on hook) 3 times.
>
> **FRONT POST SINGLE CROCHET**
> *(abbreviated FPsc)*
> Insert hook from **front** to **back** around posts of Cluster indicated *(Fig. 7, page 144)*, YO and pull up a loop, YO and draw through both loops on hook.

FRONT POST TREBLE CROCHET CLUSTER (abbreviated FPtr Cluster)

★ YO twice, insert hook from **front** to **back** around post of st indicated *(Fig. 7, page 144)*, YO and pull up a loop, (YO and draw through 2 loops on hook) twice; repeat from ★ once **more**, YO and draw through all 3 loops on hook.

CLUSTER (uses one st or sp)

★ YO, insert hook in st or sp indicated, YO and pull up a loop, YO and draw through 2 loops on hook; repeat from ★ once **more**, YO and draw through all 3 loops on hook.

SPLIT TREBLE CROCHET (abbreviated Split tr)

First Leg: YO twice, working in **front** of dc just made, insert hook from **back** to **front** in ch-2 sp indicated, YO and pull up a loop, (YO and draw through 2 loops on hook) twice (2 loops remaining on hook).

Second Leg: YO twice, insert hook from **front** to **back** in next ch-2 sp, YO and pull up a loop, (YO and draw through 2 loops on hook) twice, YO and draw through all 3 loops on hook.

PICOT

Ch 3, slip st in third ch from hook, ch 1.

DOILY

Rnd 1 (Right side)**:** Ch 7, tr in seventh ch from hook, place marker around tr just made for st placement, ch 2, (tr in same ch, ch 2) 13 times; join with slip st to fifth ch of beginning ch-7: 15 sts and 15 ch-2 sps.

Rnd 2: Slip st in first ch-2 sp, ch 1, 2 sc in same sp and in each ch-2 sp around; join with slip st to first sc: 30 sc.

Rnd 3: Ch 1, sc in same st, ch 1, (sc in next 2 sc, ch 1) around to last sc, sc in last sc; join with slip st to first sc: 30 sc and 15 ch-1 sps.

Rnd 4: Ch 1, sc in same st, sc in next ch-1 sp and in next sc, work FPtr Cluster around marked tr on Rnd 1, ★ working **behind** FPtr Cluster, sc in next sc on Rnd 3, sc in next ch-1 sp and in next sc, work FPtr Cluster around next st on Rnd 1; repeat from ★ around; join with slip st to first sc: 45 sc and 15 FPtr Clusters.

Rnd 5: Ch 1, sc in same st and in next 2 sc, skip next FPtr Cluster, (sc in next 3 sc, skip next FPtr Cluster) around; join with slip st to first sc: 45 sc.

Rnd 6: Ch 1, sc in same st, ch 3, ★ skip next sc, sc in next 2 sc, ch 3; repeat from ★ around to last 2 sc, skip next sc, sc in last sc; join with slip st to first sc: 30 sc and 15 ch-3 sps.

Rnd 7: Ch 1, sc in same st, ch 3, work Cluster in next ch-3 sp, ch 3, ★ sc in next 2 sc, ch 3, work Cluster in next ch-3 sp, ch 3; repeat from ★ around to last sc, sc in last sc; join with slip st to first sc: 30 ch-3 sps.

Rnd 8: Slip st in next 2 chs, ch 1, sc in same ch-3 sp, ch 3, (sc in next ch-3 sp, ch 3) around; join with slip st to first sc.

Rnd 9: [Slip st, ch 3 **(counts as first dc, now and throughout)**, 3 dc] in first ch-3 sp, ch 2, sc in next ch-3 sp, ch 2, ★ 4 dc in next ch-3 sp, ch 2, sc in next ch-3 sp, ch 2; repeat from ★ around; join with slip st to first dc, place marker around last ch-2 made for st placement: 75 sts and 30 ch-2 sps.

Rnd 10: Ch 3, dc in next dc, working in **front** of dc just made, work First Leg of Split tr in marked ch-2 sp, work Second Leg of Split tr, working **behind** Second Leg of Split tr, dc in next 2 dc, ch 2, work Cluster in **front** 2 legs of next sc *(Fig. 4, page 144)*, ch 2, ★ skip next ch-2 sp, dc in next 2 dc, working in **front** of dc just made, work First Leg of Split tr in last skipped ch-2 sp, work Second Leg of Split tr, working **behind** Second Leg of Split tr, dc in next 2 dc, ch 2, work Cluster in **front** 2 legs of next sc, ch 2; repeat from ★ around; join with slip st to first dc: 90 sts and 30 ch-2 sps.

Rnd 11: Ch 1, sc in same st and in next dc, sc in center 3 loops of next Split tr *(Fig. 3b, page 144)*, sc in next 2 dc and in next ch-2 sp, work FPsc around next Cluster, ★ sc in next ch-2 sp and in next 2 dc, sc in center 3 loops of next Split tr, sc in next 2 dc and in next ch-2 sp, work FPsc around next Cluster; repeat from ★ around to last ch-2 sp, sc in last ch-2 sp; join with slip st to first sc: 120 sts.

Rnd 12: Ch 1, sc in same st and in next 6 sts, place marker around last sc made for st placement, sc in each st around; join with slip st to Back Loop Only of first sc *(Fig. 1, page 143)*.

Rnd 13: Ch 1, sc in Back Loop Only of same st and each sc around; join with slip st to **both** loops of first sc.

Rnd 14: Ch 1, working in both loops, sc in same st and in next sc, 2 sc in next sc, (sc in next 7 sc, 2 sc in next sc) around to last 5 sc, sc in last 5 sc; join with slip st to first sc: 135 sc.

Rnd 15: Slip st in next sc, ch 1, sc in same st and in next sc, work Picot, sc in next 2 sc, working in **front** of previous rnds, tr in free loop of marked sc on Rnd 12 *(Fig. 2a, page 144)*, skip next sc on Rnd 14 from last sc made, sc in next 3 sc, working in **front** of previous rnds, tr in same st on Rnd 12 as last tr made, skip next sc on Rnd 14 from last sc made, ★ sc in next 2 sc, work Picot, sc in next 2 sc, skip next 7 sc on Rnd 12 from last tr made, working in **front** of previous rnds, tr in free loop of next sc, skip next sc on Rnd 14 from last sc made, sc in next 3 sc, working in **front** of previous rnds, tr in same st on Rnd 12 as last tr made, skip next st on Rnd 14 from last sc made; repeat from ★ around; join with slip st to first sc, finish off.

See Washing and Blocking, page 144.

Finished Size: 6" diameter

MATERIALS

Bedspread Weight Cotton Thread (size 10):
Ecru - 60 yards
Green - 5 yards
Blue - 5 yards
Steel crochet hook, size 7 (1.65 mm) **or** size
needed for gauge

GAUGE SWATCH: 1³/₄" square
Work same Doily through Rnd 4.

STITCH GUIDE

FRONT POST SINGLE CROCHET
(abbreviated FPsc)
Insert hook from **front** to **back** around post of dc
indicated *(Fig. 7, page 144)*, YO and pull up a
loop, YO and draw through both loops on hook.

FRONT POST TREBLE CROCHET
(abbreviated FPtr)
YO twice, insert hook from **front** to **back** around
post of FP Cluster indicated *(Fig. 7, page 144)*, YO
and pull up a loop (4 loops on hook), (YO and draw
through 2 loops on hook) 3 times.

FRONT POST CLUSTER
(abbreviated FP Cluster)
★ YO twice, insert hook from **front** to **back** around
post of dc indicated *(Fig. 7, page 144)*, YO and
pull up a loop, (YO and draw through 2 loops on
hook) twice; repeat from ★ once **more**, YO and
draw through all 3 loops on hook.

DOILY

With Ecru, ch 5; join with slip st to form a ring.

Rnd 1 (Right side)**:** Ch 3 **(counts as first dc, now
and throughout)**, 17 dc in ring; join with slip st to first
dc: 18 dc.

Note: Loop a short piece of thread around any stitch to
mark Rnd 1 as **right** side.

Rnd 2: Ch 1, sc in same st and in each dc around; join
with slip st to first sc.

Rnd 3: Ch 1, sc in same st, ch 2, (sc in next sc, ch 2)
around; join with slip st to first sc: 18 ch-2 sps.

Rnd 4: (Slip st, ch 1, 2 sc) in first ch-2 sp, work
FP Cluster around second dc on Rnd 1, place marker
around FP Cluster just made for st placement, ★ 2 sc in
next ch-2 sp on Rnd 3, work FP Cluster around next dc
on Rnd 1; repeat from ★ around; join with slip st to first
sc: 54 sts.

Rnds 5 and 6: Ch 1, sc in same st and in each st
around; join with slip st to first sc.

Rnd 7: Ch 1, work FPtr around marked FP Cluster on
Rnd 4, sc in first 3 sc on Rnd 6, ★ work FPtr around
next FP Cluster on Rnd 4, sc in next 3 sc on Rnd 6;
repeat from ★ around; join with slip st to first FPtr:
18 FPtr.

Rnd 8: Ch 1, sc in same st, ch 4, skip next 3 sc, ★ sc
in next FPtr, ch 4, skip next 3 sc; repeat from ★ around;
join with slip st to first sc: 18 ch-4 sps.

Rnd 9: (Slip st, ch 3, 4 dc) in first ch-4 sp, 5 dc in each
ch-4 sp around; join with slip st to first dc, finish off:
18 5-dc groups.

Rnd 10: With **right** side facing, join Green with sc
(see Joining With Sc, page 143) around post of
second dc of any 5-dc group *(Fig. 7, page 144)*; ch 4,
skip next dc, work FPsc around next dc, ch 4, skip next
2 dc, ★ work FPsc around next dc, ch 4, skip next dc,
work FPsc around next dc, ch 4, skip next 2 dc; repeat
from ★ around; join with slip st to first sc, finish off:
36 ch-4 sps.

Rnd 11: With **right** side facing, working in **front** of
Rnd 10 and in skipped dc on Rnd 9, join Blue with sc
around post of last dc of any 5-dc group; work FPsc
around next skipped dc, ch 4, work FPsc around next
skipped dc, ch 4, ★ work FPsc around each of next
2 skipped dc, ch 4, work FPsc around next skipped dc,
ch 4; repeat from ★ around; join with slip st to first sc,
finish off: 36 ch-4 sps.

Rnd 12: With **right** side facing and working in
ch-4 sps on Rnds 10 **and** 11, join Ecru with sc in any
ch-4 sp on Rnd 11; sc in same sp, sc in next ch-4 sp on
Rnd 10, ★ 2 sc in next ch-4 sp on Rnd 11, sc in next
ch-4 sp on Rnd 10; repeat from ★ around; join with
slip st to first sc, do **not** finish off: 108 sc.

Rnd 13: Ch 1, 2 sc in same st, sc in next 5 sc, (2 sc in
next sc, sc in next 5 sc) around; join with slip st to first
sc: 126 sc.

Rnd 14: Ch 1, sc in same st and in each sc around;
join with slip st to first sc.

Rnd 15: Ch 1, sc in same st and in next 4 sc, ch 9,
skip next 2 sc, ★ sc in next 5 sc, ch 9, skip next 2 sc;
repeat from ★ around; join with slip st to first sc: 90 sc
and 18 ch-9 sps.

Rnd 16: Slip st in next 2 sc, ch 1, sc in same st and in next ch-9 sp, (ch 3, sc in same sp) 5 times, skip next 2 sc, ★ sc in next sc and in next ch-9 sp, (ch 3, sc in same sp) 5 times, skip next 2 sc; repeat from ★ around; join with slip st to first sc, finish off.

See Washing and Blocking, page 144.

63

Finished Size: 5" diameter

MATERIALS
Bedspread Weight Cotton Thread (size 10): 55 yards
Steel crochet hook, size 7 (1.65 mm) **or** size
    needed for gauge

GAUGE SWATCH: $1^1/2$" diameter
Work same as Doily through Rnd 2.

STITCH GUIDE

BEGINNING CLUSTER
Ch 2, ★ YO, insert hook in ring, YO and pull up a loop, YO and draw through 2 loops on hook; repeat from ★ once **more**, YO and draw through all 3 loops on hook.

CLUSTER
★ YO, insert hook in ring, YO and pull up a loop, YO and draw through 2 loops on hook; repeat from ★ 2 times **more**, YO and draw through all 4 loops on hook.

FRONT POST CLUSTER
   (abbreviated FP Cluster)
★ YO, insert hook from **front** to **back** around post of st indicated *(Fig. 7, page 144)*, YO and pull up a loop, YO and draw through 2 loops on hook; repeat from ★ once **more**, YO and draw through all 3 loops on hook.

BACK POST SINGLE CROCHET
   (abbreviated BPsc)
Insert hook from **back** to **front** around post of dc indicated *(Fig. 7, page 144)*, YO and pull up a loop, YO and draw through both loops on hook.

PICOT
Ch 3, slip st in third ch from hook, ch 1.

DOILY
Ch 8; join with slip st to form a ring.

Rnd 1 (Right side)**:** Work Beginning Cluster, ch 3, (work Cluster, ch 3) 9 times; join with slip st to top of Beginning Cluster: 10 Clusters and 10 ch-3 sps.

Rnd 2: Ch 1, ★ sc in next ch-3 sp, (ch 2, sc in same sp) twice; repeat from ★ around; join with slip st to first sc: 30 sc and 20 ch-2 sps.

Rnd 3: (Slip st, ch 1, sc) in first ch-2 sp, ch 3, sc in next ch-2 sp, work FP Cluster around center leg of next Cluster on Rnd 1, ★ sc in next ch-2 sp on Rnd 2, ch 3, sc in next ch-2 sp, work FP Cluster around center leg of next Cluster on Rnd 1; repeat from ★ around; join with slip st to first sc: 10 ch-3 sps.

Rnd 4: [Slip st, ch 4 **(counts as first dc plus ch 1)**, dc] in first ch-3 sp, (ch 1, dc in same sp) 3 times, ★ dc in next ch-3 sp, (ch 1, dc in same sp) 4 times; repeat from ★ around; join with slip st to first dc: 50 dc and 40 ch-1 sps.

Rnd 5: Ch 1, work BPsc around same st, ★ ch 3, (work BPsc around next dc, ch 3) 3 times, work BPsc around each of next 2 dc; repeat from ★ around to last 4 dc, (ch 3, work BPsc around next dc) 4 times; join with slip st to first BPsc: 40 ch-3 sps.

Rnd 6: (Slip st, ch 1, sc) in first ch-3 sp, ★ ch 3, (sc in next ch-3 sp, ch 3) twice, sc in next 2 ch-3 sps; repeat from ★ around to last 3 ch-3 sps, (ch 3, sc in next ch-3 sp) 3 times; join with slip st to first sc: 30 ch-3 sps.

Rnd 7: Ch 1, sc in same st and in next ch-3 sp, (ch 3, sc in next ch-3 sp) twice, ★ sc in next 2 sc and next ch-3 sp, (ch 3, sc in next ch-3 sp) twice; repeat from ★ around to last sc, sc in last sc; join with slip st to first sc: 50 sc and 20 ch-3 sps.

Rnd 8: Ch 1, sc in same st and in next sc, 2 sc in next ch-3 sp, dc in next sc, (ch 1, dc in same st) 3 times, 2 sc in next ch-3 sp, ★ sc in next 4 sc, 2 sc in next ch-3 sp, dc in next sc, (ch 1, dc in same st) 3 times, 2 sc in next ch-3 sp; repeat from ★ around to last 2 sc, sc in last 2 sc; join with slip st to first sc: 120 sts and 30 ch-1 sps.

Rnd 9: Slip st in next sc, ch 1, sc in same st and in next 2 sc, work Picot, (sc in next ch-1 sp, work Picot) 3 times, skip next dc, sc in next 3 sc, skip next 2 sc, ★ sc in next 3 sc, work Picot, (sc in next ch-1 sp, work Picot) 3 times, skip next dc, sc in next 3 sc, skip next 2 sts; repeat from ★ around; join with slip st to first sc, finish off.

See Washing and Blocking, page 144.

Finished Size: 6^1/$_2$" square

MATERIALS

Bedspread Weight Cotton Thread (size 10): 62 yards
Steel crochet hook, size 7 (1.65 mm) **or** size
   needed for gauge

GAUGE SWATCH: 1^1/$_2$" diameter
Work same as Doily through Rnd 3.

STITCH GUIDE

CLUSTER (uses one ch-7 sp)
★ YO, insert hook in sp indicated, YO and pull up a
loop, YO and draw through 2 loops on hook;
repeat from ★ once **more**, YO and draw through all
3 loops on hook.

FRONT POST CLUSTER
   (abbreviated FP Cluster)
★ YO twice, insert hook from **front** to **back** around
post of dc indicated *(Fig. 7, page 144)*, YO and
pull up a loop, (YO and draw through 2 loops on
hook) twice; repeat from ★ once **more**, YO and
draw through all 3 loops on hook.

SPLIT FRONT POST TREBLE CROCHET
   (abbreviated Split FPtr)
YO twice, insert hook from **front** to **back** around
post of first dc of 4-dc group just worked into
(Fig. 7, page 144), YO and pull up a loop, (YO
and draw through 2 loops on hook) twice,
YO twice, insert hook from **front** to **back** around
post of last dc of same 4-dc group, YO and pull up
a loop, (YO and draw through 2 loops on hook)
twice, YO and draw through all 3 loops on hook.

BEGINNING POPCORN
Ch 3, 4 dc in ch-4 sp indicated, drop loop from
hook, insert hook in first dc of 5-dc group, hook
dropped loop and draw through.

POPCORN
5 Dc in ch-4 sp indicated, drop loop from hook,
insert hook in first dc of 5-dc group, hook dropped
loop and draw through.

PICOT
Ch 3, slip st in third ch from hook, ch 1.

DOILY

Ch 7; join with slip st to form a ring.

Rnd 1 (Right side)**:** Ch 3 **(counts as first dc, now
and throughout)**, 23 dc in ring; join with slip st to first
dc: 24 dc.

Rnd 2: Ch 1, sc in same st, ch 2, skip next dc, ★ sc in
next dc, ch 2, skip next dc; repeat from ★ around; join
with slip st to first sc: 12 ch-2 sps.

Rnd 3: (Slip st, ch 1, sc) in first ch-2 sp, work
FP Cluster around first skipped dc one rnd **below** same
ch-2, ★ sc in same sp as last sc made and in next
ch-2 sp, work FP Cluster around next skipped dc
one rnd **below** same ch-2; repeat from ★ around, sc in
same sp as last sc made; join with slip st to first sc:
12 FP Clusters and 24 sc.

Rnd 4: (Slip st, ch 1, sc) in next FP Cluster, ch 4, skip
next 2 sc, ★ sc in next FP Cluster, ch 4, skip next 2 sts;
repeat from ★ around; join with slip st to first sc:
12 ch-4 sps.

Rnd 5: (Slip st, work Beginning Popcorn) in first
ch-4 sp, ch 5, (sc in next ch-4 sp, ch 5) twice, ★ work
Popcorn in next ch-4 sp, ch 5, (sc in next ch-4 sp, ch 5)
twice; repeat from ★ 2 times **more**; join with slip st to
top of Beginning Popcorn: 4 Popcorns and 12 ch-5 sps.

Rnd 6: (Slip st, ch 1, 2 sc) in first ch-5 sp, dc in next
ch-5 sp, (ch 1, dc in same sp) 6 times, 2 sc in next
ch-5 sp, ch 7, ★ 2 sc in next ch-5 sp, dc in next ch-5 sp,
(ch 1, dc in same sp) 6 times, 2 sc in next ch-5 sp, ch 7;
repeat from ★ 2 times **more**; join with slip st to first sc:
28 sps.

Rnd 7: Slip st in next 2 sts and in next ch-1 sp, ch 1,
sc in same sp, (ch 3, sc in next ch-1 sp) 5 times, work
Cluster in next ch-7 sp, (ch 2, work Cluster in same
sp) 4 times, ★ sc in next ch-1 sp, (ch 3, sc in next
ch-1 sp) 5 times, work Cluster in next ch-7 sp, (ch 2,
work Cluster in same sp) 4 times; repeat from ★ 2 times
more; join with slip st to first sc: 36 sps.

Rnd 8: (Slip st, ch 1, sc) in first ch-3 sp, (ch 3, sc in
next ch-3 sp) 4 times, (sc, ch 3, sc) in next 4 ch-2 sps,
★ sc in next ch-3 sp, (ch 3, sc in next ch-3 sp) 4 times,
(sc, ch 3, sc) in next 4 ch-2 sps; repeat from ★ 2 times
more; join with slip st to first sc: 32 ch-3 sps.

Rnd 9: (Slip st, ch 1, sc) in first ch-3 sp, ★ ch 4, (sc in
next ch-3 sp, ch 4) twice, sc in next 2 ch-3 sps; repeat
from ★ around to last 3 ch-3 sps, (ch 4, sc in next
ch-3 sp) 3 times; join with slip st to first sc: 24 ch-4 sps.

Rnd 10: (Slip st, ch 3, 3 dc) in first ch-4 sp, 4 dc in each of next 3 ch-4 sps, (4 dc, ch 2, 4 dc) in next ch-4 sp, ★ 4 dc in each of next 5 ch-4 sps, (4 dc, ch 2, 4 dc) in next ch-4 sp; repeat from ★ 2 times **more**, 4 dc in last ch-4 sp; join with slip st to first dc: 28 4-dc groups and 4 ch-2 sps.

Rnd 11: Ch 3, dc in next dc, work Split FPtr, (working **behind** Split FPtr just made, dc in next 4 dc, work Split FPtr) 4 times, working **behind** Split FPtr just made, dc in next 2 dc, 4 dc in next ch-2 sp, dc in next 2 dc, work Split FPtr, ★ (working **behind** Split FPtr just made, dc in next 4 dc, work Split FPtr) 6 times, working **behind** Split FPtr just made, dc in next 2 dc, 4 dc in next ch-2 sp, dc in next 2 dc, work Split FPtr; repeat from ★ 2 times **more**, working **behind** Split FPtr just made, dc in next 4 dc, work Split FPtr, working **behind** Split FPtr just made, dc in last 2 dc; join with slip st to first dc: 28 Split FPtr and 128 dc.

Rnd 12: Ch 1, sc in same st and in next dc, (skip next Split FPtr, sc in next 4 dc) 4 times, ★ † skip next Split FPtr, sc in next 3 dc, 2 sc in next dc, work Split FPtr, working **behind** Split FPtr, 2 sc in next dc, sc in next 3 dc †, (skip next Split FPtr, sc in next 4 dc) 6 times; repeat from ★ 2 times **more**, then repeat from † to † once, skip next Split FPtr, sc in next 4 dc, skip next Split FPtr, sc in last 2 dc; join with slip st to first sc: 136 sc and 4 Split FPtr.

Rnd 13: Ch 1, sc in same st, (ch 3, skip next sc, sc in next sc) twice, ch 6, skip next 2 sc, (sc in next sc, ch 3, skip next sc) twice, sc in next 11 sc, ch 3, skip next sc, (sc, ch 3) twice in next Split FPtr, ★ skip next sc, sc in next 11 sc, (ch 3, skip next sc, sc in next sc) twice, ch 6, skip next 2 sc, (sc in next sc, ch 3, skip next sc) twice, sc in next 11 sc, ch 3, skip next sc, (sc, ch 3) twice in next Split FPtr; repeat from ★ 2 times **more**, skip next sc, sc in last 10 sc; join with slip st to first sc: 112 sc and 32 sps.

Rnd 14: Ch 1, sc in same st and in next ch-3 sp, ★ † work Picot, sc in next ch-3 sp, dc in next ch-6 sp, (work Picot, dc in same sp) 3 times, sc in next ch-3 sp, work Picot, sc in next ch-3 sp and in next sc, work Picot, skip next sc, sc in next 9 sc and in next ch-3 sp, work Picot, (sc, work Picot) twice in next ch-3 sp, sc in next ch-3 sp and in next 9 sc, work Picot, skip next sc †, sc in next sc and in next ch-3 sp; repeat from ★ 2 times **more**, then repeat from † to † once; join with slip st to first sc, finish off.

See Washing and Blocking, page 144.

Finished Size: 5" diameter

MATERIALS
Bedspread Weight Cotton Thread (size 10): 50 yards
Steel crochet hook, size 7 (1.65 mm) **or** size
needed for gauge

GAUGE SWATCH: 1¹/₂" diameter
Work same as Doily through Rnd 3.

STITCH GUIDE

TREBLE CROCHET *(abbreviated tr)*
YO twice, insert hook in st indicated, YO and pull up a loop (4 loops on hook), (YO and draw through 2 loops on hook) 3 times.

BEGINNING CLUSTER (uses next 2 sc)
Ch 2, ★ YO, insert hook in **next** sc, YO and pull up a loop, YO and draw through 2 loops on hook; repeat from ★ once **more**, YO and draw through all 3 loops on hook.

CLUSTER (uses next 3 sc)
★ YO, insert hook in **next** sc, YO and pull up a loop, YO and draw through 2 loops on hook; repeat from ★ 2 times **more**, YO and draw through all 4 loops on hook.

SPLIT FRONT POST TREBLE CROCHET
(abbreviated Split FPtr)
First Leg: YO twice, insert hook from **front** to **back** around post of same dc as Second Leg of last Split FPtr *(Fig. 7, page 144)*, YO and pull up a loop, (YO and draw through 2 loops on hook) twice (2 loops remaining on hook).

Second Leg: YO twice, skip next 2 dc, insert hook from **front** to **back** around post of next dc, YO and pull up a loop, (YO and draw through 2 loops on hook) twice, YO and draw through all 3 loops on hook.

SPLIT TREBLE CROCHET
(abbreviated Split tr)
First Leg: YO twice, insert hook from **top** to **bottom** in center 3 loops of same Split FPtr as Second Leg of last Split tr *(Fig. 3a, page 144)*, YO and pull up a loop, (YO and draw through 2 loops on hook) twice (2 loops remaining on hook).

Second Leg: YO twice, insert hook from **bottom** to **top** in center 3 loops of next Split FPtr *(Fig. 3b, page 144)*, YO and pull up a loop, (YO and draw through 2 loops on hook) twice, YO and draw through all 3 loops on hook.

Continued on page 100.

DOILY

Ch 10; join with slip st to form a ring.

Rnd 1 (Right side)**:** Ch 3 **(counts as first dc, now and throughout)**, 29 dc in ring; join with slip st to first dc: 30 dc.

Rnd 2: Ch 1, sc in same st, tr in next dc pulling tr to right side **now and throughout**, (sc in next dc, tr in next dc) around; join with slip st to first sc.

Rnd 3: Ch 1, sc in same st, 2 sc in next tr, (sc in next sc, 2 sc in next tr) around; join with slip st to first sc: 45 sc.

Rnd 4: Work Beginning Cluster, ch 4, (work Cluster, ch 4) around; join with slip st to top of Beginning Cluster: 15 ch-4 sps.

Rnd 5: Ch 3, 4 dc in next ch-4 sp, (dc in next Cluster, 4 dc in next ch-4 sp) around; join with slip st to first dc: 75 dc.

Rnd 6: Ch 3, dc in next 2 dc, YO twice, insert hook from **front** to **back** around post of first dc on Rnd 5 *(Fig. 7, page 144)*, YO and pull up a loop, (YO and draw through 2 loops on hook) twice (2 loops remaining on hook), work Second Leg of Split FPtr **(first Split FPtr made)**, working **behind** Second Leg of Split FPtr, dc in next 5 dc, ★ work Split FPtr, working **behind** Second Leg of Split FPtr, dc in next 5 dc; repeat from ★ 12 times **more**, work First Leg of Split FPtr, YO twice, skip last 2 dc, insert hook from **front** to **back** around post of first dc **above** First Leg of first Split FPtr, YO and pull up a loop, (YO and draw through 2 loops on hook) twice, YO and draw through all 3 loops on hook **(last Split FPtr made)**, working **behind** Second Leg of last Split FPtr, dc in last 2 dc; join with slip st to first dc: 75 dc and 15 Split FPtr.

Rnd 7: Ch 3, YO twice, working in **front** of dc just made, insert hook from **top** to **bottom** in center 3 loops of last Split FPtr made on Rnd 6 *(Fig. 3a, page 144)*, YO and pull up a loop, (YO and draw through 2 loops on hook) twice (2 loops remaining on hook), work Second Leg of Split tr **(first Split tr made)**, working **behind** Second Leg of Split tr, dc in same dc as last dc made and in next 2 dc, skip next Split FPtr, dc in next 3 dc, ★ work Split tr, working **behind** Second Leg of Split tr, dc in same dc as last dc made and in next 2 dc, skip next Split FPtr, dc in next 3 dc; repeat from ★ 12 times **more**, work First Leg of Split tr, YO twice, insert hook from **bottom** to **top** in center 3 loops of same Split FPtr as First Leg of first Split tr, YO and pull up a loop, (YO and draw through 2 loops on hook) twice, YO and draw through all 3 loops on hook **(last Split tr made)**, working **behind** Second Leg of last Split tr, dc in same dc as last dc made and in next 2 dc, skip next Split FPtr, working **behind** First Leg of first Split tr, dc in last 2 dc; join with slip st to first dc: 90 dc and 15 Split tr.

Rnd 8: Ch 1, sc in same st and in center 3 loops of next Split tr, (sc in next 6 dc and in center 3 loops of next Split tr) around to last 5 dc, sc in last 5 dc; join with slip st to first sc: 105 sc.

Rnd 9: Ch 1, sc in same st, 2 sc in next sc, (sc in next 6 sc, 2 sc in next sc) around to last 5 sc, sc in last 5 sc; join with slip st to first sc: 120 sc.

Rnd 10: Ch 1, sc in same st, tr in next sc, (sc in next sc, tr in next sc) around; join with slip st to first sc.

Rnd 11: Ch 1, sc in same st, ch 2, slip st in top of sc just made *(Fig. 6a, page 144)*, ★ sc in next 2 sts, ch 2, slip st in top of last sc made; repeat from ★ around to last tr, sc in last tr; join with slip st to first sc, finish off.

See Washing and Blocking, page 144.

66 ▬

Finished Size: 6¹/₄" diameter

MATERIALS
Bedspread Weight Cotton Thread (size 10): 75 yards
Steel crochet hook, size 7 (1.65 mm) **or** size needed for gauge

GAUGE SWATCH: 1³/₄" diameter
Work same as Doily through Rnd 9.

STITCH GUIDE

DC CLUSTER (uses one ch-2 sp)
★ YO, insert hook in ch-2 sp indicated, YO and pull up a loop, YO and draw through 2 loops on hook; repeat from ★ once **more**, YO and draw through all 3 loops on hook.

TR CLUSTER (uses one ch-7 sp)
★ YO twice, insert hook in ch-7 sp indicated, YO and pull up a loop, (YO and draw through 2 loops on hook) twice; repeat from ★ 2 times **more**, YO and draw through all 4 loops on hook.

POPCORN
4 Dc in ch-2 sp indicated, drop loop from hook, insert hook in first dc of 4-dc group, hook dropped loop and draw through.

PICOT
Ch 3, slip st in third ch from hook, ch 1.

DOILY

Rnd 1 (Right side)**:** Ch 2, 6 sc in second ch from hook; join with slip st to first sc.

Note: Loop a short piece of thread around any stitch to mark Rnd 1 as **right** side.

Rnd 2: Ch 1, 2 sc in same st and in each sc around; join with slip st to first sc: 12 sc.

Rnd 3: Ch 1, sc in same st, 2 sc in next sc, (sc in next sc, 2 sc in next sc) around; join with slip st to first sc: 18 sc.

Rnd 4: Ch 1, sc in same st and in next sc, 2 sc in next sc, (sc in next 2 sc, 2 sc in next sc) around; join with slip st to first sc: 24 sc.

Rnd 5: Ch 1, sc in same st and in next 2 sc, 2 sc in next sc, (sc in next 3 sc, 2 sc in next sc) around; join with slip st to first sc: 30 sc.

Rnd 6: Ch 1, sc in same st and in next 3 sc, 2 sc in next sc, (sc in next 4 sc, 2 sc in next sc) around; join with slip st to first sc: 36 sc.

Rnd 7: Ch 1, sc in same st and in next 4 sc, 2 sc in next sc, (sc in next 5 sc, 2 sc in next sc) around; join with slip st to first sc: 42 sc.

Rnd 8: Ch 1, sc in same st and in next sc, 2 sc in next sc, (sc in next 2 sc, 2 sc in next sc) around; join with slip st to first sc: 56 sc.

Rnd 9: Ch 1, sc in same st and in next 12 sc, 2 sc in next sc, (sc in next 13 sc, 2 sc in next sc) around; join with slip st to Back Loop Only of first sc *(Fig. 1, page 143)*: 60 sc.

Rnd 10: Ch 1, sc in Back Loop Only of same st and each sc around; join with slip st to **both** loops of first sc.

Rnd 11: Ch 1, sc in same st and in each sc around; join with slip st to first sc.

Rnd 12: Ch 5 **(counts as first dc plus ch 2, now and throughout)**, dc in same st, skip next 2 sc, ★ (dc, ch 2, dc) in next sc, skip next 2 sc; repeat from ★ around; join with slip st to first dc: 20 ch-2 sps.

Rnd 13: Slip st in first ch-2 sp, ch 5, dc in same sp, work dc Cluster in next ch-2 sp, (ch 2, work dc Cluster in same sp) twice, ★ (dc, ch 2, dc) in next ch-2 sp, work dc Cluster in next ch-2 sp, (ch 2, work dc Cluster in same sp) twice; repeat from ★ around; join with slip st to first dc: 30 ch-2 sps.

Rnd 14: Slip st in first ch-2 sp, ch 5, dc in same sp, work (dc Cluster, ch 2, dc Cluster) in next 2 ch-2 sps, ★ (dc, ch 2, dc) in next ch-2 sp, work (dc Cluster, ch 2, dc Cluster) in next 2 ch-2 sps; repeat from ★ around; join with slip st to first dc.

Rnd 15: Slip st in first ch-2 sp, ch 5, dc in same sp, (work Popcorn, ch 5, dc) in next ch-2 sp, (dc, ch 5, work Popcorn) in next ch-2 sp, ★ (dc, ch 2, dc) in next ch-2 sp, (work Popcorn, ch 5, dc) in next ch-2 sp, (dc, ch 5, work Popcorn) in next ch-2 sp; repeat from ★ around; join with slip st to first dc.

Rnd 16: Slip st in first ch-2 sp, ch 5, dc in same sp, 3 sc in next ch-5 sp, ch 7, 3 sc in next ch-5 sp, ★ (dc, ch 2, dc) in next ch-2 sp, 3 sc in next ch-5 sp, ch 7, 3 sc in next ch-5 sp; repeat from ★ around; join with slip st to first dc: 20 sps.

Rnd 17: Slip st in first ch-2 sp, ch 5, dc in same sp, work tr Cluster in next ch-7 sp, (ch 3, work tr Cluster in same sp) 4 times, ★ (dc, ch 2, dc) in next ch-2 sp, work tr Cluster in next ch-7 sp, (ch 3, work tr Cluster in same sp) 4 times; repeat from ★ around; join with slip st to first dc: 50 sps.

Rnd 18: Slip st in first ch-2 sp, ch 1, 2 sc in same sp, (2 sc, work Picot, 2 sc) in next 4 ch-3 sps, ★ 2 sc in next ch-2 sp, (2 sc, work Picot, 2 sc) in next 4 ch-3 sps; repeat from ★ around; join with slip st to first sc, finish off.

Rnd 19: With **right** side facing and working in free loops on Rnd 9 *(Fig. 2a, page 144)*, join thread with sc in first sc *(see Joining With Sc, page 143)*; work Picot, skip next 2 sc, ★ sc in next sc, work Picot, skip next 2 sc; repeat from ★ around; join with slip st to first sc, finish off.

See Washing and Blocking, page 144.

Finished Size: 6$^1/_4$" diameter

MATERIALS

Bedspread Weight Cotton Thread (size 10): 55 yards
Steel crochet hook, size 7 (1.65 mm) **or** size
   needed for gauge

GAUGE SWATCH: 1$^1/_4$" in diameter
Work same as Doily through Rnd 2.

STITCH GUIDE

FRONT POST TREBLE CROCHET
   (abbreviated FPtr)
YO twice, insert hook from **front** to **back** around
post of dc indicated *(Fig. 7, page 144)*, YO and
pull up a loop (4 loops on hook), (YO and draw
through 2 loops on hook) 3 times.

FRONT POST CLUSTER
   (abbreviated FP Cluster)
★ YO twice, insert hook from **front** to **back** around
post of dc indicated *(Fig. 7, page 144)*, YO and
pull up a loop, (YO and draw through 2 loops on
hook) twice; repeat from ★ once **more**, YO and
draw through all 3 loops on hook.

PICOT
Ch 3, slip st in third ch from hook, ch 1.

DOILY

Ch 7; join with slip st to form a ring.

Rnd 1 (Right side)**:** Ch 3 **(counts as first dc, now
and throughout)**, 23 dc in ring; join with slip st to first
dc: 24 dc.

Rnd 2: Ch 1, sc in same st, ch 2, skip next dc, ★ sc in
next dc, ch 2, skip next dc; repeat from ★ around; join
with slip st to first sc: 12 ch-2 sps.

Rnd 3: (Slip st, ch 1, 2 sc) in first ch-2 sp, (ch 3, 2 sc in
next ch-2 sp) around, ch 1, hdc in first sc to form
last ch-3 sp.

Rnd 4: Ch 1, sc in last ch-3 sp made, 7 dc in next
ch-3 sp, (sc in next ch-3 sp, 7 dc in next ch-3 sp)
around; join with slip st to first sc: 48 sts.

Rnd 5: Ch 1, sc in same st, ★ ch 3, skip next dc, sc in
next st; repeat from ★ around to last dc, skip last dc, dc
in first sc to form last ch-3 sp: 24 ch-3 sps.

Rnd 6: Ch 1, sc in last ch-3 sp made, work FP Cluster
around skipped dc one rnd **below** same ch-3, sc in
same sp on Rnd 5 as last sc made and in next ch-3 sp,
work FP Cluster around skipped dc one rnd **below** same
ch-3, sc in same sp on Rnd 5 as last sc made, ★ ch 2,
(sc in next ch-3 sp, work FP Cluster around skipped dc
one rnd **below** same ch-3, sc in same sp on Rnd 5 as
last sc made, ch 2) twice, (sc in next ch-3 sp, work
FP Cluster around skipped dc one rnd **below** same
ch-3, sc in same sp on Rnd 5 as last sc made) twice;
repeat from ★ around to last 2 ch-3 sps, (ch 2, sc in
next ch-3 sp, work FP Cluster around skipped dc
one rnd **below** same ch-3, sc in same sp on Rnd 5 as
last sc made) twice, ch 1, sc in first sc to form last
ch-2 sp: 18 ch-2 sps.

Rnd 7: Ch 1, sc in last ch-2 sp made, (ch 6, sc in next
ch-2 sp) around, ch 3, dc in first sc to form last ch-6 sp.

Rnd 8: Ch 1, sc in last ch-6 sp made, ch 3, (sc, ch 3)
twice in next ch-6 sp and in each ch-6 sp around, sc in
same sp as first sc, ch 1, hdc in first sc to form last
ch-3 sp: 36 ch-3 sps.

Rnd 9: Ch 1, sc in last ch-3 sp made, (ch 3, sc in next
ch-3 sp) around, ch 1, hdc in first sc to form
last ch-3 sp.

Rnd 10: Ch 1, sc in last ch-3 sp made, ch 4, (sc in
next ch-3 sp, ch 4) around; join with slip st to first sc.

Rnd 11: (Slip st, ch 3, 3 dc) in first ch-4 sp, place
marker around last dc made for st placement, 4 dc in
each ch-4 sp around; join with slip st to first dc: 144 dc.

Rnd 12: Ch 1, sc in same st, work FPtr around marked
dc, skip next dc from last sc made, ★ sc in next dc, skip
next dc from last FPtr made, work FPtr around next dc,
skip next dc from last sc made; repeat from ★ around;
join with slip st to first sc.

Rnd 13: Ch 1, sc in same st, work Picot, skip next
2 sts, ★ sc in next st, work Picot, skip next 2 sts; repeat
from ★ around; join with slip st to first sc, finish off.

See Washing and Blocking, page 144.

Finished Size: $6^1/_2$" diameter

MATERIALS

Bedspread Weight Cotton Thread (size 10): 68 yards
Steel crochet hook, size 7 (1.65 mm) **or** size
   needed for gauge

GAUGE SWATCH: 2" diameter
Work same as Doily through Rnd 4.

STITCH GUIDE

BACK POST SINGLE CROCHET
   (abbreviated BPsc)
Insert hook from **back** to **front** around post of dc
indicated *(Fig. 7, page 144)*, YO and pull up a
loop, YO and draw through both loops on hook.

FRONT POST CLUSTER
   (abbreviated FP Cluster)
★ YO twice, insert hook from **front** to **back** around
post of dc indicated *(Fig. 7, page 144)*, YO and
pull up a loop, (YO and draw through 2 loops on
hook) twice; repeat from ★ once **more**, YO and
draw through all 3 loops on hook.

BEGINNING CLUSTER
Ch 2, ★ YO, insert hook in ch-4 sp indicated, YO
and pull up a loop, YO and draw through 2 loops
on hook; repeat from ★ 2 times **more**, YO and
draw through all 4 loops on hook.

CLUSTER (uses one ch-4 sp)
★ YO, insert hook in ch-4 sp indicated, YO and pull
up a loop, YO and draw through 2 loops on hook;
repeat from ★ 3 times **more**, YO and draw through
all 5 loops on hook.

SPLIT DOUBLE CROCHET
   (abbreviated Split dc)
First Leg: YO, insert hook from **top** to **bottom** in
free loop of sc indicated *(Fig. 2a, page 144)*, YO
and pull up a loop, YO and draw through 2 loops
on hook (2 loops remaining on hook).

Second Leg: YO, insert hook from **bottom** to
top in free loop of sc indicated, YO and pull up a
loop, YO and draw through 2 loops on hook, YO
and draw through all 3 loops on hook.

PICOT
Ch 3, slip st in third ch from hook, ch 1.

DOILY

Rnd 1 (Right side)**:** Ch 4, 15 dc in fourth ch from
hook; join with slip st to top of beginning ch-4: 16 sts.

Rnd 2: Ch 3 **(counts as first dc)**, dc in same st, 2 dc
in next dc and in each dc around; join with slip st to first
dc: 32 dc.

Rnd 3: Ch 1, sc in same st, work FP Cluster around dc
one rnd **below** next dc, ★ working **behind** FP Cluster,
sc in next 2 dc on Rnd 2, work FP Cluster around next
dc on Rnd 1; repeat from ★ around to last dc on Rnd 2,
working **behind** last FP Cluster made, sc in last dc; join
with slip st to first sc: 16 FP Clusters and 32 sc.

Rnd 4: Ch 1, sc in same st and in next 2 sts, ch 2,
slip st in top of last sc made *(Fig. 6a, page 144)*, ★ sc
in next 3 sts, ch 2, slip st in top of last sc made; repeat
from ★ around; join with slip st to first sc: 48 sc.

Rnd 5: (Slip st, ch 1, sc) in next sc, ch 5, ★ skip next
2 sc, sc in next sc, ch 5; repeat from ★ around; join
with slip st to first sc: 16 ch-5 sps.

Rnd 6: (Slip st, ch 1, sc) in first ch-5 sp, (ch 2, sc in
same sp) twice, ★ sc in next ch-5 sp, (ch 2, sc in same
sp) twice; repeat from ★ around; join with slip st to first
sc: 32 ch-2 sps.

Rnd 7: (Slip st, ch 1, sc) in first ch-2 sp, (ch 3, sc in
next ch-2 sp) around, ch 1, hdc in first sc to form
last ch-3 sp.

Rnd 8: Ch 1, sc in last ch-3 sp made, (ch 4, sc in next
ch-3 sp) around, ch 1, dc in first sc to form last ch-4 sp;
do **not** finish off.

Continued on page 104.

Rnd 9: Work Beginning Cluster in last ch-4 sp made, ch 4, (work Cluster in next ch-4 sp, ch 4) around; join with slip st to top of Beginning Cluster.

Rnd 10: (Slip st, ch 1, sc) in first ch-4 sp, place marker around sc just made for st placement, 3 sc in same sp, 4 sc in each ch-4 sp around; join with slip st to Back Loop Only of first sc *(Fig. 1, page 143)*: 128 sc.

Rnd 11: Ch 1, sc in Back Loop Only of same st and each sc around; join with slip st to **both** loops of first sc.

Rnd 12: Ch 1, working in both loops, sc in same st and in each sc around; join with slip st to first sc.

Rnd 13: Ch 1, sc in same st and in next sc, work First Leg of Split dc in free loop of marked sc on Rnd 10, skip next 2 sc, work Second Leg of Split dc in next sc, ★ working **behind** Split dc, sc in next 4 sc on Rnd 12, work First Leg of Split dc in next sc on Rnd 10, skip next 2 sc, work Second Leg of Split dc in next sc; repeat from ★ around to last 2 sc on Rnd 12, working **behind** last Split dc made, sc in last 2 sc; join with slip st to first sc: 160 sts.

Rnd 14: Ch 1, sc in same st and in each st around; join with slip st to first sc.

Rnd 15: Ch 1, sc in same st, skip next 3 sc, dc in next sc, (ch 1, dc in same st) 4 times, skip next 3 sc, ★ sc in next sc, skip next 3 sc, dc in next sc, (ch 1, dc in same st) 4 times, skip next 3 sc; repeat from ★ around; join with slip st to first sc: 120 sts.

Rnd 16: Ch 1, (work BPsc around next dc, work Picot) 4 times, work BPsc around each of next 2 dc, ★ work Picot, (work BPsc around next dc, work Picot) 3 times, work BPsc around each of next 2 dc; repeat from ★ around to last 4 dc, (work Picot, work BPsc around next dc) 4 times; join with slip st to first BPsc, finish off.

See Washing and Blocking, page 144.

69 ▬▬▬▬

Finished Size: 9" x 5"

MATERIALS
Bedspread Weight Cotton Thread (size 10): 75 yards
Steel crochet hook, size 7 (1.65 mm) **or** size needed for gauge

GAUGE SWATCH: 2" in diameter
Work same as Doily through Rnd 3 of Center.

STITCH GUIDE

2-DC CLUSTER (uses one sp)
★ YO, insert hook in sp indicated, YO and pull up a loop, YO and draw through 2 loops on hook; repeat from ★ once **more**, YO and draw through all 3 loops on hook.

3-DC CLUSTER (uses one sp)
★ YO, insert hook in sp indicated, YO and pull up a loop, YO and draw through 2 loops on hook; repeat from ★ 2 times **more**, YO and draw through all 4 loops on hook.

BACK POST SINGLE CROCHET
(abbreviated BPsc)
Insert hook from **back** to **front** around post of st indicated *(Fig. 7, page 177)*, YO and pull up a loop, YO and draw through both loops on hook.

PICOT
Ch 3, slip st in third ch from hook, ch 1.

DOILY
CENTER
Ch 7; join with slip st to form a ring.

Rnd 1 (Right side)**:** Ch 2, work 2-dc Cluster in ring, ch 2, (work 3-dc Cluster in ring, ch 2) 9 times; join with slip st to top of first 2-dc Cluster: 10 Clusters and 10 ch-2 sps.

Note: Loop a short piece of thread around any stitch to mark Rnd 1 as **right** side.

Rnd 2: Slip st in first ch-2 sp, ch 1, (sc, ch 3, sc) in same sp and in each ch-2 sp around; join with slip st to first sc.

Rnd 3: (Slip st, ch 1, sc) in first ch-3 sp, ch 4, (sc in next ch-3 sp, ch 4) around; join with slip st to first sc.

Doily will ruffle until Rnd 6 is completed.

Rnd 4: Slip st in first ch-4 sp, ch 5, slip st in third ch from hook, ch 1, [dc in same sp, ch 2, slip st in top of last dc made *(Fig. 6a, page 144)*, ch 1] 3 times, ★ dc in next ch-4 sp, ch 2, slip st in top of last dc made, ch 1, (dc in same sp, ch 2, slip st in top of last dc made, ch 1) 3 times; repeat from ★ around; join with slip st to same ch as first slip st: 40 dc.

Rnd 5: Ch 1, work BPsc around same st, ch 2, (work BPsc around next dc, ch 2) around; join with slip st to first BPsc: 40 ch-2 sps.

Rnd 6: (Slip st, ch 2, dc) in first ch-2 sp, ch 2, (work 2-dc Cluster in next ch-2 sp, ch 2) around; join with slip st to first dc.

Rnd 7: (Slip st, ch 1, sc) in first ch-2 sp, ch 3, (sc in next ch-2 sp, ch 3) around; join with slip st to first sc, do **not** finish off.

FIRST POINT

Row 1: Slip st in first ch-3 sp, ch 1, 2 sc in same sp and in each of next 4 ch-3 sps, 3 sc in next ch-3 sp, 2 sc in each of next 5 ch-3 sps, leave remaining sps unworked: 23 sc.

Row 2: Ch 1, **turn**; sc in first 4 sc, ch 3, skip next sc, ★ sc in next sc, ch 3, skip next sc; repeat from ★ 6 times **more**, sc in last 4 sc: 15 sc and 8 ch-3 sps.

Rows 3 and 4: Turn; slip st in first 3 sc, ch 1, sc in same st and in next sc, 2 sc in next ch-3 sp, ch 3, (sc in next ch-3 sp, ch 3) across to last ch-3 sp, 2 sc in last ch-3 sp, sc in next 2 sc, leave remaining 2 sc unworked: 13 sc and 6 ch-3 sps.

Row 5: Turn; slip st in first 3 sc, ch 1, sc in same st and in next sc, 2 sc in next ch-3 sp, (ch 3, sc in next ch-3 sp) twice, 3 dc in next sc, (sc in next ch-3 sp, ch 3) twice, 2 sc in next ch-3 sp, sc in next 2 sc, leave remaining 2 sc unworked: 15 sts and 4 ch-3 sps.

Row 6: Turn; slip st in first 3 sc, ch 1, sc in same st and in next sc, 2 sc in next ch-3 sp, ch 3, sc in next ch-3 sp, ch 3, skip next 2 sts, sc in next dc, ch 3, sc in next ch-3 sp, ch 3, 2 sc in next ch-3 sp, sc in next 2 sc, leave remaining 2 sc unworked: 11 sc and 4 ch-3 sps.

Row 7: Turn; slip st in first 3 sc, ch 1, sc in same st and in next sc, 2 sc in next ch-3 sp, ch 3, (sc in next ch-3 sp, ch 3) twice, 2 sc in next ch-3 sp, sc in next 2 sc, leave remaining 2 sc unworked: 10 sc and 3 ch-3 sps.

Row 8: Turn; slip st in first 3 sc, ch 1, sc in same st and in next sc, 2 sc in next ch-3 sp, ch 3, sc in next ch-3 sp, ch 3, 2 sc in next ch-3 sp, sc in next 2 sc, leave remaining 2 sc unworked: 9 sc and 2 ch-3 sps.

Row 9: Turn; slip st in first 3 sc, ch 1, sc in same st and in next sc, 2 sc in next ch-3 sp, ch 3, 2 sc in next ch-3 sp, sc in next 2 sc, leave remaining 2 sc unworked: 8 sc and one ch-3 sp.

Row 10: Turn; slip st in first 3 sc, ch 1, sc in same st and in next sc, 3 sc in next ch-3 sp, sc in next 2 sc, leave remaining 2 sc unworked; finish off: 7 sc.

SECOND POINT

Row 1: With **right** side facing, skip next 9 ch-3 sps from First Point, join thread with sc in next ch-3 sp *(see Joining With Sc, page 143)*; sc in same sp, 2 sc in each of next 4 ch-3 sps, 3 sc in next ch-3 sp, 2 sc in each of next 5 ch-2 sps, leave remaining sps unworked: 23 sc.

Rows 2-10: Work same as First Point; at end of Row 10, do **not** finish off: 7 sc.

EDGING

Rnd 1: Ch 1, turn; sc in first sc, † skip next 2 sc, dc in next sc, (ch 1, dc in same st) 5 times, skip next 2 sc, sc in next sc, ch 3, (sc in end of next row, ch 3) 8 times, skip next row, sc in next unworked ch-3 sp on Center, (5 dc in next ch-3 sp, sc in next ch-3 sp) 4 times, ch 3, skip first row on Point, (sc in end of next row, ch 3) 8 times †, sc in first sc on last row, repeat from † to † once; join with slip st to first sc: 98 sts and 46 sps.

Rnd 2: Ch 1, do **not** turn; ★ work BPsc around next dc, (work Picot, work BPsc around next dc) twice, ch 4, slip st in third ch from hook, ch 2, work BPsc around next dc, (work Picot, work BPsc around next dc) twice, 2 sc in next ch-3 sp, (work Picot, 2 sc in next ch-3 sp) 8 times, [skip next sc, sc in next dc, work Picot, skip next dc, (sc, ch 4, slip st in top of sc just made, sc) in next dc, work Picot, skip next dc, sc in next dc] 4 times, 2 sc in next ch-3 sp, (work Picot, 2 sc in next ch-3 sp) 8 times, skip next sc; repeat from ★ once **more**; join with slip st to first BPsc, finish off.

See Washing and Blocking, page 144.

Finished Size: 7" square

MATERIALS

Bedspread Weight Cotton Thread (size 10): 79 yards
Steel crochet hook, size 7 (1.65 mm) **or** size
  needed for gauge

GAUGE SWATCH: 2" diameter
Work same as Doily through Rnd 3.

STITCH GUIDE

BACK POST SINGLE CROCHET
(abbreviated BPsc)
Insert hook from **back** to **front** around post of dc
indicated *(Fig. 7, page 144)*, YO and pull up a
loop, YO and draw through both loops on hook.

BEGINNING POPCORN
Ch 3 **(counts as first dc)**, 2 dc in sp indicated,
drop loop from hook, insert hook in first dc of
3-dc group, hook dropped loop and draw through.

POPCORN
3 Dc in ch-2 sp indicated, drop loop from hook,
insert hook in first dc of 3-dc group, hook dropped
loop and draw through.

CLUSTER
★ YO, insert hook in dc indicated, YO and pull up a
loop, YO and draw through 2 loops on hook; repeat
from ★ once **more**, YO and draw through all
3 loops on hook.

PICOT
Ch 3, slip st in third ch from hook, ch 1.

DOILY

Ch 5; join with slip st to form a ring.

Rnd 1 (Right side)**:** Ch 4 **(counts as first dc plus
ch 1)**, (dc in ring, ch 1) 15 times; join with slip st to first
dc: 16 dc and 16 ch-1 sps.

Rnd 2: Ch 1, work BPsc around same st, ch 2, (work
BPsc around next dc, ch 2) around; join with slip st to
first BPsc.

Rnd 3: (Slip st, work Beginning Popcorn) in first
ch-2 sp, (ch 3, work Popcorn in next ch-2 sp) 3 times,
ch 5, ★ work Popcorn in next ch-2 sp, (ch 3, work
Popcorn in next ch-2 sp) 3 times, ch 5; repeat from ★
2 times **more**; join with slip st to top of Beginning
Popcorn: 16 sps.

Rnd 4: Slip st in first ch-3 sp, ch 1, 2 sc in same sp
and in next 2 ch-3 sps, ch 3, (sc, ch 3) twice in next
ch-5 sp, ★ 2 sc in each of 3 ch-3 sps, ch 3, (sc, ch 3)
twice in next ch-5 sp; repeat from ★ 2 times **more**; join
with slip st to first sc: 32 sc and 12 ch-3 sps.

Rnd 5: Ch 1, sc in same st and in next 5 sc, ch 3, sc in
next ch-3 sp, 7 dc in next ch-3 sp, sc in next ch-3 sp,
ch 3, ★ sc in next 6 sc, ch 3, sc in next ch-3 sp, 7 dc in
next ch-3 sp, sc in next ch-3 sp, ch 3; repeat from ★
2 times **more**; join with slip st to first sc: 60 sts and
8 ch-3 sps.

Rnd 6: Slip st in next 2 sc, ch 1, sc in same st and in
next sc, ch 3, sc in next ch-3 sp, skip next sc, work
Cluster in next dc, (ch 2, work Cluster in next dc) 6
times, sc in next ch-3 sp, ★ ch 3, skip next 2 sc, sc in
next 2 sc, ch 3, sc in next ch-3 sp, skip next sc, work
Cluster in next dc, (ch 2, work Cluster in next dc) 6
times, sc in next ch-3 sp; repeat from ★ 2 times **more**,
ch 1, hdc in first sc to form last ch-3 sp: 32 sps.

Rnd 7: Ch 1, sc in last ch-3 sp made, (ch 3, sc in next
sp) around, ch 1, hdc in first sc to form last ch-3 sp.

Rnd 8: Ch 1, sc in last ch-3 sp made, 5 dc in next
ch-3 sp, sc in next ch-3 sp, ★ (ch 4, sc in next
ch-3 sp) 6 times, 5 dc in next ch-3 sp, sc in next
ch-3 sp; repeat from ★ 2 times **more**, (ch 4, sc in next
ch-3 sp) 5 times, ch 1, dc in first sc to form last ch-4 sp:
20 dc and 24 ch-4 sps.

Rnd 9: Ch 1, (sc, ch 3, sc) in last ch-4 sp made, skip
next 2 sts, sc in next dc, ch 3, skip next dc, sc in next
dc, (sc, ch 3, sc) in next ch-4 sp, ★ (ch 3, sc) twice in
next 5 ch-4 sps, skip next 2 sts, sc in next dc, ch 3, skip
next dc, sc in next dc, (sc, ch 3, sc) in next ch-4 sp;
repeat from ★ 2 times **more**, (ch 3, sc) twice in next
4 ch-4 sps, ch 1, hdc in first sc to form last ch-3 sp:
48 ch-3 sps.

Rnd 10: Ch 1, sc in last ch-3 sp made, (ch 3, sc in
next ch-3 sp) around, ch 1, hdc in first sc to form
last ch-3 sp.

Rnd 11: Ch 1, sc in last ch-3 sp made, 2 sc in each of
next 4 ch-3 sps, sc in next ch-3 sp, ★ (ch 4, sc in next
ch-3 sp) 7 times, 2 sc in each of next 4 ch-3 sps, sc in
next ch-3 sp; repeat from ★ 2 times **more**, (ch 4, sc in
next ch-3 sp) 6 times, ch 2, hdc in first sc to form last
ch-4 sp: 64 sc and 28 ch-4 sps.

Rnd 12: Ch 1, 2 sc in last ch-4 sp made, ★ † sc in
next 10 sc, 2 sc in next ch-4 sp, dc in next ch-4 sp,
(ch 1, dc in same sp) 5 times, [sc in next ch-4 sp, dc in
next ch-4 sp, (ch 1, dc in same sp) 5 times] twice †, 2 sc
in next ch-4 sp; repeat from ★ 2 times **more**, then
repeat from † to † once; join with slip st to first sc:
136 sts and 60 ch-1 sps.

Rnd 13: Ch 1, sc in same st and in next 13 sc, ★ † (work Picot, sc in next ch-1 sp) 5 times, [skip next dc, slip st in next sc, sc in next ch-1 sp, (work Picot, sc in next ch-1 sp) 4 times] twice, work Picot, skip next dc †, sc in next 14 sc; repeat from ★ 2 times **more**, then repeat from † to † once; join with slip st to first sc, finish off.

See Washing and Blocking, page 144.

71 ▬▬▬

Finished Size: 6" x 8³/₄"

MATERIALS

Bedspread Weight Cotton Thread (size 10): 73 yards
Steel crochet hook, size 7 (1.65 mm) **or** size
    needed for gauge

GAUGE SWATCH: 1"w x 4¹/₂"h
Work same as Doily through Rnd 2.

STITCH GUIDE

CLUSTER (uses one ch-1 sp)
★ YO, insert hook in ch-1 sp indicated, YO and pull up a loop, YO and draw through 2 loops on hook; repeat from ★ 2 times **more**, YO and draw through all 4 loops on hook.

FRONT POST TREBLE CROCHET
    (abbreviated FPtr)
YO twice, insert hook from **front** to **back** around post of dc indicated *(Fig. 7, page 144)*, YO and pull up a loop (4 loops on hook), (YO and draw through 2 loops on hook) 3 times.

FRONT POST DOUBLE CROCHET CLUSTER
    (abbreviated FPdc Cluster)
★ YO, insert hook from **front** to **back** around post of FPtr indicated *(Fig. 7, page 144)*, YO and pull up a loop, YO and draw through 2 loops on hook; repeat from ★ 2 times **more**, YO and draw through all 4 loops on hook.

FRONT POST TREBLE CROCHET CLUSTER
    (abbreviated FPtr Cluster)
★ YO twice, insert hook from **front** to **back** around post of dc indicated *(Fig. 7, page 144)*, YO and pull up a loop, (YO and draw through 2 loops on hook) twice; repeat from ★ 2 times **more**, YO and draw through all 4 loops on hook.

POPCORN
4 Dc in ch-2 sp indicated, drop loop from hook, insert hook in first dc of 4-dc group, hook dropped loop and draw through.

PICOT
Ch 3, slip st in third ch from hook, ch 1.

DOILY
Ch 30.

Rnd 1 (Right side)**:** 6 Dc in fourth ch from hook **(3 skipped chs counts as first dc)**, dc in next ch and in each ch across to last ch, 7 dc in last ch; working in free loops of beginning ch *(Fig. 2b, page 144)*, dc in next 25 chs; join with slip st to first dc: 64 dc.

Rnd 2: Ch 1, sc in same st, ch 3, skip next dc, ★ sc in next dc, ch 3, skip next dc; repeat from ★ around; join with slip st to first sc: 32 sc and 32 ch-3 sps.

Rnd 3: (Slip st, ch 1, sc) in first ch-3 sp, work FPtr Cluster around skipped dc one rnd **below** same ch-3, sc in same sp on Rnd 2 as last sc made, ★ ch 3, sc in next ch-3 sp, work FPtr Cluster around skipped dc one rnd **below** same ch-3, sc in same sp on Rnd 2 as last sc made; repeat from ★ around, dc in first sc to form last ch-3 sp: 32 ch-3 sps.

Rnd 4: Ch 1, 2 sc in last ch-3 sp made, ch 3, 4 sc in next ch-3 sp, ch 4, 4 sc in next ch-3 sp, ch 3, 2 sc in each of next 14 ch-3 sps, ch 3, 4 sc in next ch-3 sp, ch 4, 4 sc in next ch-3 sp, ch 3, 2 sc in each of last 13 ch-3 sps; join with slip st to first sc: 72 sc and 6 sps.

Rnd 5: Ch 1, sc in same st and in next sc, 3 sc in next ch-3 sp, sc in next 4 sc, 5 sc in next ch-4 sp, sc in next 4 sc, 3 sc in next ch-3 sp, sc in each sc across to next ch-3 sp, 3 sc in ch-3 sp, sc in next 4 sc, 5 sc in next ch-4 sp, sc in next 4 sc, 3 sc in next ch-3 sp, sc in each sc across; join with slip st to Back Loop Only of first sc *(Fig. 1, page 143)*: 94 sc.

Rnd 6: Ch 1, working in Back Loops Only, sc in same st and in next 2 sc, 2 sc in next sc, sc in next 7 sc, 3 sc in next sc, sc in next 7 sc, 2 sc in next sc, sc in next 30 sc, 2 sc in next sc, sc in next 7 sc, 3 sc in next sc, sc in next 7 sc, 2 sc in next sc, sc in last 27 sc; join with slip st to **both** loops of first sc: 102 sc.

Rnd 7: Working in both loops, (slip st, ch 1, sc) in next sc, ch 3, skip next sc, † (sc in next sc, ch 3) twice, skip next sc, (sc in next sc, ch 3, skip next sc) 8 times, (sc in next sc, ch 3) twice, skip next sc, (sc in next sc, ch 3, skip next sc) 6 times, sc in next 4 sc †, ch 3, skip next sc, (sc in next sc, ch 3, skip next sc) 6 times, repeat from † to † once, (ch 3, skip next sc, sc in next sc) 5 times, dc in first sc to form last ch-3 sp; do **not** finish off: 56 sc and 50 ch-3 sps.

Continued on page 108.

Rnd 8: Ch 1, sc in last ch-3 sp made, ch 3, sc in next ch-3 sp, ✝ (sc, ch 3, sc) in next ch-3 sp, (sc in next ch-3 sp, ch 3) 4 times, (sc, ch 3) twice in next ch-3 sp, sc in next ch-3 sp, (ch 3, sc in next ch-3 sp) 3 times, (sc, ch 3, sc) in next ch-3 sp, sc in next ch-3 sp, (ch 3, sc in next ch-3 sp) 6 times, sc in next 4 sc and in next ch-3 sp ✝, (ch 3, sc in next ch-3 sp) 6 times, repeat from ✝ to ✝ once, (ch 3, sc in next ch-3 sp) 4 times, dc in first sc to form last ch-3 sp: 64 sc and 46 ch-3 sps.

Rnd 9: Ch 1, sc in last ch-3 sp made, ch 3, sc in next ch-3 sp, ✝ dc in next ch-3 sp, (ch 1, dc in same sp) 4 times, sc in next ch-3 sp, (ch 3, sc in next ch-3 sp) 3 times, (sc, ch 3, sc) in next ch-3 sp, sc in next ch-3 sp, (ch 3, sc in next ch-3 sp) 3 times, dc in next ch-3 sp, (ch 1, dc in same sp) 4 times, sc in next ch-3 sp, (ch 3, sc in next ch-3 sp) 5 times, sc in next 6 sc and in next ch-3 sp ✝, (ch 3, sc in next ch-3 sp) 5 times, repeat from ✝ to ✝ once, (ch 3, sc in next ch-3 sp) 3 times, dc in first sc to form last ch-3 sp: 76 sts and 50 sps.

Rnd 10: Ch 1, sc in last ch-3 sp made, ch 3, sc in next ch 3 sp, ✝ work Cluster in next ch-1 sp, (ch 3, work Cluster in next ch-1 sp) 3 times, sc in next ch-3 sp, (ch 3, sc in next ch-3 sp) twice, dc in next ch-3 sp, (ch 1, dc in same sp) 4 times, sc in next ch-3 sp, (ch 3, sc in next ch-3 sp) twice, work Cluster in next ch-1 sp, (ch 3, work Cluster in next ch-1 sp) 3 times, sc in next ch-3 sp, (ch 3, sc in next ch-3 sp) 4 times, sc in next 8 sc and in next ch-3 sp ✝, (ch 3, sc in next ch-3 sp) 4 times, repeat from ✝ to ✝ once, (ch 3, sc in next ch-3 sp) twice, dc in first sc to form last ch-3 sp: 74 sts and 44 sps.

Rnd 11: Ch 1, sc in last ch-3 sp made, ch 3, sc in next ch-3 sp, ch 3, ✝ (sc, ch 3, sc) in next 3 ch-3 sps, (ch 3, sc in next ch-3 sp) twice, work Cluster in next ch-1 sp, (ch 3, sc in next dc, ch 3, work Cluster in next ch-1 sp) 3 times, (sc in next ch-3 sp, ch 3) twice, (sc, ch 3, sc) in next 3 ch-3 sps, (ch 3, sc in next ch-3 sp) 4 times, sc in next 10 sc and in next ch-3 sp, ch 3 ✝, (sc in next ch-3 sp, ch 3) 3 times, repeat from ✝ to ✝ once, sc in last ch-3 sp, dc in first sc to form last ch-3 sp: 82 sts and 48 ch-3 sps.

Rnd 12: Ch 1, sc in last ch-3 sp made, ch 3, sc in next ch-3 sp, ch 3, ✝ ♥ 2 sc in next ch-3 sp, sc in next ch-3 sp, working in **front** of same sp *(Fig. 5, page 144)*, work FPtr around second dc of 5-dc group 2 rnds **below**, sc in same sp on Rnd 11 as last sc made, (ch 3, sc in next ch-3 sp, working in **front** of same sp, work FPtr around next dc 2 rnds **below**, sc in same sp on Rnd 11 as last sc made) twice, 2 sc in next ch-3 sp, ch 3, (sc in next ch-3 sp, ch 3) twice ♥, (sc in next 2 ch-3 sps, ch 3) twice, (sc in next ch-3 sp, ch 3) twice, repeat from ♥ to ♥ once, 2 sc in next ch-3 sp, sc in next sc, ch 10, skip next 10 sc, sc in next sc, 2 sc in next ch-3 sp, ch 3 ✝, (sc in next ch-3 sp, ch 3) twice, repeat from ✝ to ✝ once; join with slip st to first sc: 12 FPtr, 2 loops, and 34 ch-3 sps.

Rnd 13: (Slip st, ch 1, sc) in first ch-3 sp, ✝ ch 3, sc in next ch-3 sp and in next 3 sc, ch 3, (sc, ch 3) twice in next 2 ch-3 sps, skip next 2 sts, sc in next 3 sc and in next ch-3 sp, ch 3, 2 sc in next ch-3 sp, [sc in next ch-3 sp, (ch 3, sc in same sp) twice] 3 times, 2 sc in next ch-3 sp, ch 3, sc in next ch-3 sp and in next 3 sc, ch 3, (sc, ch 3) twice in next 2 ch-3 sps, skip next 2 sts, sc in next 3 sc, (sc in next ch-3 sp, ch 3) twice, 2 sc in next ch-3 sp, dc in next loop, (ch 2, dc in same loop) 7 times, 2 sc in next ch-3 sp ✝, ch 3, sc in next ch-3 sp, repeat from ✝ to ✝ once, dc in first sc to form last ch-3 sp: 102 sts and 58 sps.

Rnd 14: Ch 1, 2 sc in last ch-3 sp made, ✝ ch 4, slip st in third ch from hook, ch 2, 2 sc in next ch-3 sp, sc in next 2 sc, skip next 2 sc, ♥ sc in next ch-3 sp, work FPdc Cluster around FPtr one rnd **below**, sc in same sp on Rnd 13 as last sc made, [(2 sc, work Picot, 2 sc) in next ch-3 sp, sc in next ch-3 sp, work FPdc Cluster around FPtr one rnd **below** same ch-3, sc in same ch-3 sp on Rnd 13 as last sc made] twice ♥, dc in next ch-3 sp, (work Picot, dc in same sp) 3 times, sc in next ch-3 sp, work Picot, sc in next ch-3 sp, (sc in next 2 sc and in next ch-3 sp, work Picot, sc in next ch-3 sp) twice, dc in next ch-3 sp, (work Picot, dc in same sp) 3 times, repeat from ♥ to ♥ once, skip next 2 sc, sc in next 2 sc, 2 sc in next ch-3 sp, ch 4, slip st in third ch from hook, ch 2, 2 sc in next ch-3 sp, work Popcorn in next ch-2 sp, (ch 4, slip st in third ch from hook, ch 2, work Popcorn in next ch-2 sp) 6 times ✝, 2 sc in next ch-3 sp, repeat from ✝ to ✝ once; join with slip st to first sc, finish off.

See Washing and Blocking, page 144.

Finished Size: $6^3/4$" diameter

MATERIALS

Bedspread Weight Cotton Thread (size 10): 80 yards
Steel crochet hook, size 7 (1.65 mm) **or** size
   needed for gauge

GAUGE SWATCH: $2^1/4$" diameter
Work same as Doily through Rnd 4.

STITCH GUIDE

TREBLE CROCHET *(abbreviated tr)*
YO twice, insert hook in sc indicated, YO and pull
up a loop (4 loops on hook), (YO and draw through
2 loops on hook) 3 times.

SPLIT TREBLE CROCHET
   (abbreviated Split tr)
First Leg: YO twice, working in **front** of previous
rnds *(Fig. 5, page 144)*, insert hook from **back** to
front in dc indicated, YO and pull up a loop, (YO
and draw through 2 loops on hook) twice (2 loops
remaining on hook).

Second Leg: YO twice, insert hook from **front** to
back in dc indicated, YO and pull up a loop, (YO
and draw through 2 loops on hook) twice, YO and
draw through all 3 loops on hook.

BEGINNING POPCORN
Ch 3, 3 dc in sp indicated, drop loop from hook,
insert hook in first dc of 4-dc group, hook dropped
loop and draw through.

POPCORN
4 Dc in sp indicated, drop loop from hook, insert
hook in first dc of 4-dc group, hook dropped loop
and draw through.

BACK POST SINGLE CROCHET
   (abbreviated BPsc)
Insert hook from **back** to **front** around post of dc
indicated *(Fig. 7, page 144)*, YO and pull up a
loop, YO and draw through both loops on hook.

PICOT
Ch 3, slip st in third ch from hook, ch 1.

DOILY

Ch 7; join with slip st to form a ring.

Rnd 1 (Right side)**:** Ch 3 **(counts as first dc, now
and throughout)**, dc in ring, place marker around dc
just made for st placement, 18 dc in ring; join with slip st
to first dc: 20 dc.

Rnd 2: Ch 1, sc in same st, ch 3, skip next dc, ★ sc in
next dc, ch 3, skip next dc; repeat from ★ around; join
with slip st to first sc: 10 ch-3 sps.

Rnd 3: (Slip st, ch 4, dc) in first ch-3 sp, (ch 1, dc in
same sp) twice, ★ dc in next ch-3 sp, (ch 1, dc in same
sp) 3 times; repeat from ★ around; join with slip st to
third ch of beginning ch-4: 30 ch-1 sps.

Rnd 4: (Slip st, ch 1, sc) in first ch-1 sp, (ch 2, sc in
next ch-1 sp) twice, work First Leg of Split tr in marked
dc on Rnd 1, ★ work Second Leg of Split tr in next
skipped dc on Rnd 1, sc in next ch-1 sp on Rnd 3,
(ch 2, sc in next ch-1 sp) twice, work First Leg of Split tr
in same st as Second Leg of last Split tr made; repeat
from ★ around, work Second Leg of Split tr in same st
as First Leg of first Split tr made; join with slip st to first
sc: 20 ch-2 sps.

Rnd 5: (Slip st, ch 1, sc) in first ch-2 sp, (ch 4, sc in
next ch-2 sp) around, tr in first sc to form last ch-4 sp.

Rnd 6: Work Beginning Popcorn in last ch-4 sp made,
(ch 3, work Popcorn in same sp) twice, 2 sc in next
ch-4 sp, ★ work Popcorn in next ch-4 sp, (ch 3, work
Popcorn in same sp) twice, 2 sc in next ch-4 sp; repeat
from ★ around; join with slip st to top of Beginning
Popcorn.

Rnd 7: (Slip st, ch 1, 2 sc) in first ch-3 sp, (ch 5, 2 sc in
next ch-3 sp) around, ch 1, tr in first sc to form last
ch-5 sp.

Rnd 8: Work Beginning Popcorn in last ch-5 sp made,
(ch 3, work Popcorn in same sp) 3 times, 2 sc in next
ch-5 sp, ★ work Popcorn in next ch-5 sp, (ch 3, work
Popcorn in same sp) 3 times, 2 sc in next ch-5 sp;
repeat from ★ around; join with slip st to top of
Beginning Popcorn: 30 ch-3 sps.

Rnd 9: (Slip st, ch 1, sc) in first ch-3 sp, (ch 4, sc in
next ch-3 sp) twice, ch 5, ★ sc in next ch-3 sp, (ch 4, sc
in next ch-3 sp) twice, ch 5; repeat from ★ around; join
with slip st to first sc.

Rnd 10: Slip st in next 2 chs, ch 1, sc in same ch-4 sp,
ch 5, sc in next ch-4 sp, dc in next ch-5 sp, (ch 1, dc in
same sp) 5 times, ★ sc in next ch-4 sp, ch 5, sc in next
ch-4 sp, dc in next ch-5 sp, (ch 1, dc in same sp) 5
times; repeat from ★ around; join with slip st to first sc,
do **not** finish off: 80 sts and 60 sps.

Continued on page 110.

Rnd 11: (Slip st, ch 1, 5 sc) in first ch-5 sp, skip next sc, work BPsc around next dc, (ch 2, work BPsc around next dc) 5 times, ★ 5 sc in next ch-5 sp, skip next sc, work BPsc around next dc, (ch 2, work BPsc around next dc) 5 times; repeat from ★ around; join with slip st to first sc: 50 sc and 50 ch-2 sps.

Rnd 12: Ch 1, sc in same st, ★ † work Picot, skip next sc, [sc, ch 4, slip st in top of sc just made *(Fig. 6a, page 144)*, sc] in next sc, work Picot, skip next sc, sc in next sc and in next ch-2 sp, 2 sc in next ch-2 sp, ch 2, 2 dc in next ch-2 sp, ch 3, slip st in top of last dc made, 2 dc in same sp, ch 2, 2 sc in next ch-2 sp, sc in next ch-2 sp, skip next BPsc †, sc in next sc; repeat from ★ 8 times **more**, then repeat from † to † once; join with slip st to first sc, finish off.

See Washing and Blocking, page 144.

73 ▮▬▬▬▬▬▬

Finished Size: 9" (point to point)

MATERIALS
Bedspread Weight Cotton Thread (size 10): 70 yards
Steel crochet hook, size 7 (1.65 mm) **or** size
    needed for gauge

GAUGE SWATCH: 1¹/₂" diameter
Work same as Doily through Rnd 4.

STITCH GUIDE

BACK POST SINGLE CROCHET
   (abbreviated BPsc)
Insert hook from **back** to **front** around post of dc indicated *(Fig. 7, page 144)*, YO and pull up a loop, YO and draw through both loops on hook.

FRONT POST SINGLE CROCHET
   (abbreviated FPsc)
Insert hook from **front** to **back** around post of FPtr indicated *(Fig. 7, page 144)*, YO and pull up a loop, YO and draw through both loops on hook.

FRONT POST TREBLE CROCHET
   (abbreviated FPtr)
YO twice, insert hook from **front** to **back** around post of st indicated *(Fig. 7, page 144)*, YO and pull up a loop (4 loops on hook), (YO and draw through 2 loops on hook) 3 times.

BEGINNING POPCORN
Ch 3 **(counts as first dc)**, 2 dc in sp indicated, drop loop from hook, insert hook in first dc of 3-dc group, hook dropped loop and draw through.

POPCORN
3 Dc in ch-4 sp indicated, drop loop from hook, insert hook in first dc of 3-dc group, hook dropped loop and draw through.

FRONT POST CLUSTER
   (abbreviated FP Cluster)
★ YO twice, insert hook from **front** to **back** around post of FPsc indicated *(Fig. 7, page 144)*, YO and pull up a loop, (YO and draw through 2 loops on hook) twice; repeat from ★ once **more**, YO and draw through all 3 loops on hook.

PICOT
Ch 2, slip st in top of last st made *(Fig. 6a, page 144)*.

DOILY
CENTER
Rnd 1 (Right side)**:** Ch 4, 11 dc in fourth ch from hook; join with slip st in top of beginning ch-4: 12 sts.

Note: Loop a short piece of thread around any stitch to mark Rnd 1 as **right** side.

Rnd 2: Ch 1, sc in same st, ch 1, (sc in next dc, ch 1) around; join with slip st to first sc: 12 sc and 12 ch-1 sps.

Rnd 3: (Slip st, ch 1, 2 sc) in first ch-1 sp, sc in next sc, (2 sc in next ch-1 sp, sc in next st) around; join with slip st to first sc: 36 sc.

Rnd 4: Ch 1, sc in same st and in next sc, work FPtr around dc 2 rnds **below** next sc, skip next sc on Rnd 3 from last sc made, ★ sc in next 2 sc on Rnd 3, work FPtr around st 2 rnds **below** next sc, skip next sc on Rnd 3 from last sc made; repeat from ★ around; join with slip st to first sc.

Rnd 5: Slip st in next 2 sts, ch 1, work FPsc around same FPtr, ★ ch 4, skip next 2 sc, work FPsc around next FPtr; repeat from ★ around to last 2 sc, ch 1, skip last 2 sc, dc in first sc to form last ch-4 sp: 12 ch-4 sps.

Rnd 6: Work Beginning Popcorn in last ch-4 sp made, ch 3, sc in same sp, (sc, ch 3, work Popcorn, ch 3, sc) in each ch-4 sp around, sc in same sp as Beginning Popcorn, ch 1, hdc in top of Beginning Popcorn to form last ch-3 sp: 24 ch-3 sps.

Rnd 7: Ch 1, sc in last ch-3 sp made, ch 3, sc in next ch-3 sp, ch 1, work FP Cluster around next FPsc one rnd **below**, ch 1, ★ sc in next ch-3 sp on Rnd 6, ch 3, sc in next ch-3 sp, ch 1, work FP Cluster around next FPsc one rnd **below**, ch 1; repeat from ★ around; join with slip st to first sc: 36 sps.

Rnd 8: Slip st in next ch, ch 1, sc in same ch-3 sp, ch 3, sc in next 2 ch-1 sps, ★ ch 3, sc in next ch-3 sp, ch 3, sc in next 2 ch-1 sps; repeat from ★ around, ch 1, hdc in first sc to form last ch-3 sp: 24 ch-3 sps.

Rnd 9: Ch 1, sc in last ch-3 sp made, ch 4, (sc in next ch-3 sp, ch 4) around; join with slip st to first sc.

Rnd 10: [Slip st, ch 3 **(counts as first dc)**, 3 dc] in first ch-4 sp, 4 dc in each ch-4 sp around; join with slip st to first dc: 96 dc.

Rnd 11: Ch 1, work BPsc around next dc, ★ ch 2, skip next dc, work BPsc around next dc; repeat from ★ around to last dc, skip last dc, hdc in first BPsc to form last ch-2 sp; do **not** finish off: 48 ch-2 sps.

FIRST POINT
Row 1: Ch 1, 2 sc in last ch-2 sp made and in each of next 4 ch-2 sps, 3 sc in each of next 2 ch-2 sps, 2 sc in each of next 5 ch-2 sps, leave remaining sps unworked: 26 sc.

Row 2: Turn; slip st in first 3 sc, ch 1, sc in same st, ch 2, skip next sc, (sc in next sc, ch 2, skip next sc) 4 times, sc in next 2 sc, (ch 2, skip next sc, sc in next sc) 5 times, leave remaining 2 sc unworked: 12 sc and 10 ch-2 sps.

Row 3: Turn; slip st in first ch-2 sp, ch 1, 2 sc in same sp and in each of next 4 ch-2 sps, sc in next 2 sc, 2 sc in each of next 5 ch-2 sps: 22 sc.

Row 4: Turn; slip st in first 3 sc, ch 1, sc in same st, ch 2, (skip next sc, sc in next sc, ch 2) 4 times, sc in next sc, (ch 2, skip next sc, sc in next sc) 4 times, leave remaining 2 sc unworked: 10 sc and 9 ch-2 sps.

Row 5: Turn; slip st in first ch-2 sp, ch 1, 2 sc in same sp and in each of next 3 ch-2 sps, 3 sc in next ch-2 sp, 2 sc in each of next 4 ch-2 sps: 19 sc.

Row 6: Turn; slip st in first 3 sc, ch 1, sc in same st, ★ ch 2, skip next sc, sc in next sc; repeat from ★ 6 times **more**, leave remaining 2 sc unworked: 8 sc and 7 ch-2 sps.

Row 7: Turn; slip st in first ch-2 sp, ch 1, 2 sc in same sp and in each of next 2 ch-2 sps, 3 sc in next ch-2 sp, 2 sc in each of next 3 ch-2 sps: 15 sc.

Row 8: Turn; slip st in first 3 sc, ch 1, sc in same st, ★ ch 2, skip next sc, sc in next sc; repeat from ★ 4 times **more**, leave remaining 2 sc unworked: 6 sc and 5 ch-2 sps.

Row 9: Turn; slip st in first ch-2 sp, ch 1, 2 sc in same sp and in next ch-2 sp, 3 sc in next ch-2 sp, 2 sc in each of next 2 ch-2 sps: 11 sc.

Row 10: Turn; slip st in first 3 sc, ch 1, sc in same st, ★ ch 2, skip next sc, sc in next sc; repeat from ★ 2 times **more**, leave remaining 2 sc unworked: 4 sc and 3 ch-2 sps.

Row 11: Turn; (slip st, ch 1, 2 sc) in first ch-2 sp, 3 sc in next ch-2 sp, 2 sc in next ch-2 sp: 7 sc.

Row 12: Turn; slip st in first 3 sc, ch 1, sc in same st, ch 2, skip next sc, sc in next sc, leave remaining 2 sc unworked: 2 sc and one ch-2 sp.

Row 13: Turn; (slip st, ch 1, 3 sc) in ch-2 sp; finish off: 3 sc.

NEXT 2 POINTS
Row 1: With **right** side facing, join thread with sc in next unworked ch-2 sp on Rnd 11 of Center *(see Joining With Sc, page 143)*; sc in same sp, 2 sc in each of next 4 ch-2 sps, 3 sc in each of next 2 ch-2 sps, 2 sc in each of next 5 ch-2 sps, leave remaining sps unworked: 26 sc.

Rows 2-13: Work same as First Point.

LAST POINT
Row 1: With **right** side facing, join thread with sc in next unworked ch-2 sp on Rnd 11 of Center; sc in same sp, 2 sc in each of next 4 ch-2 sps, 3 sc in each of next 2 ch-2 sps, 2 sc in each of next 5 ch-2 sps: 26 sc.

Rows 2-12: Work same as First Point.

Row 13: Turn; (slip st, ch 1, 3 sc) in ch-2 sp; do **not** finish off: 3 sc.

EDGING
Rnd 1: Ch 1, do **not** turn; sc in top of last sc made, ★ † (ch 4, skip next row, sc in first sc on next row) 6 times, ch 1, sc in first sc on Row 1 of next Point, ch 4, (skip next row, sc in first sc on next row, ch 4) 6 times, skip next sc †, sc in next sc; repeat from ★ 2 times **more**, then repeat from † to † once; join with slip st to first sc: 56 sps.

Rnd 2: Slip st in first ch-4 sp, ch 1, (2 sc, work Picot, 2 sc) in same sp and in next 5 ch-4 sps, ★ † sc in next ch-1 sp, (2 sc, work Picot, 2 sc) in next 6 ch-2 sps, (2 dc, work Picot, 2 dc) in next ch-4 sp, ch 5, slip st in top of last dc made, (2 dc, work Picot, 2 dc) in same sp †, (2 sc, work Picot, 2 sc) in next 6 ch-4 sps; repeat from ★ 2 times **more**, then repeat from † to † once; join with slip st to first sc, finish off.

See Washing and Blocking, page 144.

Finished Size: 6" (point to point)

MATERIALS

Bedspread Weight Cotton Thread (size 10): 52 yards
Steel crochet hook, size 7 (1.65 mm) **or** size
  needed for gauge

GAUGE SWATCH: $1^1/_4$" diameter
Work same as Doily through Rnd 2.

STITCH GUIDE

CLUSTER (uses one ch-1 sp)
★ YO, insert hook in ch-1 sp indicated, YO and pull up a loop, YO and draw through 2 loops on hook; repeat from ★ 2 times **more**, YO and draw through all 4 loops on hook.

FRONT POST CLUSTER
  (abbreviated FP Cluster)
★ YO twice, insert hook from **front** to **back** around post of dc indicated *(Fig. 7, page 144)*, YO and pull up a loop, (YO and draw through 2 loops on hook) twice; repeat from ★ once **more**, YO and draw through all 3 loops on hook.

PICOT
Ch 2, slip st in top of last sc made *(Fig. 6a, page 144)*.

DOILY

Ch 7; join with slip st to form a ring.

Rnd 1 (Right side): Ch 3 **(counts as first dc, now and throughout)**, 17 dc in ring, place marker around last dc made for st placement; join with slip st to first dc: 18 dc.

Rnd 2: Ch 1, sc in same st, ch 3, skip next dc, ★ sc in next dc, ch 3, skip next dc; repeat from ★ around; join with slip st to first sc: 9 ch-3 sps.

Rnd 3: (Slip st, ch 1, sc) in first ch-3 sp, work FP Cluster around marked dc on Rnd 1, ★ sc in same sp on Rnd 2 as last sc made and in next ch-3 sp, skip next dc on Rnd 1 from last FP Cluster made, work FP Cluster around next dc; repeat from ★ around, sc in same sp on Rnd 2 as last sc made; join with slip st to first sc: 9 FP Clusters and 18 sc.

Rnd 4: Ch 1, sc in same st, 2 sc in next FP Cluster, (sc in next 2 sc, 2 sc in next FP Cluster) around to last sc, sc in last sc: join with slip st to first sc: 36 sc.

Rnd 5: Ch 1, sc in same st, ★ ch 3, skip next sc, sc in next sc; repeat from ★ around to last sc, ch 1, skip last sc, hdc in first sc to form last ch-3 sp: 18 ch-3 sps.

Rnd 6: Ch 1, sc in last ch-3 sp made, dc in next ch-3 sp, (ch 1, dc in same sp) 3 times, sc in next ch-3 sp, ★ ch 3, sc in next ch-3 sp, dc in next ch-3 sp, (ch 1, dc in same sp) 3 times, sc in next ch-3 sp; repeat from ★ around, ch 1, hdc in first sc to form last ch-3 sp: 24 sps.

Rnd 7: Ch 1, sc in last ch-3 sp made, ch 4, work Cluster in next ch-1 sp, (ch 3, work Cluster in next ch-1 sp) twice, ★ ch 4, sc in next ch-3 sp, ch 4, work Cluster in next ch-1 sp, (ch 3, work Cluster in next ch-1 sp) twice; repeat from ★ around, ch 1, dc in first sc to form last ch-4 sp.

Rnd 8: Ch 1, sc in last ch-4 sp made, ch 4, 2 sc in next ch-4 sp, (sc, ch 3, sc) in next 2 ch-3 sps, ★ 2 sc in next ch-4 sp, ch 4, 2 sc in next ch-4 sp, (sc, ch 3, sc) in next 2 ch-3 sps; repeat from ★ around, sc in same sp as first sc; join with slip st to first sc: 18 sps.

Rnd 9: [Slip st, ch 4 **(counts as first dc plus ch 1)**, dc] in first ch-4 sp, (ch 1, dc in same sp) 4 times, 2 sc in next ch-3 sp, ch 4, 2 sc in next ch-3 sp, ★ dc in next ch-4 sp, (ch 1, dc in same sp) 5 times, 2 sc in next ch-3 sp, ch 4, 2 sc in next ch-3 sp; repeat from ★ around; join with slip st to first dc: 36 sps.

Rnd 10: (Slip st, ch 1, sc) in first ch-1 sp, (ch 3, sc in next ch-1 sp) 4 times, (ch 3, sc) 3 times in next ch-4 sp, ★ (ch 3, sc in next ch-1 sp) 5 times, (ch 3, sc) 3 times in next ch-4 sp; repeat from ★ around, ch 1, hdc in first sc to form last ch-3 sp: 48 ch-3 sps.

Rnd 11: Ch 1, sc in last ch-3 sp made, (ch 3, sc in next ch-3 sp) around, dc in first sc to form last ch-3 sp.

Rnd 12: Ch 3, dc in last ch-3 sp made, 2 dc in each of next 2 ch-3 sps, 5 dc in next ch-3 sp, (2 dc in each of next 7 ch-3 sps, 5 dc in next ch-3 sp) around to last 4 ch-3 sps, 2 dc in each of last 4 ch-3 sps; join with slip st to first dc: 114 dc.

Rnd 13: Ch 1, sc in same st and in next dc, work Picot, (sc in next 2 dc, work Picot) 3 times, 3 sc in next dc, work Picot, ★ (sc in next 2 dc, work Picot) 9 times, 3 sc in next dc, work Picot; repeat from ★ around to last 10 dc, (sc in next 2 dc, work Picot) 5 times; join with slip st to first sc, finish off.

See Washing and Blocking, page 144.

Finished Size: 6³/₄" diameter

MATERIALS
Bedspread Weight Cotton Thread (size 10): 80 yards
Steel crochet hook, size 7 (1.65 mm) **or** size
    needed for gauge

GAUGE SWATCH: 2" diameter
Work same as Doily through Rnd 3.

STITCH GUIDE

SPLIT TREBLE CROCHET
    (abbreviated Split tr)
YO twice, working in **front** of previous rnds
(Fig. 5, page 144), insert hook in first dc of
4-dc group 2 rnds **below**, YO and pull up a loop,
(YO and draw through 2 loops on hook) twice,
YO twice, insert hook in fourth dc of same group,
YO and pull up a loop, (YO and draw through
2 loops on hook) twice, YO and draw through all
3 loops on hook.

CLUSTER (uses one st or sp)
★ YO, insert hook in st or sp indicated, YO and pull
up a loop, YO and draw through 2 loops on hook;
repeat from ★ once **more**, YO and draw through all
3 loops on hook.

BEGINNING SPLIT CLUSTER
    (uses next 3 sts)
Ch 2, † YO, insert hook in **same** st, YO and pull up
a loop, YO and draw through 2 loops on hook †,
YO, skip next 2 sc, insert hook in next Cluster, YO
and pull up a loop, YO and draw through 2 loops
on hook, repeat from † to † once, YO and draw
through all 4 loops on hook.

SPLIT CLUSTER (uses next 4 sts)
YO, † insert hook in **next** Cluster, YO and pull up a
loop, YO and draw through 2 loops on hook, YO,
insert hook in **same** st, YO and pull up a loop, YO
and draw through 2 loops on hook †, YO, skip next
2 sc, repeat from † to † once, YO and draw through
all 5 loops on hook.

BACK POST SINGLE CROCHET
    (abbreviated BPsc)
Insert hook from **back** to **front** around post of dc
indicated *(Fig. 7, page 144)*, YO and pull up a
loop, YO and draw through both loops on hook.

POPCORN
4 Dc in ch-4 sp indicated, drop loop from hook,
insert hook in first dc of 4-dc group, hook dropped
loop and draw through.

PICOT
Ch 3, slip st in third ch from hook, ch 1.

DOILY
Ch 7; join with slip st to form a ring.

Rnd 1 (Right side)**:** Ch 3 **(counts as first dc, now
and throughout)**, 17 dc in ring; join with slip st to first
dc: 18 dc.

Rnd 2: Ch 1, sc in same st, ★ ch 3, skip next dc, sc in
next dc; repeat from ★ around to last dc, ch 2, skip last
dc, sc in first sc to form last ch-3 sp: 9 ch-3 sps.

Rnd 3: Ch 1, sc in last ch-3 sp made and in next sc,
★ (sc, ch 2, work Cluster, ch 2, sc) in next ch-3 sp, sc in
next sc; repeat from ★ around, (sc, ch 2, work Cluster)
in same sp as first sc, hdc in first sc to form last ch-2 sp:
18 ch-2 sps.

Rnd 4: Ch 1, sc in last ch-2 sp made, ch 4, sc in next
ch-2 sp, ★ ch 3, sc in next ch-2 sp, ch 4, sc in next
ch-2 sp; repeat from ★ around, dc in first sc to form
last ch-3 sp.

Rnd 5: Ch 3, (dc, ch 2, 2 dc) in last ch-3 sp made,
ch 2, sc in next ch-4 sp, ★ ch 2, (2 dc, ch 2) twice in
next ch-3 sp, sc in next ch-4 sp; repeat from ★ around,
ch 1, sc in first dc to form last ch-2 sp: 27 ch-2 sps.

Rnd 6: Ch 1, sc in last ch-2 sp made, ch 3, (sc in next
ch-2 sp, ch 3) around; join with slip st to first sc.

Rnd 7: (Slip st, ch 1, sc) in first ch-3 sp, ch 3, sc in
next ch-3 sp, dc in next ch-3 sp, (ch 1, dc in same sp) 4
times, ★ sc in next ch-3 sp, ch 3, sc in next ch-3 sp, dc
in next ch-3 sp, (ch 1, dc in same sp) 4 times; repeat
from ★ around; join with slip st to first sc, do **not**
finish off: 45 dc and 9 ch-3 sps.

Continued on page 114.

Rnd 8: (Slip st, ch 1, sc) in first ch-3 sp, work Split tr, sc in same sp on Rnd 7 as last sc made, skip next sc, work BPsc around next dc, (ch 3, work BPsc around next dc) 4 times, ★ sc in next ch-3 sp, work Split tr, sc in same sp on Rnd 7 as last sc made, skip next sc, work BPsc around next dc, (ch 3, work BPsc around next dc) 4 times; repeat from ★ around; join with slip st to first sc: 72 sts and 36 ch-3 sps.

Rnd 9: (Slip st, ch 1, sc) in next Split tr, ch 1, sc in next ch-3 sp, (ch 3, sc in next ch-3 sp) 3 times, ch 1, skip next 2 sts, ★ sc in next Split tr, ch 1, sc in next ch-3 sp, (ch 3, sc in next ch-3 sp) 3 times, ch 1, skip next 2 sts; repeat from ★ around; join with slip st to first sc: 45 sps.

Rnd 10: (Slip st, ch 2, dc) in first ch-1 sp, sc in next ch-3 sp, (ch 4, sc in next ch-3 sp) twice, work Cluster in next ch-1 sp, ch 3, ★ work Cluster in next ch-1 sp, sc in next ch-3 sp, (ch 4, sc in next ch-3 sp) twice, work Cluster in next ch-1 sp, ch 3; repeat from ★ around; join with slip st to first dc: 45 sts and 27 sps.

Rnd 11: Ch 2, dc in same st, sc in next ch-4 sp, ch 5, sc in next ch-4 sp, skip next sc, work Cluster in next Cluster, ch 3, sc in next ch-3 sp, ch 3, ★ work Cluster in next Cluster, sc in next ch-4 sp, ch 5, sc in next ch-4 sp, skip next sc, work Cluster in next Cluster, ch 3, sc in next ch-3 sp, ch 3; repeat from ★ around; join with slip st to first dc.

Rnd 12: Ch 2, dc in same st, 2 sc in next ch-5 sp, skip next sc, work Cluster in next Cluster, ch 3, sc in next ch-3 sp, ch 4, sc in next ch-3 sp, ch 3, ★ work Cluster in next Cluster, 2 sc in next ch-5 sp, skip next sc, work Cluster in next Cluster, ch 3, sc in next ch-3 sp, ch 4, sc in next ch-3 sp, ch 3; repeat from ★ around; join with slip st to first dc: 54 sts and 27 sps.

Rnd 13: Work Beginning Split Cluster, ch 3, sc in next ch-3 sp, work Popcorn in next ch-4 sp, (ch 3, work Popcorn in same sp) 3 times, sc in next ch-3 sp, ★ ch 3, work Split Cluster, ch 3, sc in next ch-3 sp, work Popcorn in next ch-4 sp, (ch 3, work Popcorn in same sp) 3 times, sc in next ch-3 sp; repeat from ★ around, ch 1, hdc in top of Beginning Split Cluster to form last ch-3 sp: 45 ch-3 sps.

Rnd 14: Ch 1, 2 sc in last ch-3 sp made, work Picot, (2 sc in next ch-3 sp, work Picot) around; join with slip st to first sc, finish off.

See Washing and Blocking, page 144.

Finished Size: 6$^{1}/_{2}$" diameter

MATERIALS
Bedspread Weight Cotton Thread (size 10): 85 yards
Steel crochet hook, size 7 (1.65 mm) **or** size needed for gauge

GAUGE SWATCH: 2" diameter
Work same as Doily through Rnd 5.

STITCH GUIDE

BACK POST DOUBLE CROCHET
(abbreviated BPdc)
YO, working **above** beginning ch-2, insert hook from **back** to **front** around post of dc indicated *(Fig. 7, page 144)*, YO and pull up a loop (3 loops on hook), (YO and draw through 2 loops on hook) twice.

FRONT POST DOUBLE TREBLE CROCHET
(abbreviated FPdtr)
YO 3 times, insert hook from **front** to **back** around post of dc indicated *(Fig. 7, page 144)*, YO and pull up a loop (5 loops on hook), (YO and draw through 2 loops on hook) 4 times.

CLUSTER
★ YO, insert hook in ch-5 sp indicated, YO and pull up a loop, YO and draw through 2 loops on hook; repeat from ★ 2 times **more**, YO and draw through all 4 loops on hook.

BACK POST DOUBLE CROCHET CLUSTER *(abbreviated BPdc Cluster)*
YO, † insert hook from **back** to **front** around post of dc indicated *(Fig. 7, page 144)*, YO and pull up a loop, YO and draw through 2 loops on hook †, YO, working **above** first leg, repeat from † to † once, YO and draw through all 3 loops on hook.

SPLIT FRONT POST TREBLE CROCHET
(abbreviated Split FPtr)
First Leg: YO twice, insert hook from **front** to **back** around post of dc indicated *(Fig. 7, page 144)*, YO and pull up a loop, (YO and draw through 2 loops on hook) twice (2 loops remaining on hook).

Second Leg: YO twice, insert hook from **front** to **back** around post of dc indicated, YO and pull up a loop, (YO and draw through 2 loops on hook) twice, YO and draw through all 3 loops on hook.

BEGINNING DECREASE
Pull up a loop in same st and in next sc, YO and draw through all 3 loops on hook.

DECREASE
Pull up a loop in each of next 2 sc, YO and draw through all 3 loops on hook.

PICOT
Ch 3, slip st in third ch from hook, ch 1.

DOILY
Ch 10; join with slip st to form a ring.

Rnd 1 (Right side)**:** Ch 3 **(counts as first dc, now and throughout)**, 5 dc in ring, place marker around last dc made for st placement, 24 dc in ring; join with slip st to first dc: 30 dc.

Rnd 2: Ch 1, sc in same st and in each dc around; join with slip st to first sc.

Rnd 3: Ch 1, sc in same st, ch 2, skip next sc, ★ sc in next sc, ch 2, skip next sc; repeat from ★ around; join with slip st to first sc: 15 ch-2 sps.

Rnd 4: Ch 1, sc in same st and in next ch-2 sp, work FPdtr around marked dc on Rnd 1, working **behind** FPdtr, sc in same sp on Rnd 3 as last sc made, ★ sc in next sc and in next ch-2 sp, skip next dc on Rnd 1 from last FPdtr made, work FPdtr around next dc, working **behind** FPdtr, sc in same sp on Rnd 3 as last sc made; repeat from ★ around; join with slip st to first sc: 15 FPdtr and 45 sc.

Rnd 5: Ch 1, sc in same st and in each st around; join with slip st to first sc: 60 sc.

Rnd 6: Ch 5 **(counts as first dc plus ch 2)**, skip next sc, ★ dc in next sc, ch 2, skip next sc; repeat from ★ around; join with slip st to first dc: 30 dc and 30 ch-2 sps.

Rnd 7: Ch 1, sc in same st and in next ch-2 sp, ch 2, slip st in top of last sc made *(Fig. 6a, page 144)*, sc in same ch-2 sp, ★ sc in next dc, (sc, ch 2, slip st in top of last sc made, sc) in next ch-2 sp; repeat from ★ around; join with slip st to first sc: 90 sc.

Rnd 8: Ch 1, slip st from **back** to **front** around post of first dc on Rnd 6 *(Fig. 7, page 144)*, ch 2, work BPdc around same st, ch 2, (work BPdc Cluster around next dc on Rnd 6, ch 2) around; join with slip st to first BPdc: 30 ch-2 sps.

Rnd 9: (Slip st, ch 3, 2 dc) in first ch-2 sp, 3 dc in each ch-2 sp around; join with slip st to first dc: 90 dc.

Rnd 10: Ch 1, sc in same st and in each dc around; join with slip st to first sc.

Rnd 11: Ch 1, sc in same st, ch 2, ★ skip next sc, sc in next 2 sc, ch 2; repeat from ★ around to last 2 sc, skip next sc, sc in last sc; join with slip st to first sc: 60 sc and 30 ch-2 sps.

Rnd 12: (Slip st, ch 1, sc) in first ch-2 sp, work First Leg of Split FPtr around first dc on Rnd 9, skip next dc, work Second Leg of Split FPtr around next dc, working **behind** Split FPtr, sc in same sp on Rnd 11 as last sc made and in next 2 sc, ★ sc in next ch-2 sp, work First Leg of Split FPtr around next dc on Rnd 9 from Second Leg of last Split FPtr made, skip next dc, work Second Leg of Split FPtr around next dc, working **behind** Split FPtr, sc in same sp on Rnd 11 as last sc made and in next 2 sts; repeat from ★ around; join with slip st to first sc: 30 Split FPtr and 120 sc.

Rnd 13: (Slip st, ch 1, sc) in next Split FPtr, ch 5, skip next 4 sc, ★ sc in next Split FPtr, ch 5, skip next 4 sts; repeat from ★ around; join with slip st to first sc: 30 ch-5 sps.

Rnd 14: Slip st in next 2 chs, ch 1, 2 sc in same ch-5 sp, work Cluster in next ch-5 sp, (ch 3, work Cluster in same sp) 3 times, ★ 2 sc in next ch-5 sp, work Cluster in next ch-5 sp, (ch 3, work Cluster in same sp) 3 times; repeat from ★ around; join with slip st to first sc: 60 Clusters, 30 sc, and 45 ch-3 sps.

Rnd 15: Work beginning decrease, (sc, work Picot, sc) in next 3 ch-3 sps, skip next Cluster, ★ decrease, (sc, work Picot, sc) in next 3 ch-3 sps, skip next Cluster; repeat from ★ around; join with slip st to top of beginning decrease, finish off.

See Washing and Blocking, page 144.

Finished Size: $6^1/_4$" square

MATERIALS

Bedspread Weight Cotton Thread (size 10): 75 yards
Steel crochet hook, size 7 (1.65 mm) **or** size
  needed for gauge

GAUGE SWATCH: 2" diameter
Work same as Doily through Rnd 3.

STITCH GUIDE

TREBLE CROCHET *(abbreviated tr)*
YO twice, insert hook in dc indicated, YO and pull
up a loop (4 loops on hook), (YO and draw through
2 loops on hook) 3 times.

DOUBLE TREBLE CROCHET
(abbreviated dtr)
YO 3 times, insert hook in free loop of sc indicated
(Fig. 2a, page 144), YO and pull up a loop
(5 loops on hook), (YO and draw through 2 loops
on hook) 4 times.

SPLIT DOUBLE CROCHET
(abbreviated Split dc)
First Leg: YO, insert hook in free loop of sc
indicated *(Fig. 2a, page 144)*, YO and pull up a
loop, YO and draw through 2 loops on hook
(2 loops remaining on hook).

Second Leg: YO, insert hook in free loop of sc
indicated, YO and pull up a loop, YO and draw
through 2 loops on hook, YO and draw through all
3 loops on hook.

BACK POST CLUSTER
(abbreviated BP Cluster)
YO, † insert hook from **back** to **front** around post
of dc indicated *(Fig. 7, page 144)*, YO and pull up
a loop, YO and draw through 2 loops on hook †,
YO, working **above** first leg, repeat from † to †
once, YO and draw through all 3 loops on hook.

FRONT POST CLUSTER
(abbreviated FP Cluster)
★ YO 3 times, insert hook from **front** to **back**
around post of dc indicated *(Fig. 7, page 144)*, YO
and pull up a loop, (YO and draw through 2 loops
on hook) 3 times; repeat from ★ once **more**, YO
and draw through all 3 loops on hook.

PICOT
Ch 3, slip st in third ch from hook, ch 1.

DOILY

Ch 14; join with slip st to form a ring.

Rnd 1 (Right side)**:** Ch 3 **(counts as first dc, now
and throughout)**, 5 dc in ring, place marker around
last dc made for st placement, 26 dc in ring; join with
slip st to first dc: 32 dc.

Rnd 2: Ch 1, sc in same st, ch 3, skip next dc, ★ sc in
next dc, ch 3, skip next dc; repeat from ★ around; join
with slip st to first sc: 16 sc and 16 ch-3 sps.

Rnd 3: (Slip st, ch 1, sc) in first ch-3 sp, work
FP Cluster around marked dc on Rnd 1, ★ working
behind FP Cluster, sc in same sp on Rnd 2 as last sc
made and in next ch-3 sp, skip next dc on Rnd 1 from
last FP Cluster made, work FP Cluster around next dc;
repeat from ★ around, working **behind** last FP Cluster
made, sc in same sp on Rnd 2 as last sc made; join with
slip st to first sc: 32 sc and 16 FP Clusters.

Rnd 4: Ch 1, sc in same st, 2 sc in next FP Cluster, (sc
in next 2 sc, 2 sc in next FP Cluster) around to last sc, sc
in last sc; join with slip st to first sc: 64 sc.

Rnd 5: Ch 1, sc in same st, place marker around sc just
made for st placement, sc in each sc around; join with
slip st to Back Loop Only of first sc *(Fig. 1, page 143)*.

Rnd 6: Ch 1, sc in Back Loop Only of same st and
each sc around; join with slip st to **both** loops of first sc.

Rnd 7: Ch 1, working in both loops, sc in same st,
★ ch 2, skip next sc, sc in next sc; repeat from ★ around
to last sc, skip last sc, hdc in first sc to form last ch-2 sp:
32 ch-2 sps.

Rnd 8: Ch 3, 2 dc in last ch-2 sp made, 3 dc in each
ch-2 sp around; join with slip st to first dc: 96 dc.

Rnd 9: Ch 1, sc in same st, tr in next dc pulling tr to right side, sc in next dc, working in **front** of previous rnds *(Fig. 5, page 144)*, dtr in free loop of marked sc on Rnd 5, ★ sc in next dc on Rnd 8, tr in next dc pulling tr to right side, sc in next dc, skip next sc on Rnd 5, working in **front** of previous rnds, dtr in free loop of next sc; repeat from ★ around; join with slip st to first sc: 128 sts.

Rnd 10: Ch 1, sc in same st, (skip next tr, sc in next 3 sts) around to last 3 sts, skip next tr, sc in last 2 sts; join with slip st to Back Loop Only of first sc: 96 sc.

Rnd 11: Ch 1, sc in Back Loop Only of same st and each sc around; join with slip st to **both** loops of first sc.

Rnd 12: Ch 1, working in both loops, sc in same st, ch 3, skip next sc, sc in next 2 sc, (ch 3, skip next sc, sc in next sc) 5 times, ch 5, ★ skip next 2 sc, (sc in next sc, ch 3, skip next sc) 5 times, sc in next 2 sc, (ch 3, skip next sc, sc in next sc) 5 times, ch 5; repeat from ★ 2 times **more**, skip next 2 sc, sc in next sc, (ch 3, skip next sc, sc in next sc) 3 times, ch 1, skip last sc, hdc in first sc to form last ch-3 sp: 44 sps.

Rnd 13: Ch 1, sc in last ch-3 sp made, ch 3, sc in next ch-3 sp, ★ † work First Leg of Split dc in free loop of sc 2 rnds **below** next sc *(Fig. 2a, page 144)*, work Second Leg of Split dc in next sc, (sc in next ch-3 sp on Rnd 12, ch 3) 3 times, sc in next 2 ch-3 sps, dc in next ch-5 sp, (ch 1, dc in same sp) 6 times, sc in next 2 ch-3 sps †, (ch 3, sc in next ch-3 sp) 3 times; repeat from ★ 2 times **more**, then repeat from † to † once, ch 3, sc in last ch-3 sp, ch 1, hdc in first sc to form last ch-3 sp: 28 dc, 4 Split dc, and 24 ch-3 sps.

Rnd 14: Ch 1, sc in last ch-3 sp made, ch 3, sc in next ch-3 sp, ★ † skip next sc, (dc, ch 3, dc) in next Split dc, sc in next ch-3 sp, (ch 3, sc in next ch-3 sp) twice, skip next 2 sc, work BP Cluster around next dc, (ch 2, work BP Cluster around next dc) 6 times, sc in next ch-3 sp †, (ch 3, sc in next ch-3 sp) twice; repeat from ★ 2 times **more**, then repeat from † to † once, dc in first sc to form last ch-3 sp: 8 dc and 44 sps.

Rnd 15: Ch 1, 3 sc in last ch-3 sp made and in next ch-3 sp, ★ † skip next sc, sc in next dc, ch 2, (sc, ch 2) twice in next ch-3 sp, sc in next dc, 3 sc in each of next 2 ch-3 sps, (dc, ch 3, dc) in next 6 ch-2 sps †, 3 sc in each of next 2 ch-3 sps; repeat from ★ 2 times **more**, then repeat from † to † once; join with slip st to first sc: 36 sps.

Rnd 16: Ch 1, sc in same st and in next 5 sc, ★ † 2 sc in next ch-2 sp, (dc, work Picot, dc) in next ch-2 sp, 2 sc in next ch-2 sp, skip next sc, sc in next 6 sc, (sc, work Picot, sc) in next ch-3 sp, (work Picot, sc) twice in next 5 ch-3 sps, skip next dc †, sc in next 6 sc; repeat from ★ 2 times **more**, then repeat from † to † once; join with slip st to first sc, finish off.

See Washing and Blocking, page 144.

78

Finished Size: 7¹/₂" (point to point)

MATERIALS
Bedspread Weight Cotton Thread (size 10): 70 yards
Steel crochet hook, size 7 (1.65 mm) **or** size needed for gauge

GAUGE SWATCH: 2" diameter
Work same as Doily through Rnd 2.

STITCH GUIDE

BEGINNING POPCORN
Ch 3 **(counts as first dc, now and throughout)**, 3 dc in ring, drop loop from hook, insert hook in first dc of 4-dc group, hook dropped loop and draw through.

POPCORN
4 Dc in ring, drop loop from hook, insert hook in first dc of 4-dc group, hook dropped loop and draw through.

BACK POST SINGLE CROCHET
(abbreviated BPsc)
Insert hook from **back** to **front** around post of dc indicated *(Fig. 7, page 144)*, YO and pull up a loop, YO and draw through both loops on hook.

SPLIT FRONT POST TREBLE CROCHET
(abbreviated Split FPtr)
First Leg: YO twice, insert hook from **front** to **back** around post of dc indicated *(Fig. 7, page 144)*, YO and pull up a loop, (YO and draw through 2 loops on hook) twice (2 loops remaining on hook).

Second Leg: YO twice, insert hook from **front** to **back** around post of dc indicated, YO and pull up a loop, (YO and draw through 2 loops on hook) twice, YO and draw through all 3 loops on hook.

PICOT
Ch 1, slip st in top of last sc made *(Fig. 6a, page 144)*.

DOILY
CENTER
Ch 7; join with slip st to form a ring.

Rnd 1 (Right side)**:** Work Beginning Popcorn, ch 3, (work Popcorn, ch 3) 7 times; join with slip st to top of Beginning Popcorn, do **not** finish off: 8 ch-3 sps.

Note: Loop a short piece of thread around any stitch to mark Rnd 1 as **right** side.

Continued on page 118.

117

Rnd 2: (Slip st, ch 3, 4 dc) in first ch-3 sp, 5 dc in each ch-3 sp around; join with slip st to first dc: 8 5-dc groups.

Rnd 3: Ch 3, dc in next 2 dc, ★ † work First Leg of Split FPtr around first dc of 5-dc group just worked into, work Second Leg of Split FPtr around last dc of same 5-dc group †, working **behind** Split FPtr, dc in same st as last dc made and in next 5 dc; repeat from ★ 6 times **more**, then repeat from † to † once, working **behind** last Split FPtr made, dc in same st as last dc made and in last 2 dc; join with slip st to first dc: 48 dc and 8 Split FPtr.

Rnd 4: Ch 1, ★ work BPsc around next dc, ch 5, skip next 3 sts, work BPsc around next dc, ch 3, skip next 2 sts; repeat from ★ around; join with slip st to first BPsc: 16 sps.

Rnd 5: Slip st in next 3 chs and in same ch-5 sp, ch 4, (dc, ch 1, dc) in same sp, ch 2, sc in next ch-3 sp, ch 2, ★ dc in next ch-5 sp, (ch 1, dc in same sp) 4 times, ch 2, sc in next ch-3 sp, ch 2; repeat from ★ around, (dc, ch 1) twice in same sp as beginning ch-4; join with slip st to third ch of beginning ch-4: 48 sps.

Rnd 6: (Slip st, ch 1, sc) in first ch-1 sp, ch 3, (sc in next 2 sps, ch 3) twice, ★ (sc in next ch-1 sp, ch 3) twice, (sc in next 2 sps, ch 3) twice; repeat from ★ around to last ch-1 sp, sc in last ch-1 sp, ch 1, hdc in first sc to form last ch-3 sp: 32 ch-3 sps.

Rnd 7: Ch 1, 3 sc in last ch-3 sp made, 2 sc in next ch-3 sp, ch 2, sc in next ch-3 sp, ch 2, ★ 2 sc in next ch-3 sp, 5 sc in next ch-3 sp, 2 sc in next ch-3 sp, ch 2, sc in next ch-3 sp, ch 2; repeat from ★ around to last ch-3 sp, 2 sc in last ch-3 sp and in same sp as first sc; join with slip st to Back Loop Only of first sc *(Fig. 1, page 143)*: 80 sc and 16 ch-2 sps.

Rnd 8: Ch 3, working in Back Loops Only, dc in next 4 sc, 2 dc in next ch-2 sp, dc in next sc, 2 dc in next ch-2 sp, dc in next 4 sc, ★ 3 dc in next sc, dc in next 4 sc, 2 dc in next ch-2 sp, dc in next sc, 2 dc in next ch-2 sp, dc in next 4 sc; repeat from ★ around, 2 dc in same st as first dc; join with slip st to first dc, do **not** finish off: 128 dc.

FIRST POINT

Row 1: Ch 1, sc in same st, working in both loops, ★ ch 2, skip next dc, sc in next dc; repeat from ★ 5 times **more**, skip next dc, hdc in next dc, leave remaining dc unworked: 6 ch-2 sps.

Row 2: Ch 2, **turn**; sc in first ch-2 sp, (ch 2, sc in next ch-2 sp) 4 times, hdc in last ch-2 sp: 5 ch-2 sps.

Row 3: Ch 2, turn; sc in first ch-2 sp, (ch 2, sc in next ch-2 sp) 3 times, hdc in last ch-2 sp: 4 ch-2 sps.

Row 4: Ch 2, turn; sc in first ch-2 sp, (ch 2, sc in next ch-2 sp) twice, hdc in last ch-2 sp: 3 ch-2 sps.

Row 5: Ch 2, turn; sc in first ch-2 sp, ch 2, sc in next ch-2 sp, hdc in last ch-2 sp: 2 ch-2 sps.

Row 6: Ch 2, turn; sc in first ch-2 sp, hdc in last ch-2 sp: one ch-2 sp.

Row 7: Ch 3, turn; slip st in ch-2 sp; finish off: one ch-3 sp.

NEXT 6 POINTS

Row 1: With **right** side facing and working in both loops, skip next unworked dc on Center from last Point made and join thread with sc in next dc *(see Joining With Sc, page 143)*; ★ ch 2, skip next dc, sc in next dc; repeat from ★ 5 times **more**, skip next dc, hdc in next dc, leave remaining dc unworked: 6 ch-2 sps.

Rows 2-7: Work same as First Point.

LAST POINT

Row 1: With **right** side facing and working in both loops, skip next unworked dc on Center from last Point made and join thread with sc in next dc; ★ ch 2, skip next dc, sc in next dc; repeat from ★ 5 times **more**, skip next dc, hdc in next dc, leave last dc unworked: 6 ch-2 sps.

Rows 2-6: Work same as First Point.

Row 7: Ch 1, turn; hdc in ch-2 sp to form ch-3 sp; do **not** finish off: one ch-3 sp.

EDGING

Rnd 1: Ch 1, do **not** turn; sc in last ch-3 sp made, ★ † (ch 2, sc in end of next row) 6 times, sc in next unworked dc on Rnd 8 of Center and in end of first row on next Point, ch 2, (sc in end of next row, ch 2) 5 times †, sc in next ch-3 sp; repeat from ★ 6 times **more**, then repeat from † to † once; join with slip st to first sc: 96 ch-2 sps.

Rnd 2: Slip st in first ch-2 sp, ch 1, (sc, work Picot, sc) in same sp and in next 5 ch-2 sps, skip next sc, slip st in next sc, (sc, work Picot, sc) in next 6 ch-2 sps, ch 3, slip st in third ch from hook, ch 1, ★ (sc, work Picot, sc) in next 6 ch-2 sps, skip next sc, slip st in next sc, (sc, work Picot, sc) in next 6 ch-2 sps, ch 3, slip st in third ch from hook, ch 1; repeat from ★ around; join with slip st to first sc, finish off.

See Washing and Blocking, page 144.

Finished Size: 5" diameter

MATERIALS

Bedspread Weight Cotton Thread (size 10): 35 yards
Steel crochet hook, size 7 (1.65 mm) **or** size
   needed for gauge

GAUGE SWATCH: 2" diameter
Work same as Doily through Rnd 3.

STITCH GUIDE

2-DC CLUSTER
★ YO, insert hook in sp indicated, YO and pull up a
loop, YO and draw through 2 loops on hook; repeat
from ★ once **more**, YO and draw through all
3 loops on hook.

3-DC CLUSTER
★ YO, insert hook in sp indicated, YO and pull up a
loop, YO and draw through 2 loops on hook; repeat
from ★ 2 times **more**, YO and draw through all
4 loops on hook.

BACK POST SINGLE CROCHET
(abbreviated BPdc)
Insert hook from **back** to **front** around post of dc
indicated *(Fig. 7, page 144)*, YO and pull up a
loop, YO and draw through both loops on hook.

FRONT POST CLUSTER
(abbreviated FP Cluster)
★ YO, insert hook from **front** to **back** around posts
of both BPsc one rnd **below** *(Fig. 7, page 144)*,
YO and pull up a loop, YO and draw through
2 loops on hook; repeat from ★ once **more**, YO
and draw through all 3 loops on hook.

SPLIT FRONT POST TREBLE CROCHET
(abbreviated Split FPtr)
YO twice, insert hook from **front** to **back** around
post of first dc of 5-dc group on Rnd 3 *(Fig. 7,
page 144)*, YO and pull up a loop, (YO and draw
through 2 loops on hook) twice, YO twice, insert
hook from **front** to **back** around post of last dc of
same group, YO and pull up a loop, (YO and draw
through 2 loops on hook) twice, YO and draw
through all 3 loops on hook.

DOILY

Ch 8; join with slip st to form a ring.

Rnd 1 (Right side)**:** Ch 2, work 2-dc Cluster in ring,
(ch 2, work 3-dc Cluster in ring) 9 times, ch 1, sc in top
of first 2-dc Cluster to form last ch-2 sp: 10 ch-2 sps.

Rnd 2: Ch 1, sc in last ch-2 sp made, (sc, ch 2, sc) in
each ch-2 sp around, sc in same sp as first sc, hdc in
first sc to form last ch-2 sp.

Rnd 3: Ch 3 **(counts as first dc)**, 4 dc in same sp,
5 dc in each ch-2 sp around; join with slip st to first dc:
50 dc.

Rnd 4: Ch 1, sc in same st, ch 3, skip next dc, sc in
next dc, ch 3, ★ skip next dc, sc in next 2 dc, ch 3, skip
next dc, sc in next dc, ch 3; repeat from ★ around to last
2 dc, skip next dc, sc in last dc; join with slip st to first
sc: 20 ch-3 sps.

Rnd 5: (Slip st, ch 1, 2 sc) in first ch-3 sp, work
Split FPtr, 2 sc in next ch-3 sp on Rnd 4, ch 3, ★ 2 sc in
next ch-3 sp, work Split FPtr, 2 sc in next ch-3 sp on
Rnd 4, ch 3; repeat from ★ around; join with slip st to
first sc: 50 sts and 10 ch-3 sps.

Rnd 6: Slip st in next 2 sts, ch 1, sc in same st, dc in
next ch-3 sp, (ch 1, dc in same sp) 5 times, skip next
2 sc, ★ sc in next Split FPtr, dc in next ch-3 sp, (ch 1, dc
in same sp) 5 times, skip next 2 sts; repeat from ★
around; join with slip st to first sc: 60 dc.

Rnd 7: Ch 1, ★ work BPsc around next dc, (ch 3, work
BPsc around next dc) 5 times, skip next sc; repeat from
★ around; join with slip st to first BPsc: 50 ch-3 sps.

Rnd 8: (Slip st, ch 1, sc) in first ch-3 sp, ch 3, (sc in
next ch-3 sp, ch 3) 3 times, ★ sc in next 2 ch-3 sps,
ch 3, (sc in next ch-3 sp, ch 3) 3 times; repeat from ★
around to last ch-3 sp, sc in last ch-3 sp; join with slip st
to first sc.

Rnd 9: (Slip st, ch 1, sc) in first ch-3 sp, (ch 4, sc in
next ch-3 sp) 3 times, work FP Cluster, ★ sc in next
ch-3 sp on Rnd 8, (ch 4, sc in next ch-3 sp) 3 times,
work FP Cluster; repeat from ★ around; join with slip st
to first sc: 10 FP Clusters and 30 ch-4 sps.

Rnd 10: (Slip st, ch 1, 2 sc) in first ch-3 sp, ch 4, (sc,
ch 4) twice in next ch-4 sp, 2 sc in next ch-4 sp, skip
next sc, sc in next FP Cluster, ch 3, slip st in top of last
sc made *(Fig. 6a, page 144)*, ★ 2 sc in next ch-4 sp,
ch 4, (sc, ch 4) twice in next ch-4 sp, 2 sc in next
ch-4 sp, skip next sc, sc in next FP Cluster, ch 3, slip st
in top of last sc made; repeat from ★ around; join with
slip st to first sc, finish off.

See Washing and Blocking, page 144.

Finished Size: 7¹/₂" diameter

MATERIALS

Bedspread Weight Cotton Thread (size 10): 75 yards
Steel crochet hook, size 7 (1.65 mm) **or** size
    needed for gauge

GAUGE SWATCH: 1³/₄" diameter
Work same as Doily through Rnd 3.

STITCH GUIDE

SPLIT FRONT POST TREBLE CROCHET
(abbreviated Split FPtr) (uses 2 dc)
First Leg: YO twice, insert hook from **front** to
back around post of dc indicated *(Fig. 7,
page 144)*, YO and pull up a loop, (YO and draw
through 2 loops on hook) twice (2 loops remaining
on hook).

Second Leg: YO twice, insert hook from **front** to
back around post of dc indicated, YO and pull up a
loop, (YO and draw through 2 loops on hook) twice,
YO and draw through all 3 loops on hook.

POPCORN (uses next 3 sc)
2 Dc in each of next 3 sc, drop loop from hook,
insert hook in first dc of 6-dc group, hook dropped
loop and draw through.

SMALL PICOT
Ch 3, slip st in third ch from hook, ch 1.

LARGE PICOT
Ch 4, slip st in third ch from hook, ch 2.

DOILY

Ch 7; join with slip st to form a ring.

Rnd 1 (Right side)**:** Ch 3 **(counts as first dc)**, 2 dc in
ring, ch 2, (3 dc in ring, ch 2) 5 times; join with slip st to
first dc: 18 dc and 6 ch-2 sps.

Rnd 2: Ch 1, sc in same st, sc in next 2 dc and in next
ch-2 sp, work First Leg of Split FPtr around center dc of
first 3-dc group, ★ work Second Leg of Split FPtr
around center dc of next 3-dc group, sc in same sp as
last sc made, sc in next 3 dc and in next ch-2 sp, work
First Leg of Split FPtr around same st as Second Leg of
last Split FPtr made; repeat from ★ around, working
above First Leg of first Split FPtr made, work
Second Leg of Split FPtr around same st, sc in same sp
as last sc made; join with slip st to first sc: 36 sts.

Rnd 3: (Slip st, ch 1, sc) in next sc, ch 4, skip next
2 sc, ★ sc in next st, ch 4, skip next 2 sc; repeat from ★
around; join with slip st to first sc: 12 ch-4 sps.

Rnd 4: (Slip st, ch 3, dc, ch 2, 2 dc) in first ch-4 sp,
ch 2, (2 dc, ch 2) twice in each ch-4 sp around; join with
slip st to first dc: 24 ch-2 sps.

Rnd 5: Slip st in next dc and in next ch-2 sp, ch 3, (dc,
ch 2, 2 dc) in same sp, ch 2, sc in next ch-2 sp, ch 2,
★ (2 dc, ch 2) twice in next ch-2 sp, sc in next ch-2 sp,
ch 2; repeat from ★ around; join with slip st to first dc:
36 ch-2 sps.

Rnd 6: Slip st in next dc and in next ch-2 sp, ch 3, (dc,
ch 2, 2 dc) in same sp, ch 2, (sc in next ch-2 sp, ch 2)
twice, ★ (2 dc, ch 2) twice in next ch-2 sp, (sc in next
ch-2 sp, ch 2) twice; repeat from ★ around; join with
slip st to first dc: 48 ch-2 sps.

Rnd 7: Slip st in next dc and in next ch-2 sp, ch 3, (dc,
ch 2, 2 dc) in same sp, ch 3, sc in next 3 ch-2 sps, ch 3,
★ (2 dc, ch 2, 2 dc) in next ch-2 sp, ch 3, sc in next
3 ch-2 sps, ch 3; repeat from ★ around; join with slip st
to first dc: 36 sc and 36 sps.

Rnd 8: Slip st in next dc and in next ch-2 sp, ch 3, (dc,
ch 2, 2 dc) in same sp, ch 3, sc in next ch-3 sp, ch 1,
work Popcorn, ch 1, sc in next ch-3 sp, ch 3, ★ (2 dc,
ch 2, 2 dc) in next ch-2 sp, ch 3, sc in next ch-3 sp,
ch 1, work Popcorn, ch 1, sc in next ch-3 sp, ch 3;
repeat from ★ around; join with slip st to first dc:
12 Popcorns and 60 sps.

Rnd 9: Slip st in next dc and in next ch-2 sp, ch 3, (dc,
ch 2, 2 dc) in same sp, ch 3, sc in next ch-3 sp, dc in
next ch-1 sp, ch 4, dc in next ch-1 sp, sc in next
ch-3 sp, ch 3, ★ (2 dc, ch 2, 2 dc) in next ch-2 sp, ch 3,
sc in next ch-3 sp, dc in next ch-1 sp, ch 4, dc in next
ch-1 sp, sc in next ch-3 sp, ch 3; repeat from ★ around;
join with slip st to first dc: 72 dc and 48 sps.

Rnd 10: Ch 2, hdc in next dc, 3 dc in next ch-2 sp,
hdc in next 2 dc, ch 3, sc in next ch-3 sp, (2 hdc, 3 dc,
2 hdc) in next ch-4 sp, sc in next ch-3 sp, ch 3, ★ hdc in
next 2 dc, 3 dc in next ch-2 sp, hdc in next 2 dc, ch 3,
sc in next ch-3 sp, (2 hdc, 3 dc, 2 hdc) in next ch-4 sp,
sc in next ch-3 sp, ch 3; repeat from ★ around; join with
slip st to top of beginning ch-2: 192 sts and
24 ch-3 sps.

Rnd 11: Ch 1, sc in same st, ★ † work Small Picot,
skip next hdc, sc in next dc, work Large Picot, skip next
dc, sc in next dc, work Small Picot, skip next hdc, sc in
next hdc, 2 sc in next ch-3 sp, skip next sc, sc in next
hdc, work Small Picot, skip next hdc, sc in next dc, work
Large Picot, skip next dc, sc in next dc, work
Small Picot, skip next hdc, sc in next hdc, 2 sc in next
ch-3 sp †, sc in next hdc; repeat from ★ 10 times **more**,
then repeat from † to † once **more**; join with slip st to
first sc, finish off.

See Washing and Blocking, page 144.

Finished Size: $5^1/_2$" diameter

MATERIALS
Bedspread Weight Cotton Thread (size 10): 35 yards
Steel crochet hook, size 7 (1.65 mm) **or** size
    needed for gauge

GAUGE SWATCH: $1^1/_4$" diameter
Work same as Doily through Rnd 3.

STITCH GUIDE

2-DC CLUSTER
★ YO, insert hook in sp indicated, YO and pull up a
loop, YO and draw through 2 loops on hook; repeat
from ★ once **more**, YO and draw through all
3 loops on hook.

3-DC CLUSTER
★ YO, insert hook in sp indicated, YO and pull up a
loop, YO and draw through 2 loops on hook; repeat
from ★ 2 times **more**, YO and draw through all
4 loops on hook.

BACK POST SINGLE CROCHET
(abbreviated BPsc)
Insert hook from **back** to **front** around post of dc
indicated **(Fig. 7, page 144)**, YO and pull up a
loop, YO and draw through both loops on hook.

PICOT
Ch 2, slip st in top of last dc made **(Fig. 6a,
page 144)**.

DOILY
Ch 10; join with slip st to form a ring.

Rnd 1 (Right side)**:** Ch 2, work 2-dc Cluster in ring,
(ch 3, work 3-dc Cluster in ring) 11 times, ch 1, hdc in
top of 2-dc Cluster to form last ch-3 sp: 12 ch-3 sps.

Rnd 2: Ch 1, sc in last ch-3 sp made, (sc, ch 3, sc) in
each ch-3 sp around, sc in same sp as first sc, ch 1, hdc
in first sc to form last ch-3 sp.

Rnd 3: Ch 1, sc in last ch-3 sp made, dc in next
ch-3 sp, (ch 1, dc in same sp) 5 times, ★ sc in next
ch-3 sp, dc in next ch-3 sp, (ch 1, dc in same sp) 5
times; repeat from ★ around; join with slip st to first sc:
30 ch-1 sps.

Rnd 4: Slip st in next dc and in next ch-1 sp, ch 1, sc
in same sp, ch 3, (sc in next ch-1 sp, ch 3) around; join
with slip st to first sc.

Rnd 5: [Slip st, ch 3 **(counts as first dc)**, 2 dc] in
first ch-3 sp, 3 dc in next ch-3 sp, ch 2, 3 dc in each of
next 2 ch-3 sps, dc in next ch-3 sp, ★ 3 dc in each of
next 2 ch-3 sps, ch 2, 3 dc in each of next 2 ch-3 sps,
dc in next ch-3 sp; repeat from ★ around; join with
slip st to first dc: 78 dc and 6 ch-2 sps.

Rnd 6: Ch 1, ★ † work BPsc around next dc, (ch 4,
skip next dc, work BPsc around next dc) twice, sc in
next ch-2 sp, work BPsc around next dc, (ch 4, skip
next dc, work BPsc around next dc) twice †, ch 4, skip
next 3 dc; repeat from ★ 4 times **more**, then repeat
from † to † once, ch 1, skip last 3 sts, dc in first BPsc to
form last ch-4 sp: 42 sts and 30 ch-4 sps.

Rnd 7: Ch 1, sc in last ch-4 sp made, (ch 4, sc in next
ch-4 sp) twice, skip next BPsc, (dc, ch 4, dc) in next sc,
sc in next ch-4 sp, ★ (ch 4, sc in next ch-4 sp) 4 times,
skip next BPsc, (dc, ch 4, dc) in next sc, sc in next
ch-4 sp; repeat from ★ around to last ch-4 sp, ch 4, sc
in last ch-4 sp, ch 1, dc in first sc to form last ch-4 sp:
30 ch-4 sps.

Rnd 8: Ch 1, 3 sc in last ch-4 sp made and in next
ch-4 sp, ★ † (sc, ch 3, sc) in next ch-4 sp, skip next sc,
dc in next dc, ch 3, (sc, ch 3) twice in next ch-4 sp, dc
in next dc, (sc, ch 3, sc) in next ch-4 sp †, 3 sc in each
of next 2 ch-4 sps; repeat from ★ 4 times **more**, then
repeat from † to † once; join with slip st to first sc:
84 sts and 30 ch-3 sps.

Rnd 9: Ch 1, sc in same st and in next 6 sc, ★ † sc in
next ch-3 sp, skip next sc, dc in next dc, ch 3, slip st in
second ch from hook, ch 2, sc in next ch-3 sp, dc in
next ch-3 sp, (work Picot, dc in same sp) 3 times, sc in
next ch-3 sp, ch 3, slip st in second ch from hook, ch 2,
dc in next dc †, sc in next ch-3 sp and in next 8 sc;
repeat from ★ 4 times **more**, then repeat from † to †
once, sc in next ch-3 sp and in last sc; join with slip st to
first sc, finish off.

See Washing and Blocking, page 144.

Finished Size: 6" (point to point)

MATERIALS

Bedspread Weight Cotton Thread (size 10): 78 yards
Steel crochet hook, size 7 (1.65 mm) **or** size
needed for gauge

GAUGE SWATCH: 1³/₄" diameter
Work same as Doily through Rnd 3.

STITCH GUIDE

BACK POST SINGLE CROCHET
(abbreviated BPsc)
Insert hook from **back** to **front** around post of dc
indicated *(Fig. 7, page 144)*, YO and pull up a
loop, YO and draw through both loops on hook.

BEGINNING DC CLUSTER
Ch 2, ★ YO, insert hook in sp indicated, YO and
pull up a loop, YO and draw through 2 loops on
hook; repeat from ★ once **more**, YO and draw
through all 3 loops on hook.

DC CLUSTER
★ YO, insert hook in ring, YO and pull up a loop,
YO and draw through 2 loops on hook; repeat from
★ 2 times **more**, YO and draw through all 4 loops
on hook.

TR CLUSTER *(uses one sc)*
★ YO twice, insert hook in front 2 legs of sc
indicated *(Fig. 4, page 144)*, YO and pull up a
loop, (YO and draw through 2 loops on hook) twice;
repeat from ★ once **more**, YO and draw through all
3 loops on hook.

SPLIT TREBLE CROCHET
(abbreviated Split tr)
First Leg: YO twice, insert hook from **back** to
front in dc Cluster indicated, YO and pull up a
loop, (YO and draw through 2 loops on hook) twice
(2 loops remaining on hook).

Second Leg: YO twice, skip next Cluster, insert
hook from **front** to **back** in dc Cluster indicated,
YO and pull up a loop, (YO and draw through
2 loops on hook) twice, YO and draw through all
3 loops on hook.

SPLIT FRONT POST TREBLE CROCHET
(abbreviated Split FPtr)
First Leg: YO twice, insert hook from **front** to
back around post of dc indicated *(Fig. 7,
page 144)*, YO and pull up a loop, (YO and draw
through 2 loops on hook) twice (2 loops remaining
on hook).

Second Leg: YO twice, insert hook from **front** to
back around post of dc indicated, YO and pull up a
loop, (YO and draw through 2 loops on hook) twice,
YO and draw through all 3 loops on hook.

SCALLOP
Work Beginning dc Cluster in top of last sc made
(Fig. 6a, page 144), ch 4, (slip st, work Beginning
dc Cluster) in top of last Beginning dc Cluster made
(Fig. 6b, page 144).

PICOT
Ch 3, slip st in third ch from hook, ch 1.

DOILY

Ch 7; join with slip st to form a ring.

Rnd 1 (Right side)**:** Work Beginning dc Cluster in ring,
ch 2, (work dc Cluster, ch 2) 11 times, place marker
around last dc Cluster made for st placement; join with
slip st to top of Beginning dc Cluster: 12 Clusters and
12 ch-2 sps.

Rnd 2: (Slip st, ch 1, sc) in first ch-2 sp, (ch 4, sc in
next ch-2 sp) around, ch 1, dc in first sc to form
last ch-4 sp.

Rnd 3: Ch 1, sc in last ch-4 sp made, working in **front**
of Rnd 2 *(Fig. 5, page 144)*, work First Leg of Split tr
in marked dc Cluster on Rnd 1, skip next dc Cluster,
work Second Leg of Split tr in next dc Cluster, sc in
same sp on Rnd 2 as last sc made, ch 3, sc in next
ch-4 sp, working in **front** of Second Leg of last Split tr
made, work First Leg of Split tr in skipped dc Cluster on
Rnd 1, skip next dc Cluster, ★ work Second Leg of
Split tr in next dc Cluster, sc in same sp on Rnd 2 as last
sc made, ch 3, sc in next ch-4 sp, working in **front** of
Second Leg of last Split tr made, work First Leg of
Split tr in same st as Second Leg of next-to-the-last
Split tr made; repeat from ★ around to last ch-4 sp,
work Second Leg of Split tr in same st as First Leg of
first Split tr made, sc in same sp on Rnd 2 as last sc
made, ch 3, sc in last ch-4 sp, working in **front** of
Second Leg of last Split tr made, work First Leg of
Split tr in same st as Second Leg of next-to-the-last
Split tr made, skip next dc Cluster, working **behind**
First Leg of first Split tr made, work Second Leg of
Split tr in same st as First Leg of second Split tr made, sc
in same sp on Rnd 2 as last sc made, dc in first sc to
form last ch-3 sp.

Rnd 4: Ch 3 **(counts as first dc)**, (dc, ch 2, dc) in last ch-3 sp made, place marker around last dc made for st placement, dc in same sp, (2 dc, ch 2, 2 dc) in each ch-3 sp around; join with slip st to first dc: 48 dc and 12 ch-2 sps.

Rnd 5: Slip st in next dc and in next ch-2 sp, ch 1, sc in same sp, ch 7, (sc in next ch-2 sp, ch 7) around; join with slip st to first sc.

Rnd 6: (Slip st, ch 1, sc, ch 2, sc) in first ch-7 sp, work First Leg of Split FPtr around marked dc on Rnd 4, skip next 2 dc, work Second Leg of Split FPtr around next dc, (sc, ch 2) twice in same sp on Rnd 5 as last sc made, ★ (sc, ch 2, sc) in next ch-7 sp, work First Leg of Split FPtr around next dc on Rnd 4, skip next 2 dc, work Second Leg of Split FPtr around next dc, (sc, ch 2) twice in same sp on Rnd 5 as last sc made; repeat from ★ around; join with slip st to first sc: 36 ch-2 sps.

Rnd 7: (Slip st, ch 1, sc) in first ch-2 sp, ch 5, sc in next ch-2 sp, 2 sc in next ch-2 sp, ★ sc in next ch-2 sp, ch 5, sc in next ch-2 sp, 2 sc in next ch-2 sp; repeat from ★ around; join with slip st to first sc: 48 sc and 12 ch-5 sps.

Rnd 8: [Slip st, ch 4 **(counts as first dc plus ch 1)**, dc] in first ch-5 sp, (ch 1, dc in same sp) 5 times, work tr Cluster in next sc on Rnd 5 (between Split tr), ★ dc in next ch-5 sp on Rnd 7, (ch 1, dc in same sp) 6 times, work tr Cluster in next sc on Rnd 5 (between Split tr); repeat from ★ around; join with slip st to first dc: 96 sts and 72 ch-1 sps.

Rnd 9: Ch 1, work BPsc around same st, (ch 3, work BPsc around next dc) 6 times, skip next tr Cluster, ★ work BPsc around next dc, (ch 3, work BPsc around next dc) 6 times, skip next tr Cluster; repeat from ★ around; join with slip st to first BPsc.

Rnd 10: (Slip st, ch 1, sc) in first ch-3 sp, 2 sc in next ch-3 sp, 3 sc in each of next 2 ch-3 sps, 2 sc in next ch-3 sp, ★ sc in next 2 ch-3 sps, 2 sc in next ch-3 sp, 3 sc in each of next 2 ch-3 sps, 2 sc in next ch-3 sp; repeat from ★ around to last ch-3 sp, sc in last ch-3 sp; join with slip st to first sc: 144 sc.

Rnd 11: (Slip st, ch 1, sc) in next sc, work Picot, skip next 2 sc, sc in next sc, work Scallop, skip next 2 sc, sc in next sc, work Picot, skip next 2 sc, sc in next sc, pull up a loop in next 2 sc, YO and draw through all 3 loops on hook, ★ sc in next sc, work Picot, skip next 2 sc, sc in next sc, work Scallop, skip next 2 sc, sc in next sc, work Picot, skip next 2 sc, sc in next sc, pull up a loop in next 2 sts, YO and draw through all 3 loops on hook; repeat from ★ around; join with slip st to first sc, finish off.

See Washing and Blocking, page 144.

83 ▮▬▬▬

Finished Size: 5¹/₄" diameter

MATERIALS
Bedspread Weight Cotton Thread (size 10): 58 yards
Steel crochet hook, size 7 (1.65 mm) **or** size needed for gauge

GAUGE SWATCH: 2" diameter
Work same as Doily through Rnd 6.

STITCH GUIDE

> **TREBLE CROCHET** *(abbreviated tr)*
> YO twice, insert hook in st indicated, YO and pull up a loop (4 loops on hook), (YO and draw through 2 loops on hook) 3 times.
>
> **FRONT POST CLUSTER**
> *(abbreviated FP Cluster)*
> ★ YO twice, insert hook from **front** to **back** around post of dc indicated *(Fig. 7, page 144)*, YO and pull up a loop, (YO and draw through 2 loops on hook) twice; repeat from ★ once **more**, YO and draw through all 3 loops on hook.

DOILY
Rnd 1 (Right side)**:** Ch 4, 11 dc in fourth ch from hook; join with slip st to top of beginning ch-4: 12 sts.

Rnd 2: Ch 1, (sc, tr) in same st and in each dc around pulling tr to right side **now and throughout**; join with slip st to first sc: 24 sts.

Rnd 3: Ch 1, sc in same st and in each st around; join with slip st to first sc.

Rnd 4: Ch 1, sc in same st, 2 sc in next sc, (sc in next sc, 2 sc in next sc) around; join with slip st to first sc: 36 sc.

Rnd 5: Ch 1, sc in same st, tr in next sc, (sc in next sc, tr in next sc) around; join with slip st to first sc.

Rnd 6: Ch 1, sc in same st, 2 sc in next tr, (sc in next sc, 2 sc in next tr) around; join with slip st to first sc: 54 sts.

Rnd 7: Ch 5 **(counts as first dc plus ch 2)**, skip next sc, ★ dc in next sc, ch 2, skip next sc; repeat from ★ around; join with slip st to first dc: 27 dc and 27 ch-2 sps.

Rnd 8: Ch 1, sc in same st, 2 sc in next ch-2 sp, (sc in next dc, 2 sc in next ch-2 sp) around; join with slip st to first sc, do **not** finish off: 81 sc.

Continued on page 124.

Rnd 9: Ch 1, sc in same st and in each sc around; join with slip st to first sc.

Rnd 10: (Slip st, ch 1, sc) in next sc, ch 1, sc in next sc, working in **front** of previous rnds *(Fig. 5, page 144)*, work FP Cluster around next dc on Rnd 7, skip next sc on Rnd 9 from last sc made, ★ sc in next sc, ch 1, sc in next sc, working in **front** of previous rnds, work FP Cluster around next dc on Rnd 7, skip next sc on Rnd 9 from last st made; repeat from ★ around; join with slip st to first sc: 27 ch-1 sps.

Rnd 11: (Slip st, ch 1, sc) in first ch-1 sp, (ch 4, sc in next ch-1 sp) around, ch 2, hdc in first sc to form last ch-4 sp.

Rnd 12: Ch 1, sc in last ch-4 sp made, ch 1, ★ (sc, ch 2, sc) in next ch-4 sp, ch 1; repeat from ★ around, sc in same sp as first sc, ch 1, sc in first sc to form last ch-2 sp.

Rnd 13: Ch 1, sc in last ch-2 sp made, ch 5, skip next ch-1 sp, ★ sc in next ch-2 sp, ch 5, skip next ch-1 sp; repeat from ★ around; join with slip st to first sc: 27 ch-5 sps.

Rnd 14: Slip st in first ch-5 sp, ch 1, (sc, hdc, 3 dc, hdc, sc) in same sp and in each ch-5 sp around; join with slip st to first sc, finish off.

See Washing and Blocking, page 144.

84 ▮▬

Finished Size: 6¹/₄" diameter

MATERIALS
Bedspread Weight Cotton Thread (size 10): 85 yards
Steel crochet hook, size 7 (1.65 mm) **or** size needed for gauge

GAUGE SWATCH: 1³/₄" diameter
Work same as Doily through Rnd 4.

STITCH GUIDE

TREBLE CROCHET *(abbreviated tr)*
YO twice, insert hook in st indicated, YO and pull up a loop (4 loops on hook), (YO and draw through 2 loops on hook) 3 times.

POPCORN
4 Dc in ch-2 sp indicated, drop loop from hook, insert hook in first dc of 4-dc group, hook dropped loop and draw through.

FRONT POST CLUSTER
(abbreviated FP Cluster) (uses one dc)
★ YO twice, insert hook from **front** to **back** around post of dc indicated *(Fig. 7, page 144)*, YO and pull up a loop, (YO and draw through 2 loops on hook) twice; repeat from ★ once **more**, YO and draw through all 3 loops on hook.

SPLIT FRONT POST CLUSTER
(abbreviated Split FP Cluster)
[YO twice, insert hook from **front** to **back** around post of last dc of same 6-dc group on Rnd 8 *(Fig. 7, page 144)*, YO and pull up a loop, (YO and draw through 2 loops on hook) twice] 2 times (3 loops remaining on hook), [YO twice, insert hook from **front** to **back** around post of first dc of next 6-dc group, YO and pull up a loop, (YO and draw through 2 loops on hook) twice] 2 times, YO and draw through all 5 loops on hook.

SMALL PICOT
Ch 2, slip st in second ch from hook, ch 1.

LARGE PICOT
Ch 3, slip st in third ch from hook, ch 1.

DOILY

Ch 6; join with slip st to form a ring.

Rnd 1 (Right side)**:** Ch 1, 12 sc in ring; join with slip st to Back Loop Only of first sc *(Fig. 1, page 143)*.

Note: Loop a short piece of thread around any stitch to mark Rnd 1 as **right** side.

Rnd 2: Ch 1, working in Back Loops Only, sc in same st, 2 sc in next sc, (sc in next sc, 2 sc in next sc) around; join with slip st to **both** loops of first sc: 18 sc.

Rnd 3: Ch 1, working in both loops, sc in same st, ch 3, skip next sc, ★ sc in next sc, ch 3, skip next sc; repeat from ★ around; join with slip st to first sc: 9 ch-3 sps.

Rnd 4: [Slip st, ch 3 **(counts as first dc)**, 4 dc] in first ch-3 sp, 5 dc in each ch-3 sp around; join with slip st to first dc: 45 dc.

Rnd 5: Ch 1, sc in same st, ★ ch 2, skip next dc, sc in next dc, ch 2, skip next dc, sc in next 2 dc; repeat from ★ around to last 4 dc, (ch 2, skip next dc, sc in next dc) twice; join with slip st to first sc: 27 sc and 18 ch-2 sps.

Rnd 6: Ch 1, sc in same st, ch 4, work Popcorn in next ch-2 sp, ch 3, work Popcorn in next ch-2 sp, ch 4, ★ sc in next 2 sc, ch 4, work Popcorn in next ch-2 sp, ch 3, work Popcorn in next ch-2 sp, ch 4; repeat from ★ around to last sc, sc in last sc; join with slip st to first sc: 27 sps.

Rnd 7: Slip st in next 2 chs, ch 1, sc in same ch-4 sp, (sc, ch 3, sc) in next ch-3 sp, sc in next ch-4 sp, ch 5, ★ sc in next ch-4 sp, (sc, ch 3, sc) in next ch-3 sp, sc in next ch-4 sp, ch 5; repeat from ★ around; join with slip st to first sc: 18 sps.

Rnd 8: Slip st in next sc and in next ch-3 sp, ch 1, 2 sc in same sp, dc in next ch-5 sp, (ch 1, dc in same sp) 5 times, ★ 2 sc in next ch-3 sp, dc in next ch-5 sp, (ch 1, dc in same sp) 5 times; repeat from ★ around; join with slip st to first sc: 45 ch-1 sps.

Rnd 9: Slip st in next 2 sts and in next ch-1 sp, ch 1, sc in same sp, (ch 3, sc in next ch-1 sp) around, ch 2, sc in first sc to form last ch-3 sp.

Rnd 10: Ch 1, sc in last ch-3 sp made and in next ch-3 sp, skip first dc of 6-dc group on Rnd 8, work FP Cluster around next dc, ★ † sc in same sp on Rnd 9 as last sc made, (ch 3, sc in next ch-3 sp, work FP Cluster around next dc, sc in same sp on Rnd 9 as last sc made) 3 times, sc in next ch-3 sp, work Split FP Cluster, sc in same sp on Rnd 9 as last sc made †, sc in next ch-3 sp, work FP Cluster around next dc of 6-dc group on Rnd 8; repeat from ★ 7 times **more**, then repeat from † to † once; join with slip st to first sc: 9 Split FP Clusters, 36 FP Clusters, and 27 ch-3 sps.

Rnd 11: Slip st in next 3 sts and in next ch-3 sp, ch 1, 2 sc in same sp, (ch 5, 2 sc in next ch-3 sp) twice, skip next 4 sts, (tr, ch 5, tr) in next Split FP Cluster, ★ 2 sc in next ch-3 sp, (ch 5, 2 sc in next ch-3 sp) twice, skip next 4 sts, (tr, ch 5, tr) in next Split FP Cluster; repeat from ★ around; join with slip st to first sc: 27 ch-5 sps.

Rnd 12: Slip st in next sc and in next ch-5 sp, ch 1, [3 sc, ch 2, slip st in top of last sc made *(Fig. 6a, page 144)*, 3 sc] in same sp and in next ch-5 sp, in next ch-5 sp work (2 dc, Small Picot, 2 dc, Large Picot, 2 dc, Small Picot, 2 dc), ★ (3 sc, ch 2, slip st in top of last sc made, 3 sc) in next 2 ch-5 sps, in next ch-5 sp work (2 dc, Small Picot, 2 dc, Large Picot, 2 dc, Small Picot, 2 dc); repeat from ★ around; join with slip st to first sc, finish off.

TRIM

With **right** side facing and working in free loops of sc on Rnd 1 *(Fig. 2a, page 144)*, join thread with slip st in any sc; ch 3, slip st in same st, ch 3, (slip st, ch 3) twice in each sc around; join with slip st to first slip st, finish off.

See Washing and Blocking, page 144.

85 ▰

Finished Size: 5¹/₂" diameter

MATERIALS
Bedspread Weight Cotton Thread (size 10): 42 yards
Steel crochet hook, size 7 (1.65 mm) **or** size needed for gauge

GAUGE SWATCH: 1¹/₄" diameter
Work same as Doily through Rnd 2.

STITCH GUIDE

2-DC CLUSTER (uses one st or sp)
★ YO, insert hook in st or sp indicated, YO and pull up a loop, YO and draw through 2 loops on hook; repeat from ★ once **more**, YO and draw through all 3 loops on hook.

3-DC CLUSTER
★ YO, insert hook in sp indicated, YO and pull up a loop, YO and draw through 2 loops on hook; repeat from ★ 2 times **more**, YO and draw through all 4 loops on hook.

SMALL PICOT
Ch 2, slip st in top of last sc made *(Fig. 6a, page 144)*.

LARGE PICOT
Ch 3, slip st in third ch from hook, ch 1.

DOILY

Ch 7; join with slip st to form a ring.

Rnd 1 (Right side)**:** Ch 2, work 2-dc Cluster in ring, ch 3, (work 3-dc Cluster in ring, ch 3) 7 times; join with slip st to top of first 2-dc Cluster: 8 Clusters and 8 ch-3 sps.

Rnd 2: Ch 1, sc in same st, (sc, ch 3, sc) in next ch-3 sp, ★ sc in next Cluster, (sc, ch 3, sc) in next ch-3 sp; repeat from ★ around; join with slip st to first sc: 24 sc and 8 ch-3 sps.

Rnd 3: Ch 2, dc in same st and in next ch-3 sp, (ch 1, dc in same sp) 4 times, skip next sc, ★ work 2-dc Cluster in next sc, dc in next ch-3 sp, (ch 1, dc in same sp) 4 times, skip next sc; repeat from ★ around; join with slip st to first dc: 40 dc and 32 ch-1 sps.

Rnd 4: (Slip st, ch 1, sc) in next dc, (sc in next ch-1 sp and in next dc) 4 times, skip next st, ★ sc in next dc, (sc in next ch-1 sp and in next dc) 4 times, skip next st; repeat from ★ around; join with slip st to first sc, do **not** finish off: 72 sc.

Continued on page 126.

Rnd 5: Slip st in next sc, ch 1, sc in same st and in next 2 sc, 3 sc in next sc, sc in next 3 sc, ★ ch 1, skip next 2 sc, sc in next 3 sc, 3 sc in next sc, sc in next 3 sc; repeat from ★ to last 2 sts, skip last 2 sts, sc in first sc to form last ch-1 sp: 72 sc and 9 ch-1 sps.

Rnd 6: Ch 1, sc in last ch-1 sp made, ch 3, skip next 2 sc, sc in next sc, ch 3, (skip next sc, sc in next sc, ch 3) twice, ★ sc in next ch-1 sp, ch 3, skip next 2 sc, sc in next sc, ch 3, (skip next sc, sc in next sc, ch 3) twice; repeat from ★ around; join with slip st to first sc: 32 ch-3 sps.

Rnd 7: (Slip st, ch 1, sc) in first ch-3 sp, (ch 4, sc in next ch-3 sp) 3 times, ★ sc in next ch-3 sp, (ch 4, sc in next ch-3 sp) 3 times; repeat from ★ around; join with slip st to first sc: 24 ch-4 sps.

Rnd 8: Slip st in next ch, ch 1, 2 sc in same ch-4 sp, (dc, ch 3, dc) in next sc, sc in next ch-4 sp, (dc, ch 3, dc) in next sc, 2 sc in next ch-4 sp, ch 3, ★ 2 sc in next ch-4 sp, (dc, ch 3, dc) in next sc, sc in next ch-4 sp, (dc, ch 3, dc) in next sc, 2 sc in next ch-4 sp, ch 3; repeat from ★ around; join with slip st to first sc: 24 ch-3 sps.

Rnd 9: Slip st in next 2 sts and in next ch-3 sp, ch 1, 2 sc in same sp, ★ † skip next dc, (dc, ch 5, dc) in next sc, 2 sc in next ch-3 sp, work 2-dc Cluster in next ch-3 sp, (ch 2, work 2-dc Cluster in same sp) 3 times †, 2 sc in next ch-3 sp; repeat from ★ 7 times **more**, then repeat from † to † once; join with slip st to first sc: 32 sps.

Rnd 10: (Slip st, ch 1, sc) in next sc, ★ † in next ch-5 sp work (sc, Small Picot, sc, Large Picot, sc, Small Picot, sc), skip next dc, sc in next sc, (sc, work Large Picot, sc) in next 3 ch-3 sps, skip next Cluster and next sc †, sc in next sc; repeat from ★ 7 times **more**, then repeat from † to † once; join with slip st to first sc, finish off.

See Washing and Blocking, page 144.

86 ▰

Finished Size: 6" diameter

MATERIALS
Bedspread Weight Cotton Thread (size 10): 52 yards
Steel crochet hook, size 7 (1.65 mm) **or** size needed for gauge

GAUGE SWATCH: $1^3/4$" diameter
Work same as Doily through Rnd 6.

STITCH GUIDE

2-DC CLUSTER (uses one sp)
★ YO, insert hook in sp indicated, YO and pull up a loop, YO and draw through 2 loops on hook; repeat from ★ once **more**, YO and draw through all 3 loops on hook.

3-DC CLUSTER (uses one ch-3 sp)
★ YO, insert hook in ch-3 sp indicated, YO and pull up a loop, YO and draw through 2 loops on hook; repeat from ★ 2 times **more**, YO and draw through all 4 loops on hook.

SPLIT TREBLE CROCHET
   (abbreviated Split tr)
First Leg: YO twice, working in **front** of previous rnds *(Fig. 5, page 144)*, insert hook in st indicated, YO and pull up a loop, (YO and draw through 2 loops on hook) twice (2 loops remaining on hook).

Second Leg: YO twice, insert hook in sc indicated, YO and pull up a loop, (YO and draw through 2 loops on hook) twice, YO and draw through all 3 loops on hook.

FRONT POST CLUSTER
   (abbreviated FP Cluster)
★ YO twice, insert hook from **front** to **back** around post of center dc of 3-dc group on Rnd 13 *(Fig. 7, page 144)*, YO and pull up a loop, (YO and draw through 2 loops on hook) twice; repeat from ★ once **more**, YO and draw through all 3 loops on hook.

PICOT
Ch 2, slip st in second ch from hook, ch 1.

DOILY
Ch 8; join with slip st to form a ring.

Rnd 1 (Right side)**:** Ch 1, 12 sc in ring; join with slip st to first sc.

Rnd 2: Ch 1, sc in same st, 2 sc in next sc, (sc in next sc, 2 sc in next sc) around; join with slip st to first sc: 18 sc.

Rnd 3: Ch 1, sc in same st and in each sc around; join with slip st to first sc.

Rnd 4: Ch 1, sc in same st, 2 sc in next sc, (sc in next sc, 2 sc in next sc) around; join with slip st to first sc: 27 sc.

Rnd 5: Ch 1, sc in same st and in next sc, 2 sc in next sc, (sc in next 2 sc, 2 sc in next sc) around, place marker in last sc made for st placement; join with slip st to first sc: 36 sc.

Rnd 6: Ch 1, sc in same st, ★ ch 3, skip next sc, sc in next sc; repeat from ★ around to last sc, ch 1, skip last sc, hdc in first sc to form last ch-3 sp: 18 ch-3 sps.

Rnd 7: Ch 2, work 2-dc Cluster in last ch-3 sp made, ch 4, sc in next ch-3 sp, ch 4, ★ work 3-dc Cluster in next ch-3 sp, ch 4, sc in next ch-3 sp, ch 4; repeat from ★ around; join with slip st to top of first 2-dc Cluster.

Rnd 8: (Slip st, ch 1, 2 sc) in first ch-4 sp, work First Leg of Split tr in marked sc on Rnd 5, skip next unworked sc, ★ work Second Leg of Split tr in next unworked sc, 2 sc in next ch-4 sp on Rnd 7, ch 5, 2 sc in next ch-4 sp, work First Leg of Split tr in same st on Rnd 5 as Second Leg of last Split tr made, skip next unworked sc; repeat from ★ around to last ch-4 sp, work Second Leg of Split tr in same st on Rnd 5 as First Leg of first Split tr made, 2 sc in last ch-4 sp, ch 5; join with slip st to first sc: 45 sts and 9 ch-5 sps.

Rnd 9: Ch 1, sc in same st, ch 5, skip next 3 sts, sc in next sc, 5 sc in next ch-5 sp, ★ sc in next sc, ch 5, skip next 3 sts, sc in next sc, 5 sc in next ch-5 sp; repeat from ★ around; join with slip st to first sc: 9 ch-5 sps.

Rnd 10: (Slip st, ch 1, 5 sc) in first ch-5 sp, ch 2, skip next 3 sc, (sc, ch 3, sc) in next sc, ch 2, ★ 5 sc in next ch-5 sp, ch 2, skip next 3 sc, (sc, ch 3, sc) in next sc, ch 2; repeat from ★ around; join with slip st to first sc: 63 sc and 27 sps.

Rnd 11: Ch 1, sc in same st, ch 3, (skip next sc, sc in next sc, ch 3) twice, skip next ch-2 sp, sc in next ch-3 sp, ch 3, skip next ch-2 sp, ★ sc in next sc, ch 3, (skip next sc, sc in next sc, ch 3) twice, skip next ch-2 sp, sc in next ch-3 sp, ch 3, skip next ch-2 sp; repeat from ★ around; join with slip st to first sc: 36 ch-3 sps.

Rnd 12: (Slip st, ch 1, sc) in first ch-3 sp, (ch 4, sc in next ch-3 sp) around, ch 1, dc in first sc to form last ch-4 sp.

Rnd 13: Ch 3 **(counts as first dc)**, 2 dc in last ch-4 sp made, (ch 1, 3 dc in next ch-4 sp) around, sc in first dc to form last ch-1 sp: 108 dc and 36 ch-1 sps.

Rnd 14: Ch 1, sc in last ch-1 sp made, (ch 4, sc in next ch-1 sp) around, ch 1, dc in first sc to form last ch-4 sp.

Rnd 15: Ch 1, 2 sc in last ch-4 sp made, work 2-dc Cluster in next ch-4 sp, (ch 3, work 2-dc Cluster in same sp) twice, ★ 2 sc in next ch-4 sp, work 2-dc Cluster in next ch-4 sp, (ch 3, work 2-dc Cluster in same sp) twice; repeat from ★ around; join with slip st to first sc: 36 ch-3 sps.

Rnd 16: Slip st in next 2 sts and in next ch-3 sp, ch 1, 3 sc in same sp, work Picot, 3 sc in next ch-3 sp, work FP Cluster, ★ 3 sc in next ch-3 sp, work Picot, 3 sc in next ch-3 sp, work FP Cluster; repeat from ★ around; join with slip st to first sc, finish off.

See Washing and Blocking, page 144.

87

Finished Size: 5$\frac{1}{4}$" diameter

MATERIALS
Bedspread Weight Cotton Thread (size 10): 39 yards
Steel crochet hook, size 7 (1.65 mm) **or** size needed for gauge

GAUGE SWATCH: 2" diameter
Work same as Doily through Rnd 3.

STITCH GUIDE

SPLIT TREBLE CROCHET
(abbreviated Split tr)
First Leg: YO twice, working in **front** of last 2 rnds *(Fig. 5, page 144)*, insert hook in dc indicated, YO and pull up a loop, (YO and draw through 2 loops on hook) twice (2 loops remaining on hook).

Second Leg: YO twice, insert hook in dc indicated, YO and pull up a loop, (YO and draw through 2 loops on hook) twice, YO and draw through all 3 loops on hook.

BEGINNING CLUSTER (uses one ch-1 sp)
★ YO, insert hook in ch-1 sp indicated, YO and pull up a loop, YO and draw through 2 loops on hook; repeat from ★ once **more**, YO and draw through all 3 loops on hook.

CLUSTER (uses one ch-1 sp)
★ YO, insert hook in ch-1 sp indicated, YO and pull up a loop, YO and draw through 2 loops on hook; repeat from ★ 2 times **more**, YO and draw through all 4 loops on hook.

DOILY

Ch 7; join with slip st to form a ring.

Rnd 1 (Right side)**:** Ch 3 **(counts as first dc)**, 21 dc in ring, place marker around last dc made for st placement, 2 dc in ring; join with slip st to first dc: 24 dc.

Rnd 2: Ch 1, sc in same st, ★ ch 3, skip next dc, sc in next dc; repeat from ★ around to last dc, ch 1, skip last dc, hdc in first sc to form last ch-3 sp: 12 ch-3 sps.

Rnd 3: Ch 1, sc in last ch-3 sp made, (ch 5, sc in next ch-3 sp) around, ch 2, dc in first sc to form last ch-5 sp; do **not** finish off.

Continued on page 128.

Rnd 4: Ch 1, sc in last ch-5 sp made, work First Leg of Split tr in marked dc on Rnd 1, ★ work Second Leg of Split tr in next skipped dc, sc in same sp on Rnd 3 as last sc made, ch 7, sc in next ch-5 sp, work First Leg of Split tr in same st as Second Leg of last Split tr made; repeat from ★ around, work Second Leg of Split tr in same st as First Leg of first Split tr made, sc in same sp on Rnd 3 as last sc made, ch 7; join with slip st to first sc.

Rnd 5: Slip st in next 2 sts and in next ch-7 sp, ch 1, sc in same sp, (ch 3, sc in same sp) 4 times, ★ sc in next ch-7 sp, (ch 3, sc in same sp) 4 times; repeat from ★ around; join with slip st to first sc: 48 ch-3 sps.

Rnd 6: (Slip st, ch 1, sc) in first ch-3 sp, (ch 4, sc in next ch-3 sp) 3 times, ★ sc in next ch-3 sp, (ch 4, sc in next ch-3 sp) 3 times; repeat from ★ around; join with slip st to first sc: 36 ch-4 sps.

Rnd 7: (Slip st, ch 1, sc) in first ch-4 sp, dc in next ch-4 sp, (ch 1, dc in same sp) 5 times, ★ sc in next 2 ch-4 sps, dc in next ch-4 sp, (ch 1, dc in same sp) 5 times; repeat from ★ around to last ch-4 sp, sc in last ch-4 sp; join with slip st to first sc: 60 ch-1 sps.

Rnd 8: Slip st in next dc and in next ch-1 sp, ch 2, work Beginning Cluster in same sp, (ch 2, work Cluster in next ch-1 sp) 4 times, ★ work Cluster in next ch-1 sp, (ch 2, work Cluster in next ch-1 sp) 4 times; repeat from ★ around; join with slip st to top of Beginning Cluster: 48 ch-2 sps.

Rnd 9: Slip st in first ch-2 sp, ch 1, (sc, ch 2, sc) in same sp and in each ch-2 sp around; join with slip st to first sc, finish off.

See Washing and Blocking, page 144.

88 ▬▬▬

Finished Size: 6^1/$_2$" diameter

MATERIALS

Bedspread Weight Cotton Thread (size 10): 60 yards
Steel crochet hook, size 7 (1.65 mm) **or** size needed for gauge

GAUGE SWATCH: 1^3/$_4$" diameter
Work same as Doily through Rnd 3.

STITCH GUIDE

BEGINNING CLUSTER
Ch 2, YO, insert hook in both loops of next sc, YO and pull up a loop, YO and draw through 2 loops on hook, YO, insert hook in Front Loop Only of next sc **(Fig. 1, page 143)**, YO and pull up a loop, YO and draw through 2 loops on hook, YO and draw through all 3 loops on hook.

CLUSTER
YO, insert hook in free loop of same st as last leg of last Cluster made **(Fig. 2a, page 144)**, YO and pull up a loop, YO and draw through 2 loops on hook, YO, insert hook in **both** loops of next sc, YO and pull up a loop, YO and draw through 2 loops on hook, YO, insert hook in Front Loop Only of next sc **(Fig. 1, page 143)**, YO and pull up a loop, YO and draw through 2 loops on hook, YO and draw through all 4 loops on hook.

3-DC CLUSTER
YO, working in **front** of previous rnd **(Fig. 5, page 144)**, insert hook in front 2 legs of sc one rnd **below (Fig. 4, page 144)**, YO and pull up a loop, YO and draw through 2 loops on hook, ★ YO, insert hook in **same** st, YO and pull up a loop, YO and draw through 2 loops on hook; repeat from ★ once **more**, YO and draw through all 4 loops on hook.

SPLIT FRONT POST TREBLE CROCHET
(abbreviated Split FPtr)
First Leg: YO twice, insert hook from **front** to **back** around post of dc indicated **(Fig. 7, page 144)**, YO and pull up a loop, (YO and draw through 2 loops on hook) twice (2 loops remaining on hook).

Second Leg: YO twice, insert hook from **front** to **back** around post of next dc, YO and pull up a loop, (YO and draw through 2 loops on hook) twice, YO and draw though all 3 loops on hook.

128

BEGINNING DECREASE
(uses 2 dc and one ch-1 sp)

YO, insert hook in next dc, YO and pull up a loop, YO and draw through 2 loops on hook, YO, insert hook in next ch-1 sp, YO and pull up a loop, YO and draw through 2 loops on hook, YO, insert hook in Front Loop Only of next dc, YO and pull up a loop, YO and draw through 2 loops on hook, YO and draw through all 4 loops on hook.

DECREASE (uses 2 dc and one ch-1 sp)

YO, insert hook in free loop of last dc worked into, YO and pull up a loop, YO and draw through 2 loops on hook, YO, insert hook in next ch-1 sp, YO and pull up a loop, YO and draw through 2 loops on hook, YO, insert hook in Front Loop Only of next dc, YO and pull up a loop, YO and draw through 2 loops on hook, YO and draw through all 4 loops on hook.

ENDING DECREASE
(uses 2 dc and one ch-1 sp)

YO, insert hook in free loop of last dc worked into, YO and pull up a loop, YO and draw through 2 loops on hook, YO, insert hook in next ch-1 sp, YO and pull up a loop, YO and draw through 2 loops on hook, YO, insert hook in **both** loops of next dc, YO and pull up a loop, YO and draw through 2 loops on hook, YO and draw through all 4 loops on hook.

PICOT
Ch 2, slip st in top of last sc made *(Fig. 6a, page 144)*.

DOILY

Ch 14; join with slip st to form a ring.

Rnd 1 (Right side)**:** Ch 1, 30 sc in ring; join with slip st to Back Loop Only of first sc *(Fig. 1, page 143)*.

Rnd 2: Work Beginning Cluster, (ch 3, work Cluster) around to last sc, working second leg of last Cluster in last sc and last leg in free loop of first sc, ch 1, hdc in top of Beginning Cluster to form last ch-3 sp: 15 ch-3 sps.

Rnd 3: Ch 1, sc in last ch-3 sp made, (sc, ch 3, sc) in each ch-3 sp around, sc in same sp as first sc, ch 1, hdc in first sc to form last ch-3 sp.

Rnd 4: Ch 3 **(counts as first dc)**, dc in last ch-3 sp made, (2 dc, ch 2, 2 dc) in each ch-3 sp around, 2 dc in same sp as first dc, hdc in first dc to form last ch-2 sp: 60 dc and 15 ch-2 sps.

Rnd 5: Ch 1, sc in last ch-2 sp made, work First Leg of Split FPtr around first dc of last 2-dc group made, work Second Leg of Split FPtr, sc in same sp as last sc made, ch 4, ★ sc in next ch-2 sp, work First Leg of Split FPtr around first dc of next 2-dc group, work Second Leg of Split FPtr, sc in same sp as last sc made, ch 4; repeat from ★ around; join with slip st to first sc: 15 Split FPtr and 15 ch-4 sps.

Rnd 6: (Slip st, ch 1, sc) in next Split FPtr, ch 3, (sc, ch 3) twice in next ch-4 sp, skip next sc, ★ sc in next Split FPtr, ch 3, (sc, ch 3) twice in next ch-4 sp, skip next sc; repeat from ★ around; join with slip st to first sc: 45 ch-3 sps.

Rnd 7: (Slip st, ch 1, sc) in first ch-3 sp, ch 3, sc in next ch-3 sp, ch 3, ★ sc in next 2 ch-3 sps, ch 3, sc in next ch-3 sp, ch 3; repeat from ★ around to last ch-3 sp, sc in last ch-3 sp; join with slip st to first sc: 30 ch-3 sps.

Rnd 8: (Slip st, ch 1, sc) in first ch-3 sp, ch 4, sc in next ch-3 sp, ch 1, work 3-dc Cluster, ch 1, ★ sc in next ch-3 sp, ch 4, sc in next ch-3 sp, ch 1, work 3-dc Cluster, ch 1; repeat from ★ around; join with slip st to first sc: 15 3-dc Clusters and 15 ch-4 sps.

Rnd 9: (Slip st, ch 4, dc) in first ch-4 sp, (ch 1, dc in same sp) 5 times, skip next sc, sc in next 3-dc Cluster, skip next ch-1 sp, ★ dc in next ch-4 sp, (ch 1, dc in same sp) 6 times, skip next sc, sc in next 3-dc Cluster, skip next ch-1 sp; repeat from ★ around; join with slip st to third ch of beginning ch-4: 120 sts and 90 ch-1 sps.

Rnd 10: (Slip st, ch 1, sc) in first ch-1 sp, ch 3, work beginning decrease, ch 3, (work decrease, ch 3) twice, work ending decrease, ch 3, sc in next ch-1 sp, ★ skip next dc, sc in next sc and in next ch-1 sp, ch 3, work beginning decrease, ch 3, (work decrease, ch 3) twice, work ending decrease, ch 3, sc in next ch-1 sp; repeat from ★ around to last 3 sts, skip next dc, sc in next sc, skip last st; join with slip st to first sc: 75 ch-3 sps.

Rnd 11: Slip st in next 2 chs, ch 1, sc in same ch-3 sp, (2 sc, work Picot, 2 sc) in next ch-3 sp, (sc, ch 3, slip st in third ch from hook, ch 1, sc) in next ch-3 sp, (2 sc, work Picot, 2 sc) in next ch-3 sp, ★ sc in next 2 ch-3 sps, (2 sc, work Picot, 2 sc) in next ch-3 sp, (sc, ch 3, slip st in third ch from hook, ch 1, sc) in next ch-3 sp, (2 sc, work Picot, 2 sc) in next ch-3 sp; repeat from ★ around to last ch-3 sp, sc in last ch-3 sp; join with slip st to first sc, finish off.

See Washing and Blocking, page 144.

Finished Size: 8^1/$_2$" diameter

MATERIALS

Bedspread Weight Cotton Thread (size 10): 83 yards
Steel crochet hook, size 7 (1.65 mm) **or** size
   needed for gauge

GAUGE SWATCH: 1^7/$_8$" diameter
Work same as Doily through Rnd 6.

STITCH GUIDE

TREBLE CROCHET (abbreviated tr)
YO twice, insert hook in sc indicated, YO and pull
up a loop (4 loops on hook), (YO and draw through
2 loops on hook) 3 times.

TRIPLE TREBLE CROCHET
   (abbreviated tr tr)
YO 4 times, insert hook in ch-3 sp indicated, YO
and pull up a loop (6 loops on hook), (YO and draw
through 2 loops on hook) 5 times.

FRONT POST DOUBLE CROCHET
   (abbreviated FPdc)
YO, insert hook from **front** to **back** around post of
dc indicated **(Fig. 7, page 144)**, YO and pull up a
loop (3 loops on hook), (YO and draw through
2 loops on hook) twice.

FRONT POST TREBLE CROCHET
   (abbreviated FPtr)
YO twice, insert hook from **front** to **back** around
post of FPdc indicated **(Fig. 7, page 144)**, YO and
pull up a loop (4 loops on hook), (YO and draw
through 2 loops on hook) 3 times.

DECREASE (uses next 3 ch-3 sps)
YO, skip next 2 ch-3 sps, insert hook in next
ch-3 sp, YO and pull up a loop, YO and draw
through 2 loops on hook, YO, insert hook in first
skipped ch-3 sp, YO and pull up a loop, YO and
draw through 2 loops on hook, YO and draw
through all 3 loops on hook.

CLUSTER (uses next 5 sts)
★ † YO, insert hook in **next** dc, YO and pull up a
loop, YO and draw through 2 loops on hook †;
repeat from ★ once **more**, YO, insert hook from
back to **front** around post of next tr tr **(Fig. 7,
page 144)**, YO and pull up a loop, YO and draw
through 2 loops on hook, repeat from † to † twice,
YO and draw through all 6 loops on hook, ch 3,
slip st in top of st just made **(Fig. 6b, page 144)**.

DOILY

Ch 10; join with slip st to form a ring.

Rnd 1 (Right side)**:** Ch 3 **(counts as first dc, now
and throughout)**, 23 dc in ring; join with slip st to first
dc: 24 dc.

Rnd 2: Ch 1, sc in same st, work FPdc around next dc,
(sc in next dc, work FPdc around next dc) around; join
with slip st to Back Loop Only of first sc **(Fig. 1,
page 143)**.

Rnd 3: Ch 1, working in Back Loops Only, sc in same
st, 2 sc in next FPdc, (sc in next sc, 2 sc in next FPdc)
around; join with slip st to **both** loops of first sc: 36 sc.

Rnd 4: Ch 1, sc in same st and in both loops of each sc
around; join with slip st to first sc.

Rnd 5: Ch 1, sc in same st and in next sc, 2 sc in next
sc, (sc in next 2 sc, 2 sc in next sc) around; join with
slip st to first sc: 48 sc.

Rnd 6: Ch 1, sc in same st, work FPtr around first
FPdc on Rnd 2, skip next sc on Rnd 5 from last sc
made, sc in next sc, tr in free loop of next sc on Rnd 2
(Fig. 2a, page 144), ★ skip next sc on Rnd 5 from last
sc made, sc in next sc, work FPtr around next FPdc on
Rnd 2, skip next sc on Rnd 5 from last sc made, sc in
next sc, tr in free loop of next sc on Rnd 2; repeat from
★ around; join with slip st to first sc.

Rnd 7: Ch 1, sc in same st, ★ ch 3, skip next st, sc in
next sc; repeat from ★ around to last tr, ch 1, skip last tr,
hdc in first sc to form last ch-3 sp: 24 ch-3 sps.

Rnd 8: Ch 3, dc in last ch-3 sp made, sc in next
ch-3 sp, ch 3, sc in next ch-3 sp, ★ (2 dc, ch 2, 2 dc) in
next ch-3 sp, sc in next ch-3 sp, ch 3, sc in next
ch-3 sp; repeat from ★ around, 2 dc in same sp as first
dc, ch 1, sc in first dc to form last ch-2 sp: 16 sc and
16 sps.

Rnd 9: Ch 3, dc in last ch-2 sp made, ch 3, skip next
2 dc, sc in next sc, (sc, ch 3, sc) in next ch-3 sp, sc in
next sc, ch 3, ★ (2 dc, ch 2, 2 dc) in next ch-2 sp, ch 3,
skip next 2 dc, sc in next sc, (sc, ch 3, sc) in next
ch-3 sp, sc in next sc, ch 3; repeat from ★ around, 2 dc
in same sp as first dc, ch 1, sc in first dc to form last
ch-2 sp: 32 sps.

Rnd 10: Ch 3, dc in last ch-2 sp made, ch 3, 2 sc in
next ch-3 sp, (sc, ch 3, sc) in next ch-3 sp, 2 sc in next
ch-3 sp, ch 3, ★ (2 dc, ch 2, 2 dc) in next ch-2 sp, ch 3,
2 sc in next ch-3 sp, (sc, ch 3, sc) in next ch-3 sp, 2 sc
in next ch-3 sp, ch 3; repeat from ★ around, 2 dc in
same sp as first dc, ch 1, sc in first dc to form last
ch-2 sp.

Rnd 11: Ch 3, (dc, ch 2, 2 dc) in last ch-2 sp made, ch 3, 2 sc in next ch-3 sp, (sc, ch 3, sc) in next ch-3 sp, 2 sc in next ch-3 sp, ch 3, ★ 2 dc in next ch-2 sp, (ch 2, 2 dc in same sp) twice, ch 3, 2 sc in next ch-3 sp, (sc, ch 3, sc) in next ch-3 sp, 2 sc in next ch-3 sp, ch 3; repeat from ★ around, 2 dc in same sp as first dc, ch 1, sc in first dc to form last ch-2 sp: 40 sps.

Rnd 12: Ch 3, dc in last ch-2 sp made, ★ † ch 3, (2 dc, ch 2, 2 dc) in next ch-2 sp, ch 3, 2 sc in next ch-3 sp, (sc, ch 3, sc) in next ch-3 sp, 2 sc in next ch-3 sp, ch 3 †, (2 dc, ch 2, 2 dc) in next ch-2 sp; repeat from ★ 6 times **more**, then repeat from † to † once, 2 dc in same sp as first dc, ch 1, sc in first dc to form last ch-2 sp: 48 sps.

Rnd 13: Ch 3, dc in last ch-2 sp made, ★ † ch 3, sc in next ch-3 sp, ch 3, (2 dc, ch 2, 2 dc) in next ch-2 sp, ch 3, 2 sc in next ch-3 sp, (sc, ch 3, sc) in next ch-3 sp, 2 sc in next ch-3 sp, ch 3 †, (2 dc, ch 2, 2 dc) in next ch-2 sp; repeat from ★ 6 times **more**, then repeat from † to † once, 2 dc in same sp as first dc, ch 1, sc in first dc to form last ch-2 sp: 56 sps.

Rnd 14: Ch 3, dc in last ch-2 sp made, ★ † ch 3, 2 sc in next ch-3 sp, sc in next sc, 2 sc in next ch-3 sp, ch 3, (2 dc, ch 2, 2 dc) in next ch-2 sp, ch 3, 2 sc in next ch-3 sp, (sc, ch 3, sc) in next ch-3 sp, 2 sc in next ch-3 sp, ch 3 †, (2 dc, ch 2, 2 dc) in next ch-2 sp; repeat from ★ 6 times **more**, then repeat from † to † once, 2 dc in same sp as first dc, ch 1, sc in first dc to form last ch-2 sp.

Rnd 15: Ch 3, dc in last ch-2 sp made, ★ † ch 3, 2 sc in next ch-3 sp, ch 7, 2 sc in next ch-3 sp, ch 3, (2 dc, ch 2, 2 dc) in next ch-2 sp, decrease †, (2 dc, ch 2, 2 dc) in next ch-2 sp; repeat from ★ 6 times **more**, then repeat from † to † once, 2 dc in same sp as first dc, ch 2; join with slip st to first dc: 40 sps.

Rnd 16: Slip st in next dc and in next ch-3 sp, ch 1, 2 sc in same sp, ★ † ch 3, (sc, ch 3) 4 times in next ch-7 sp, 2 sc in next ch-3 sp, ch 4, 2 dc in next ch-2 sp, working **behind** previous rnd *(Fig. 5, page 144)*, tr tr in skipped ch-3 sp on Rnd 14, 2 dc in next ch-2 sp on Rnd 15 †, ch 4, 2 sc in next ch-3 sp; repeat from ★ 6 times **more**, then repeat from † to † once, tr in first sc to form last ch-4 sp: 56 sps.

Rnd 17: Ch 1, 4 sc in last ch-4 sp made, ★ † sc in next ch-3 sp, (dc, ch 2, slip st in second ch from hook, ch 1, dc) in next ch-3 sp, (dc, ch 3, slip st in second ch from hook, ch 2, dc) in next ch-3 sp, (dc, ch 2, slip st in second ch from hook, ch 1, dc) in next ch-3 sp, sc in next ch-3 sp, 4 sc in next ch-4 sp, ch 3, work Cluster, ch 3 †, 4 sc in next ch-4 sp; repeat from ★ 6 times **more**, then repeat from † to † once; join with slip st to first sc, finish off.

See Washing and Blocking, page 144.

Finished Size: 9¹/₂" diameter

MATERIALS

Bedspread Weight Cotton Thread (size 10): 118 yards
Steel crochet hook, size 7 (1.65 mm) **or** size needed for gauge

GAUGE SWATCH: 2¹/₂" diameter
Work same as Doily through Rnd 5.

STITCH GUIDE

TREBLE CROCHET *(abbreviated tr)*
YO twice, insert hook in ch-3 sp indicated, YO and pull up a loop (4 loops on hook), (YO and draw through 2 loops on hook) 3 times.

BACK POST DOUBLE CROCHET
(abbreviated BPdc)
YO, insert hook from **back** to **front** around post of dc indicated *(Fig. 7, page 144)*, YO and pull up a loop, (YO and draw through 2 loops on hook) twice.

SMALL PICOT
Ch 3, slip st in second ch from hook, ch 2.

LARGE PICOT
Ch 5, slip st in third ch from hook, ch 2.

DOILY

Rnd 1 (Right side)**:** Ch 2, sc in second ch from hook, (ch 3, sc in same ch) 5 times, ch 1, hdc in first sc to form last ch-3 sp: 6 ch-3 sps.

Rnd 2: Ch 1, sc in last ch-3 sp made, (ch 4, sc in next ch-3 sp) around, ch 1, dc in first sc to form last ch-4 sp.

Rnd 3: Ch 1, (sc, ch 3) twice in last ch-4 sp made, (sc, ch 3) 3 times in each ch-4 sp around, sc in same sp as first sc, ch 1, hdc in first sc to form last ch-3 sp: 18 ch-3 sps.

Rnd 4: Ch 1, sc in last ch-3 sp made, (ch 3, sc in next ch-3 sp) around, dc in first sc to form last ch-3 sp.

Rnd 5: Ch 3 **(counts as first dc, now and throughout)**, 2 dc in last ch-3 sp made, 4 dc in next ch-3 sp, (3 dc in next ch-3 sp, 4 dc in next ch-3 sp) around; join with slip st to first dc: 63 dc.

Rnd 6: Ch 1, sc in same st and in each dc around; join with slip st to first sc, do **not** finish off.

Continued on page 132.

Rnd 7: Ch 1, sc in same st and in next 5 sc, 2 sc in next sc, (sc in next 6 sc, 2 sc in next sc) around; join with slip st to first sc: 72 sc.

Rnd 8: Ch 3, dc in same st, ch 2, skip next 2 sc, sc in next sc, ch 5, skip next 2 sc, sc in next sc, ch 2, skip next 2 sc, ★ (2 dc, ch 2) twice in next sc, skip next 2 sc, sc in next sc, ch 5, skip next 2 sc, sc in next sc, ch 2, skip next 2 sc; repeat from ★ around, 2 dc in same st as first dc, ch 1, sc in first dc to form last ch-2 sp: 32 sps.

Rnd 9: Ch 3, dc in last ch-2 sp made, ch 2, sc in next ch-2 sp, 7 dc in next ch-5 sp, sc in next ch-2 sp, ch 2, ★ (2 dc, ch 2) twice in next ch-2 sp, sc in next ch-2 sp, 7 dc in next ch-5 sp, sc in next ch-2 sp, ch 2; repeat from ★ around, 2 dc in same sp as first dc, ch 1, sc in first dc to form last ch-2 sp: 88 dc and 24 ch-2 sps.

Rnd 10: Ch 3, dc in last ch-2 sp made, ★ † ch 2, sc in next ch-2 sp, skip next sc, work BPdc around next dc, (ch 1, work BPdc around next dc) 6 times, sc in next ch-2 sp, ch 2 †, (2 dc, ch 2) twice in next ch-2 sp; repeat from ★ 6 times **more**, then repeat from † to † once, 2 dc in same sp as first dc, ch 1, sc in first dc to form last ch-2 sp: 80 sps.

Rnd 11: Ch 3, (dc, ch 2, 2 dc) in last ch-2 sp made, ★ † ch 2, sc in next 2 sps, ch 3, (sc in next ch-1 sp, ch 3) 4 times, sc in next 2 sps, ch 2 †, (2 dc, ch 2) 3 times in next ch-2 sp; repeat from ★ 6 times **more**, then repeat from † to † once, 2 dc in same sp as first dc, ch 1, sc in first sc to form last ch-2 sp.

Rnd 12: Ch 3, dc in last ch-2 sp made, ★ † ch 3, (2 dc, ch 2) twice in next ch-2 sp, sc in next 2 sps, ch 3, (sc in next ch-3 sp, ch 3) 3 times, sc in next 2 sps, ch 2 †, (2 dc, ch 2, 2 dc) in next ch-2 sp; repeat from ★ 6 times **more**, then repeat from † to † once, 2 dc in same sp as first dc, ch 1, sc in first dc to form last ch-2 sp: 72 sps.

Rnd 13: Ch 3, dc in last ch-2 sp made, ★ † ch 3, sc in next ch-3 sp, ch 3, (2 dc, ch 2) twice in next ch-2 sp, sc in next 2 sps, ch 3, (sc in next ch-3 sp, ch 3) twice, sc in next 2 sps, ch 2 †, (2 dc, ch 2, 2 dc) in next ch-2 sp; repeat from ★ 6 times **more**, then repeat from † to † once, 2 dc in same sp as first dc, ch 1, sc in first dc to form last ch-2 sp.

Rnd 14: Ch 3, dc in last ch-2 sp made, ★ † ch 3, 2 sc in next ch-3 sp, ch 6, 2 sc in next ch-3 sp, ch 3, (2 dc, ch 2) twice in next ch-2 sp, sc in next 2 sps, ch 3, sc in next ch-3 sp, ch 3, sc in next 2 sps, ch 2 †, (2 dc, ch 2, 2 dc) in next ch-2 sp; repeat from ★ 6 times **more**, then repeat from † to † once, 2 dc in same sp as first dc, ch 1, sc in first dc to form last ch-2 sp.

Rnd 15: Ch 3, dc in last ch-2 sp made, ★ † ch 3, 2 sc in next ch-3 sp, sc in next ch-6 sp, (ch 3, sc in same sp) 3 times, 2 sc in next ch-3 sp, ch 3, (2 dc, ch 2) twice in next ch-2 sp, sc in next 2 sps, ch 3, sc in next 2 sps, ch 2 †, (2 dc, ch 2, 2 dc) in next ch-2 sp; repeat from ★ 6 times **more**, then repeat from † to † once, 2 dc in same sp as first dc, ch 1, sc in first dc to form last ch-2 sp: 80 sps.

Rnd 16: Ch 3, dc in last ch-2 sp made, ★ † ch 3, 2 sc in next ch-3 sp, ch 11, skip next 3 ch-3 sps, 2 sc in next ch-3 sp, ch 3, (2 dc, ch 2) twice in next ch-2 sp, sc in next 3 sps, ch 2 †, (2 dc, ch 2, 2 dc) in next ch-2 sp; repeat from ★ 6 times **more**, then repeat from † to † once, 2 dc in same sp as first dc, hdc in first dc to form last ch-2 sp: 48 sps and 8 loops.

Rnd 17: Ch 1, 2 sc in last ch-2 sp made, ★ † ch 5, 2 sc in next ch-3 sp, sc in next loop, working in **front** of same loop *(Fig. 5, page 144)*, tr in first skipped ch-3 sp on Rnd 15, 2 sc in same loop on Rnd 16 as last sc made, working in **front** of same loop, tr in same sp on Rnd 15 as last tr made, sc in same loop on Rnd 16 as last sc made, (working in **front** of same loop, tr in **next** skipped ch-3 sp on Rnd 15, 2 sc in same loop on Rnd 16 as last sc made, working in **front** of same loop, tr in same sp on Rnd 15 as last tr made, sc in same loop on Rnd 16 as last sc made) twice, 2 sc in next ch-3 sp, ch 5, 2 sc in next ch-2 sp, skip next 2 ch-2 sps †, 2 sc in next ch-2 sp; repeat from ★ 6 times **more**, then repeat from † to † once; join with slip st to first sc: 192 sts and 16 ch-5 sps.

Rnd 18: Slip st in next sc and in next ch-5 sp, ch 1, 5 sc in same sp, ★ † sc in next 4 sts, work Small Picot, skip next 2 sc, sc in next tr, skip next sc, sc in next tr, work Large Picot, skip next 2 sc, sc in next tr, skip next sc, sc in next tr, work Small Picot, skip next 2 sc, sc in next 4 sts, 5 sc in next ch-5 sp, work Large Picot †, 5 sc in next ch-5 sp; repeat from ★ 6 times **more**, then repeat from † to † once; join with slip st to first sc, finish off.

See Washing and Blocking, page 144.

Finished Size: 7¹/₂" diameter

MATERIALS

Bedspread Weight Cotton Thread (size 10): 62 yards
Steel crochet hook, size 7 (1.65 mm) **or** size
needed for gauge

GAUGE SWATCH: 2" diameter
Work same as Doily through Rnd 2.

STITCH GUIDE

TREBLE CROCHET *(abbreviated tr)*
YO twice, insert hook in ch-3 sp indicated, YO and
pull up a loop (4 loops on hook), (YO and draw
through 2 loops on hook) 3 times.

2-DC CLUSTER (uses one sp)
★ YO, insert hook in sp indicated, YO and pull up a
loop, YO and draw through 2 loops on hook;
repeat from ★ once **more**, YO and draw through
all 3 loops on hook.

3-DC CLUSTER (uses one sp)
★ YO, insert hook in sp indicated, YO and pull up a
loop, YO and draw through 2 loops on hook;
repeat from ★ 2 times **more**, YO and draw through
all 4 loops on hook.

DECREASE (uses next 6 sc)
† YO, insert hook in **next** sc, YO and pull up a
loop, YO and draw through 2 loops on hook †, skip
next sc, repeat from † to † twice, skip next sc,
repeat from † to † once, YO and draw through all
5 loops on hook.

PICOT
Ch 3, slip st in third ch from hook, ch 1.

DOILY

Ch 8; join with slip st to form a ring.

Rnd 1 (Right side)**:** Ch 2, work 2-dc Cluster in ring,
(ch 3, work 3-dc Cluster in ring) 9 times, ch 1, hdc in
top of first 2-dc Cluster to form last ch-3 sp:
10 ch-3 sps.

Rnd 2: Ch 3 **(counts as first dc)**, dc in last ch-3 sp
made, (2 dc, ch 2, 2 dc) in each ch-3 sp around, 2 dc in
same sp as first dc, ch 1, sc in first dc to form last
ch-2 sp: 40 dc and 10 ch-2 sps.

Rnd 3: Ch 1, sc in last ch-2 sp made and in next 4 dc,
★ (sc, ch 2, sc) in next ch-2 sp, sc in next 4 dc; repeat
from ★ around, sc in same sp as first sc, ch 1, sc in first
sc to form last ch-2 sp: 60 sc and 10 ch-2 sps.

Rnd 4: Ch 1, sc in last ch-2 sp made and in next 6 sc,
★ (sc, ch 2, sc) in next ch-2 sp, sc in next 6 sc; repeat
from ★ around, sc in same sp as first sc, hdc in first sc
to form last ch-2 sp: 80 sc and 10 ch-2 sps.

Rnd 5: Ch 5 **(counts as first dc plus ch 2, now
and throughout)**, dc in last ch-2 sp made, ch 3, skip
next sc, decrease, ch 3, ★ (dc, ch 2, dc) in next ch-2 sp,
ch 3, skip next sc, decrease, ch 3; repeat from ★
around; join with slip st to first dc: 30 sps.

Rnd 6: (Slip st, ch 5, dc) in first ch-2 sp, ch 3, 2 sc in
each of next 2 ch-3 sps, ch 3, ★ (dc, ch 2, dc) in next
ch-2 sp, ch 3, 2 sc in each of next 2 ch-3 sps, ch 3;
repeat from ★ around; join with slip st to first dc.

Rnd 7: (Slip st, ch 5, dc, ch 2, dc) in first ch-2 sp,
ch 3, (sc in next ch-3 sp, ch 3) twice, ★ dc in next
ch-2 sp, (ch 2, dc in same sp) twice, ch 3, (sc in next
ch-3 sp, ch 3) twice; repeat from ★ around; join with
slip st to first dc: 50 sps.

Rnd 8: (Slip st, ch 5, dc) in first ch-2 sp, ch 4, (dc,
ch 2, dc) in next ch-2 sp, ch 3, sc in next 3 ch-3 sps,
ch 3, ★ (dc, ch 2, dc) in next ch-2 sp, ch 4, (dc, ch 2,
dc) in next ch-2 sp, ch 3, sc in next 3 ch-3 sps, ch 3;
repeat from ★ around; join with slip st to first dc.

Rnd 9: (Slip st, ch 5, dc) in first ch-2 sp, ★ † ch 4, sc
in next ch-4 sp, ch 4, (dc, ch 2, dc) in next ch-2 sp, skip
next ch-3 sp, tr in next ch-3 sp, ch 4, working in **front**
of last tr made, tr in skipped ch-3 sp †, (dc, ch 2, dc) in
next ch-2 sp; repeat from ★ 8 times **more**, then repeat
from † to † once; join with slip st to first dc.

Rnd 10: (Slip st, ch 5, dc) in first ch-2 sp, ★ † ch 3, sc
in next ch-4 sp, ch 4, sc in next ch-4 sp, ch 3, (dc,
ch 2, dc) in next ch-2 sp, sc in next ch-4 sp †, (dc, ch 2,
dc) in next ch-2 sp; repeat from ★ 8 times **more**, then
repeat from † to † once; join with slip st to first dc.

Rnd 11: Slip st in first ch-2 sp, ch 7, ★ † sc in next
ch-3 sp, work 2-dc Cluster in next ch-4 sp, (ch 2, work
2-dc Cluster in same sp) 4 times, sc in next ch-3 sp,
ch 4 †, dc in next 2 ch-2 sps, ch 4; repeat from ★
8 times **more**, then repeat from † to † once, dc in last
ch-2 sp; join with slip st to third ch of beginning ch-7:
60 sps.

Rnd 12: (Slip st, ch 1, 4 sc) in first ch-4 sp, (sc, work
Picot, sc) in next 4 ch-2 sps, 4 sc in next ch-4 sp, work
Picot, ★ 4 sc in next ch-4 sp, (sc, work Picot, sc) in next
4 ch-2 sps, 4 sc in next ch-4 sp, work Picot; repeat
from ★ around; join with slip st to first sc, finish off.

See Washing and Blocking, page 144.

Finished Size: $7^1/_2$"w x $6^3/_4$"h

MATERIALS
Bedspread Weight Cotton Thread (size 10): 48 yards
Steel crochet hook, size 7 (1.65 mm) **or** size
   needed for gauge

GAUGE SWATCH: $2^1/_2$" square
Work same as First Motif.

STITCH GUIDE

TREBLE CROCHET *(abbreviated tr)*
YO twice, insert hook in sc indicated, YO and pull
up a loop (4 loops on hook), (YO and draw through
2 loops on hook) 3 times.

BEGINNING CLUSTER (uses one ch-3 sp)
Ch 3, ★ YO, insert hook in ch-3 sp indicated, YO
and pull up a loop, YO and draw through 2 loops
on hook; repeat from ★ once **more**, YO and draw
through all 3 loops on hook.

CLUSTER (uses one ch-3 sp)
★ YO, insert hook in ch-3 sp indicated, YO and pull
up a loop, YO and draw through 2 loops on hook;
repeat from ★ 2 times **more**, YO and draw through
all 4 loops on hook.

DECREASE
Pull up a loop in next 2 joining sps, YO and draw
through all 3 loops on hook.

SMALL PICOT
Ch 2, slip st in top of last st made *(Fig. 6a,
page 144)*.

LARGE PICOT
Ch 3, slip st in third ch from hook, ch 1.

FIRST MOTIF

Rnd 1 (Right side): Ch 5, (dc in fifth ch from hook,
ch 1) 11 times; join with slip st to fourth ch of beginning
ch-5: 12 sts and 12 sps.

Note: Loop a short piece of thread around any stitch to
mark Rnd 1 as **right** side.

Rnd 2: (Slip st, ch 1, sc) in first ch-1 sp, (ch 3, sc in
next ch-1 sp) around, dc in first sc to form last ch-3 sp.

Rnd 3: Work Beginning Cluster in last ch-3 sp made,
(ch 4, work Cluster in next ch-3 sp) around, ch 3, sc in
top of Beginning Cluster to form last ch-4 sp.

Rnd 4: Ch 1, sc in last ch-4 sp made, ★ sc in next
ch-4 sp, (ch 3, sc in same sp) twice; repeat from ★
around, (sc, ch 3, sc) in same sp as first sc, ch 1, hdc in
first sc to form last ch-3 sp: 24 ch-3 sps.

Rnd 5: Ch 3 **(counts as first dc, now and
throughout)**, dc in last ch-3 sp made, ch 2, sc in next
ch-3 sp, (ch 3, sc in next 2 ch-3 sps) twice, ch 2,
★ (2 dc, ch 2) twice in next ch-3 sp, sc in next ch-3 sp,
(ch 3, sc in next 2 ch-3 sps) twice, ch 2; repeat from ★
2 times **more**, 2 dc in same sp as first dc, ch 2; join
with slip st to first dc, finish off.

SECOND MOTIF
Rnds 1-4: Work same as First Motif: 24 ch-3 sps.

Rnd 5 (Joining rnd)**:** Ch 3, dc in last ch-3 sp made,
ch 2, sc in next ch-3 sp, (ch 3, sc in next 2 ch-3 sps)
twice, ch 2, ★ (2 dc, ch 2) twice in next ch-3 sp, sc in
next ch-3 sp, (ch 3, sc in next 2 ch-3 sps) twice, ch 2;
repeat from ★ once **more**, 2 dc in next ch-3 sp, ch 1,
holding Motifs with **wrong** sides together, slip st in
corresponding corner ch-2 sp on **First Motif**, ch 1,
2 dc in same sp as last dc made on **new Motif**, ch 2, sc
in next ch-3 sp, ch 1, skip next ch-2 sp on **First Motif**,
sc in next ch-3 sp, ch 1, sc in next 2 ch-3 sps on **new
Motif**, ch 1, sc in next ch-3 sp on **First Motif**, ch 1, sc
in next 2 ch-3 sps on **new Motif**, ch 2, 2 dc in same sp
as first dc, ch 1, skip next ch-2 sp on **First Motif**, slip st
in next corner ch-2 sp, ch 1; join with slip st to first dc,
finish off.

THIRD MOTIF
Rnds 1-4: Work same as First Motif: 24 ch-3 sps.

Rnd 5 (Joining rnd)**:** Ch 3, dc in last ch-3 sp made,
ch 2, sc in next ch-3 sp, (ch 3, sc in next 2 ch-3 sps)
twice, ch 2, ★ (2 dc, ch 2) twice in next ch-3 sp, sc in
next ch-3 sp, (ch 3, sc in next 2 ch-3 sps) twice, ch 2;
repeat from ★ once **more**, 2 dc in next ch-3 sp, ch 1,
holding Motifs with **wrong** sides together, slip st in
joining slip st on **Second Motif**, place marker in slip st
just made for st placement, ch 1, 2 dc in same sp as last
dc made on **new Motif**, ch 2, sc in next ch-3 sp, ch 1,
skip next ch-2 sp on **Second Motif**, sc in next ch-3 sp,
ch 1, sc in next 2 ch-3 sps on **new Motif**, ch 1, sc in
next ch-3 sp on **Second Motif**, ch 1, sc in next
2 ch-3 sps on **new Motif**, ch 2, 2 dc in same sp as first
dc, ch 1, skip next ch-2 sp on **Second Motif**, slip st in
next corner ch-2 sp, ch 1; join with slip st to first dc,
finish off.

EDGING

Rnd 1: With **right** side facing, join thread with sc in ch-2 sp **before** marked slip st *(see Joining With Sc, page 143)*; ch 4, working **around** slip sts *(Fig. 5, page 144)*, pull up a loop in each of next 3 joining sps, YO and draw through all 4 loops on hook, ch 4, (sc in next sp, ch 4) 4 times, [3 sc in next corner ch-2 sp, ch 4, (sc in next sp, ch 4) 4 times] twice, decrease, ch 4, (sc in next sp, ch 4) 4 times, (dc, ch 7, dc) in next corner ch-2 sp, ch 4, (sc in next sp, ch 4) 4 times, decrease, ch 4, [(sc in next sp, ch 4) 4 times, 3 sc in next ch-2 sp, ch 4] twice, sc in next sp, (ch 4, sc in next sp) twice, tr in first sc to form last ch-4 sp: 41 sps.

Rnd 2: Ch 3, 6 dc in last ch-4 sp made, sc in next 2 ch-4 sps, (7 dc in next ch-4 sp, sc in next ch-4 sp) twice, [ch 7, sc in next ch-4 sp, (7 dc in next ch-4 sp, sc in next ch-4 sp) twice] 2 times, ch 4, sc in next ch-4 sp, (7 dc in next ch-4 sp, sc in next ch-4 sp) twice, 13 dc in next ch-7 sp, sc in next ch-4 sp, (7 dc in next ch-4 sp, sc in next ch-4 sp) twice, ch 4, sc in next ch-4 sp, (7 dc in next ch-4 sp, sc in next ch-4 sp) twice, ch 7, sc in next ch-4 sp, (7 dc in next ch-4 sp, sc in next ch-4 sp) twice, ch 7, sc in next ch-4 sp, 7 dc in next ch-4 sp, sc in last ch-4 sp; join with slip st to first dc: 149 sts.

Rnd 3: Ch 1, sc in same st, (work Large Picot, skip next dc, sc in next dc) twice, ch 3, skip next 3 sts, sc in sp **before** next sc, ch 3, skip next 3 sts, sc in next dc, (work Large Picot, skip next dc, sc in next dc) twice, slip st in next sc, sc in next dc, (work Large Picot, skip next dc, sc in next dc) 3 times, ♥ sc in next ch-7 sp, working in **front** of same sp *(Fig. 5, page 144)*, tr in first sc of next 3-sc group one rnd **below**, ★ (sc, work Small Picot, sc) in same sp on Rnd 2 as last sc made, working in **front** of same sp, tr in **next** sc one rnd **below**; repeat from ★ once **more**, sc in same sp on Rnd 2 as last sc made ♥, skip next sc, sc in next dc, (work Large Picot, skip next dc, sc in next dc) twice, skip next 2 dc, (4 dc, work Small Picot, 3 dc) in next sc, skip next 2 dc, sc in next dc, (work Large Picot, skip next dc, sc in next dc) twice, repeat from ♥ to ♥ once, skip next sc, † sc in next dc, (work Large Picot, skip next dc, sc in next dc) 3 times, slip st in next sc, sc in next dc, (work Large Picot, skip next dc, sc in next dc) 3 times †, (3 sc, work Small Picot, 2 sc) in next ch-4 sp, skip next sc, repeat from † to † once, slip st in next sc, (sc in next dc, work Large Picot, skip next dc) 3 times, (dc, work Large Picot, dc) in next dc, (work Large Picot, skip next dc, sc in next dc) 3 times, slip st in next sc, repeat from † to † once, (3 sc, work Small Picot, 2 sc) in next ch-4 sp, repeat from † to † once, repeat from ♥ to ♥ once, skip next sc, sc in next dc, (work Large Picot, skip next dc, sc in next dc) twice, skip next 2 dc, (4 dc, work Small Picot, 3 dc) in next sc, skip next 2 dc, sc in next dc, (work Large Picot, skip next dc, sc in next dc) twice, repeat from ♥ to ♥ once, skip next sc, sc in next dc, (work Large Picot, skip next dc, sc in next dc) 3 times, slip st in last sc; join with slip st to first sc, finish off.

See Washing and Blocking, page 144.

93 ▰▬▬

Finished Size: $6^1/_4$" (point to point)

MATERIALS
Bedspread Weight Cotton Thread (size 10): 75 yards
Steel crochet hook, size 7 (1.65 mm) **or** size needed for gauge

GAUGE SWATCH: $2^1/_2$" diameter
Work same as Doily through Rnd 5.

STITCH GUIDE

SPLIT FRONT POST TREBLE CROCHET
(abbreviated Split FPtr)
First Leg: YO twice, insert hook from **front** to **back** around post of sc indicated *(Fig. 7, page 144)*, YO and pull up a loop, (YO and draw through 2 loops on hook) twice (2 loops remaining on hook).

Second Leg: YO twice, insert hook from **front** to **back** around post of sc indicated, YO and pull up a loop, (YO and draw through 2 loops on hook) twice, YO and draw through all 3 loops on hook.

BEGINNING POPCORN
Ch 3, 3 dc in ch-2 sp indicated, drop loop from hook, insert hook in first dc of 4-dc group, hook dropped loop and draw through.

POPCORN
4 Dc in ch-2 sp indicated, drop loop from hook, insert hook in first dc of 4-dc group, hook dropped loop and draw through.

PICOT
Ch 4, slip st in third ch from hook, ch 2.

DOILY

Ch 7; join with slip st to form a ring.

Rnd 1 (Right side)**:** Ch 2, 23 hdc in ring; join with slip st to top of beginning ch-2: 24 sts.

Rnd 2: Ch 1, sc in same st, ch 2, skip next hdc, ★ sc in next hdc, ch 2, skip next hdc; repeat from ★ around; join with slip st to first sc: 12 ch-2 sps.

Rnd 3: (Slip st, ch 1, sc) in first ch-2 sp, ch 3, (sc in next ch-2 sp, ch 3) around; join with slip st to first sc.

Rnd 4: [Slip st, ch 3 **(counts as first dc, now and throughout)**, 3 dc] in first ch-3 sp, 4 dc in each ch-3 sp around; join with slip st to first dc, do **not** finish off: 48 dc.

Continued on page 136.

Rnd 5: Ch 1, sc in same st and in next dc, work First Leg of Split FPtr around first sc on Rnd 3, ★ work Second Leg of Split FPtr around next sc, sc in next 4 dc on Rnd 4, work First Leg of Split FPtr around same sc as Second Leg of last Split FPtr made; repeat from ★ around to last 2 dc on Rnd 4, working **above** First Leg of first Split FPtr made, work Second Leg of Split FPtr around same sc, sc in last 2 dc on Rnd 4; join with slip st to first sc: 60 sts.

Rnd 6: Ch 1, sc in same st and in next sc, ch 2, ★ skip next Split FPtr, sc in next 4 sc, ch 2; repeat from ★ around to last 3 sts, skip next Split FPtr, sc in last 2 sc; join with slip st to first sc: 48 sc and 12 ch-2 sps.

Rnd 7: Slip st in next sc and in next ch-2 sp, work Beginning Popcorn in same sp, ch 4, skip next sc, sc in next 2 sc, ch 4, ★ work Popcorn in next ch-2 sp, ch 4, skip next sc, sc in next 2 sc, ch 4; repeat from ★ around; join with slip st to top of Beginning Popcorn: 24 ch-4 sps.

Rnd 8: (Slip st, ch 1, sc) in first ch-4 sp, ch 5, sc in next ch-4 sp, ch 3, ★ sc in next ch-4 sp, ch 5, sc in next ch-4 sp, ch 3; repeat from ★ around; join with slip st to first sc.

Rnd 9: (Slip st, ch 4, dc) in first ch-5 sp, (ch 1, dc in same sp) 4 times, hdc in next ch-3 sp, ★ dc in next ch-5 sp, (ch 1, dc in same sp) 5 times, hdc in next ch-3 sp; repeat from ★ around; join with slip st to third ch of beginning ch-4: 84 sts and 60 ch-1 sps.

Rnd 10: Ch 1, sc in same st, (sc in next ch-1 sp and in next dc) twice, 3 sc in next ch-1 sp, sc in next dc, (sc in next ch-1 sp and in next dc) twice, skip next hdc, ★ sc in next dc, (sc in next ch-1 sp and in next dc) twice, 3 sc in next ch-1 sp, sc in next dc, (sc in next ch-1 sp and in next dc) twice, skip next hdc; repeat from ★ around; join with slip st to first sc: 156 sc.

Rnd 11: Slip st in next 2 sc, ch 1, sc in same st, ch 3, (skip next sc, sc in next sc, ch 3) 4 times, skip next 4 sts, ★ sc in next sc, ch 3, (skip next sc, sc in next sc, ch 3) 4 times, skip next 4 sts; repeat from ★ around; join with slip st to first sc: 60 ch-3 sps.

Rnd 12: (Slip st, ch 1, sc) in first ch-3 sp, ch 2, 2 dc in next ch-3 sp, work Picot, 2 dc in next ch-3 sp, ch 2, ★ sc in next 3 ch-3 sps, ch 2, 2 dc in next ch-3 sp, work Picot, 2 dc in next ch-3 sp, ch 2; repeat from ★ around to last 2 ch-3 sps, sc in last 2 ch-3 sps; join with slip st to first sc, finish off.

See Washing and Blocking, page 144.

Finished Size: 5$^{1}/_{4}$" diameter

MATERIALS

Bedspread Weight Cotton Thread (size 10): 65 yards
Steel crochet hook, size 7 (1.65 mm) **or** size needed for gauge

GAUGE SWATCH: 1$^{5}/_{8}$" diameter
Work same as Doily through Rnd 2.

STITCH GUIDE

TREBLE CROCHET *(abbreviated tr)*
YO twice, insert hook in ch-6 sp indicated, YO and pull up a loop (4 loops on hook), (YO and draw through 2 loops on hook) 3 times.

BEGINNING DECREASE (uses next 2 dc)
Ch 2, ★ YO, insert hook in **next** dc, YO and pull up a loop, YO and draw through 2 loops on hook; repeat from ★ once **more**, YO and draw through all 3 loops on hook.

DECREASE (uses next 2 dc)
YO, insert hook in same st as third leg of last decrease made, YO and pull up a loop, YO and draw through 2 loops on hook, ★ YO, insert hook in **next** dc, YO and pull up a loop, YO and draw through 2 loops on hook; repeat from ★ once **more**, YO and draw through all 4 loops on hook.

ENDING DECREASE (uses last dc)
YO, insert hook in same st as third leg of last decrease made, YO and pull up a loop, YO and draw through 2 loops on hook, YO, insert hook in last dc, YO and pull up a loop, YO and draw through 2 loops on hook, YO, insert hook in same st as first leg of Beginning decrease, YO and pull up a loop, YO and draw through 2 loops on hook, YO and draw through all 4 loops on hook.

BEGINNING CLUSTER (uses one ch-2 sp)
Ch 2, ★ YO, insert hook in sp indicated, YO and pull up a loop, YO and draw through 2 loops on hook; repeat from ★ once **more**, YO and draw through all 3 loops on hook.

CLUSTER (uses one ch-2 sp)
★ YO, insert hook in ch-2 sp indicated, YO and pull up a loop, YO and draw through 2 loops on hook; repeat from ★ 2 times **more**, YO and draw through all 4 loops on hook.

PICOT
Ch 3, slip st in third ch from hook, ch 1.

DOILY

Ch 8; join with slip st to form a ring.

Rnd 1 (Right side)**:** Ch 3 **(counts as first dc, now and throughout)**, 23 dc in ring; join with slip st to first dc: 24 dc.

Rnd 2: Work Beginning decrease, ch 4, (decrease, ch 4) around to last dc, work Ending decrease, ch 4; join with slip st to top of Beginning decrease: 12 ch-4 sps.

Rnd 3: (Slip st, ch 1, sc) in first ch-4 sp, (ch 2, sc in same sp) twice, ★ sc in next ch-4 sp, (ch 2, sc in same sp) twice; repeat from ★ around; join with slip st to first sc: 24 ch-2 sps.

Rnd 4: (Slip st, work Beginning Cluster) in first ch-2 sp, ch 4, sc in next ch-2 sp, ch 4, ★ work Cluster in next ch-2 sp, ch 4, sc in next ch-2 sp, ch 4; repeat from ★ around; join with slip st to top of Beginning Cluster.

Rnd 5: (Slip st, ch 1, sc) in first ch-4 sp, 3 dc in next sc, sc in next ch-4 sp, ch 1, ★ sc in next ch-4 sp, 3 dc in next sc, sc in next ch-4 sp, ch 1; repeat from ★ around; join with slip st to first sc: 60 sts and 12 ch-1 sps.

Rnd 6: Ch 1, sc in same st and in each st and each ch-1 sp around; join with slip st to first sc: 72 sc.

Rnd 7: Ch 1, sc in same st, ch 5, skip next 3 sc, ★ sc in next sc, ch 5, skip next 3 sc; repeat from ★ around; join with slip st to first sc: 18 ch-5 sps.

Rnd 8: Slip st in first ch-5 sp, ch 1, (sc, hdc, 3 dc, hdc, sc) in same sp and in each ch-5 sp around; join with slip st to first sc: 18 petals.

Rnd 9: Ch 2, working **behind** Rnd 8 and in skipped sc on Rnd 6 *(Fig. 5, page 144)*, slip st in first 2 skipped sc on Rnd 6, ch 1, sc in same st, (ch 6, sc in center sc of next 3 skipped sc) around, ch 3, dc in first sc to form last ch-6 sp: 18 ch-6 sps.

Rnd 10: Ch 4 **(counts as first tr)**, (2 dc, sc) in last ch-6 sp made, (sc, 2 dc, tr, 2 dc, sc) in next ch-6 sp and in each ch-6 sp around, (sc, 2 dc) in same sp as first tr; join with slip st to first tr: 18 petals.

Rnd 11: Ch 1, sc in same st, ch 3, dc in center dc of next petal on Rnd 8, ch 3, ★ sc in next tr on Rnd 10, ch 3, dc in center dc of next petal on Rnd 8, ch 3; repeat from ★ around; join with slip st to first sc: 36 ch-3 sps.

Rnd 12: Ch 1, sc in same st, dc in next dc, (ch 1, dc in same st) 4 times, ★ sc in next sc, dc in next dc, (ch 1, dc in same st) 4 times; repeat from ★ around; join with slip st to first sc: 108 sts and 72 ch-1 sps.

Rnd 13: Ch 1, sc in same st, work Picot, skip next ch-1 sp, (sc in next ch-1 sp, work Picot) twice, skip next 2 dc, ★ sc in next sc, work Picot, skip next ch-1 sp, (sc in next ch-1 sp, work Picot) twice, skip next 2 dc; repeat from ★ around; join with slip st to first sc, finish off.

See Washing and Blocking, page 144.

Finished Size: 5$\frac{1}{2}$" diameter

MATERIALS

Bedspread Weight Cotton Thread (size 10): 62 yards
Steel crochet hook, size 7 (1.65 mm) **or** size
   needed for gauge

GAUGE SWATCH: 2" diameter
Work same as Doily through Rnd 3.

STITCH GUIDE

TREBLE CROCHET *(abbreviated tr)*
YO twice, insert in sp indicated, YO and pull up a loop (4 loops on hook), (YO and draw through 2 loops on hook) 3 times.

BEGINNING 4-DC POPCORN
Ch 3 **(counts as first dc)**, 3 dc in sp indicated, drop loop from hook, insert hook in first dc of 4-dc group, hook dropped loop and draw through.

4-DC POPCORN
4 Dc in sp indicated, drop loop from hook, insert hook in first dc of 4-dc group, hook dropped loop and draw through.

7-TR POPCORN
7 Tr in ch-3 sp indicated, drop loop from hook, insert hook in first tr of 7-tr group, hook dropped loop and draw through.

PICOT
Ch 2, slip st in second ch from hook, ch 1.

DOILY

Ch 8; join with slip st to form a ring.

Rnd 1 (Right side)**:** Work Beginning 4-dc Popcorn in ring, (ch 3, work 4-dc Popcorn in ring) 9 times, ch 1, hdc in top of Beginning 4-dc Popcorn to form last ch-3 sp: 10 ch-3 sps.

Rnd 2: Ch 1, sc in last ch-3 sp made, (ch 4, sc in next ch-3 sp) around, ch 1, dc in first sc to form last ch-4 sp.

Rnd 3: Ch 1, (sc, ch 3, sc) in last ch-4 sp made, ★ sc in next ch-4 sp, (ch 3, sc in same sp) twice; repeat from ★ around, sc in same sp as first sc, ch 1, hdc in first sc to form last ch-3 sp: 20 ch-3 sps.

Rnd 4: Ch 1, sc in last ch-3 sp made, (ch 3, sc in next ch-3 sp) around, dc in first sc to form last ch-3 sp.

Rnd 5: Ch 3 **(counts as first dc)**, 2 dc in last ch-3 sp made, (ch 1, 3 dc in next ch-3 sp) around, sc in first dc to form last ch-1 sp; do **not** finish off: 60 dc and 20 ch-1 sps.

Continued on page 138.

Rnd 6: Ch 1, sc in last ch-1 sp made and in next dc, ch 3, ★ skip next dc, sc in next dc, sc in next ch-1 sp and in next dc, ch 3; repeat from ★ around to last 2 dc, skip next dc, sc in last dc; join with slip st to first sc.

Rnd 7: Ch 1, sc in same st, ch 5, work 7-tr Popcorn in next ch-3 sp, ★ ch 5, skip next sc, sc in next sc, ch 5, work 7-tr Popcorn in next ch-3 sp; repeat from ★ around to last sc, ch 2, skip last sc, dc in first sc to form last ch-5 sp: 40 ch-5 sps.

Rnd 8: Ch 1, sc in last ch-5 sp made, ch 1, 2 sc in next ch-5 sp, ch 3, ★ 2 sc in next ch-5 sp, ch 1, 2 sc in next ch-5 sp, ch 3; repeat from ★ around, sc in same sp as first sc; join with slip st to first sc.

Rnd 9: (Slip st, ch 1, sc) in first ch-1 sp, ch 2, dc in next ch-3 sp, (work Picot, dc in same sp) 3 times, ch 2, ★ sc in next ch-1 sp, ch 2, dc in next ch-3 sp, (work Picot, dc in same sp) 3 times, ch 2; repeat from ★ around; join with slip st to first sc, finish off.

See Washing and Blocking, page 144.

96 ▬

Finished Size: 5" (point to point)

MATERIALS
Bedspread Weight Cotton Thread (size 10): 50 yards
Steel crochet hook, size 7 (1.65 mm) **or** size
    needed for gauge

GAUGE SWATCH: 1¹/₂" diameter
Work same as Doily through Rnd 4.

STITCH GUIDE

FRONT POST DOUBLE CROCHET
(abbreviated FPdc)
YO, insert hook from **front** to **back** around post of dc indicated *(Fig. 7, page 144)*, YO and pull up a loop (3 loops on hook), (YO and draw through 2 loops on hook) twice.

FRONT POST DOUBLE TREBLE CROCHET
(abbreviated FPdtr)
YO 3 times, insert hook from **front** to **back** around post of dc indicated *(Fig. 7, page 144)*, YO and pull up a loop (5 loops on hook), (YO and draw through 2 loops on hook) 4 times.

POPCORN
4 Dc in ch-2 sp indicated, drop loop from hook, insert hook in first dc of 4-dc group, hook dropped loop and draw through.

SPLIT DOUBLE TREBLE CROCHET
(abbreviated Split dtr)
First Leg: YO 3 times, insert hook from **back** to **front** in next ch-4 sp **between** Popcorn on Rnd 5 and 2 sc on Rnd 6, YO and pull up a loop, (YO and draw through 2 loops on hook) 3 times (2 loops remaining on hook).

Second Leg: YO 3 times, insert hook from **front** to **back** in next ch-4 sp **between** 2 sc and Popcorn, YO and pull up a loop, (YO and draw through 2 loops on hook) 3 times, YO and draw through all 3 loops on hook.

DECREASE
Pull up a loop in next 2 sc, YO and draw through all 3 loops on hook.

DOILY
Ch 6; join with slip st to form a ring.

Rnd 1 (Right side)**:** Ch 3 **(counts as first dc, now and throughout)**, 19 dc in ring; join with slip st to first dc: 20 dc.

Rnd 2: Ch 1, sc in same st, ★ ch 2, skip next dc, sc in next dc; repeat from ★ around to last dc, ch 1, skip last dc, sc in first sc to form last ch-2 sp: 10 ch-2 sps.

Rnd 3: Ch 1, sc in last ch-2 sp made and in next sc, sc in next ch-2 sp, ch 2, work FPdtr around second dc on Rnd 1, ch 2, sc in same sp on Rnd 2 and in next sc, ★ sc in next ch-2 sp, ch 2, skip next dc on Rnd 1, work FPdtr around next dc, ch 2, sc in same sp on Rnd 2 and in next sc; repeat from ★ 7 times **more**, sc in same ch-2 sp as first sc, ch 2, skip next dc on Rnd 1, work FPdtr around next dc, hdc in first sc to form last ch-2 sp: 20 ch-2 sps.

Rnd 4: Ch 1, sc in last ch-2 sp made, ch 1, sc in next ch-2 sp, (sc, ch 2, sc) in next FPdtr, ★ sc in next ch-2 sp, ch 1, sc in next ch-2 sp, (sc, ch 2, sc) in next FPdtr; repeat from ★ around; join with slip st to first sc: 20 sps.

Rnd 5: (Slip st, ch 1, sc) in first ch-1 sp, ch 4, work Popcorn in next ch-2 sp, ★ ch 4, sc in next ch-1 sp, ch 4, work Popcorn in next ch-2 sp; repeat from ★ around, ch 1, dc in first sc to form last ch-4 sp, place marker around ch-4 just made for st placement.

Rnd 6: Ch 1, 2 sc in last ch-4 sp made, ch 3, 2 sc in next ch-4 sp, ch 2, ★ 2 sc in next ch-4 sp, ch 3, 2 sc in next ch-4 sp, ch 2; repeat from ★ around; join with slip st to first sc: 40 sc.

Rnd 7: Ch 3, dc in next sc, 3 dc in next ch-3 sp, dc in next 2 sc, 2 dc in next ch-2 sp, ★ dc in next 2 sc, 3 dc in next ch-3 sp, dc in next 2 sc, 2 dc in next ch-2 sp; repeat from ★ around; join with slip st to first dc: 90 dc.

Rnd 8: Ch 1, sc in same st, work FPdc around next dc, (sc in next dc, work FPdc around next dc) around; join with slip st to first sc.

Rnd 9: Ch 1, sc in same st and in next 3 sts, YO 3 times, insert hook from **back** to **front** in marked ch-4 sp **between** Popcorn on Rnd 5 and 2 sc on Rnd 6, YO and pull up a loop, (YO and draw through 2 loops on hook) 3 times (2 loops remaining on hook), work Second Leg of Split dtr **(first Split dtr made)**, ★ sc in same st on Rnd 8 and in next 9 sts, work Split dtr; repeat from ★ around to last 5 sts on Rnd 8, sc in same st and in last 5 sts; join with slip st to first sc: 100 sc and 10 Split dtr.

Rnd 10: Ch 1, sc in same st, skip next 3 sc, dc in next Split dtr, (ch 1, dc in same st) 4 times, skip next 3 sc, sc in next sc, ch 5, skip next 2 sc, ★ sc in next sc, skip next 3 sc, dc in next Split dtr, (ch 1, dc in same st) 4 times, skip next 3 sc, sc in next sc, ch 5, skip next 2 sc; repeat from ★ around; join with slip st to first sc: 50 sps.

Rnd 11: Slip st in next dc, ch 5 **(counts as first dc plus ch 2)**, dc in next dc, ch 2, (dc, ch 2) twice in next dc, dc in next dc, ch 2, dc in next dc, 2 sc in next ch-5 sp, skip next sc, ★ (dc in next dc, ch 2) twice, (dc, ch 2) twice in next dc, dc in next dc, ch 2, dc in next dc, 2 sc in next ch-5 sp, skip next sc; repeat from ★ around; join with slip st to first dc.

Rnd 12: Ch 1, sc in same st, (2 sc in next ch-2 sp, sc in next dc) twice, 3 sc in next ch-2 sp, sc in next dc, (2 sc in next ch-2 sp, sc in next dc) twice, decrease, ★ sc in next dc, (2 sc in next ch-2 sp, sc in next dc) twice, 3 sc in next ch-2 sp, sc in next dc, (2 sc in next ch-2 sp, sc in next dc) twice, decrease; repeat from ★ around; join with slip st to first sc, finish off.

See Washing and Blocking, page 144.

97 ▰

Finished Size: 5¼" (point to point)

MATERIALS
Bedspread Weight Cotton Thread (size 10): 55 yards
Steel crochet hook, size 7 (1.65 mm) **or** size
   needed for gauge

GAUGE SWATCH: 1½" diameter
Work same as Doily through Rnd 4.

STITCH GUIDE

FRONT POST DOUBLE CROCHET
   (abbreviated FPdc)
YO, insert hook from **front** to **back** around post of dc indicated **(Fig. 7, page 144)**, YO and pull up a loop (3 loops on hook), (YO and draw through 2 loops on hook) twice.

FRONT POST DOUBLE TREBLE CROCHET
   (abbreviated FPdtr)
YO 3 times, insert hook from **front** to **back** around post of dc indicated **(Fig. 7, page 144)**, YO and pull up a loop (5 loops on hook), (YO and draw through 2 loops on hook) 4 times.

BEGINNING CLUSTER (uses one ch-2 sp)
Ch 2, ★ YO, insert hook in ch-2 sp indicated, YO and pull up a loop, YO and draw through 2 loops on hook; repeat from ★ once **more**, YO and draw through all 3 loops on hook.

CLUSTER (uses one ch-2 sp)
★ YO, insert hook in ch-2 sp indicated, YO and pull up a loop, YO and draw through 2 loops on hook; repeat from ★ 2 times **more**, YO and draw through all 4 loops on hook.

SPLIT TREBLE CROCHET
   (abbreviated Split tr) (uses 2 ch-5 sps)
YO twice, insert hook in ch-5 sp **before** sc 2 rnds **below**, YO and pull up a loop, (YO and draw through 2 loops on hook) twice, YO twice, insert hook in next ch-5 sp **after** sc, YO and pull up a loop, (YO and draw through 2 loops on hook) twice, YO and draw through all 3 loops on hook.

DOILY
Ch 6; join with slip st to form a ring.

Rnd 1 (Right side)**:** Ch 3 **(counts as first dc)**, 4 dc in ring, place marker around last dc made for st placement, 19 dc in ring; join with slip st to first dc: 24 dc.

Rnd 2: Ch 1, sc in same st, ch 2, skip next dc, ★ sc in next dc, ch 2, skip next dc; repeat from ★ around; join with slip st to first sc: 12 ch-2 sps.

Rnd 3: (Slip st, ch 1, sc) in first ch-2 sp, work FPdtr around marked dc on Rnd 1, ★ sc in same sp on Rnd 2 and in next ch-2 sp, skip next dc on Rnd 1, work FPdtr around next dc; repeat from ★ around, sc in same sp on Rnd 2; join with slip st to first sc: 24 sc and 12 FPdtr.

Rnd 4: Ch 1, sc in same st, 2 sc in next FPdtr, (sc in next 2 sc, 2 sc in next FPdtr) around to last sc, sc in last sc; join with slip st to Back Loop Only of first sc **(Fig. 1, page 143)**, do **not** finish off: 48 sc.

Continued on page 140.

Rnd 5: Ch 1, sc in Back Loop Only of same st and each sc around; join with slip st to **both** loops of first sc.

Rnd 6: Ch 1, working in both loops, sc in same st, ch 2, skip next sc, ★ sc in next sc, ch 2, skip next sc; repeat from ★ around; join with slip st to first sc: 24 ch-2 sps.

Rnd 7: (Slip st, work Beginning Cluster) in first ch-2 sp, ch 3, sc in next ch-2 sp, ch 3, ★ work Cluster in next ch-2 sp, ch 3, sc in next ch-2 sp, ch 3; repeat from ★ around; join with slip st to top of Beginning Cluster.

Rnd 8: (Slip st, ch 1, 2 sc) in first ch-3 sp, ch 5, (2 sc in each of next 2 ch-3 sps, ch 5) around to last ch-3 sp, 2 sc in last ch-3 sp; join with slip st to first sc: 48 sc and 12 ch-5 sps.

Rnd 9: Ch 1, sc in same st and in next sc, sc in next ch-5 sp, (ch 2, sc in same sp) 3 times, ★ sc in next 4 sc and in next ch-5 sp, (ch 2, sc in same sp) 3 times; repeat from ★ around to last 2 sc, sc in last 2 sc; join with slip st to first sc: 96 sc and 36 ch-2 sps.

Rnd 10: Slip st in next 2 sc and in next ch-2 sp, work Beginning Cluster in same sp, ch 5, sc in next ch-2 sp, ch 5, ★ work Cluster in next 2 ch-2 sps, ch 5, sc in next ch-2 sp, ch 5; repeat from ★ around to last ch-2 sp, work Cluster in last ch-2 sp; join with slip st to top of Beginning Cluster: 24 Clusters and 24 ch-5 sps.

Rnd 11: (Slip st, ch 1, 3 sc) in first ch-5 sp, ch 4, 3 sc in next ch-5 sp, skip next Cluster, dc in sp **before** next Cluster, ★ 3 sc in next ch-5 sp, ch 4, 3 sc in next ch-5 sp, skip next Cluster, dc in sp **before** next Cluster; repeat from ★ around; join with slip st to first sc: 84 sts and 12 ch-4 sps.

Rnd 12: Ch 1, sc in same st and in next 2 sc, 5 sc in next ch-4 sp, (sc in next 7 sts, 5 sc in next ch-4 sp) around to last 4 sts, sc in last 4 sts; join with slip st to first sc: 144 sc.

Rnd 13: Ch 1, sc in same st and in next 5 sc, work Split tr, sc in same st on Rnd 12 and in next 5 sc, work FPdc around dc one rnd **below**, ★ sc in next 6 sc on Rnd 12, work Split tr, sc in same st on Rnd 12 and in next 5 sc, work FPdc around dc one rnd **below**; repeat from ★ around; join with slip st to first sc: 144 sc, 12 FPdc, and 12 Split tr.

Rnd 14: Ch 1, sc in same st and in next 5 sc, 2 sc in next Split tr, sc in next 6 sc, skip next FPdc, ★ sc in next 6 sc, 2 sc in next Split tr, sc in next 6 sc, skip next FPdc; repeat from ★ around; join with slip st to first sc, finish off.

See Washing and Blocking, page 144.

98▬

Finished Size: 6" diameter

MATERIALS
Bedspread Weight Cotton Thread (size 10): 62 yards
Steel crochet hook, size 7 (1.65 mm) **or** size
   needed for gauge

GAUGE SWATCH: $1^3/4$" diameter
Work same as Doily through Rnd 3.

STITCH GUIDE

TREBLE CROCHET *(abbreviated tr)*
YO twice, insert hook in sc indicated, YO and pull up a loop (4 loops on hook), (YO and draw through 2 loops on hook) 3 times.

SPLIT TREBLE CROCHET
   (abbreviated Split tr)
First Leg: YO twice, working in **front** of previous rnd *(Fig. 5, page 144)*, insert hook from **top** to **bottom** in free loop of sc indicated *(Fig. 2a, page 144)*, YO and pull up a loop, (YO and draw through 2 loops on hook) twice (2 loops remaining on hook).

Second Leg: YO twice, insert hook from **bottom** to **top** in free loop of sc indicated, YO and pull up a loop, (YO and draw through 2 loops on hook) twice, YO and draw through all 3 loops on hook.

BEGINNING CLUSTER (uses next 2 sc)
Ch 2, ★ YO, insert hook in **next** sc, YO and pull up a loop, YO and draw through 2 loops on hook; repeat from ★ once **more**, YO and draw through all 3 loops on hook.

CLUSTER (uses next 2 sc)
YO, insert hook in same st as third leg of last Cluster made, YO and pull up a loop, YO and draw through 2 loops on hook, ★ YO, insert hook in **next** sc, YO and pull up a loop, YO and draw through 2 loops on hook; repeat from ★ once **more**, YO and draw through all 4 loops on hook.

FRONT POST CLUSTER
   (abbreviated FP Cluster)
★ YO, insert hook from **front** to **back** around post of dc indicated *(Fig. 7, page 144)*, YO and pull up a loop, YO and draw through 2 loops on hook; repeat from ★ 2 times **more**, YO and draw through all 4 loops on hook.

SCALLOP

Ch 2, ★ YO, insert hook in top of last sc made *(Fig. 6a, page 144)*, YO and pull up a loop, YO and draw through 2 loops on hook; repeat from ★ once **more**, YO and draw through all 3 loops on hook, ch 2, slip st in top of last st made *(Fig. 6b, page 144)*, ch 2, † YO, insert hook in same st, YO and pull up a loop, YO and draw through 2 loops on hook †; repeat from † to † once **more**, YO and draw through all 3 loops on hook.

PICOT

Ch 2, slip st in top of last sc made *(Fig. 6a, page 144)*.

DOILY

Ch 10; join with slip st to form a ring.

Rnd 1 (Right side)**:** Ch 1, 30 sc in ring; join with slip st to first sc.

Rnd 2: Work Beginning Cluster, ch 3, (work Cluster, ch 3) around working third leg of last Cluster in same st as beginning ch-2; join with slip st to top of Beginning Cluster: 15 Clusters and 15 ch-3 sps.

Rnd 3: (Slip st, ch 1, 2 sc) in first ch-3 sp, place marker around last sc made for st placement, sc in same sp, 3 sc in each ch-3 sp around; join with slip st to Back Loop Only of first sc *(Fig. 1, page 143)*: 45 sc.

Rnd 4: Ch 3 **(counts as first dc, now and throughout)**, working in Back Loops Only, dc in next 2 sc, ch 1, (dc in next 3 sc, ch 1) around; join with slip st to first dc: 45 dc and 15 ch-1 sps.

Rnd 5: Ch 3, work FP Cluster around next dc, working in both loops, dc in next dc, working in **front** of previous rnd *(Fig. 5, page 144)* and in free loops of sc on Rnd 3 *(Fig. 2a, page 144)*, work First Leg of Split tr in marked sc on Rnd 3, skip next 2 sc, ★ work Second Leg of Split tr in next sc, working **behind** Split tr, dc in next dc on Rnd 4, work FP Cluster around next dc, dc in next dc, working in **front** of previous rnd, work First Leg of Split tr in same st as Second Leg of last Split tr made, skip next 2 sc; repeat from ★ around, work Second Leg of last Split tr in same st as First Leg of first Split tr made; join with slip st to first dc: 60 sts.

Rnd 6: Ch 1, sc in same st, 2 sc in next FP Cluster, sc in next 2 sts, place marker around last sc made for st placement, sc in same st and in next 3 sts, 2 sc in next Split tr, (sc in next 3 sts, 2 sc in next Split tr) around; join with slip st to Back Loop Only of first sc: 76 sc.

Rnd 7: Ch 1, sc in Back Loop Only of same st and each sc around; join with slip st to **both** loops of first sc.

Rnd 8: Ch 1, working in both loops, sc in same st, ch 2, skip next sc, ★ sc in next sc, ch 2, skip next sc; repeat from ★ around; join with slip st to first sc: 38 sc and 38 ch-2 sps.

Rnd 9: Ch 1, sc in same st and in next ch-2 sp, working in **front** of previous rnds, tr in free loop of marked sc on Rnd 6 *(Fig. 2a, page 144)*, ★ working **behind** tr just made, sc in next sc on Rnd 8 and in next ch-2 sp, working in **front** of previous rnds, skip next sc on Rnd 6 from last tr made, tr in free loop of next sc; repeat from ★ around; join with slip st to first sc: 114 sts.

Rnd 10: Ch 1, sc in same st and in each st around; join with slip st to first sc.

Rnd 11: Ch 1, sc in same st, tr in next sc pulling tr to right side, (sc in next sc, tr in next sc pulling tr to right side) around; join with slip st to first sc.

Rnd 12: Ch 1, sc in same st and in each st around; join with slip st to first sc.

Rnd 13: Ch 1, sc in same st, ch 2, skip next sc, ★ sc in next sc, ch 2, skip next sc; repeat from ★ around; join with slip st to first sc: 57 sc and 57 ch-2 sps.

Rnd 14: (Slip st, ch 1, sc) in first ch-2 sp, (ch 3, sc in next ch-2 sp) around, dc in first sc to form last ch-3 sp.

Rnd 15: Ch 1, (sc, work Picot, sc) in last ch-3 sp made, sc in next ch-3 sp, work Scallop, sc in next ch-3 sp, ★ (sc, work Picot, sc) in next ch-3 sp, sc in next ch-3 sp, work Scallop, sc in next ch-3 sp; repeat from ★ around; join with slip st to first sc, finish off.

See Washing and Blocking, page 144.

99

Finished Size: 6¹/₄" diameter

MATERIALS

Bedspread Weight Cotton Thread (size 10): 55 yards
Steel crochet hook, size 7 (1.65 mm) **or** size
needed for gauge

GAUGE SWATCH: 2" diameter
Work same as Doily through Rnd 3.

STITCH GUIDE

BACK POST SINGLE CROCHET
(abbreviated BPsc)
Insert hook from **back** to **front** around post of dc
indicated *(Fig. 7, page 144)*, YO and pull up a
loop, YO and draw through both loops on hook.

FRONT POST CLUSTER
(abbreviated FP Cluster)
★ YO twice, insert hook from **front** to **back** around
post of dc indicated *(Fig. 7, page 144)*, YO and
pull up a loop, (YO and draw through 2 loops on
hook) twice; repeat from ★ once **more**, YO and
draw through all 3 loops on hook.

PICOT
Ch 3, slip st in third ch from hook, ch 1.

DOILY

Rnd 1 (Right side)**:** Ch 5, (dc, ch 1) 11 times in fifth ch
from hook **(4 skipped chs count as first dc plus
ch 1)**; join with slip st to first dc: 12 ch-1 sps.

Rnd 2: (Slip st, ch 1, sc) in first ch-1 sp, ch 2, (sc in
next ch-1 sp, ch 2) around; join with slip st to first sc.

Rnd 3: Ch 1, sc in same st and in next ch-2 sp, work
FP Cluster around next dc on Rnd 1, sc in same sp on
Rnd 2 as last sc made, ★ sc in next sc and in next
ch-2 sp, work FP Cluster around next dc on Rnd 1, sc in
same sp on Rnd 2 as last sc made; repeat from ★
around; join with slip st to first sc: 48 sts.

Rnd 4: Slip st in next 2 sts, ch 1, sc in same st, ★ ch 5,
skip next 3 sc, sc in next FP Cluster; repeat from ★
around, ch 3, skip next 3 sts, hdc in first sc to form last
ch-5 sp: 12 ch-5 sps.

Rnd 5: Ch 5 **(counts as first dc plus ch 2, now
and throughout)**, sc in last ch-5 sp made, [sc, ch 2,
(dc, ch 2) twice, sc] in each ch-5 sp around, (sc, ch 2,
dc) in same sp as first dc, ch 1, sc in first dc to form last
ch-2 sp: 36 ch-2 sps.

Rnd 6: Ch 5, dc in last ch-2 sp made, ch 5, skip next
2 ch-2 sps, ★ (dc, ch 2, dc) in next ch-2 sp, ch 5, skip
next 2 ch-2 sps; repeat from ★ around; join with slip st
to first dc: 24 dc and 24 sps.

Rnd 7: Ch 1, sc in same st, 2 sc in next ch-2 sp, sc in
next dc, 5 sc in next ch-5 sp, ★ sc in next dc, 2 sc in
next ch-2 sp, sc in next dc, 5 sc in next ch-5 sp; repeat
from ★ around; join with slip st to first sc: 108 sc.

Rnd 8: Ch 1, sc in same st and in next 5 sc, (sc, ch 1,
sc) in next sc, ★ sc in next 8 sc, (sc, ch 1, sc) in next sc;
repeat from ★ around to last 2 sc, sc in last 2 sc; join
with slip st to first sc: 120 sc and 12 ch-1 sps.

Rnd 9: Ch 1, sc in same st and in each sc and each
ch-1 sp around; join with slip st to first sc: 132 sc.

Rnd 10: Slip st in next 4 sc, ch 1, sc in same st and in
next 2 sc, 2 sc in next sc, sc in next 3 sc, ch 10, skip
next 4 sc, ★ sc in next 3 sc, 2 sc in next sc, sc in next
3 sc, ch 10, skip next 4 sts; repeat from ★ around; join
with slip st to first sc: 96 sc and 12 loops.

Rnd 11: Slip st in next 3 sc, ch 1, sc in same st and in
next sc, dc in next loop, (ch 1, dc in same loop) 9 times,
skip next 3 sc, ★ sc in next 2 sc, dc in next loop, (ch 1,
dc in same loop) 9 times, skip next 3 sts; repeat from ★
around; join with slip st to first sc: 144 sts.

Rnd 12: Slip st in next sc, ch 1, ★ work BPsc around
next dc, ch 2, work BPsc around next dc, (work Picot,
work BPsc around next dc) 7 times, ch 2, work BPsc
around next dc, ch 1, skip next 2 sts; repeat from ★
around; join with slip st to first BPsc, finish off.

See Washing and Blocking, page 144.

GENERAL INSTRUCTIONS

ABBREVIATIONS

BPdc	Back Post double crochet(s)
BPsc	Back Post single crochet(s)
ch(s)	chain(s)
dc	double crochet(s)
dtr	double treble crochet(s)
FP	Front Post
FPdc	Front Post double crochet(s)
FPdtr	Front Post double treble crochet(s)
FPsc	Front Post single crochet(s)
FPtr	Front Post treble crochet(s)
FPtr tr	Front Post triple treble crochet(s)
hdc	half double crochet(s)
mm	millimeters
Rnd(s)	Round(s)
sc	single crochet(s)
sp(s)	space(s)
st(s)	stitch(es)
tr	treble crochet(s)
tr tr	triple treble crochet(s)
YO	yarn over

★ — work instructions following ★ as many **more** times as indicated in addition to the first time.

† to † **or** ♥ to ♥ — work all instructions from first † to second † **or** from first ♥ to second ♥ as **many** times as specified.

( ) or **[ ]** — work enclosed instructions **as many** times as specified by the number immediately following **or** work all enclosed instructions in the stitch or space indicated **or** contains explanatory remarks.

colon (:) — the number(s) given after a colon at the end of a row or round denote(s) the number of stitches you should have on that row or round.

CROCHET TERMINOLOGY	
UNITED STATES	**INTERNATIONAL**
slip stitch (slip st)	= single crochet (sc)
single crochet (sc)	= double crochet (dc)
half double crochet (hdc)	= half treble crochet (htr)
double crochet (dc)	= treble crochet (tr)
treble crochet (tr)	= double treble crochet (dtr)
double treble crochet (dtr)	= triple treble crochet (ttr)
triple treble crochet (tr tr)	= quadruple treble crochet (qtr)
skip	= miss

GAUGE

Exact gauge is **essential** for proper size. Before beginning your Doily, make the sample swatch given in the individual instructions in the thread and hook specified. After completing the swatch, measure it, counting your stitches and rounds carefully. If your swatch is larger or smaller than specified, **make another, changing hook size to get the correct gauge**. Keep trying until you find the size hook that will give you the specified gauge.

THREAD

The photographed items were made using bedspread weight cotton thread (size 10). Any of the following brands may be used with good results:

Anchor "Mercer Crochet"
DMC "Baroque"
DMC "Cebelia"
DMC "Cordonnet"
DMC "Traditions"
Grandma's Best
J. & P. Coats "Knit-Cro-Sheen"
J. & P. Coats "South Maid"
Lily "Daisy"
Opera

JOINING WITH SC

When instructed to join with sc, begin with a slip knot on hook. Insert hook in stitch or space indicated, YO and pull up a loop, YO and draw through both loops on hook.

BACK OR FRONT LOOP ONLY

Work only in loop(s) indicated by arrow *(Fig. 1)*.

Fig. 1

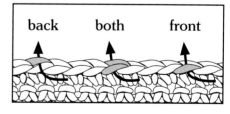

STEEL CROCHET HOOKS															
U.S.	00	0	1	2	3	4	5	6	7	8	9	10	11	12	13	14
Metric - mm	3.50	3.25	2.75	2.25	2.10	2.00	1.90	1.80	1.65	1.50	1.40	1.30	1.10	1.00	0.85	0.75

FREE LOOPS

After working in Back or Front Loops Only on a row or round, there will be a ridge of unused loops. These are called the free loops. Later, when instructed to work in the free loops of the same round, work in these loops (*Fig. 2a*).

When instructed to work in free loops of a chain, work in loop indicated by arrow (*Fig. 2b*).

Fig. 2a

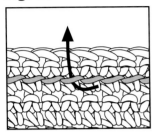

Fig. 2b

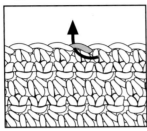

WORKING IN CENTER 3 LOOPS OF A STITCH

When instructed to work in center 3 loops of a stitch, work in loops indicated by arrow (*Fig. 3a or 3b*).

Fig. 3a

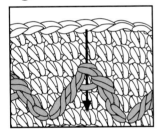

Fig. 3b

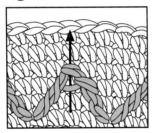

WORKING IN FRONT 2 LEGS OF A STITCH

When instructed to work in front 2 legs of a stitch, work in loops indicated by arrow (*Fig. 4*).

Fig. 4

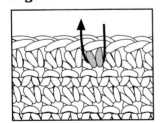

WORKING IN FRONT, AROUND, OR BEHIND A STITCH

Work in stitch or space indicated, inserting hook in direction of arrow (*Fig. 5*).

Fig. 5

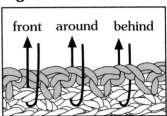

front   around   behind

WORKING IN TOP OF A STITCH

When instructed to work in top of a stitch, work in loops indicated by arrow (*Fig. 6a or 6b*).

Fig. 6a

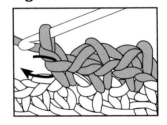

Fig. 6b

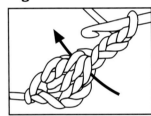

POST STITCH

Work around post of stitch indicated, inserting hook in direction of arrow (*Fig. 7*).

Fig. 7

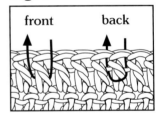

front   back

WASHING AND BLOCKING

For a more professional look, pieces should be washed and blocked. Using a mild detergent and warm water and being careful not to rub, twist, or wring, gently squeeze suds through the piece. Rinse several times in cool, clear water. Roll piece in a clean terry towel and gently press out the excess moisture. Lay piece on a flat surface and shape to proper size; where needed, pin in place using rust-proof pins. Allow to dry **completely**.